HOLOCAUST II?

HOLOCAUST II?

Saving Israel
From Suicide

ANDREW J. HURLEY

MISSION PUBLISHING, INC. / 1990

Design and typography by Jim Cook/Santa Barbara

LIBRARY OF CONGRESS CATALOGING-IN-PUBLICATION DATA
Hurley, Andrew J., 1917-
    Holocaust II?: saving Israel from suicide / Andrew J. Hurley.
        p.   c.m.
    Includes bibliographical references (p.).
    ISBN 0-9625696-0-7: $22.95
    1. Jewish-Arab relations. 2. United States—Foreign relations—
Israel. 3. Israel—Foreign relations—United States. 4. American
Israel Public Affairs Committee. 5. United States—Foreign
relations—1945-   . I. Title. II. Title: Holocaust two. III. Title:
Holocaust 2.
DS119.7.H852   1990   90-32912
956.94—dc20   CIP

Published by Mission Publishing, Inc.
5266 Tujunga
North Hollywood, California 91601

Dedicated to Peace

ACKNOWLEDGMENTS

Some of the ideas expressed in this book have been in my thoughts for many years, but it is doubtful if they would ever have been seen in print without the dedicated efforts of those persons whose contributions I wish to acknowledge here.

I am profoundly grateful to my wife, Louise, who encouraged me to undertake the writing of this book and to persevere to its completion. Her aid in research and her honest critique of the author's work were invaluable, and her efforts in coordinating all aspects of producing the book were above and beyond the call of duty.

Particular recognition is given to Janice Hine, whose skills and special talents enabled her to decipher the author's heiroglyphics to produce the original manuscript.

Special thanks are also due to Helen McKenna for her professional services in editing the initial stages of the book.

I am grateful to Alyson Montgomery and Carrie Courter for their dedication to the task in typing and proofreading a difficult text.

Finally, much credit is due to Barbara Schanberger, who expertly performed the job of researching and organizing the source notes.

Contents

INTRODUCTION

How the Book Was Written

FIRST, AND MOST IMPORTANT, the book has been written in a race against time. One of the major challenges has been to keep ahead of current events.

The subject matter of the book is so highly controversial and emotionally charged that writing it has involved special problems. The format, therefore, has been determined more by necessity than by choice, and, in some respects, departs from customary book structure.

As many writers and speakers have learned, it is virtually impossible for a non-Jewish author or speaker to write or say anything having to do with Israel or the Jewish people that cannot be interpreted by someone as veiled, if not blatant, anti-Semitism. The only completely safe course to follow is to write or say nothing on the subject, which is the conventional wisdom.

An alternative may be to support and establish a position upon the basis of sources and authorities that have unimpeachable credentials and are immune to any suggestion of anti-Semitism.

The latter course has been the choice adopted for this book. Accordingly, with few exceptions, this book relies almost exclusively on the following sources and authorities:

1. Well-known and highly respected Israeli and Jewish writers.
2. Members, or former members, of the Israeli government.
3. Well-known and generally accepted historians.
4. Responsible and objective news media, i.e., the *Jerusalem Post* (International Edition), the *Los Angeles Times,* the *New York Times, Newsweek, U.S. News & World Report, Fortune, Business Week, The Wall Street Journal,* network television, etc.

5. Members of Congress and the Executive Branch of the United States government.
6. The Congressional Record and other public documents.
7. The *Encyclopedia Judaica* and *The Encyclopedia Britannica.*

To avoid a charge that the sources and authorities have been misquoted, selectively quoted, or quoted out of context, the quoted material relied upon to support various positions taken in this book has been set forth verbatim and in detail.

This approach also serves to reduce the number of source or reference notes at the end of the book since, in most cases, the sources are set forth in the text itself. This gives the reader the benefit of knowing immediately, before reading the material, the authority relied upon by the author for the position taken and conclusion reached.

PREFACE

THIS BOOK IS CONCERNED with the Israeli-Palestinian crisis and the threat it poses to the survival of Israel and to world peace.

It is not primarily intended as a literary work—but rather as a means of advancing a *plan for peace in the Middle East.*

Many of the positions taken in this book reflect, not only the views of the author, but also the opinions of many prominent Israelis, as well as those of important members of the American Jewish Community.

The following, in summary form, are the contentions of the author as set forth in this book:

1. The present Likud government of Israel is embarked on a suicidal course which, if allowed to continue, will lead inevitably to the destruction of Israel.
2. Today, as so often in its tragic history, Israel is the victim of the folly of its leaders.
3. The survival of Israel is too important to leave solely in the hands of the Likud government.
4. The continuance in power of the Likud government, despite its disastrous policies, has been made possible by the well-meaning but misguided and blind support of the American Jewish Establishment. Acting through the Israeli Lobby, it has frustrated and defeated efforts on the part of the U.S. and others to bring peace to Israel and the Middle East.
5. The American Jewish leadership is not listening to the urgent voices of reason from Israel, i.e., Abba Eban, Yehoshafat Harkabi, Simha Flapan, Amos Perlmutter, and many others, who are alarmed and fear for Israel's survival.

6. The time has come when the Israeli people desperately need the intervention of the Diaspora to save Israel *from its government* before it is too late.

7. The historic events that have occurred in the Middle East over the past year have provided an unprecedented opportunity to bring about a peaceful settlement of the central issue—the future of the West Bank, Gaza, and a Palestinian state.

The intent and purpose of this book is to offer a *solution* to the Middle East crisis and to outline a plan for peace between Israel and the Palestinians, which will provide for Israel the security it needs, and at the same time will satisfy the right of the Palestinian people to an independent sovereign state.

As the U.S. government continues to be intimidated and paralyzed by the Israeli Lobby, and the American Jewish leadership continues to remain aloof from this crisis, all that stands between Israel and catastrophe is the voice of the *American Jewish Community.*

If American Jewry does not respond at this critical moment in Israel's history, they must be prepared to accept the inevitability of a new Holocaust *with the Jews of Israel among the victims.*

HOLOCAUST II?

CHAPTER I

The March of Folly

IN HER RECENT BOOK entitled *The March of Folly,* distinguished author-historian, the late Barbara Tuchman, explains what the
title of her book is intended to mean:

> A phenomenon noticeable throughout history regardless of place or
> period is the pursuit by governments of policies contrary to their own
> interests. Mankind, it seems, makes a poorer performance of govern-
> ment than of almost any other human activity. In this sphere, wisdom,
> which may be defined as the exercise of judgment acting on experience,
> common sense, and available information, is less operative and more
> frustrated than it should be. Why do holders of high office so often act
> contrary to the way reason points and enlightened self-interest suggests?
> Why does intelligent mental process seem so often not to function?[1]

She defines it as the "pursuit of policy contrary to self-interest." As a
classic example, she cites the case of Rehoboam, King of Israel, son of King
Solomon, who succeeded to his father's throne in 926 B.C.[2]

Rehoboam, a headstrong and ambitious ruler, ignored the advice of his
father's prudent counselors and provoked the northern ten tribes of Israel
into revolt under a new leader, Jeroboam. Only the tribes of Judah and
Benjamin stayed loyal to Rehoboam, with the result that the Hebrew
kingdom was bitterly divided. The historic rupture never healed; it destroyed forever the unity of Eretz Israel (Land of Israel) and proved a
turning point in the political and religious history of the Hebrews.[3]

Tuchman goes on to cite other instances in history where human blindness to consequences has caused many avoidable catastrophes and summarizes the far-reaching consequences of Rehoboam's folly:

> The kingdom of Judah, containing Jerusalem, lived on as the land of the Jewish people. It suffered conquest, too, and exile by the waters of Babylon, then revival, civil strife, foreign sovereignty, rebellion, another conquest, another farther exile and dispersion, oppression, ghetto and massacre—but not disappearance. *The alternative course that Rehoboam might have taken, advised by the elders and so lightly rejected, exacted a long revenge that has left its mark for 2800 years.*[4] [Emphasis supplied]

Thus the ancient land of Eretz Israel was not conquered from without, but was torn apart by *internal* dissension.

The theme of recurrent tragedy, above referred to by Tuchman, has been the cruel fate of the Jewish people throughout its history. However, most of these tragedies were self-inflicted and the result of the folly, foolhardiness, and ambition of its leaders. Once again the people of Israel are being betrayed by their leaders, it is the pied pipers of the Likud government who are today marching the people of Israel to certain disaster.

FOLLY MARCHES ON

As we have seen, beginning in 926 B.C., Eretz Israel was divided into two rival and hostile kingdoms: "Israel" in the north and "Judah" (including Jerusalem) in the south, each torn by bitter dynastic struggles and enmities. After his successful revolt from Judah, Jeroboam dedicated his efforts to making his new kingdom of Israel, completely independent of Judah under Rehoboam. To keep his people from going to Jerusalem to worship, he established new sanctuaries for worship at Bethel and Dan. He removed from the religious rituals all Judean reminders and changed the old festival dates to new ones. He set up two golden calves in the sanctuaries for the people to worship, thus transforming completely the spiritual meaning of the worship of Yahve (God).

Politically and spiritually alienated from Judah, the kingdom of Israel suffered through repeated revolutions and assassinations. Nine dynasties were established in little more than two hundred years. Nineteen kings followed each other, usually compelled to fight a bloody path to the throne.[5]*

*A History of the Jews, by Abram Leon Sachar, Ph.D., President of Brandeis University.

THE ASSYRIANS

In the year 734 B.C., the Kingdom of Israel (the northern ten tribes) under King Pekah joined a league of other kings in defiance of Assyria, the then dominant empire in the Middle East.

The Assyrian king, Tilgath-Pileser III, responded by launching a ruthless military campaign to crush the alliance. The Kingdom of Israel was quickly invaded by the Assyrians and thousands of its most important inhabitants were uprooted and scattered throughout the Assyrian empire. What had been the Kingdom of Israel was renamed "Samaria" by its Assyrian conquerors.[6]

Within a decade, two successive invasions by Assyrian kings, Shalmaneser V and Sargon II, completed the destruction of the northern kingdom. The remaining population was deported and scattered by the Assyrians to the four winds and disappeared from history as the "Ten Lost Tribes of Israel."[7]

As was their custom with difficult conquests, the Assyrians transplanted and resettled into Samaria new and alien peoples in place of the Israelites. These non-Jewish inhabitants, called "Samaritans," were largely composed of Cathaeans, Babylonians, Elamites, and Sushanites.

ISAIAH

Having witnessed the fate of Israel and the consequences of defying the Assyrian Empire, the surviving Kingdom of Judah prudently decided to follow the path of peace. For a time King Hezekiah of Judah wisely counseled his people to live and prosper in the sight of God, to build cities, to carry on commerce, and avoid war.

Thus for a time Judah escaped the fate of other neighboring countries, many of which suffered ruin and desolation as a consequence of war and defeat at the hands of the Assyrians. Nevertheless, the militant factions at Hezekiah's court were conspiring to stage a rebellion and conclude an alliance with Egypt and the Philistines to overthrow the Assyrians. The more King Hezekiah hesitated, the more the militants clamored for action.

The prophet Isaiah begged Hezekiah to profit by the fate of the Kingdom of Israel and other Assyrian victims. Desperately, Isaiah appealed over the heads of the "war party" to the good sense of the people. He walked around Jerusalem in bare feet, in sackcloth, prophesying that those who plotted to join the war against Assyria would be destroyed.

In spite of Isaiah's pleas in 714 B.C., Hezekiah under pressure from the militants joined the alliance against the Assyrians.

The vindication of Isaiah's foresight and the consequences of Hezekiah's folly came in 701 B.C. Sennachireb, the Assyrian king, attacked the league and crushed the rebellion. His armies spread fire and destruction throughout Judah and besieged Jerusalem. Finally a truce was arranged under which the Kingdom of Judah lost most of its territories. The city was plundered, Hezekiah's daughters were carried off to Nineveh, and he was left with only his crown and the ruined city of Jerusalem.[8]

JEREMIAH

A century later, the Assyrian empire in its turn was overthrown by the Babylonians under the great King Nebuchadnezzar. In his reign of forty-three years, Nebuchadnezzar spread the civilization of the new Babylon throughout the world. History records his reign as a time of relative peace and prosperity.

As long as the Kingdom of Judah submitted peacefully to Babylon, Nebuchadnezzar did not interfere with its internal affairs. However, a militant rebel faction in Judah was soon scheming with surrounding nations for a war to break loose from Babylon. This time it was the Prophet Jeremiah who pleaded for peace, insisting that Judah, wedged between mighty nations, could find salvation only by remaining outside of alliances and coalitions and that any thought of rebellion was foolhardy.[9]

Because of his warnings, Jeremiah became the most unpopular man in Jerusalem. He was ridiculed by the priests, denounced by the militants, and condemned by the people. He sent copies of his sermons, pleading for peace, to the king who angrily destroyed them. Jeremiah barely escaped execution as a traitor. The king defied the might of Babylon and prepared for war.

While Jeremiah was still preaching the cause of peace, the Babylonian King Nebuchadnezzar swept down and overwhelmed the kingdom of Judah. The king, and most of the leading citizens, were taken captive and transported to Babylon.

THE BABYLONIAN CAPTIVITY

Incredibly, the surviving militants in Jerusalem were plotting a new rebellion against Babylon. Again, Jeremiah vainly preached peace and repentance. In a final act of exasperation Nebuchadnezzar descended again with his armies upon Jerusalem. Jeremiah advised King Zedekiah to surrender, and for this advice Jeremiah was starved, beaten, and left to die. After a two and a half year siege, Jerusalem was taken, the temple burned to the ground, the city utterly destroyed, and the population taken as captives to Babylon.

The Jews remained in Babylon for approximately fifty years after the destruction of Jerusalem, until Cyrus the Persian conquered Babylon. Cyrus, a generous king, gave the Jewish exiles permission to return to their home and rebuild the Temple. A majority of them, however, preferred to live in Babylon rather than return to Jerusalem. As a result, Babylon developed into, and remained, a great center of Jewish culture for the next millennium.[10]

Other Jewish communities in Babylon, instead of returning to Jerusalem, chose to emigrate to Egypt, where they became populous and powerful in the centuries to come.

The rebuilding of the Temple in Jerusalem was begun almost immediately by the returnees from Babylon. The Samaritans (the people who had been settled by the Assyrians in Samaria on the West Bank of the Jordan and who had replaced the ten tribes of Israel) offered to help rebuild the Temple. Their offer was scornfully rejected by the Jews who refused to have anything to do with them. The Samaritan population was despised by the Jews as a "mongrel race." Jews were not only forbidden to intermarry with them, but were denied any social or religious contact with them. Even commercial transactions were severely limited. Samaritans were considered enemies of Judah or, at least, friends of the enemies of the Jews.

Bitter at their rejection and resentful of the attitude of the Jews toward them, the Samaritans built their own temple at Mount Gerizim at Shechem (today known as Nablus, a city on the West Bank of the Jordan). When Antiochus of Syria invaded Judea in 168 B.C., the Samaritans, as an expression of revenge for their ostracism, rededicated their temple at Mount Gerizim to the Greek god Zeus. Forty years later, following the restoration of the Jewish (Hasmonean) monarchy, John Hyrcanus destroyed the Samaritan temple.

The Jews and Samaritans lived side by side in a relationship of mutual hatred and distrust for many centuries.

The pious talk of the present-day Likud government of Israel about reclaiming the "sacred land of Samaria" on the West Bank is an historical travesty.

In 332 B.C. Alexander the Great burst upon the world scene, and in his short life conquered the entire Persian empire. Upon Alexander's death, the empire was divided among his senior generals. Ptolemy became ruler of Egypt, and its capital city of Alexandria attracted large numbers of Jews, who prospered under the privileges extended to them by him. Over the years, the Jewish community grew powerful and at one time comprised almost forty percent of the population of Alexandria, the second largest city in the Mediterranean world.

In the case of Palestine, however, this favorable situation came to an end with the triumph of Antiochus of Syria over the Ptolemian armies and in 201 B.C. Judah came under the control of the Selucids.

The Selucid dynasty (also founded by one of Alexander's generals) attempted to impose Greek customs and religious practices upon the Jews to whom "Hellenism" was anathema.

The Jews of Palestine revolted under the famous leader Judas Maccabaeus, who conducted a brilliant guerrilla campaign against the Syrians. Judas reconquered Jerusalem and reconsecrated the Temple in 165 B.C., an event celebrated today as "Hannukah." Thus began the Jewish (Hasmonean) dynasty of the Maccabees.

THE JEWISH KINGDOM RESTORED

The first years of the Jewish kingdom under the Maccabees were spiritually rich and materially prosperous. Then came a tragic turn in the fate of Judah. This is described in the following passage from Abram Sachar's *A History of the Jews* referred to earlier:

Material prosperity continued under John Hyrcanus (son of Simon Maccabaeus), who succeeded to the headship of the State when Simon, his father, was treacherously assassinated. Perhaps there was now too much prosperity; Hyrcanus' head was turned by ambitions to play a role in the eastern Mediterranean world. He created a mercenary army, with which he proceeded to carve out an empire. He subjugated the Samaritans and destroyed their temple. He gave Israel's ancient enemies, the Edomites, the alternative of exile or conversion to Judaism. *It was a sorry commentary upon the perverseness of human nature that Hyrcanus was already spreading his faith by the point of the sword,* although he was only one generation removed from those who had poured out life and fortune for religious freedom. His son, Aristobulus, continued and improved upon his example. He pushed his conquests up through Galilee and ultimately crowned himself king. He reintroduced the dreadful Oriental custom of destroying the members of his family who could become a threat to the security of his throne.

Meantime a formidable party had developed that vigorously opposed the policy of the rulers and their abandonment of Hasmonean idealism, called the Pharisees.[11] [Emphasis supplied]

The Pharisees were opposed by the Sadducees who supported the royal policy of imperialism. Their opposition reached the point of civil war in the reign of Alexander Jannaeus who succeeded his brother, Aristobulus. Jannaeus inaugurated a persecution in which six thousand Pharisees lost their lives. Sachar describes the state of anarchy in Judah in these words:

> For six years the civil strife continued. Jannaeus was merciless when opposed. At one time eight hundred rebels who had held a fortress against him were crucified and the throats of their wives and children were cut before their dying eyes. Eight thousand others were driven into Egyptian exile. Even in the worst days of the Israelite monarchy there had been no such bloody bickering.
>
> After the death of Jannaeus, his wife, Alexandra, who succeeded to the throne, reversed his policy and favoured the Pharisees. For a moment there was peace in Judah. The exiles returned, foreign wars ceased, and the old faith was practiced without hindrance. But the Pharisees had been too sorely outraged to allow their enemies to escape without punishment. Firm in their belief that their rancor was virtue, they instituted a series of persecutions and judicial murders which opened every old wound.[12]
>
> The Roman general Pompey was creating an empire in the East for the new mistress of the Mediterranean and looked greedily upon the fortresses of south-western Asia. Both warring factions in Judea appealed to him in 64 B.C. to judge between them, and after a show of deliberation he supported Aristobulus and bade his rival begone. He sent to Rome the magnificent golden vine which the grateful Aristobulus sent him as a present.
>
> *Next year the Pharisees begged Pompey to abolish the kingship altogether, take control of the country, and remove the curse of dynastic war. Pompey acted with alacrity and sent his legions to take over the Holy City.*[13] [Emphasis supplied]

Thus the end of the Jewish Kingdom of Judah came with an *invitation* to the Romans to take over Jerusalem and Judea.

Sachar concludes this sad chapter with the following observation:

Freedom was again crushed because the Jews had not learned how to use it. The selfishness of the ruling houses and the strife of political and religious factions exhausted the strength of the State. A curse seemed to lie on the Jews which prevented them from reaching the highest levels of moral power except when they were hammered and beaten by oppression.[14]

HEROD THE GREAT

A quarter of a century after Rome assumed control over Judea, the state was still in turmoil. The people suffered from the interminable feuds of the Hasmonean princes—but also from the civil strife and upheaval in Rome itself.

It was during this period that Herod supplanted the declining Hasmonean dynasty. Herod turned out to be one of the ablest rulers in Jewish history and brought peace to Judah. His reign was a genuine Augustan Age for Palestine. He respected the scruples of the Pharisees and, as far as he was able, did not allow any offensive statues into Jerusalem and even omitted his own image from the coinage. He built a magnificent temple, far more beautiful than the already legendary Temple of Solomon.

Upon the death of Herod, the last phase of stable Jewish rule effectively ended. Instead, there followed a period of great and rising tension, the reasons for which were not clear to the Romans. Rome's method of governing the empire was considered liberal for the times. Certainly this was the view of the six million or more Jews in the Diaspora who were treated as a special people accorded many privileges not allowed any other national or ethnic group in the empire.[15]

They had their own courts and system of taxation and were the only people not required to offer sacrifices to the emperor or recognize his divinity. The Roman Legions were not allowed to enter Jerusalem with their Eagle standards for fear of giving offense to the Jews who prohibited "graven images." Most of the Jews in Palestine did not see Romans as oppressors or enemies of their religion. However, a substantial minority of zealots and other extreme militants in Palestine were unreconciled to the Romans' rule and from time to time committed violent acts of defiance.

Ultimately, the Romans found the Jews to be ungovernable, even under their own rulers, and the people too turbulent to handle without direct Roman supervision. A procurator was therefore placed in control, responsible directly to the emperor. Still the country was rife with rebellion. There were three different factions in the Jewish population opposed to the Romans, but bitter enemies of each other.

THE ROMAN WARS

The Roman wars began when the fortress at Masada, which was occupied by a Roman garrison, was captured by one group of rebels and the Romans put to the sword.

The Roman soldiers, at the fortress Antonia, offered to surrender and be allowed to leave the country. The terms were accepted by the Jews—but as soon as the Romans had laid down their arms they were savagely slaughtered.

The tragic story of the siege and destruction of Jerusalem by the Roman Legions under Titus is well known.

For the purpose of this book Sachar's account is referred to here:

The city was magnificently fortified, protected externally by a triple circle of walls and internally by numerous towers and defenses. And the Jews fired by holy zeal were determined not to give in to the Romans while the breath of life remained in them. Titus implored the city to surrender but the Roman emissaries were killed.

Courage and defiance went for naught, however, in the face of the cursed factional strife which cropped up again even in the most critical moments of Jewish national life.

Three factions fought each other divided by temperament, by personal animosities, by disputes over war methods. One held the upper tower, one the lower, and the other the Temple area in between. None co-operated with another, riots and assassinations were frequent, while the most powerful legions in the world pounded at the gates.[16]

The zealots refused any Roman offers of truce or surrender. They firmly believed that God would not let Jerusalem fall. Finally in A.D. 70, after incredible suffering, Jerusalem was captured and destroyed. Almost a million Jews died or were sold into slavery.

The great Jewish historian-general, Josephus, in his account "The Jewish War," which was written to show the total impossibility that the war against Rome could have succeeded, blames the war and the disaster on the nationalist militant factions among the Jews.

Josephus wrote that because of their actions, "out of all the cities under Roman rule it was the lot of ours [Jerusalem] to attain the highest felicity, and to fall to the lowest depths of calamity."[17]

For almost half a century after the destruction of Jerusalem, the Jews lived at peace, enjoying equal political rights with the non-Jewish subjects of Rome and enjoying the general prosperity of the times.

As Sachar describes it:

> The Jews gradually adjusted themselves to the tragedy that had come upon them. The fall of the Temple and the dissolution of the State destroyed all of the outward symbols by which the religious and national life of the people had been regulated. Fortunately Judaism was not dependent for existence on a sanctuary and sacrifices. The life-blood of the nation was the law and the traditions which had grown up about it. *The truest defenders of the faith were now, not the desperate Zealots who sacrificed themselves with sublime stupidity,* but the scribes and sages who devoted their lives to teaching the masses the meaning of the ancient heritage. Such was Johanan ben Zakkai, who established an academy at Jabneh at the very moment that the physical State was being destroyed. The light which smoldered out in Jerusalem was again rekindled.[18] [Emphasis supplied]

Nevertheless, an irreconcilable minority of Jews kept alive an opposition which no prosperity could smother. They remained quiet so long as revolt seemed useless—but at the first sign of imperial weakness their hopes drove them to sedition.

In A.D. 115 the emperor Trajan was heavily involved in a military campaign against the still unconquered Parthians and at the same time was faced with a rebellion in other parts of the empire. Sachar continues:

> The Jews of Egypt, taking advantage of Roman difficulties, began to riot against their Roman and Greek enemies, and their disturbances grew into a formidable rebellion. This had hardly been suppressed when even more serious disturbances occurred in Cyrene and in Cyprus. The Roman historian Dio Cassius paints a sensational picture of the uprisings. The Jews wiped out nearly half a million people in both places, eating their flesh, besmearing themselves with their blood, sawing them asunder, feeding them to wild beasts! The account is the distorted version of a prejudiced historian, but evidently the Jews were in the grip of a wild and irresponsible fanaticism, which drenched Cyprus and Cyrene with blood. Trajan was compelled to send one of his ablest generals to cope with the fury of the Jews. The devastation was complete; when the last embers of

the rebellion had been extinguished, it was necessary to rebuild Cyprus from its foundations. No Jew was thereafter permitted to set foot on the island.[19]

Trajan died in A.D. 117 and was succeeded by Hadrian, whom the Jews welcomed as a second "Cyrus." Without malice toward the Jews or an understanding of the possible consequences, Hadrian issued two edicts, one to build a new city on the ruins of Jerusalem, to be called "Aelia Capitolina" and another to outlaw, what he considered a barbaric practice, mutilation. He mistakenly included circumcision in that category.

Sachar dramatically describes the reaction:

Both edicts set the Jews afire and they rose in their final rebellion against Rome, one of the most serious and protracted in Roman history.

Led by the venerable Rabbi Akiba and a brilliant young warrior, Simon Bar-Kokba, the might of Rome was forgotten. The Jews believed that this last stand against the Romans was like no other. It was the prelude to the establishment of God's kingdom on earth and, to some of his followers, Bar-Kokba was thought to be the Messiah. [20]

The amazing zeal of the aroused nation brought them unexpected success in the early months of the rebellion. They completely routed the Roman legions and cleared the country of the enemy. Hadrian was obliged to recall from Britain his best general Severus to put down the revolt. [21]

In a lengthy campaign of attrition the rebels were finally isolated and destroyed. Both Bar Kokba and Akiba were executed. The Romans, who had suffered heavy casualties and were in no mood for leniency, began a campaign of extermination which finally ended the tragedy.

Sachar concludes his powerful theme:

The Jewish casualties were much greater than attended the destruction of the state in A.D. 70. It is not improbable that a half million lives were sacrificed in the hopeless cause. Those who escaped death were rushed to the slave markets of the East or to the gladiatorial arenas of the chief cities of the West. On the site of the sanctuary a temple was built in honor of Jupiter Capitolina. The very name of Judah was discarded and the province which had given the Roman legions so much trouble was renamed Syria Palestine. Jews were forbidden on pain of death to ever set foot in Jerusalem.[22]

This prohibition continued until Rome itself fell.

It is a remarkable story. One can only speculate on the course of Jewish history, had the advice and pleas of the peacemakers (Isaiah, Jeremiah, Josephus and, finally, Rabbi Yochanan Ben Zakki) been heeded, instead of those of the fanatical zealots or the power-hungry demagogues. Throughout the ages, who of these proved to be the true friends of the Jewish people? Of this great drama, how much was rooted in faith—how much the consequences of folly?

The eminent professor and Israeli historian Yehoshafat Harkabi has pondered this matter and has written a book entitled *Facing Reality* in which he points out the remarkable parallel between Israel's situation today and that which existed prior to the destruction of Jerusalem by the Romans.[23]

Professor Harkabi's views are summarized in an Associated Press report appearing in the *Los Angeles Times,* October 18, 1988 edition, from which the following is quoted:

ISRAELI HISTORIAN WARNS
OF PERIL IN MASADA'S EXAMPLE

TEL AVIV—An Israeli historian has ignited a controversy by arguing that a much-heralded Jewish revolt against the Romans—far from being a glorious chapter in Jewish history—was self-destructive fanaticism and a bitter lesson for modern Israel.

The revolt was followed by the mass suicide on Masada in A.D. 73 and Gen. Shimon Bar-Kokba's rebellion nearly 60 years later.

A small but articulate group of scholars, writers and politicians has long contended that in the cold light of modern scrutiny the revolt was lunacy, rather than glorious.

The debate has been lifted out of the realm of pure history and plunged into the political battlefield because Israel today faces many of the same themes that confronted the rebel against Rome 1,911 years ago—among them survival, liberty and religion.

Occurred at Opportune Time

The way a generation of school children have been told it, the Jews revolted because they considered the Roman occupation brutal and in contempt of Jewish religious sensibilities. After a glorious fight of the few Jews against the many Romans, the story goes, the rebellion was crushed, Jerusalem was sacked, and the last thousand defenders committed suicide atop the mountain fortress of Masada.

But the rebellion smoldered on, and in A.D. 132 a Jewish general, Shimon Bar-Kokba, captured Jerusalem and held it for three years until the Romans vanquished his army and sent the Jews into an exile that was to last until the rebirth of Israel in 1948.

In his 107-page book, *Facing Reality,* Harkabi portrays the revolt as a disaster from start to finish, whipped up by rabble-rousing zealots blind to the realities of power in the Roman Empire.

The result, he writes, was the destruction of Jerusalem and the slaughter of 500,000 of the 1.3 million Jews living there.

The argument is not entirely new. But coming from Harkabi, an eminent scholar, former military intelligence chief and a pillar of the Establishment, it caused a sensation among intellectuals.

In an oblique, understated style, Harkabi suggests that his country may be treading the same dangerous waters as did the rebels against Rome. He discerns the same two camps today that existed in Bar-Kokba's time: what he calls the "realistic" and "sane" camp and the "blind," "euphoric," "unrealistic" one.

Harkabi does not deny that by "blind" and "euphoric" he is referring to Israel's present-day extreme nationalists who would annex the occupied West Bank of the Jordan River in defiance of world opinion.

Parallels to Modern Times Seen
Harkabi sees parallels between the Israelis who minimize the weight of the superpowers, and the zealots who misread the might of Rome; who tell Jews to ignore the outside world and trust in God alone; who, *after having annexed the West Bank and its million Arabs, would then lean back on the Messianic dream of a mass Jewish migration to Israel to correct the demographic imbalance.*

He likens the euphoria that overcame Israel after the 1967 Six-Day War to the ecstasy of the zealots after their own early victories.

"The problem is not where Bar-Kokba erred," Harkabi writes. "The problem is how we came to worship his error, and how it affects our national thinking."

But Amos Eylon, a prominent writer and political commentator, says *it is high time someone challenged "the angels of death and destruction like Bar-Kokba" who had become Israel's "hallowed symbols of national renewal."*

[13]

In a spectacular play called *The War of the Jews*, leftist playwright Joshua Sobol portrays the zealots as bloodthirsty demagogues shot through with personal hatred and greed. To Sobol, as to Harkabi, the voice of sanity comes from Yochanan Ben-Zakkai, the rabbinical sage who opposed the revolt and made a separate peace with Rome in return for being allowed to go on teaching the Bible to his disciples.

Israeli television entered the dispute by airing a debate called "If I Were There," in which six politicians of various political bent were asked how they would have conducted the revolt. To the amazement of many, all but one said they would have surrendered rather than lead their people to their death.

"None of us has the right, morally or otherwise, to lead our people knowingly to its doom" one said.

Moderator Israel Segal summed it up succinctly: "The dilemma that faced that generation and the problems that accompanied the revolt confront us today, too, it seems." [24] [Emphasis supplied]

CHAPTER II

The Diaspora and Eretz Israel

ALTHOUGH THE JEWS of Judea, who survived the destruction of Jerusalem in A.D. 70 and the Bar-Kokba revolt in A.D. 135, were widely dispersed by the Romans, the main Jewish Diaspora which has existed throughout the centuries was not the result of these events.

Today the word *Diaspora* is sometimes used among Jews as a convenient means of distinguishing between the Jews living in Israel and those living in other parts of the world.

However, to use the word *Diaspora* as it is also frequently used, to create the idea that it represents the "scattered remnants" of the Jewish people "exiled" from their homeland in "Eretz Israel" (The Land of Israel) is, historically, without foundation.

As we have seen, a *majority* of the Jews who had been taken away into Babylonian captivity preferred not to return to Israel when Cyrus the Persian liberated the Jews in Babylon and encouraged them to return to Palestine. This majority, who made the decision to stay in Babylon rather than return to Israel, became a prosperous and powerful community and a center of Jewish culture and learning for many centuries. Others, as has been mentioned, migrated to Egypt where eventually their number exceeded one million.

Before A.D. 70, when the second Temple was in its highest glory, the vast majority of Jews, *by choice,* did not, and never had, lived in Eretz Israel. They were not *exiles* in any sense of the word. Centuries before the fall of

Jerusalem their ancestors had emigrated from Israel *voluntarily* and had colonized the major centers of population around the Mediterranean and beyond. These Jewish communities were highly successful and prosperous.[1]

Paul Johnson, in his *History of the Jews,* states:

At the time of the Claudian census in A.D. 48 some 6,944,000 Jews were within the confines of the Roman Empire, plus what Josephus calls the "myriads and myriads" in Babylonia and elsewhere beyond it. One calculation is that during the Herodian period there were about *eight million* Jews in the world, of whom 2,350,000 to 2,500,000 lived in Palestine, the Jews thus constituting about 10 per cent of the Roman Empire. *This expanding nation and teeming Diaspora were the sources of Jerusalem's wealth and influence.*[2]

The Diaspora, through which Paul and others traveled, was vast. The Roman geographer, Strabo, said that the Jews were a power throughout the inhabited world. There were a million of them in Egypt alone. *In Alexandria, perhaps the world's greatest city after Rome itself, they formed a majority in two out of five quarters.* They were numerous in Cyrene and Berenice, in Pergamum, Miletus, Sardis, in Phrygian Apamea, Cyprus, Antioch, Damascus and Ephesus, and on both shores of the Black Sea. They had been in Rome for 200 years and now formed a substantial colony there; and from Rome they had spread all over urban Italy, and then into Gaul and Spain and across the sea into north-west Africa.[3] [Emphasis supplied]

The ubiquity of Jewish communities in the ancient world has caused speculation by Nathan Ausubel in his *Book of Jewish Knowledge* that some Jews *may not have left Egypt* with Moses in the Exodus.

He quotes Philo, the Hellenistic Jewish philosopher, as writing:

So populous are the Jews that no one country can hold them and therefore they settle in very many of the most prosperous countries in Europe and Asia, both on the islands and on the mainland.[4]

It should be pointed out that during the period of the Hasmonean dynasty, which lasted almost two hundred years, the Kingdom of Judah was a sovereign and independent state to which any Jew could have migrated or returned if he wished to do so.

As noted in the previous chapter, the reason that the Hasmonean dynasty ended was because the Jews *invited* the Romans to take over control of Judea to establish order in the Kingdom which was torn by dynastic struggle and factionalism.

The Diaspora Jews living throughout the Roman Empire, in most cases, were not persecuted by the Romans. They were in fact a privileged people in the empire.[5]

As mentioned earlier, the Roman authorities were so sensitive to Jewish religious feelings that the Roman legions could not carry their Eagle-headed standards into Jerusalem. The Jews of the ancient world who comprised ten percent of the population of the entire Roman Empire were not living in "ghettos," which were unknown until the year 1570, or as persecuted "exiles."[6]

This is even more true in modern times. The Jews have always been an enterprising and resourceful people who, in most cases, have moved to various places in the world in search of opportunity rather than refuge.

Certainly, there have been tragic times when Jewish communities have been *driven* into exile—but this by no means accounts for or explains the distribution of the Jewish population in the world today.

It is estimated that the distribution of the Jewish population of the world, in the year 1980, was approximately as follows: *Out of a total world population of 13.5 million Jews,* about 3.5 million lived in Israel. By far, the largest Jewish community is in the United States (5,750,000) and this, combined with important Jewish communities in Canada (310,000), Argentina (250,000), Brazil (130,000), and Mexico (40,000), and a dozen smaller groups, means that nearly half of world Jewry (6.6 million) is now in the Americas.

The next largest Jewish community, after the U.S. and Israel, is Soviet Russia's, with about 1,750,000. There are still sizable communities in Hungary and Rumania (30,000), and a total of 130,000 in Marxist eastern Europe. In western Europe there are a little over 1,250,000 Jews, the principal communities being in France (670,000), Britain (360,000), West Germany (42,000), Belgium (41,000), Italy (35,000), the Netherlands (28,000), and Switzerland (21,000). In Africa, outside the South African Republic (105,000) there are now few Jews except in the diminished communities of Morocco (17,000) and Ethiopia (perhaps 5,000). In Asia there are still about 35,000 Jews in Persia and 21,000 in Turkey. The Australian and New Zealand communities together add a further 75,000.[7]

It is obvious that the vast majority of the Jews of the world don't consider themselves in "exile" and have no intention of returning to live in their "homeland," Eretz Israel.

Since the coming of modern Zionism, which is discussed in the next chapter, certain Zionist leaders, particularly Zeev Jabotinsky who founded the Zionist-Revisionist party, have made as their principal objectives the conquest of all of Palestine and the expulsion or subjugation of the Arab population *in order to make room for a new "aliya" (Ingathering of the Exiles) to Israel.*

In recent years, this has been the sacred doctrine of the Gush Emunim (Bloc of the Faithful), a religious party of the extreme right and a major element in contemporary Israeli politics.

The Gush Emunim is the primary ideological force behind the Likud government's policies on the West Bank and Gaza.

THE ALIYA

The presence and continued expansion of Israeli settlements on occupied Palestinian lands is the most volatile, emotional, and intractable issue involved in the Israeli-Palestinian conflict. It is why the Intifada began and why the Israeli settlers have retaliated with "vigilante" raids against Arab villages.

Yet the policy itself is based upon the fiction of an aliya from the Diaspora, which is expected to populate the West Bank and Gaza after the Arabs are driven out.

In referring to the Zionist-Revisionist movement, started by Jabotinsky, Johnson has this to say:

On these grounds he founded the Union of Zionist-Revisionists to use the full resources of Jewish capitalism to bring to Palestine "the largest number of Jews within the shortest period of time." He attracted an enormous following in eastern Europe, especially in Poland, where the Revisionist militant youth wing, Betar—of which the young Menachem Begin became the organizer—wore uniforms, drilled, and learned to shoot. The object was to achieve the Jewish state in one sudden, irresistible act of will. In fact, *all three Jewish leaders (Zionist) overestimated the actual willingness of Jews to emigrate to Palestine during the 1920s.* After the turmoil of the immediate post-war years, especially the pogroms in Poland and the Ukraine, the Jews like everyone else shared in the prosperity of the decade. The urge to take ships to Haifa abated. During the 1920s the Jewish population of Palestine did, indeed, double, to 160,000. But the total number of immigrants was only 100,000 of which 25 per cent did not stay. So the net rate of immigration was a mere 8,000 a year. *Indeed, in 1927, the peak year of twenties prosperity, only 2,713 came and more than 5,000 left.* In 1929, the water-shed year in the world economy, arrivals (to Eretz Israel) and departures just about balanced.

Therein lay a great missed opportunity, and the makings of tragedy. During the calm years, when Palestine was relatively open, *the Jews would not come.*[8] [Emphasis supplied]

In a full-page article appearing in the *Jerusalem Post,* October 7, 1978, edition entitled "The General With a Phantom Army," Meir Merhav exposes the specious arguments used by Ariel Sharon and Menachem Begin about the massive aliya that will settle the West Bank. The following is an excerpt from the article:

Most Israelis, and our politicians most of all, have always kept up a lot of sanctimonious pretense about aliya. Like God and motherhood, everybody has always been for it. There has been little realistic thinking of what the prospects of significant immigration really are. There has been little practical effort to maximize the relatively limited existing potential for aliya.

More importantly, what seems to have been forgotten—not only by Ariel Sharon and Hanan Porat, but by the chief ideologue of *Greater Israel, Menachem Begin himself*—is that in the entire history of Zionism and of the State of Israel there has never been a mass immigration except in the wake of catastrophe. Jews motivated by ideals, whether secularly Zionist or religious, have always come in a trickle of small numbers. And many of them, simply because they were idealists, often became discouraged and left when reality soured their dreams.

Even when catastrophe overwhelmed entire Jewish communities, the majority of them *sought refuge not in Israel, but elsewhere.* Perhaps no more than 60,000 German Jews out of a total of some 300,000 who left Germany in 1933-39 could have come to Israel. Perhaps the British would not have allowed in more. *But many of them did not even consider the possibility* of coming here. The same is true of other Jewish communities.

Today, physical disaster does not threaten Jews anywhere. Even if it did, in one country or another, *there would always be a preference for a refuge other than Israel.* Even among Russian Jews, who are the most persecuted today in the national sense, 50-60 percent of those who are allowed to leave the Soviet Union choose to go to a place other than Israel.

We may not like these facts, but we cannot ignore them. We must realize that, the world being what it is, we cannot expect any large-scale immigration from the Diaspora. If, unpredictably, large numbers of Jews anywhere should be expelled and turn to Israel, we would of course take them in. But meanwhile we must settle down to being a Jewish state of four million by the end of the century.[9] [Emphasis supplied]

The above article from the *Jerusalem Post* was written eleven years ago, at a time when more than half of the Jews allowed to leave the Soviet Union decided to go to some country other than Israel.

Today the immigration situation has deteriorated to the point that in some years more Jews are leaving Israel than are arriving. More than 300,000 former Israelis live in the U.S. and Canada.

The latest figures available for 1988 (*Jerusalem Post,* June 20, 1988) show that *90 percent* of Jews leaving the Soviet Union *refuse* to go to Israel. The situation has become so alarming that the Likud government has put into effect a plan to *force* Jews leaving the Soviet Union to go to Israel. This is done by putting them on a plane bound for Israel and allowing no stopover. The term "refusenik" now has a new meaning.[10]

Time magazine, November 22, 1986, reports on the problem in an article entitled "Soviet Jews: Israel Wants Them All," from which the following has been excerpted:

LET OUR PEOPLE GO has been the compelling slogan of a massive campaign to win for the U.S.S.R.'s 3 million Jews the right of free emigration. Yielding reluctantly to worldwide pressure, the Kremlin has granted exit permits to about 125,000 Jews since 1970. *No other Soviet minority has been allowed to leave the country in any significant numbers.*

Halfway House. To the dismay and embarrassment of Israeli officials, a growing number of Russian Jews are reluctant to go to Israel. While the vast majority of refugees in the early 1970s went to Israel, 59% of those who arrived at the halfway house for emigrants in Vienna last month expressed a desire to settle in the U.S. Now a long-simmering dispute between Israelis and some Jewish organizations over the destination of the refugees may jeopardize the future of Jewish emigration from the Soviet Union.

To Israeli officials, the refugees' lack of interest in becoming citizens of the Jewish state seems like rank ingratitude and an affront to Zionist faith.

Unable to stem the tide of about 10,000 Russian Jews who have already emigrated to the U.S., *the Israeli government has moved to force most refugees in the future to come to Israel.* As the Israelis explain it, their basic problem is with the way station in Vienna, where Russian Jews arrive in the West by train. Nearly all emigrants must travel on Israeli visas to meet Soviet requirements for exit. Those wishing to proceed to the U.S., however, may stop in Vienna and request rerouting to the U.S. They apply to the Hebrew Immigrant Aid Society (HIAS) and other American humanitarian organizations for financial and practical assistance.

These America-bound refugees receive money raised nationwide among American Jews. The U.S. government since 1973 has contributed $13 million to their support. Some angry Israelis have dubbed those who seek this aid "defectors" or "dropouts." Josef Almogi, chairman of the Jewish Agency, which supervises all immigration to Israel, complains that "those who drop out enjoy better conditions."

They can stay in Europe three to six months at the expense of American agencies that then get them refugee visas to go on to America, Canada, or wherever.

An early Israeli attempt to stop the dropouts involved trying to establish an air link between Moscow and Tel Aviv. *In that way, Russian Jews might be flown directly to Israel, thus eliminating the Vienna stopover and the refugees' option to go elsewhere.*[11] (Emphasis supplied.)

An article in the *Jerusalem Post* of June 18, 1988, expressed dissatisfaction in the manner that U.S. Jewish leaders are dealing with the problem. The article is entitled "Erase Disgrace of Drop-Outs."

U.S. Jewish leaders must be confronted fearlessly by Israelis and told that Soviet Jews seeking to leave the USSR on Israeli visas must come to Israel.

The disgrace of the mass exodus of Soviet Jews under the guise of immigrating to Israel must cease immediately, Absorption Minister Ya'acov Tsur insisted. The struggle for Soviet Jewry, he continued, is a national, Zionist endeavour of the first order.

The benefits extended to former Soviet Jews by the U.S. government and the enticements offered them by U.S. Jewry place Israel in a position of cynical competition with that Jewry, Tsur asserted.

The real crunch will probably come next year, however, as the number of Russian Jews emigrating to the "golden medina" continues to climb, and as U.S. government funding for refugee resettlement begins to drop. HIAS [the Hebrew Immigration Aid Society] estimates that, in 1989, 25-30,000 Russian Jews will apply for admission to the U.S. as refugees.

A large portion of what HIAS, the JDC and federations spend on Soviet Jewish immigrants has come from the U.S. federal budget. In the past, when the number of Jewish refugees admitted to the U.S. rose, Jewish organizations would run to Congress for additional dollars.[12] [Emphasis supplied]

Why is it that so many Soviet Jewish emigres refuse to go to Israel and by a wide margin prefer the U.S. instead?

As long ago as July 1979, the *Los Angeles Times,* July 6 edition, published an article in which Alexander Dranov, who had emigrated from the Soviet Union in 1978, expressed his opinion regarding the feelings and attitudes of the Jewish emigres.

The following are excerpts from his interesting explanation:

Many Israelis cannot understand why it is that many Soviet Jews do not wish to emigrate to Israel, why it is that many seem to lack patriotic feelings for their "historical motherland," why it is that many seem to possess materialistic ideas about America. I would like to explain.

The most compelling reason for emigrating from the Soviet Union is to get away from an oppressive society—oppressive not only to Jews, though to the Jews more than any others, but oppressive also in all the countless ways that you don't have to be Jewish to experience. *Perhaps the chief form of oppression is simply the constant shortage of anything making a good and normal life: food, money, clothes, cars, apartments, information, the hope for a better future.*

In addition, Israel's geographic position is not particularly attractive to many Soviet Jews. To many, Israel does not seem to be Western enough and, indeed for Soviet Jews, particularly those from developed urban centers like Leningrad, Moscow, and Kiev, Israel seems almost Oriental. The climate is another factor. Many Soviet Jews are simply afraid of the heat of the deserts that make up much of Israel's territory. In America, they are convinced, the climate is more moderate.

Even more important is the image that many Soviet Jews have of Israel as a country that is less than free and democratic than is the United States. To many it even resembles the Soviet Union in some ways. This image is fairly strong, and it includes real and imaginary things. Compulsory military training and service, an overtly religious society and rumors of restrictions on leaving the country are all upsetting to a Soviet Jew.

It is perhaps understandable why many Soviet Jews would prefer to emigrate to a rich and free country with a reputation for stability, peace, a high standard of living, work opportunities and, perhaps most important of all, the right to be "left alone." For a Russian, the joy not to care a damn about anything political is a precious joy. The opportunity to be free from any obligation, from having to be anything—not even a Jew, if one so chooses—is synonymous with freedom in the minds of many Soviet Jews. America's diverse and developed culture, *famous cities and a temperate climate explain the tendency of Soviet Jews to prefer the United States over Israel.*[13] [Emphasis supplied.]

Noteworthy in Dranov's article is the remarkable statement that the chief form of "oppression" in the Soviet Union is not, as we thought, the lack of religious freedom, but rather the constant shortage of consumer goods, i.e., food, money, clothes, cars, apartments, etc.

Another objection of many Soviet emigres to going to Israel, he says, is "the climate—it's too hot." This is something that God seems to have overlooked in selecting a suitable promised land.

On the other hand, Dranov points out that the Soviet Jews prefer to emigrate to a rich and free country with a reputation for stability, a high standard of living and work opportunities.

It appears that nothing has changed in the last ten years since Dranov wrote his article. The *Los Angeles Times,* June 23, 1989, reports that the Anti-Defamation League and other Jewish agencies are trying hard to induce Soviet Jewish emigres to go to Israel but are having little success.

The *Times* concludes the report in these words:

But the Soviets are not buying. Israel's climate is too hot, says one. Its people are too religious, complains another. Hebrew is too hard to learn, says a third. A fourth young man feels the streets of Israel are unsafe. He wants to settle in Detroit.[14]

[23]

The tragedy of all this is that the Shamir-Sharon plan for the West Bank and Gaza is to dispossess the Palestinian people of land upon which their ancestors have lived for centuries (and to which they are passionately attached) upon the pretext of making room for people whose ancestors may have lived there two or three thousand years ago, *but who themselves have never lived there and do not want to live there, unless forced to by the Israeli government.*

*   *   *

Author's Note: The foregoing chapter was written in June of 1989, before the dramatic upheavals in Eastern Europe occurred. As of this writing (March 1990) the political instability currently prevalent in Eastern Europe has caused some concern among the Jewish population of certain Soviet-bloc nations about the possibility of a revival of indigenous anti-Semitism. This is happening at a time when the U.S. has decided that Jewish citizens of the Soviet Union can no longer be properly classified for immigration purposes as oppressed people and thus entitled to the status of refugees. The consequence has been to reduce and limit the number of Soviet immigrants accepted into the U.S. annually. Therefore, this recent combination of circumstances has resulted in a significant increase in the number of Soviet Jews immigrating to Israel. The effect of this immigration has been to exacerbate the already grave crisis in the Middle East and to underscore the central issue discussed later in this book, namely, whether European immigrants are more entitled to live in Palestine than Palestinians.

CHAPTER III

The Zionist Movement: 1887-1948

MODERN ZIONISM as a movement did not originate with the Holocaust survivors—but had a long and eventful history which began in the last century. Nevertheless, the Nazi persecutions and Hitler's "final solution," which aroused the sympathies of the world for the Jewish people, were the operative events which culminated in the creation of the State of Israel.

However, as Amos Perlmutter* points out in his book entitled *Israel: The Partitioned State,* the present political discords and rivalries within Israel today are simply a continuation and perpetuation of earlier divisions in the Zionist movement:

> Israel may be territorially secure, but old themes, voices, and faces still seem to echo from the past. The debate over autonomy, the Palestinians, settlements and the West Bank, and over secure boundaries is a variation on old debates that went by other names and were waged in World Zionist Congress meetings decades ago, in the political halls of the pre-state entity that was the Yishuv, in the first Knesset, and in the Knessets flush with undreamt-of military victories. To have heard Begin expound

---

* Amos Perlmutter is a professor of government at American University in Washington, D.C. He is a noted author, editor, and historian and has served as a member of the Israeli Delegation to the United Nations.

passionately on Eretz Israel, the old biblical lands of Israel, was to hear again the voice of Revisionist Zionism and its long-dead founder, Zeev Jabotinsky. When hearing the leader of the Labor Party, Prime Minister Shimon Peres, complain about Begin's autocratic ways, one must remember how fiercely Labor's founder and father, David Ben-Gurion, tried to stamp out the followers of Revisionist Zionism, and recall how deep the struggle really goes. Old themes, old fears, and old drives are still very much alive in today's Israel—frontiers, security, the Arab question, Palestine, Eretz Israel, internal political struggles, and the world at large.[1]

Perlmutter's scholarly analysis of the philosophical and political history of Zionism is enlightening—but discouraging, when one realizes that the same issues and conflicts which existed almost a century ago are no closer to resolution today. Indeed, the fears, obsessions, and ambitions, which dominated earlier debates, have since been magnified and intensified by two world wars, the Holocaust, five Arab-Israeli wars, and the recent Palestinian uprising.

Perlmutter in his book summarizes the situation in these words:

The question after the 1984 elections is not of one government or another's survival. Israel appears once again to be defining and redefining its territorial aspirations, which is the essence of the politics of security of the third partitioned state. As in the days before statehood, the same question is being asked and debated: What are the final boundaries of the state?

The answers to that question are, it is hoped, to be found in this book. Different men throughout Israel's history and pre-history have answered this question differently. *For Theodore Herzl,* there were no boundaries, no real country or state, only the passionate notion that *the Jews must find a homeland of their own.* For Chaim Weizmann, the Jewish state was indelibly tied to the British Mandatory, which existed like some protective umbrella overhead. For David Ben-Gurion, neither a fundamentalist nor a visionary, the boundaries of the state were flexible, never finally fixed, dependent on the nature and need of the historical moment. *For Zeev Jabotinsky, who violently opposed the idea of any sort of partition, and even more so for Menachem Begin, the caretaker of Jabotinsky's ideas, the state meant unpartitioned Eretz Israel,* complete Israel, the old biblical lands of Judea and Samaria, in which there is no room for real Palestinian autonomy, let alone a Palestinian state.

Thus, the political history of Israel and its institutions becomes a description of a great debate over boundaries, argued by great men who then enacted imperfect resolutions of that debate. As we can see in Israel today, in Lebanon, and in the West Bank, the debate goes on.[2] [Emphasis supplied]

Therefore, even a limited understanding of the political and religious forces at work in Israel today requires some historical perspective.

THE BEGINNINGS

The acknowledged Father of modern Zionism, Theodore Herzl, was a journalist born in Budapest in 1860, and an "assimilated Jew." His historic role is remarkable, considering the fortuitous circumstances under which it began.

As a journalist, he took on as an assignment the notorious Dreyfus case. The case was an international sensation involving Alfred Dreyfus, a Jewish French army officer, who had been falsely accused of treason by a Gentile officer who was later proven to be the guilty party.

The trial caused the latent anti-Semitic emotions in the French army and in the French people to surface violently. This convinced Herzl that emancipation and assimilation had failed the Jews of Europe, and that the only solution was for the Jews to have a homeland of their own. He was not concerned about the particular location of such a homeland, only that it would be "Jewish" and a place where Jews could live in peace and security.

However, he met strong opposition from many assimilated, as well as Orthodox Jews, the latter of whom believed that only the coming of the Messiah could bring about a new Zion.

Nevertheless, Herzl persevered in his idea and carried his dream to as many of the courts of Europe as would receive him. He also enlisted the aid of influential Jewish financiers whenever and wherever he could find them. Impressed with his sincerity, the British offered to give him Uganda for a Jewish homeland.

Herzl found his greatest support among the East European Jews—who had been suffering persecution and pogroms at the hands of the Russian czar. With these East European Jews as a base, he began to organize the movement which became known as the World Zionist Organization. In 1892 he called a meeting of the World Zionist Congress in Basel, Switzerland, at which meeting he was elected president of the organization.

His suggestion of a Jewish homeland in Uganda was met with such bitter

[27]

opposition by the delegates that it threatened the very survival of the movement. Finally, the delegates rejected the idea of any place other than Palestine as the Jewish homeland.

The dissensions and divisions among Socialist Zionists, Religious Zionists, and Secular Zionists soon made a battleground of the Zionist movement, and the personal attacks upon some of Herzl's programs may have contributed to his early death on July 3, 1904.

At the time of Herzl's death, Palestine was, as it had been for more than four hundred years, part of the Ottoman Empire. Of a population of approximately 700,000, Jews numbering 35,000 resided mostly in Jerusalem and the port cities and engaged principally in commerce. The remaining 665,000 were mainly Arabs.

For centuries there had been no organized Jewish immigration into Palestine except for a small "Lovers of Zion" movement among Russian Jews in 1882. Notwithstanding the numerical odds presented by a large indigenous Arab population, the early Zionists *intended to establish an undivided Jewish hegemony over the entire territory of Palestine.* They recognized the Arab problem—but decided it could be solved later, after they achieved their primary objective—a Jewish state.

After Herzl's death, the Zionist movement continued its momentum under new leaders, each of these leaders, as we have seen, holding very different ideas and philosophies as to how their common purpose—a completely Jewish Palestine—might best be accomplished.[3]

Closest to Herzl's ideas was Chaim Weizmann, who believed that a Jewish homeland could best be established through the power and influence of the British Empire. Consequently, he assiduously cultivated such prominent persons as David Lloyd George, Winston Churchill, and Anthony Balfour.

At first Zeev Jabotinsky was a supporter of Weizmann's British solution—but later broke away to found the movement known as *Revisionist Zionism.* This movement declared Britain to be the enemy, and laid claim to all ancient biblical lands, including Judea and Samaria. The more extreme elements later dominated the movement and, as described by Perlmutter:

They would achieve a black fame as violent terrorists actively fighting the British. *Ironically, the legacy of Jabotinsky, as embodied by former prime minister Menachem Begin, still lives in Israel today and still wreaks emotional havoc.*[4] [Emphasis supplied]

However, the leader who would ultimately have the greatest impact and be responsible for bringing about the reality of a Jewish homeland and the State of Israel was David Ben-Gurion, the head of the *Socialist Zionist* movement. Although all three heirs to the Zionist movement were united in their devotion to Zionism and admiration of Herzl, they agreed on very little else.

Gradually, Chaim Weizmann emerged to the forefront of Zionist leadership. His purpose was to reconcile Zionist aspirations with British imperialism. Weizmann cared little for the indigenous Arabs of Palestine. He believed that Arabs and Jews must live separately since, in his opinion, the Arabs would reduce the standard of living of the Jews. He felt that the Jewish settlements would lag if there was cooperation and fraternization among Jews and Arabs. He doubted whether Arabs had patriotic feelings and saw them as nothing but backward, scheming, deceptive, and untrustworthy.[5]

The Zionist movement, as a nationalistic movement, was uncompromisingly committed to these fundamental tenets:

1. Establishment of a Jewish state in Eretz Israel ("the historical land") as the territorial center of the Jewish nation *in direct opposition to the Arab claims to the land.*
2. Creation of a Jewish majority in Palestine.
3. Separation from the Arabs. In calling for Jewish statehood, and the restoration of Jewish culture, the Zionists sought to establish a clear-cut position isolated from Arab and Muslim cultural values and social structure. *The conscious aim was to create an independent and autonomous Jewish national culture and social system in Eretz Israel which would be fortified by erecting political, economic, social, and cultural walls designed to separate Jews* from the Arab population which they would rule.[6]

THE BALFOUR DECLARATION

With the advent of World War I in 1914 and the Ottoman Empire's decision to join Germany and Austria-Hungary against the Allies, the first real opportunity came to bring the Zionist dream into reality. A victory for the Allies was expected to result in the dismemberment of the Ottoman Empire, leaving the fate of Palestine in the hands of the victors, Britain and France.

Britain needed all the help she could get in her struggle with Germany.

Britain enlisted the aid of the Arabs against Turkey, and an Arab army under British General Allenby and T.E. Lawrence (Lawrence of Arabia) achieved spectacular victories in the Middle East, including the capture of Jerusalem. Relying on British assurances, the Arabs had no doubt that their sacrifices and military successes would justify Britain's recognition and support of Arab nationalism.

At the same time, however, the British wanted to use the Jews as a wedge against France by creating a British (League of Nations) Mandate over Palestine. They reasoned that this could best be accomplished by reaching an understanding with the Zionist leaders.

The result was the famous "Balfour Declaration of 1917," which was simply a short note from Anthony Balfour, British Foreign Minister, to Lord Rothschild. It is quoted here in its entirety:

Dear Lord Rothschild:

I have much pleasure in conveying to you, on behalf of His Majesty's Government, the following declaration of sympathy with Jewish Zionist aspirations which has been submitted to and approved by the Cabinet.

His Majesty's Government views with favour the establishment in Palestine of a national home for the Jewish people, and will use their best endeavours to facilitate the achievement of this object, *it being clearly understood that nothing shall be done which may prejudice the civil and religious rights of existing non-Jewish communities in Palestine,* or the rights and political status enjoyed by Jews in any other country.

I should be grateful if you would bring this declaration to the knowledge of the Zionist Federation.[7] [Emphasis supplied]

Anthony Balfour

This ambiguous document was the first official recognition of the Zionists' political objectives and may be said to be the only claim up to that time to the legitimacy of a future Jewish state. However, the Arabs saw in the Balfour Declaration official support for the Jews, and even a promise of an eventual Jewish state within their midst. Indeed, publication of the Balfour Declaration marked the moment that Palestinian Arab nationalism, quiescent but pregnant with possibility until then, took the offensive against the Zionists. The Socialist Zionists in Palestine knew the Balfour Declaration for what it was—both a lifeline of legitimacy for the Jews, and an endless and potentially murderous source of enmity between Arab and Jew.

In the meantime, as a result of the Russian pogroms of 1905, an additional 20,000 Jews migrated to Palestine, among whom was David Ben-Gurion. To the Zionists, any concession to the idea of dividing the Palestine territory between Arabs and Jews was simply a *pretext* to be used until the final achievement of Jewish sovereignty *over all of "Eretz Israel."*

Although a small moderate faction of Zionists thought it possible for Jews and Arabs to live together peacefully in an integrated society, the militant nationalist rejectionists vehemently opposed this theory. Their approach was pessimistic and condescending. Professor Yoseph Klausner, a prominent historian of ancient Jewish history at the Hebrew University in Jerusalem, and eventually a prominent revisionist scholar, argued that the Arabs and Jews were irreconcilable. He saw integration between the two as culturally dangerous, fearing that the Jews would "descend from their high culture into the semi-primitive Arab culture." Zeev Jabotinsky, at that time second only to Weizmann in the World Zionist leadership, also saw the prospect of future conflict and struggle, but he, like many Zionist leaders, underestimated the strength and ferocity of Arab nationalism.[8]

The Zionist movement and its implications for the indigenous Arab population of Palestine were apparent as far back as 1910, when the Ottoman Empire announced its opposition to new Jewish settlements. Well before 1914, the Arabs were very aware of Zionist aims to take control of their country and voiced their adamant opposition to the Jewish plans for new settlements. From the start, the Arabs distinguished between "foreign Jews," meaning Zionist European, and the indigenous "Ottoman Jews," a small number of whom had shared Palestine with the Arabs for centuries.

As previously noted, the roots of the Arab-Zionist conflict antedated the Balfour Declaration, but when the declaration was actually made, the Arab resistance solidified in the form of Palestinian Arab nationalist opposition. Despite many warnings from the Arabs, all of the Zionist leaders underestimated the Arab nationalist movement and its intensity. To the Arabs, the Balfour Declaration was a betrayal of Arab nationalism and, while promising to protect their rights, was simply an attempt to legitimize Jewish political domination over Palestine in complete disregard to the *numerical superiority of the Arabs and the Wilsonian principles of majority rule and self-determination.*[9]

To the British and their Palestinian Mandate, it was obvious that there was no compromise position which would accommodate both the Zionist and Palestinian claims and aspirations. The "partition" of Palestine was an alternative, but not a solution, since it antagonized both Jews and Palestinians.

Gradually, British policy began to drift away from the Balfour Declaration in favor of limiting Jewish immigration into Palestine. Recognizing the mounting crisis in Palestine, Britain issued a report on July 7, 1937, which, in part, stated:

> Arab nationalism is as intense a force as Jewish. *The Arab leaders' demand for national self-government and the shutting down of the Jewish National Home has remained unchanged since 1920.* Like Jewish nationalism, Arab nationalism is stimulated by the educational system and by the growth of the Youth movement. It has also been greatly encouraged by the recent Anglo-Egyptian and Franco-Syrian treaties. The gulf between the races is thus already wide and will continue to widen if the present Mandate is maintained.[10] [Emphasis supplied]

The British report concluded with another proposed partition plan, which found no support on either side—and ignited acrimonious debate throughout the Zionist movement worldwide. *The Socialist Zionist Labor movement,* however, was willing to accept the principle of partition as a *temporary* and *intermediate* step toward full Jewish hegemony and a state comprising *all of Palestine.*

Revisionist Zionism's leader, Zeev Jabotinsky, was the labor movement's chief antagonist and one of the principal opponents of partition. *Jabotinsky believed that the Zionist goal must be to establish a Jewish state comprising all of pre-1922 Palestine, including Transjordan.* He based the Revisionist program on three goals:

1. The gradual transformation of Palestine (including Transjordan) into a Jewish commonwealth; that is, into a self-governing commonwealth under the auspices of an established Jewish majority.
2. To create the tools for building this commonwealth, including a regular army, a system of state control over customs and taxation, and the nationalization of all land.
3. To harness the Balfour Declaration to Zionist aims through active political and diplomatic work.

Jabotinsky opposed the concept of a Jewish enclave and isolation from the rest of Palestine. He believed that the *one national group*—the Jews—

would surpass the other—the Arabs—because their culture, values, and commitments were superior, and that a Jewish state would dominate and rule all of Eretz Israel.[11]

It is clear that the Arabs' hostility toward aggressive Zionism had nothing to do with the fact that the "aggressors" were ethnically "Jewish." The same hostility would have been aroused in the Arab population had the immigrants (invaders to the Arabs) been Swedish. The Arabs' response to Zionism was a purely human reaction toward a movement whose unconcealed purpose was to take over and rule the country in which they had been born and in which their ancestors had lived for centuries. Also, to make matters worse, this was happening at a time when the Palestinians' own nationalist dreams (they believed) were nearing the point of fulfillment.

BRITISH WHITE PAPER

As previously noted, the basic strategy of nearly all segments of the Zionist movement was to win the population battle with the Arabs first, after which Jewish hegemony and domination of Palestine would be established. In effect, the Arabs were to be overwhelmed by the Jewish immigrants and, hopefully, induced either to migrate or, if necessary, be expelled from Palestine to some other Arab state or community. Gradually, what had always been clear to the Palestinians became apparent to the British, namely, that the Zionists were distorting the intent and purpose of the Balfour Declaration by unwarranted interpretations. Accordingly, in the spring of 1939, the British issued its famous "White Paper," which was intended to clarify the ambiguities in the Balfour Declaration and to restate British policy on Palestine in unmistakable terms.

A portion of the "White Paper" is set forth below:

Unauthorized statements have been made to the effect that the purpose in view is to create a wholly Jewish Palestine. Phrases have been used such as "Palestine is to become as Jewish as England is English." *His Majesty's government regard any such expectation as impracticable and have no such aim in view.* Nor have they at any time contemplated ... *the disappearance or the subordination of the Arab population,* language or culture in Palestine. They would draw attention to the fact that the terms of the Balfour Declaration referred to, do not contemplate that *Palestine as a whole* should be converted into a Jewish National Home but that such a home should be founded *in Palestine.* But this statement has not removed doubts, and *His Majesty's government therefore now declares unequivocally that it is not part of their policy that Palestine should become a Jewish State.*[12] [Emphasis supplied]

The White Paper then sets forth certain specific provisions limiting Jewish immigration over the next five years.

Within months *after* the issuance of the White Paper, in the spring of 1939, the war with Nazi Germany broke out. Therefore, the White Paper did not address the later and graver problems of Jewish refugees from Hitler's "final solution," and the British continued to limit Jewish immigration into Palestine, in strict accord with the White Paper quotas. This infuriated the Zionists who considered launching an all-out guerrilla war against the British Mandate. The dilemma faced by Ben-Gurion and the Socialist Zionists was that the Nazi threat was far greater than the British and, as more became known concerning the magnitude of the Holocaust, it became clear that outright hostilities against the British were unwise as long as the Nazis constituted the principal danger.

Accordingly, a middle course was decided upon—the Jews would accumulate arms and military equipment and organize their military strength, but would not provoke the British into all-out war. Instead, the Jews would continue to evade the British immigration restrictions and to fortify the settlements then in place and continue to open new settlements regardless of land restrictions. It would be open defiance of the White Paper—but not warfare.

However, to the militant Zionists of the *Revisionist* faction who had opposed the British Mandate even before the White Paper was issued, it became a call to arms to be pursued with assassinations, robberies, and assorted acts of terrorism.

In the meantime, however, as the momentum of World War II seemed to be going against the British and the Nazi tide was lapping at the gates of Cairo, thousands of Jews volunteered to serve in the Allied forces against Germany. All of this made the British more amenable toward Zionism, and they began helping to train and arm the Haganah (the military arm of the Socialist Zionists). This help included courses in explosives, mines, artillery, etc., even though the British recognized the risk that the Haganah might later use this training against them.

The death in 1940 of Zeev Jabotinsky, founder of the Revisionist party, opened the way for Israel's most militant terrorist, Abraham Stern, the predecessor of Menachem Begin and Yitzhak Shamir. Stern, a wild-eyed fanatic, began feverishly to organize commandos, build up arms caches, and recruit immigrants from Europe. Stern was committed to Israel's "eternal aspirations," which included the building of the third Temple, transferring the Arab Palestinians out of Palestine and expelling the British. To this last purpose he even sought an alliance with Nazi Germany to destroy the British Mandate.

Stern envisioned a Jewish Fatherland with the borders of Israel (according to the "Torah") to extend from the *Nile to the Euphrates*.† This was to be achieved by a Jewish army, with the help of the underground and the Diaspora. Stern considered the Socialist Zionists, and especially Ben-Gurion and Weizmann, to be traitors. To many moderate Zionists the "Stern gang" was a particularly murderous group of terrorists, and they frequently assisted the British in rounding them up. Stern was finally trapped by the British and killed. Although an outcast from moderate Zionism, he was also a symbol of a growing revolt that Menachem Begin would come to embody. After his death, Stern was succeeded by another terrorist, Yitzhak Shamir, who took over leadership of the Stern gang (later called the Lehi).[13]

As the German threat receded, the British became more aggressive in their efforts to enforce the White Paper policy. They turned back several refugee ships from Europe in which, tragically, Jewish lives were lost. In no way, of course, could anything that the British did or did not do regarding immigration change materially the course or magnitude of the Holocaust once it was underway. Nevertheless, the perceived callousness of the British toward the Jewish refugees aroused a feeling of great bitterness among the Jews and this set the final stage for the forced abandonment of the British Mandate. The British army of occupation was now facing a guerrilla war— but it never clearly understood whom it was fighting.

THE JEWISH UNDERGROUND AND TERRORISM

In April 1942, Menachem Begin arrived in Palestine as a member of the "Andres Free Polish Army." He obtained a release from the army to assume control of the forces of Revisionist Zionism which included elements of the Irgun and Lehis underground.

Begin's objective was to use terrorism as the means of making British presence in Palestine intolerable to Britain. With passionate intensity, Begin led the fight against the British in Palestine. His mind-set, which he retained even as prime minister, was an obsession with Britain's "guilt" in the Holocaust. Begin wrote:

---

† From the Nile to the Euphrates includes present-day Lebanon, Jordan, Syria, and Iraq.

One cannot say that those who shaped British policy did not want to save the Jews; it would be more correct to say that *they very eagerly wanted the Jews not to be saved.* . . . They were highly interested in achieving the maximum reduction in the number of Jews liable to seek to enter the land of Israel.[14] [Emphasis supplied]

Begin officially launched his war against the British on February 1, 1944. His battle plan was simple—an unrestricted campaign of terror. The most infamous of these terrorist acts was the bombing under Begin's orders of the King David Hotel (the British headquarters) on July 22, 1946, in which eighty people died. A particularly cruel deed perpetrated by the Etzel (Irgun) is described by Perlmutter as follows:

Begin's Etzel forces had kidnapped two young British sergeants, conscripts with no particular animosity toward the Jews, in retaliation for the capture of three Etzel men. In effect, the British were being held hostage. Then, on July 29, 1947, the Etzel men were hanged by the British in Acre Prison.

The drama that had been playing out for months was coming to a grisly climax. Parents of the sergeants had pleaded for their lives. British officials called the "hostage" system heinous. In many ways, this was another misperception on the part of the British. The mandatory viewed Etzel and the underground groups as terrorists fighting an illegal war. Begin saw it as a real war and viewed their fighters as legitimate soldiers. Etzel Chief of Staff Amichal Paglin said that "we had nothing against the two boys personally. We just wanted to stop the hangings."

After the Etzel fighters were hanged, even Zionist supporters pleaded with the Etzel to spare the two British soldiers. The plea fell on deaf ears. Immediately upon hearing the news of the hangings, the two sergeants, hooded, were placed on chairs and a noose was put around their necks. Etzel men kicked the chairs away. The bodies were transported to a eucalyptus grove nearby and hung upside down from a tree for the British to find. The area around the bodies was booby-trapped and mined.[15]

Johnson, in his book entitled *History of the Jews,* expresses the opinion that the Jewish underground introduced the "first use of scientific terrorism in the modern world" and that *Menachem Begin was its most accomplished practitioner.*[16]

In his final commentary on this period, Perlmutter gives Menachem Begin's terrorist activities a major share of the credit for driving out the British:

Etzel often confused with Lehi, of course performed numerous acts of violence against the British, not all of them as grisly or horrifying as the King David bombing or the hanging of the British sergeants. These included a daring raid on the supposedly impregnable Acre Prison to release Lehi and Etzel prisoners. *What was most important was that the acts were played out to the world, and it would not be wrong to say that they played as key a role in pushing the hamstrung, weary, frustrated British out of Palestine* as did the combined efforts of the Haganah and Palmach, and the political tenacity of Ben-Gurion and Weizmann.

Looking back at the struggle against the mandatory from the standpoint of modern times, there is no denying the importance of both the more moderate forces of Ben-Gurion and *the terrorist forces of Etzel and Begin. Begin provided the often horrific spark which would stir and incite the British to the point where they were ready to leave Palestine.* Ben-Gurion, often in politically ruthless ways, kept the forces of resistance together, and molded the state-in-being that was to become Israel.[17] [Emphasis supplied]

However, the Lehi, led by Yitzhak Shamir, was too extreme even for Begin's taste. Among other terrorist acts, it was responsible for the murder in 1944 of Lord Moyne, British Minister for Middle East Affairs, and on April 26, 1944, the cold-blooded killing of six sleeping British paratroopers. Later, Shamir's Lehi planned and carried out the assassination of Count Folke Bernadotte, the United Nations envoy.[18]

It is clear that throughout the history of the Zionist movement the major factions were agreed on only one thing—they wanted *all* of Palestine, not a "partitioned" Palestine except as a first step toward total control. In essence this meant that a homeland for the Jews meant no homeland for the Palestinians.

As we have seen, one proposed solution had long been to "partition" Palestine between Jews and Arabs in an attempt to accommodate both the Jews and Palestinian national movements. The insoluble problem continued to be that neither side wanted partition—each claiming the entire country of Palestine.

In 1942, the Socialist Zionists, led by Ben-Gurion, reluctantly began to move toward accepting a partition of Palestine—but only as a first step in achieving a Jewish state encompassing all of Palestine.

Ben-Gurion's philosophy is summarized in the recent book by Simha Flapan, entitled *The Birth of Israel, Myths and Realities:*

Ben-Gurion's long-range objective was quite clear: "Just as I do not see the proposed Jewish state as a final solution to the problems of the Jewish people," he told his party members, *"so I do not see partition as the final solution of the Palestine question. Those who reject partition are right in their claim that this country cannot be partitioned because it constitutes one unit,* not only from a historical point of view but also from that of nature and economy."

Addressing the Zionist Executive, he again emphasized the tactical nature of his support for partition and his assumption that "after the formation of a large army in the wake of the establishment of the state, we will abolish partition and expand to the whole of Palestine." He reiterated this position in a letter to his family during that same period. *"A Jewish state is not the end but the beginning . . . we shall organize a sophisticated defense force—an elite army. I have no doubt that our army will be one of the best in the world. And then I am sure that we will not be prevented from settling in other parts of the country,* either through mutual understanding and agreement with our neighbors, or by other means."

In May 1942, Ben-Gurion convened a Zionist conference in New York City that was attended by some six hundred delegates, including leaders from Palestine and from the European movements. The main thrust of the resulting Biltmore Program (named after the hotel where the meeting took place) was that "Palestine be established as a Jewish commonwealth integrated into the structure of the new democratic world." The British Mandate, it was declared, could no longer assure the establishment of the national home. Significantly, the subject of borders was not mentioned in the final resolution. *Yet the implications of the commonwealth plan were obvious: Palestine was to be a Jewish state. The Arabs were no longer a party to negotiations and had no role in determining the future of the country.*

With the support of the increasingly influential and militant American Zionists in a coalition against the more liberal, conciliatory elements in the movement, Ben-Gurion gained passage of the resolution. The Biltmore Program became the official policy of the World Zionist movement and heralded Ben-Gurion's ascent to unchallenged leadership. On his return to Palestine after the conference, *Ben-Gurion continued to emphasize that Biltmore referred to a Jewish state in the whole of Palestine.* At a meeting of the Histadrut Council at Kfar Vitkin, he explained that "this is why we formulated our demand not as a Jewish state in Palestine, *but Palestine as a Jewish state,*" and he specifically advised not to identify the Biltmore Program with a Jewish state *in part* of Palestine.[19] [Emphasis supplied]

On August 5, 1946, the Executive Board of the Jewish Agency met in Paris and adopted the concept of "partition" as the official policy of the Zionist movement.

Ben-Gurion knew that President Truman was opposed both to a Jewish state in Palestine and to partition. Truman was, however, sympathetic to the refugee problem of the Holocaust survivors.

Perlmutter calls attention to a popular misconception that associates Zionism primarily with the victims of the Holocaust:

Ben-Gurion and the Zionists then decided to combine the Holocaust and independence, the plight of Jewish displaced persons and survivors of the camps with the concept of partition. Even for the Zionists this was something of a departure, *for they had come late to the issue of the plight of the victims of the Holocaust. The pursuit of a displaced persons policy had not been one of the Zionists' major goals (no matter how much some historians like to insist it was.)* Now, in 1946, the plight of the displaced persons in British camps coincided with pragmatic politics on several levels. On the most immediate front, immigration to Eretz Israel was always a major Zionist concern, and the survivors of European Jewry represented hundreds of thousands of potential Jewish settlers who had nowhere else to go since the gates of most countries, including the United States, were closed to them. The displaced persons therefore also represented a practical way to mix humanitarian concerns with pragmatic politics. This was especially true in finding a way to get the United States involved in the Palestine problem. The British, without meaning to, were eminently cooperative.[20] [Emphasis supplied]

As efforts to involve the United States grew, the political pressure on President Truman increased.

Truman, as did almost everyone else, felt great sympathy for the Jewish refugees from Europe. He was also much less sure of the Jewish vote than

Roosevelt had been. For the coming 1948 election, he needed the endorsement of Jewish organizations in such swing-states as New York, Pennsylvania, and Illinois. Once the British renounced their mandate, Truman pushed for the creation of a Jewish state in Palestine. In May 1947, the Palestine problem came before the United Nations. The majority produced a new partition plan—there would be Jewish and Arab states, plus an international zone in Jerusalem. *Being aware of Zionist ambitions for all of Palestine, neither the American State Department, nor the British Foreign Office wanted a Jewish state.* They foresaw disaster for the West if one were created. The British War Office and the U.S. Defense Department were also strongly opposed.

PARTITION AND THE BIRTH OF ISRAEL

Nevertheless, on November 29, 1947, thanks to Truman's vigorous backing, the plan was adopted by the General Assembly, 33 votes to 13, with 10 abstentions.[21]

The Partition Plan contains, among others, the following provisions:

1. The basic premise underlying the partition proposal is that *the claims to Palestine of the Arabs and Jews, both possessing validity, are irreconcilable, and that among all of the solutions advanced partition will provide the most realistic and practicable settlement,* and is the most likely to afford a workable basis for meeting in part the claims and national aspirations of both parties.
2. It is a fact that both of these peoples have their historic roots in Palestine, and that both make vital contributions to the economic and cultural life of the country. The partition solution takes these considerations fully into account.
3. *The basic conflict in Palestine is a clash of two intense nationalisms.* Regardless of the historical origins of the conflict, the rights and wrongs of the promises and counter-promises, and the international intervention incident to the Mandate, there are now in Palestine some 650,000 Jews and some 1,200,000 Arabs, who are dissimilar in their ways of living and, for the time being, separated by political interests which render difficult full and effective political cooperation among them, whether voluntary or induced by constitutional arrangements.
4. *Only by means of partition can these conflicting national aspirations find substantial expression and qualify both peoples to take their*

places as independent nations in the international community and in the United Nations.

5. The partition solution provides that finality, which is a most urgent need, is the solution. Every other proposed solution would tend to induce the two parties to seek modification in their favour by means of persistent pressure. The grant of independence to both States, however, would remove the basis for such efforts.

6. Partition is based on a realistic appraisal of the actual Arab-Jewish relations in Palestine. Full political cooperation would be indispensable to the effective functioning of any single-State scheme, such as the federal State proposal, except in those cases which frankly envisage either an Arab or a Jewish dominated State.

7. Partition is the only means available by which political and economic responsibility can be placed squarely on both Arabs and Jews, with the prospective result that, confronted with responsibility for bearing fully the consequences of their own actions, a new and important element of political amelioration would be introduced. In the proposed federal State solution, this factor would be lacking.

8. Jewish immigration is the central issue in Palestine today and is one factor, above all others, that rules out the necessary cooperation between the Arab and Jewish communities in a single State. The creation of a Jewish State under a partition scheme is the only hope of removing this issue from the arena of conflict.

9. It is recognized that partition has been strongly opposed by Arabs, but it is felt that the opposition would be lessened by a *solution which definitively fixes the extent of territory to be allotted to the Jews* with its implicit limitation on immigration. *The fact that the solution carries the sanction of the United Nations involves a finality which should allay Arab fears of further expansion of the Jewish State.* [Emphasis supplied]

Although the partition resolution of the United Nations General Assembly, referred to above, constitutes the *de jure* foundation for the State of Israel, it is clear that the Zionists had no intention of abiding by either the letter or the spirit of the U.N. resolution.

Menachem Begin, leader of the Irgun, declared that the *"bisection of our homeland is illegal and will never be recognized."* Begin's Hezut party, founded in 1948, argued for a Jewish state not only in all of Palestine—but in Jordan as well, *"even if it has to be won by blood and fire."*[22]

None of the Zionist parties accepted the U.N. resolution as anything but a temporary expedient.

As the late Simha Flapan,‡ in his recent book, *The Birth of Israel, Myths and Realities,* describes it:

> In short, acceptance of the UN Partition Resolution *was an example of Zionist pragmatism par excellence. It was a tactical acceptance,* a vital step in the right direction—*a springboard for expansion* when circumstances proved more judicious. And indeed, in the period between the UN vote on November 29, 1947, and the declaration of the State of Israel on May 14, 1948, a number of developments helped to produce the judicious circumstances that would enable the embryonic Jewish State to expand its borders.[23]

Overall Zionist strategy never wavered from its basic position—all of Palestine was to be Jewish and *no Palestinian state* would be allowed, *regardless of the U.N. resolution.* On Friday, May 14, 1948, Ben-Gurion read out the Scroll of Independence:

> By virtue of our national and intrinsic right and on the strength of the resolution of the United Nations General Assembly, we hereby declare the establishment of a Jewish state in Palestine, which shall be known as the State of Israel.[24]

---

‡Simha Flapan was National Secretary of Israel's MAPAM party, and director of its Arab Affairs Department. He was founder and editor-in-chief of the Middle East monthly *New Outlook,* and founder and director of the Jewish-Arab Institute and the Israeli Peace Research Institute. He also lectured as a Fellow at the Harvard University Center for International Affairs, as a Visiting Scholar at the Harvard Center for Middle East Studies, and as a Foreign Associate of the Roya Institute of International Affairs in London.

CHAPTER IV

The Arab-Israeli Wars

THE CROWNING achievement and the culminating event in the history of Zionism was the founding of the State of Israel. It was also the *casus belli* of the "War of Independence," 1948-1949, the first of five Arab-Israeli wars. For the purposes of this book, it is the only one of these wars which will be discussed in any detail, because it is the source of the Palestinian refugee problem, one of the most difficult issues to be dealt with in resolving the Middle East crisis.

THE WAR OF INDEPENDENCE AND ISRAELI MYTHOLOGY

The popularly accepted version of the War of Independence, in Israel and elsewhere, may be summarized as follows:

No sooner had the young nation of Israel declared itself as a State, it was set upon (in its cradle, so to speak) by powerful enemies determined upon its destruction. Only after a heroic defense, involving brilliant tactics and unsurpassed bravery, did Israel succeed in defeating and humiliating the Arab hordes. The imagery associated with the Israeli victory is that of a David desperately facing a Goliath and triumphing against great odds.

This account of the War of Independence has been told and retold with frequent embellishments to where it is now accepted (according to the late Simha Flapan) in Israeli society as historical truth *and hardened into a dangerous ideological shield.*

This version of the events surrounding the founding of Israel and the

War of Independence may never have been questioned or challenged except for the recent release and declassification of many state documents and military archives, including the secret war diaries of Ben-Gurion. The particular significance of these recent revelations is that they cast an entirely new light on the crucial question concerning the Palestinian refugees.

This long-debated question is (1) whether, when the 1948-49 war started, the Palestinian refugees voluntarily abandoned their lands and homes not intending to return, so that Israel was entitled to seize and confiscate their homes and property, or (2) whether the Palestinians fled for their lives in a panic because of the threats and attacks by the Israeli army, and the terrorist atrocities committed by the Irgun, under Begin, and the Lehi, under Shamir, which were intended to terrify them into leaving.

This question may have remained unanswerable had the Israeli government's archives and Ben-Gurion's war diaries not been declassified.

Simha Flapan, in his recently published book entitled *The Birth of Israel, Myths and Realities,* undertakes to answer this crucial question. What is revealed by these newly declassified archives and diaries, Flapan says, is a "historian's Pandora's box." His book sets forth seven "Foundation Myths" which, when the truth is known, profoundly alters the prevailing perception of the crucial events surrounding the birth of Israel.

In the realm of mythology, Flapan includes such popular beliefs as (1) that the Arabs forced the 1948 war on the peaceful Israelis, (2) that the Arab armies were a unified and powerful coalition determined to destroy Israel, and (3) that Israel was a David fighting Goliath for survival. It is also untrue, says Flapan, that Israel's hand has always been extended in peace.

Except for a brief period, Israel was the real Goliath in the War of Independence and has continued as such in the Middle East ever since.

Flapan states his purpose in his introduction:

It is the purpose of this book to debunk these myths, not as an academic exercise but as a contribution to a better understanding of the Palestinian problem and to a more constructive approach to its solution.

There is also a personal issue—for me as for tens of thousands of Israelis, ardent Zionists and socialists, whose public and private lives have been built on a belief in those myths, along with a belief in Zionism and the State of Israel as embodying not only the national liberation of the Jewish people but the great humanitarian principles of Judaism and enlightened mankind. True, we did not always agree with many official policies and even opposed them publicly. And developments since 1967 have created realities contradictory to these beliefs. But we still believed that Israel was born out of the agony of a just and inevitable war, guided by the principles of human dignity, justice, and equality. Perhaps it was naivete. *Perhaps it was the effect of the Holocaust that made us unable, unwilling to be fundamentally critical of our country and ourselves. Whatever its sources, the truth cannot be shunned.* It must be used even now in the service of the same universal principles that inspired us in our younger days.[1] [Emphasis supplied]

Flapan has the same grave concern regarding Israel's future, as is expressed in this book:

To what extent does the growing support for the theocratic racist Rabbi Meir Kahane—*who talks openly of deporting the Palestinians from Israel and the West Bank and Gaza—have its roots in the events of 1948?*

Like most Israelis, I had always been under the influence of certain myths that had become accepted as historical truth. And since myths are central to the creation of structures of thinking and propaganda, these myths had been of paramount importance in shaping Israeli policy for more than three and a half decades.

Israel's myths are located at the core of the nation's self-perception. Even though Israel has the most sophisticated army in the region and possesses an advanced atomic capability, it continues to regard itself in terms of the Holocaust, as the victim of an unconquerable bloodthirsty enemy. Thus whatever Israelis do, whatever means we employ to guard our gains or to increase them, we justify as last-ditch self-defense. We can, therefore, do no wrong. *The myths of Israel forged during the formation of the state have hardened into this impenetrable, and dangerous, ideological shield.* Yet what emerged from my reading was that while it was precisely during the period between 1948 and 1952 that most of these myths gained credence, the documents at hand not only failed to substantiate them, they openly contradicted them.[2] [Emphasis supplied]

Of the various "Foundation Myths," discussed by Flapan, this book is primarily concerned with Myth Three, which Flapan states as follows:

Myth Three: The flight of the Palestinians from the country, both before and after the establishment of the State of Israel, came in response to a call by the Arab leadership to leave temporarily, in order to return with the victorious Arab armies. They fled despite the efforts of the Jewish leadership to persuade them to stay. *In fact, the flight was prompted by Israel's political and military leaders, who believed that Zionist coloniza-tion and statehood necessitated the "transfer" of Palestinian Arabs to Arab countries.*[3] [Emphasis supplied]

The importance of the truth concerning this myth is that it deals with the issue of the Palestinian refugees, which has festered and remained unresolved for forty years. It is a bitter and emotionally charged issue, that is as alive today as it was then, and one that must be faced and dealt with if peace is ever to be attained.[4]

WAR, TERROR, AND REFUGEES: 1948-1949

On May 15, 1948, the day after the Scroll of Independence of Israel was read, a disorganized and loosely-led collection of Arab soldiers from differ-ent countries attacked Israel with disastrous consequence to the Arabs. This gave the Israelis the very opportunity for which they were waiting. The Israeli version of the events that followed is one of the "Foundation Myths," which Flapan discusses at length in his book.

The Palestinians were opposed in principle to the U.N. partition reso-lution and considered it unjust, since it gave the Jews (with only 35 percent of the population), 55 percent of the country's territory. Furthermore, it cut off the Palestinian state from the Red Sea and from Syria, and provided only one approach to the Mediterranean.

Flapan also points out that:

> The Palestinians also failed to see why they should be made to pay for the Holocaust (the ultimate crime against humanity, committed in Europe by Europeans).... They failed to see why it was *not* fair for the Jews to be in a minority in a unitary Palestinian state, while it *was* fair for almost half of the Palestinian population—the indigenous majority on its own ancestral soil—to be converted overnight into a minority under alien rule in the envisaged Jewish state according to partition.[5]

Despite these feelings, the masses of Palestinians *accepted the partition as irreversible and a fait accompli.* This is confirmed by an unequivocal statement by Ben-Gurion in a report to Sharett on March 14, 1948: "It is now clear, without the slightest doubt, that were we to face the Palestinians alone, everything would be all right. *The decisive majority of them do not want to fight us,* and all of them together are unable to stand up to us even at the present state of our organization and equipment."[6]

The Palestinians did not want, or believe in, a war. Instead, they attempted to protect themselves against warfare by the only means at their disposal: local agreements with their Jewish neighbors against mutual attacks, provocations, and hostile acts. Hundreds of such "nonaggressive pacts" were arranged. They were signed between Arab villages and neighboring Jewish Kibbutzim; between Jewish and Arab workers in places of common employment like ports, army camps, railways, oil refineries, and the postal service; and between Jewish and Arab businessmen, merchants, plantation owners, and others.[7]

As the local Arab population demonstrated a relative passivity, the move to sign nonaggressive pacts with Jewish neighbors spread all over the country.[8]

Nearly all the Arab affairs experts at the Jewish Agency, regardless of political outlook, agreed that most Palestinians, particularly the peasants and urban property owners, *were not interested in a war against the Jews.*[9] There was no Palestinian uprising in response to the Jewish state, and not a single Jewish settlement was attacked by them.

According to Flapan, the evidence is so overwhelming that the question arises how the myth of a Palestinian jihad against the Jews could survive so long. One reason, he said, is the *"efficiency of the Israeli propaganda campaign."*[10]

Israel's overriding strategy was *the elimination of the Palestinian people as contenders for and even as inhabitants of the same territory and the denial of their right to be an independent state. These objectives took precedence over peace.* As it turned out, their attainment actually made peace impossible, transforming the Israel-Palestine conflict into an even more intense Israeli-Palestinian confrontation marked by a feverish arms race and five wars in thirty-four years.[11] The 1948-49 war, then, was a golden opportunity for Israel to advance its territorial ambitions, as well as to reduce the Arab population to a fraction of its former numbers. Thus Israel could achieve, under the banner of a "defensive" war, sweeping changes in its boundaries and a drastic reduction in the Palestinian population, its two main objectives.

To implement its strategy, Israel allowed its terrorist factions, led by Menachem Begin and Yitzhak Shamir, to have a free rein to pursue their terrorist activities.[12] Together with the Israeli army they carried out the War of Independence which included:

1. Raids upon peaceful and defenseless Arab villages involving murder, torture, rape, and pillage.
2. Psychological warfare to convince the Arab villagers that the best thing for their safety would be to flee their villages and come back when the hostilities ended.
3. Direct expulsion of village inhabitants by razing their homes and occupying their lands.
4. Destruction of the fabric of Palestinian life by wrecking the economy and denying to the remaining Arabs the source of subsistence.
5. Confiscation of all the property of the refugees and refusing to let many return to their land and homes.

The exodus of Palestinian Arabs, both forced and voluntary, began with the publication of the U.N. partition resolution on November 29, 1947, and continued even after the armistice agreements were signed in the summer of 1949. Between 600,000 and 700,000 Palestinian Arabs were evicted or fled from areas that were either allocated to the Jewish state or occupied by Jewish forces during the fighting (and later integrated de facto into Israel).[13] *During and after the exodus, every effort was made—from the razing of villages to the promulgation of laws—to prevent their return.*[14]

There is overwhelming circumstantial evidence showing that a design was being implemented by the Haganah, and later the IDF (Israel Defense Force), to reduce the number of Arabs in the Jewish state to a minimum, to make use of most of their lands and properties, and to resettle Jewish immigrants on the confiscated lands.[15]

As a result, hundreds of thousands of Palestinians were intimidated and terrorized and caused to flee in panic. Still others were driven out by the Israeli Army which, under the leadership of Ben-Gurion, planned and executed the expulsion in the wake of the U.N. partition.[16]

The Israeli leadership, including Ben-Gurion, were all of one mind: that "the Arabs understood only the language of force and any proposals for compromise would be taken for weakness." They all accepted Ben-Gurion's view that the State of Israel should be demographically homogeneous and *geographically as extensive as possible.*[17]

The Israeli propaganda was also effective as a psychological weapon. The Haganah disseminated leaflets to Arab villages which said:

We have no wish to fight ordinary people who want to live in peace, but only the army and forces which are preparing to invade Palestine.

Therefore ... all people who do not want this war must leave together with their women and children in order to be safe.

This is going to be a cruel war, with no mercy or compassion. There is no reason why you should endanger yourselves.[18] [Emphasis supplied]

Lest this notice be taken as a compassionate gesture, rather than a cynical method of causing evacuation of Arab villages, it is important to know something of what had just happened in the infamous Dir Yassin massacre.
The following are quotations from Flapan's book:

The village of Dir Yassin was located in a largely Jewish area in the vicinity of Jerusalem and *had signed a nonaggression pact with its Jewish neighbors as early as 1942.*
Yet for the entire day of April 9, 1948, Irgun and LEHI soldiers carried out the slaughter in a cold and premeditated fashion. In a 1979 article dealing with the later forced evacuation of Lydda and Ramleh, *New York Times* reporter David Shipler cites Red Cross and British documents to the effect *that the attackers "lined men, women, and children up against walls and shot them,"* so that Dir Yassin *"remains a name of infamy in the world." When they had finished, they looted the village and fled.*[19] [Emphasis supplied]

Following this, Menachem Begin sent out an 'order of the day' to his band of terrorists: "Accept my congratulations on this splendid act of conquest. . . . As at Dir Yassin, so everywhere we will attack and smite the enemy, God, God, thou has chosen us for conquest."[20]
Flapan continues:

The ruthlessness of the attack on Dir Yassin *shocked Jewish and world public opinion alike, drove fear and panic into the Arab population, and led to the flight of unarmed civilians from their homes all over the country.* David Shaltiel, the head of the Haganah in Jerusalem, condemned the massacre of Arab civilians in the sharpest terms. He charged that the splinter groups had not launched a military operation but had chosen one of the quiet villages in the area that had never been connected with any of the attacks since the start of hostilities. But according to the Irgun, Shaltiel had approved of the attack. And years later, the historian of the Haganah, Aryeh Yitzhaki, wrote that the *operation in Dir Yassin was in line with dozens of attacks carried out at that time by the Haganah and Palmach, in the course of which houses full of elderly people, women, and children were blown up.* (Less well-known than Dir Yassin but no less brutal was the massacre in Duweima, near Hebron, carried out on October 29, 1948, by Former LEHI members and revealed by the Israeli journalist Yoela Har-Shefi in 1984.)

Former mayor of Jerusalem Khalidi called the attack on Dir Yassin senseless, especially in view of the pacific nature of the village and its relations with its Jewish neighbors. But from another perspective, it made perfect sense. More panic was sown among the Arab population by this operation than by anything that had happened up to then. *Dir Yassin is considered by most historians to have been the direct reason for the flight of the Arabs from Haifa on April 21 and from Jaffa on May 4.*[21] [Emphasis supplied]

Ben-Gurion made it clear, however, that even though the Arab areas which he considered important to the new state had been brought under Israeli control, there still remained the problem of their inhabitants. On May 11, he noted in his diary that he had given orders for the destruction of an "Arab island" in the Jewish-populated area.[22]

The most significant elimination of these "Arab islands" took place two months after Israel's Declaration of Independence. In one of the gravest episodes of this tragic story, on July 12-13, 1948, as many as fifty thousand Arabs were driven out of their homes in Lydda and Ramleh.

In Lydda, the exodus took place on foot. In Ramleh, the IDF provided buses and trucks. Originally, all males had been rounded up and enclosed in a compound, but after some shooting was heard, and construed by Ben-Gurion to be the beginning of an Arab legion counteroffensive, he stopped the arrests and ordered the speedy eviction of all the Arabs, including women, children, and the elderly. In explanation, he said that "those who made war on us bear responsibility after their defeat."

With the population gone, *the Israeli soldiers proceeded to loot the two towns in an outbreak of mass pillaging* that the officers could neither prevent nor control.

This was not the first time that Israeli soldiers had engaged in looting; nor was looting a problem confined to the army. *Jewish civilians also rushed to plunder Arab towns and villages once they were emptied of their inhabitants.*

Ben-Gurion had shown considerable concern over the phenomenon even before the events at Ramleh and Lydda. On June 16, he wrote: *"There is a moral defect in our ranks that I never suspected existed: I refer to the mass looting, in which all sections of the population participated.* This is not only a moral defect but a grave military defect." Six weeks earlier, on May 1, Ben-Gurion had noted that, in Haifa, professional thieves took part in the looting initiated by the Irgun, and that booty had also been found in the possession of Haganah commanders. He described other unsavory aspects of the operations as well: *"There was a search for Arabs; they were seized, beaten, and also tortured."* In October, he again referred to large-scale looting by the Haganah in Beersheba, which would appear to indicate *that his previous exhortations had not been effective.* Flapan adds this comment: *"His moral revulsion, however, did not lead him either to insist that offenders be brought to trial or to abandon the strategy of evictions."* Indeed, very few soldiers and civilians were tried for looting or indiscriminate killing.[23]

Ben-Gurion believed strongly that economic warfare against the Palestinian Arabs would also be an important tactic. This is explained in the following quotations from Flapan:

> In a letter to Sharett . . . Ben-Gurion focused on economic issues, observing that "the important difference with [the riots of] 1937 is the increased vulnerability of the Arab urban economy. *Haifa and Jaffa are at our mercy. We can 'starve them out.'* Motorized transport, which has also become an important factor in *their life, is to a large extent at our mercy."*
>
> *The destruction of the Palestinian urban bases, along with the conquest and evacuation (willing or unwilling) of nearby villages, undermined the whole structure of Palestinian life* in many parts of the country, especially in the towns. Ben-Gurion's advisers urged closing stores, barring raw materials from factories, and various other measures. Yadin, the army's head of operations, advised that "we must paralyze Arab transportation and commerce, and harass them in country and town. This is the way to lower their morale." And Sasson proposed "damaging Arab commerce—even if Jewish commerce will be damaged. We can tolerate it, they cannot . . . we must not hit here and there, but at all transportation at once, all commerce and so on."[24]

Within weeks, the urban disintegration of the Palestinian Arabs was a fait accompli. Ben-Gurion's tactics had succeeded. As he explained it:

> The strategic objective [of the Jewish forces] was to destroy the urban communities, which were the most organized and politically conscious sections of the Palestinian people. This was not done by house-to-house

fighting inside the cities and towns, but by the conquest and destruction of the rural areas surrounding most of the towns. This technique led to the collapse and surrender of Haifa, Jaffa, Tiberias, Safed, Acre, Beit-Shan, Lydda, Ramleh, Majdal, and Beersheba. Deprived of transportation, food, and raw materials, the urban communities underwent a process of disintegration, chaos, and hunger which forced them to surrender.[25] [Emphasis supplied]

The Israeli claim that most Palestinians abandoned their homes and left voluntarily *is Israeli propaganda*. According to Flapan:

Indeed, from the point of view of military logistics, the contention that the Palestinian Arab leadership appealed to the Arab masses to leave their homes in order to open the way for the invading armies, after which they would return to share in the victory, makes no sense at all. The Arab armies, coming long distances and operating in or from the Arab areas of Palestine, needed the help of the local population for food, fuel, water, transport, manpower, and information.

The recent publication of thousands of documents in the state and Zionist archives, as well as Ben-Gurion's war diaries, shows that there is no evidence to support Israeli claims. In fact, the declassified material contradicts the "order" theory, for among these new sources are documents testifying to the considerable efforts of the AHC [Arab Higher Committee] and the Arab states to constrain the flight.[26]

For its part, the Haganah avoided outright massacres like Dir Yassin but, through destruction of property, harassment, and rumor-mongering, was no less determined to evacuate the Arab population and prevent its return. Indeed, by the end of the 1947-48 war, IDF's *burning, blowing up, and mining of the ruins accounted for the destruction of 350 Arab villages and townlets situated in areas assigned to the Jewish state or those conquered during the fighting. Thousands upon thousands of houses, workshops, storerooms, cattle pens, nurseries, and orchards were destroyed, while livestock was seized and equipment looted or burned.* The operation, executed with a strict efficiency, *was inexplicable* since most of these villages were not engaged in heavy fighting against the Jewish forces and most of the inhabitants had fled either in fear of a "new Dir Yassin" or in response to "friendly advice" from Jewish neighbors.[27] [Emphasis supplied]

A more sophisticated form of pressure was achieved by legislation regarding property, particularly the Absentees' Property Law of 1950. This law, first promulgated in December 1948, stated that any Arabs who left their places of residence between November 29, 1947, and September 1, 1948, either to go to areas outside Palestine or to areas within Palestine that were occupied by active Arab military forces, would be considered absentees and their property subject to appropriation by the Custodian of Enemy Property (an office soon replaced by the Custodian of Absentees' Property). Even Arabs who had traveled to visit relatives or to escape areas of fighting were considered absentees.[28]

A detailed account of exactly how "abandoned" Arab property assisted in the absorption of the new immigrants was prepared by *Joseph Schechtman, an expert on population transfer who helped create the myth of "voluntary" exodus. "The amount of this property,"* he wrote in 1952, is *"very considerable."*

Two million nine hundred and ninety thousand dunams (739,750 acres) of formerly Arab-owned land, including olive and orange groves, vineyards, citrus orchards, and assorted tree gardens, became totally deserted as a result of the Arab mass flight. Of this Arab land, 2,070,270 dunams were of good quality, 136,530 of medium quality, and 751,730 dunams were of poor soil. In addition, 73,000 dwelling rooms in abandoned Arab houses, and 7,800 shops, workshops, and storerooms became ownerless in towns and villages.

Bank accounts estimated to total 5 million Palestinian pounds, and left in Arab and non-Arab banks, were frozen by the Israeli government. All of this Arab absentee property, movable and immovable, was entrusted to an official "custodian."

It is difficult to overestimate the tremendous role this lot of abandoned Arab property has played in the settlement of hundreds of thousands of Jewish immigrants who have reached Israel since the proclamation of the state in May 1948. Forty-seven new rural settlements established on the sites of abandoned Arab villages had, by October 1949, already absorbed 25,255 new immigrants. By the spring of 1950 over 1 million dunams (250,000 acres) had been leased by the custodian to Jewish settlements and individual farmers for the raising of grain crops.

Large tracts of land belonging to Arab absentees have also been leased to Jewish settlers, old and new, for the raising of vegetables. In the south alone, 15,000 dunams of vineyards and fruit trees have been leased to cooperative settlements.[29]

This has saved the Jewish Agency and the government millions of dollars. While the average cost of establishing an immigrant family in a new settlement was from $7,500 to $9,000, the cost of doing so in abandoned Arab villages did not exceed $1,500.[30]

THE MYTH OF VOLUNTARY EXODUS

To justify these actions the *myth* was created and heavily propagandized that the Palestinians had left their homes *voluntarily* or were encouraged to do so by the Arab countries. Having thus "abandoned their homes, farms, orchards" to the Israelis, it was proper for the Israelis to confiscate and occupy them. This Flapan refutes in great detail:

> Palestinian sources offer further evidence that even earlier, in March and April, the Arab Higher Committee, broadcasting from Damascus, demanded that the population stay put and announced that Palestinians of military age must return from the Arab countries. All Arab officials in Palestine were also asked to remain at their posts.
>
> Why did such pleas have so little impact? *They were outweighed by the cumulative effect of Zionist pressure tactics that ranged from economic and psychological warfare to the systematic ousting of the Arab population by the army and terrorism.*[31] [Emphasis supplied]

Flapan continues:

> The myth of voluntary Palestinian exodus, in response to Arab "orders from above," has survived with an astounding perseverance. In retrospect, the myth can be seen as the *inevitable result of the denial of the Palestinians' right to national independence and statehood, a principle that guided Zionist policies from the beginning.*
>
> Political in origin, the myth became an important component in the prevailing *self-image of the new state.* First of all, it served to *cover the traces of the unsavory methods employed by the authorities—from the confiscation of food, raw materials, medicaments, and land, to acts of terror and intimidation, the creation of panic, and finally, forcible expulsion—and thus to exorcise the feelings of guilt in many sectors of society, especially the younger generation.* Many of them bore the burden of the operations that caused the Arab flight. They personally implemented the instructions to destroy whole villages, forcing men, women, and children to leave their homes for some unknown destination beyond the borders. Many of them took part in operations where they rounded up all able-

[54]

bodied men and then crowded them into trucks for deportation. Their feelings of moral frustration and revulsion were not easily eradicated.[32] [Emphasis supplied]

The fact that the *Israelis were responsible* for the mass exodus of the Arab refugees is attested to by the IDF's own intelligence estimates.

As of June 1, 1948, 370,000 Arabs had left the country, from both the Jewish parts and the Arab parts conquered by the Jews. Jewish attacks on Arab centers, particularly large villages, townlets, or cities, accounted for about 55 percent of those who left: terrorist acts of the Irgun and Lehi, 15 percent; whispering campaigns (psychological warfare), about 2 percent; evacuations ordered by the IDF, another 2 percent; and general fear, about 10 percent.

It is clear from these statistics that *84 percent left in direct response to Israeli actions,* while only *5 percent left* on orders from Arab bands. The remaining 11 percent are not accounted for in this estimate, and may refer to those who left voluntarily. (The total reflects only about 50 percent of the entire exodus, since a similar number were to leave the country within the next six months.)

Flapan concludes his discussion of Myth Three with the following:

Was there any significant opposition to official policy? On many occasions, the forceful expulsion of the Palestinian population generated protests in liberal and progressive circles against the violation of elementary human rights. News of the expulsions, of brutal treatment, of looting, and of the terrible suffering of Arabs forced to leave their homes and properties were reported by witnesses, among them religious dignitaries, doctors and nurses, church-school teachers, journalists, Quakers, members of the staff of U.N. mediator Count Bernadotte, and people from the International Red Cross who moved in after the fighting. Their reports and appeals to international bodies to stop the bloodshed and help victims generated stormy debates in the press, as well as in the British Parliament and the U.S. Congress. Indeed, the tragedy of the refugees was at the center of Bernadotte's report and recommendations.[33]*

The foregoing, therefore, is the truth concerning the historical background of one of the most emotional and bitter issues involved in the Israeli-Palestinian conflict—the Palestinian refugees. As mentioned earlier,

*Count Bernadotte, chief U.N. envoy, was assassinated by the Lehi terrorist band under the leadership of Yitzhak Shamir.

this is an issue that has remained unresolved for more than forty years.

The importance of the disclosures from Ben-Gurion's war diaries and other recently declassified documents cannot be overestimated.

The conclusions reluctantly arrived at by Flapan in his book *The Birth of Israel: Myths and Realities* are so startling, and the implications so far-reaching, that Flapan's own words have been used as much as possible in stating the facts, which from any other source than Simha Flapan would be unbelievable.

His book is essential reading for anyone desiring a true perspective on the Israeli-Palestinian crisis, and especially the plight of the Palestinian refugees.

THE 1956 SINAI WAR

Following the War of Independence, no progress was made in solving the Palestinian refugee problem and an uneasy period of no war and no peace lasted until the Sinai war with Egypt in 1956.

In 1952, a military junta overthrew the Egyptian monarchy which led to the dictatorship of Gamal Abdel Nasser.

As a matter of policy, Egypt had always denied Israeli ships the right to use the Suez Canal. However, in 1956, Nasser also closed off Israel's access to the Gulf of Aqaba through the Straits of Tiran. Israel retaliated by launching a pre-emptive strike into the Sinai and, in conjunction with French and English forces, captured the Suez Canal and also opened the sea route to Aqaba. Under the agreement which ended the fighting, Israel agreed to withdraw from the Sinai on condition that Egypt would not remilitarize it and that U.N. peace-keeping forces be deployed in the Sinai to police the truce agreement. This arrangement lasted until 1967.

THE 1967 SIX-DAY WAR

On May 15, 1967, Nasser abruptly invaded and remilitarized the Sinai and again closed the Straits of Tiran to Israeli shipping. He ordered the U.N. peace-keeping force to leave the Sinai and the U.N. force quickly complied. Jordan, Iraq, and Syria expressed their support of Egypt.

On June 5, 1967, Israel launched a surprise air attack on Egypt and completely destroyed the Egyptian air force on the ground. In six days, the Israeli army captured and occupied all of Jerusalem, the entire West Bank and Gaza, and the Syrian Golan Heights, and reoccupied all of the Egyptian Sinai.

Following the cessation of hostilities, *the United Nations* adopted the famous *Resolution 242.* Among the basic provisions of the resolution was the recognition by the parties of the *"inadmissibility of acquiring territories by war, and the necessity for the withdrawal of Israeli armed forces from territories occupied in the 1967 Six-Day War."*

The status of these conquered and occupied territories, which were populated by more than a million and a half Palestinians, became the fundamental issue involved in the Middle East conflict. This issue (except for the Sinai question, which was settled by the Camp David Accords) remains unresolved after twenty-two years.

The Israeli victory in the 1967 war also had other far-reaching consequences. Most importantly, it caused the Israeli people to have a new feeling about themselves. The euphoria which accompanied this spectacular victory caused many to believe that Israel was "invincible."

Johnson, in his *History of the Jews,* describes this new attitude, particularly as it affected the rise of the radical nationalist "Land of Israel" movement:

There were many Jews who saw Israel's repeated victories as a moral mandate for wider boundaries. For pious Jews it was the hand of providence, for secular Jews, a form of manifest destiny. In 1968 the Sephardi Chief Rabbi argued that it was a religious obligation not to return the newly conquered territories. The same year the Kibbutz Dati, representing the religious collectives, intoned a prayer for Independence Day: *"Extend the boundaries of our land, just as Thou has promised our forefathers, from the river Euphrates to the river of Egypt.* Build your holy city, Jerusalem, capital of Israel; and there may your temple be established as in the days of Solomon." Dr. Harold Fisch, rector of Bar-Ilan University, insisted: "There is only one nation to whom the land belongs in trust and by covenant promise, and that is the Jewish people. No temporary demographic changes can alter this basic fact which is the bedrock of the Jewish faith; just as one wife does not have two husbands so one land does not have two sovereign nations in possession of it." *The 1967 victory also produced a multi-party movement known as the Land of Israel, which argued that it was not within the moral authority of the Israeli state, representing only Israeli citizens,* to give up any conquered portion of the Promised Land, since this was the property of the entire Jewish people, *and must be* preserved for their eventual ingathering or Aliya.[34] [Emphasis supplied]

Six years had passed since the U.N. Resolution 242 was adopted, which required Israel to withdraw its forces from the lands conquered and occupied in the 1967 war.

Although Israel had ostensibly accepted the resolution, no effort was being made by Israel to comply with its terms or to withdraw its forces from the Sinai and the West Bank and Gaza.

Anwar Sadat, then President of Egypt following Nasser's death, was under great pressure from the Egyptian militarists to renew the war with Israel and recapture the Sinai.

On October 6, 1973, the Egyptian army crossed the Suez Canal in force and attacked and broke through the Israeli "Bar Lev Line." Simultaneously, the Syrians broke through the Israeli lines on the Golan Heights. This brief war is described by Johnson:

An element of technological surprise in the effectiveness of Arab anti-tank and anti-aircraft missiles enabled them to inflict disturbing losses on Israeli planes and armor. For the first time in the quarter-century of the state's existence, Israel faced the possibility of a major defeat and even of a second holocaust. But the Syrian advance had been stemmed on 9 October; the next day, in response to desperate Israeli pleas, the American President, Richard Nixon, began an emergency airlift of advanced weapons. Two days afterwards the Israeli forces began an audacious counter-attack on Egypt, crossing on to the West Bank of the Canal, and threatening to cut off all the advancing Egyptian forces in Sinai. This was the turning-point and Israel moved swiftly towards a victory as decisive as that of 1967, when a cease-fire came into force on 24 October.[35]

The last of the five Israeli wars, "The War in Lebanon," 1982-83, will be discussed briefly in Chapter X in its chronological sequence.

CHAPTER V

The Search for Peace

NOT LONG AFTER the October 1973 war between Israel, Syria, and Egypt, President Gerald Ford took office with the Middle East situation high on his agenda. The failure of previous administrations to achieve a peaceful settlement of the Middle East conflict had not been for any lack of effort on the part of the U.S. Every administration since and including Nixon's has vainly tried to develop a plan or program to bring about a peaceful solution to the dangerous deadlock between Israel and the Palestinians, which poses a constant threat to world peace.

While it may appear that the issues dividing the Palestinians and the Israelis are highly complex, the chief problem is not their "complexity," but the simple fact that the fundamental positions of the two antagonists, as they stand, *are irreconcilable.* Given the situation, the repeated efforts of the U.S. to mediate the dispute have been frustrated because there never has been any prospect of success.

Without exception, each new administration has begun with high hopes of bringing about a peaceful resolution of the Israeli-Palestinian impasse—but finally gives up in the face of Israeli "intransigence," or Palestinian "factionalism"—but mostly because of the lack of *political will* on the part of the U.S. This continuing exercise in futility is referred to euphemistically as the "peace process."

The humiliation suffered by Egypt in the Six-Day War of 1967 was eased by the fact, mentioned earlier, that the Egyptian army, in the 1973 war, had successfully crossed the Suez Canal, breached the Israeli defenses, inflicted heavy casualties, and might have won the war had not the U.S. come to Israel's rescue by a massive airlift of arms, armor, and planes from the U.S. and from our NATO military arsenal.

It is generally agreed that only because of Egypt's initial military successes in the war, which saved Egypt's pride, could Sadat, in 1977, have made his dramatic peace overtures to Israel without appearing as a supplicant.

Following the 1973 war, Israel intensified its colonization efforts in the occupied West Bank, Gaza, and Sinai by hastening the building of new settlements.

The Arabs were powerless to do anything other than to ask the U.N. to condemn the Israeli West Bank settlements as being against international law and the U.N. Resolution 242 and to request the U.S. to require Israel to return the occupied territories—all of which Israel simply ignored.

At the same time, the Arabs played into Israel's hands by carrying out sporadic acts of terrorism and by allowing the extreme faction of the PLO to continue to demand the destruction of Israel.

PLO Chairman Arafat was prepared to recognize Israel's existence in exchange for the Israeli withdrawal from the occupied lands. He was fearful, however, that if he made such an open concession without an Israeli commitment in return, his life, or at least his leadership of the PLO, would be in jeopardy. For that reason, Arafat was forced to perform a high wire act that frustrated all efforts of mediators to pin him down to a specific and firm position.

While Arafat's vacillations exasperated the forces working toward peace, it was the best of both worlds for the Israelis. The Israeli strategy was to win the game by "ball control."

By simply holding on to the ball (the occupied territories) and by progressively increasing their grip on the territories by building new settlements on Palestinian lands, they would eventually win the game. With enough settlements, the West Bank and Gaza would belong to Israel by a *fait accompli*. Israel didn't need or want a peace conference, *because it could only result in Israel having to give up something it had already decided to keep.*

With lavish help from the U.S., Israel had now become, by far, the strongest military power for its size in the world and it had defeated the Arabs in four wars. As we have seen in Chapter III, the Jewish underground had "written the book" on "terrorism" and how to rid a country of an oppressive occupying power without the use of conventional military forces.

[60]

Begin and Shamir have gained a well-deserved reputation as the most successful terrorists of this century.

Now that the Israeli army of occupation was in the same position as the British army of occupation had been, and the Palestinians were in the same position that the Jewish underground had been, it seemed to the Palestinians that their course was obvious.

Encouraged by the successful example of the Irgun terrorists under Begin, and the Lehi terrorists under Shamir, the Palestinians tried to imitate their success, hoping that terrorist acts would have the same effect of driving out the Israeli occupiers as the Jewish terrorists had on driving out the British occupiers.

The plan was a failure mostly because the rules of the game had changed. Begin and Shamir had now decided that terrorism was a *bad thing* and loudly and constantly condemned it at every opportunity. Since Israel has unparalleled access to the world media, the Palestinians got a bad press.

THE FORD ADMINISTRATION

During the Ford administration, a great deal of time and diplomatic effort were involved in shuttle diplomacy on the part of Secretary of State Henry Kissinger, for the purpose of stabilizing the temporary frontiers of the belligerents in the 1973 war along the cease-fire lines.

Unfortunately little was, or could be, accomplished in resolving the basic territorial issues existing among the belligerents. U.S. policy, also favored by the U.N., consisted of making efforts to reconvene the Geneva conference at which, hopefully, all parties and issues would be at the negotiating table so that a comprehensive solution to the Middle East problems could be achieved.

Since the principal issues to be resolved concerned the Palestinian situation (1) in the West Bank and Gaza, (2) the refugee problem, and (3) the status of Jerusalem, the Palestinians would necessarily have to be represented at any such conference. For this purpose the Palestinians regarded the Palestine Liberation Organization as their proper representative. Israel, as usual, flatly refused to attend any meeting or conference with representatives of the PLO on the grounds that they were a "terrorist" organization bent upon the destruction of Israel.

THE CARTER PEACE OFFENSIVE

As the Carter administration took office in January of 1977, the respective positions staked out by the belligerents had not changed since the end of the Six-Day War, 1967.

1. Israel still occupied the Sinai, the West Bank and Gaza, all of Jerusalem, and the Golan Heights.
2. Israel refused to return any of the captured territories (with the possible exception of part of the Sinai) on the grounds that the possession of the occupied territories was required in order to provide "defensible borders" necessary for Israel's security.
3. Under no circumstances would Israel allow a Palestinian state to exist next to it, also for reasons of security.
4. Israel could not and *would not give up a single foot of the West Bank and Gaza* because these were part of Eretz Israel, land given by God to Abraham in perpetuity.

Hardly anyone outside of Israel considered this last argument as a serious contention and assumed that, since Israel had accepted (or pretended to accept) Resolutions 242 and 338, which called for a return of the occupied territories, it was only a bargaining stance.

The main Arab position, in simple terms, was to insist:

1. That the occupied territories be returned pursuant to U.N. Resolutions 242 and 338.
2. That the West Bank and Gaza be the basis for an independent Palestinian state.*
3. That the Israeli settlements on the West Bank were an obstacle to peace and contrary to international law, which prohibited an occupying power from settling its own citizens on occupied land.

Israel's strategy was (1) to deflect or fend off any peace overtures from any source by refusing even to appear in the same room with representatives of the PLO, and (2) to express a ready willingness to negotiate a peaceful settlement of the Palestinian questions, "if only there was someone to negotiate with."

Begin was even more emphatic in confusing matters. In a memorable statement, he announced that everything is "negotiable," but there are certain things he *would never agree to.* (This comment certainly deserves a place beside Samuel Goldwyn's famous remark, "An oral contract is not worth the paper it is written on.")

---

* The question of the future status of Jerusalem and the Syrian Golan Heights are peripheral issues not discussed in this book, in order to concentrate on the core issues of the West Bank and Gaza.

As Jimmy Carter's inauguration day approached, January 20, 1977, the media was full of reports proclaiming that the political climate in the Middle East was more favorable for peace than it had been for twenty-five years, and that the problems of the Middle East were ripe for a solution.

Both President Carter and Secretary of State Cyrus Vance (and Zbigniew Brzeszinski, National Security Advisor) were eagerly looking to the Arab-Israeli stalemate as an opportunity for a major foreign policy coup. Carter's idealism and Vance's and Brzeszinski's experience seemed to complement each other so that it was thought that the U.S. was in a strong position to accept the leadership of a peace offensive in the Middle East.

Accordingly, almost immediately after the Carter inauguration, Secretary of State Vance left on a peace mission to the Middle East.

On February 7, 1977, the *Wall Street Journal* carried a report of Vance's trip, a portion of which is quoted here:

VANCE'S MIDEAST TRIP MAY LEAD TO PATH
FOR RENEWAL OF ARAB-ISRAELI PEACE TALKS

DAMASCUS—The Carter administration's first foray into Middle East diplomacy apparently has produced some new ideas about how to get serious peace negotiations started.

But so far, what has come out is more a sense of direction than a specific plan to get Arabs and Israelis into a Geneva conference later this year. And because fresh ideas often fail in this troubled region, this effort, too, may never produce concrete results.

"There is a very hard and difficult road ahead," Secretary Vance cautioned at a news conference here early Monday, before he was to return to Washington to report on his trip to President Carter.

Some Old Facts: According to Mr. Vance, his fact-finding journey rediscovered some rather old facts. The main ones are that Arabs and Israelis disagree sharply about the "core" issues of a possible final Middle East settlement, namely the nature of what peace means, the extent of Israeli withdrawals from occupied territory, and how to settle the Palestinian issue.

Still, Secretary Vance professed some muted optimism at the end of his week-long trip.

There also seems to be a serious effort under way among Arab leaders to overcome Israel's refusal to have the PLO at the Geneva conference, which Mr. Vance hopes will begin in the second half of 1977. Israel con-

tends the PLO is merely a terrorist organization without political standing rather than the sole spokesman of the Palestinian cause, as Arab
governments assert publicly.

Procedural Problem: Unfortunately, all this involves mainly a procedural problem that must be settled before a Geneva conference can begin.
It does little for the central issues of Middle East peace, which apparently
remains as intractable as ever. For example, the Arabs still insist upon
complete return of all occupied territory while Israel, just as adamantly,
insists it will never return everything.

Thus, the best the Americans hope for this year is to get the negotiation process started. They don't expect any substantial issue to be settled
during 1977.[1]

On February 14, 1977, the *Los Angeles Times* published a news item on
the Vance trip from which the following excerpt is taken:

As Kissinger used to say and Carter advisers now repeat, "moderates"
are in control in the key Arab states confronting Israel, *and this alone
presents an opportunity Israel cannot afford to miss.*

*As a result, Israel is likely to find that Vance and the Carter adminis-
tration, again following the lead of Kissinger and the Ford administration, perceive the key obstacle to a settlement no longer as the question
of Arabs refusing to grant Israel the right to exist.*

Instead, the crux of the problem is being defined in terms of the
seventeen-year-old dilemma of the Palestinians: how to devise a formula
in which the "legitimate interests" of the Palestinians can be preserved
side by side with the integrity of Israel.

In a recent interview with the *New York Times,* Vance noted that the
Palestinians have begun to show signs of moderating their position that
their own rights of nationhood demand Israel's destruction.

Vance said, "Such moderation would be a helpful step, if true."

On paper, therefore, there appears to be an unprecedented degree of
flexibility among Arab leaders, who have advertised their willingness to
negotiate in a sustained "peace offensive" which has kept the Israelis off
balance diplomatically and has cast them in an uncomfortable posture of
intransigence.

Depending on his perspective, Vance is likely to find an accumulation
of signals from Arab leaders indicating that *the momentum toward a
settlement is irresistible and that the only missing ingredient is U.S.*

pressure to bring the Israelis to Geneva negotiations.[2] [Emphasis supplied]

The above *Los Angeles Times* report has been quoted simply to emphasize the point that, if the reader were not aware that the date of the report was February 14, 1977, it would read like yesterday's newspaper. Even in 1977, these issues, which grew out of the 1967 Six-Day War, had been festering for more than ten years. They have now remained unresolved for more than twenty-two years.

In a thoughtful and persuasive article appearing in the *Los Angeles Times* on March 9, 1977, Ira Handelman, a professor at the University of Southern California, and Yoav Peled, an Israeli and a professor of political science at UCLA, *addressed a plea to the American supporters of Israel (in particular the Jewish community) to recognize the new climate and opportunities for peace and to support the U.S. negotiating efforts.*

The article entitled *Time for an Eye Checkup, Israel Watchers* is set forth here in part:

Momentum seems to be building for a peace settlement in the Middle East. Both the Arab nations and Israel have expressed a desire to reconvene the Geneva conference this year, as have the United States, the Soviet Union, and U.N. Secretary General Kurt Waldheim.

However, a major stumbling block remains: the role of the Palestine Liberation Organization.

The Arab states insist that the PLO must have a part in the peace conference, whether as an independent delegation, as part of a combined Palestinian-Jordanian group or within a unified Arab mission.

Israel, on the other hand, adamantly refuses to negotiate with the PLO, insisting that the Palestinian issue should be resolved through bilateral talks with Jordan.

The only country capable of breaking this stalemate is the United States. While the Carter Administration would like to see the talks resume after the Israeli elections in May, it still supports Israel's refusal to deal with the PLO—unless the Palestinians modify their covenant (constitution) to recognize Israel's right to exist.

Many observers now believe that the Palestinian National Council, when it meets this month, will attempt to accommodate the American demand.

If that occurs, the United States might well abandon its opposition to PLO participation. But since the Israeli government is unlikely to go along, the result could be a confrontation between Jerusalem and Washington.

Israel's American supporters could help to obviate such a confrontation, but to do so, many among them will have to overcome their preconceptions about the Middle East.

For years, many of Israel's friends in this country—Jews and non-Jews alike—have entertained a simplistic, black-and-white view of the Arab-Israeli conflict. In their minds, Israel was an almost perfect state, a close-knit democracy struggling for survival against overwhelming forces of darkness and barbarism. The Arabs, on the other hand, were perceived as a single-minded horde of 100 million, determined to destroy Israel and drive the Jews into the sea. Paradoxically, Israel—particularly after 1967—was thought to be militarily invincible, while the Arabs, though numerically superior, were portrayed as militarily incompetent pawns of the Soviet Union.

Thus, for Americans sympathetic to Israel, taking a position on every issue connected with the conflict was easy. Whatever Israel did was right; whatever the Arabs did was wrong.

More recently, the public perception of Israel has been shaken by revelations of internal dissension, acute social problems and corruption in high places.

Americans whose support of Israel has been based on an idealized vision of the Jewish state can react to these developments in one of three ways. They can "punish" Israel for not living up to their fantasies by withholding their support, *they can cling to the old myths and fight every differing viewpoint as anti-Zionist or anti-Semitic propaganda, or they can take a more realistic view of the Middle Eastern situation and try to understand the legitimate fears, aspirations, and grievances of both sides.*

Clearly, the best interests of both the United States and Israel would be served by the latter response. One way to express this new view is to drop the simplistic notion that the PLO is nothing more than a gang of terrorist murderers.

True, like other national liberation movements, the PLO has frequently resorted to violence but, notwithstanding the reprehensible nature of some of its actions, it is a mistake to confuse the PLO's political ends with its violent means.

The primary purpose of the terrorist acts was to bring the Palestinians' cause to world attention. Now that their position has been almost universally recognized—the PLO maintains offices in about 150 capitals—the number of violent incidents has drastically declined.

American supporters of Israel who deny the reality of this development—or belittle its significance—are doing Israel a great disservice.

In any future American-Israeli confrontation over PLO participation at Geneva, it would be impossible for Israel's supporters to play a constructive role if they fail to recognize the changes that have occurred in PLO thinking since 1973.

If pro-Israel groups in the United States fail to face up to this new reality, public debate and discussion will be left to the ideologists and extremists.[3] [Emphasis supplied]

The valuable advice given and the wisdom shown in the foregoing article was ignored by the Israeli partisans in this country at a crucial time when the course of Israel's foreign policy was about to undergo a radicalization with the election, several months later, of the Likud party under the leadership of Menachem Begin. As Handelman and Peled predicted, the ideologists and extremists took over.

In the spring of 1977, Israel was in the midst of a strongly contested election campaign between Prime Minister Yitzhak Rabin, of the Labor party, and Menachem Begin, of the Likud.

Prime Minister Rabin was eager to meet the new U.S. president. A report on Prime Minister Rabin's meeting with President Carter was carried in the *Los Angeles Times* of March 8, 1977, a portion of which is set out below:

RABIN REAFFIRMS DESIRE
FOR PEACE—ON ISRAEL'S TERMS

WASHINGTON—Israeli Prime Minister Yitzhak Rabin, apparently buoyed by his first meeting with President Carter, reaffirmed Tuesday his nation's willingness to press toward a Middle East peace settlement later this year—*but only terms favorable to Israel.*

Only "defensible borders" between Israel and her Arab neighbors will be acceptable, Rabin told a news conference after his two days of talks here. "And those borders in no way coincide with the boundaries at the beginning of the six-day war."

"Fake solutions" would be unacceptable, Rabin told a crowd of American and Israeli reporters crammed into a reception room at Blair House, the official guest house across the street from the White House. "We are talking about genuine peace."

In almost every respect, the requirements for "genuine peace" that Rabin prescribed reflected bedrock Israeli positions that have been unchanged since the six-day war of 1967. They surprised nobody:

All boundaries to be negotiated and "defensible," no acceptance of U.S. guarantees of security as a substitute for self-defense, no negotiation with Palestinians except within the framework of Israeli talks with Jordan.[4] [Emphasis supplied]

In the late spring of 1977, a drastic change occurred in the political climate and power structure in Israel. To the surprise and shock of most observers, the Labor party, which had dominated the government since the foundation of Israel, had been defeated by the militant Likud party headed by Menachem Begin.

In July of 1977, Prime Minister Begin made his first official visit to Washington to meet President Carter. The meeting ended with broad smiles and optimistic remarks by both Begin and Carter, which surprised Carter aides since they knew that little, if any, progress had been made. This was somewhat puzzling, since only a few weeks before, the White House had issued stern warnings to Begin that he must be more flexible in his upcoming meeting with Carter.

Time magazine, in an article appearing in the August 1, 1977, edition, asked rhetorically what had happened to Carter's announced firm position on the Middle East, and then proceeded to answer its own question:

Ever since his meeting with U.S. Jews (TIME, July 18) Carter had softened his attitude toward Israel without technically changing his position. Example: lately there has not been any mention of a "home-land" for Palestinians but instead reference to a Palestinian region tied to Jordan. He obviously wanted to avoid a meeting with Begin that ended in open disagreement. Besides, recalling Carter's earlier disastrous encounter with Rabin, one official explained, "Carter must have realized that his tough attitude toward Rabin did not pay off. Instead of movement, he got Israel to dig in its heels. Carter must have seen that to get the best results, he must play the pussycat—and he was the pussycat."

But what results Carter got, apart from a friendly atmosphere that might prove to be useful later, is not clear. As far as is known, *Carter simply did not choose to press his earlier prescriptions for Israeli concessions, including the Palestinian homeland and substantial withdrawal from occupied territories to pre-1967 boundaries.* Begin in turn sidestepped the thornier issues.[5] [Emphasis supplied]

It is obvious from the results of President Carter's meetings with Rabin and Begin, that the Israeli partisans in this country were not heeding the advice of Handelman and Peled, to the effect that Israel's best interest would be served by supporting U.S. efforts in the Middle East, and that failure to do so would be a great disservice to Israel.

In late summer 1977, Secretary Vance made a second trip to the Middle East where his worst fears were confirmed. The results of his trip are summarized in a report appearing in *U.S. News & World Report* entitled "After Vance's Trip: Peace No Closer in Mid-east":

Despite six months of intensive work, with President Carter deeply involved, the U.S. still is as far away as ever from achieving a negotiated peace between Israel and the Arab countries.

Hard line in Israel. In terms of significant agreements, nevertheless, Vance collected no more this time than from his first Mideast trip last February. He told a news conference in Jerusalem: "In the discussions here in Israel, we did not narrow the gap any further."

Vance had hoped that he could move the two sides close enough together to warrant a full-scale peace conference in Geneva in October, a development Carter optimistically had predicted after his meeting in Washington in July with Israel's new and conservative Prime Minister, Menachem Begin.

Instead, Begin greeted the Secretary in Jerusalem with a hard-line stance that seemed to rule out a return to the Geneva talks any time soon.

Israel, Begin insisted, would never sit down at the conference table with the Palestine Liberation Organization, *as demanded by Arab nations, even if the PLO formally recognizes Israel's right to exist as an independent country.*

The Prime Minister was equally adamant in declaring that Israel *would never give up the occupied West Bank of the Jordan River* for creation of a Palestinian homeland, an Arab proposal publicly supported by Carter.

Said one Israeli Foreign Ministry official *after the Vance-Begin talks:* "*We will never give back the West Bank to anybody.* If Washington pressures us to do so, the peace process collapses, and the United States loses."[6] [Emphasis supplied]

The Wall Street Journal of August 11, 1977, summarizes the results of Secretary Vance's trip in an article entitled *"Vance Concedes That Talks*

With Begin Didn't Narrow Gap Between Israel, Arabs," the pertinent portion of which is quoted as follows:

> JERUSALEM—Chances of a Mideast peace conference this year—never bright—seem dimmer than ever as Secretary of State Cyrus Vance concludes a six-nation tour of the region today.
>
> His effort to close the negotiating gap between Arabs and Israelis has had only limited success. *Substantial, perhaps irreconcilable, differences remain on key issues.* These include the extent of Israeli withdrawal from occupied territories, how to resolve the Arab Palestinian problem, and the nature of future peaceful relations between the two sides.
>
> The peacemaking effort hasn't halted. Next month at the United Nations General Assembly meeting, Mr. Vance will hold a series of meetings with Arab and Israeli foreign ministers in hopes of closing the gaps between their positions.
>
> His chances of success, however, are problematical. Despite progress on some matters, two days of talks here with Prime Minister Menachem Begin, who is deeply suspicious of Arab motives, didn't bring the sides much closer, Mr. Vance conceded.[7] [Emphasis supplied]

The *U.S. News & World Report,* September 5, 1977, edition, gives its analysis of *the reason for Prime Minister Begin's uncompromising attitude:*

> Carter's public statements on the shape of a Mideast agreement apparently have done much to convince the Arabs that the U.S. is genuinely interested in a "just peace" and that they can expect fair treatment from Washington. *As a result, the Arab position today appears more moderate than ever before.* "We believe," Vance said in Israel, "that the Arabs are sincere in their desire for peace, and we conveyed this to Mr. Begin."
>
> *Keys to Begin's stand. What is behind the uncompromising attitude Vance found in Israel, a nation that only a few weeks ago worried over worsening relations with the U.S.?*
>
> The amiable reception that Carter gave Begin in Washington did much to strengthen the new Prime Minister's position at home. Polls show him riding high, and his image as a statesman continues to grow— enabling him to stand firm in his position.
>
> *Also, Israeli officials are convinced Begin has the support of a large part of the Jewish community in the U.S. They believe, therefore, that Begin can successfully resist Carter, even in Congress, if the U.S.*

attempts to pressure Israel into making concessions to the Arabs.
[Emphasis supplied]

The same edition of *U.S. News & World Report,* September 5, 1977, summarizes the situation:

Secretary of State Vance returns from Mideast making plain he feels *Israel is being obstructionist. Carter tells the nation at his press conference that Israel acts illegally in settling West Bank.*

Why hasn't Carter reacted more strongly to Israeli Prime Minister Begin's tough independent line? Best guess: *President is unwilling just now to risk provoking U.S. Jewish Community.*[8] [Emphasis supplied]

This strange and sudden reticence of the Carter administration was not lost on the moderate Arab countries.

A report to the *Los Angeles Times* from Cairo datelined September 4, 1977, states in part as follows:

Amid signs of growing Arab disillusionment with the Carter Administration, foreign ministers of the Arab League met in Cairo Saturday to hammer out a unified strategy. In the words of one observer, it "will force President Carter to the moment of truth" on the issues of Israeli settlements and dialogue with the Palestinians.

Although the Carter Administration has condemned Israel's recent establishment of new West Bank settlements and made conditional overtures to the PLO, which the Palestinians rejected, even the moderate Arab countries, such as Egypt, have expressed disappointment that the American stance so far has appeared to be more talk than action.

"We admire President Carter's statements—even Yasser Arafat (the PLO leader) has spoken admiringly of them—but we are beginning to see what he said as more posturing than policy," an Arab source said. *"The Americans condemn the Israeli settlements, but instead of punishing Israel with pressure that only America can exert, they reward Israel with more arms shipments."*

Arab anger over the establishment of more Israeli settlements on the West Bank was further exacerbated here Friday by word from Israel that Ariel Sharon, the Israeli agriculture minister, was proposing an intensive long-range West Bank settlement policy, coupled with a doubling of the Israeli population to sustain it.[9] [Emphasis supplied]

Notwithstanding Carter's condemnations, Israel continued to accelerate the pace of the settlement program on the West Bank in order to advance its policy of putting "facts on the ground."

In its September 19, 1977, edition, *Time* magazine reflects upon the discouragement and disillusionment of the Carter administration:

> *Time* learned last week that despite official denials Israel has started, in addition to the three officially declared new settlements, another three new settlements in the past month, and a fourth is in the process of being manned. Moreover, the controversial plan of Agriculture Minister Ariel Sharon to settle 2 million Jews in occupied lands has the official support of Premier Menachem Begin's government. "We will continue to settle, and settling is a long process which must be carried out," said Sharon in an interview last week with Jerusalem Bureau Chief Donald Neff and Correspondent David Halevy. *"Anyone who thinks that this government is going to withdraw from the West Bank is suffering delusions."*
>
> Even though Carter says he has private assurances from all of the leaders that they will be more flexible than their public stance, hopes for a renewed Geneva are dimmer than ever. In an interview with Syndicated Columnist Trude B. Feldman that appears in a number of Jewish publications around the country this week, the President seemed sobered by the procedural difficulties in bringing the two sides together. "Dozens of other foreign policy matters have suffered to some degree because I've expended so much time on this issue," he said. "If our efforts fail this year, it'll be difficult for us to continue to devote that much time and energy to the Mideast."[10]

Nevertheless, Carter continued doggedly to pursue his hopes for a Geneva conference that would somehow include Palestinian representation.

Time magazine, in the October 10, 1977, edition reports:

THE PALESTINIAN PROBLEM

GENEVA: U.S. policy is shifting on whether to deal with the PLO.

"It is obvious to me that there can be no Middle Eastern peace settlement without adequate Palestinian representation." So said President Carter at his Washington press conference, echoing a theme he had stated many times before. But then Carter went a significant step further.

If the Palestine Liberation Organization endorsed United Nations resolutions that implicitly accept Israel's right to exist, he promised, "then we will begin to meet with them and to search for some accommodation and some reasonable approach to the Palestinian question."

Arabs hailed the President's statement: Israelis were furious. In Jerusalem's view, Carter was backing away from a long-standing agreement that the U.S. would never deal with the PLO as long as it was committed to the destruction of Israel. More than that, the Israelis detected that they were coming under heavy pressure from their closest ally in the world— an ally that was significantly modifying its policy in the Middle East.

The Israeli perception is basically correct. Ever since his Clinton, Mass., call last March for a Palestinian "homeland," *Jimmy Carter has become more and more convinced that the Palestinian issue is, as President Hafez Assad of Syria calls it, "the mother question" in the Middle East.* Carter also feels that answering that question is of vital importance to America's "national interests" and the key to a successful resumption of peace negotiations in Geneva.[11] [Emphasis supplied]

Notwithstanding the virtual impossibility of a "negotiated" peace at Geneva, the U.S. still was pushing both sides to the conference table.

In a report in the October 24, 1977, issue *Newsweek* concludes by saying:

U.S. officials remained confident that a Geneva conference could still be launched before the end of the year. "We have a 40-60 chance of seeing all the Arab parties accept the working paper more or less unscathed," one top U.S. aide said last week. Experienced Middle East diplomats were less optimistic. They feared that the Dayan-Carter working paper had disillusioned more militant Arab leaders, *persuading them that no U.S. President—regardless of his expressed sympathy for the Arab cause—could withstand pressure from a powerful pro-Israel lobby.* Consequently, Carter may have to do a lot more persuading before Arabs and Israelis sit down together at Geneva.[12] [Emphasis supplied]

In an article in the *Los Angeles Times* entitled "The Fairy Tale Status of U.S.-Israeli Ties," Arie Lova Eliav, a member of the Israeli Parliament, offers some perceptive observations:

After Secretary of State Vance's recent visit to Israel, I rose to deliver a speech to the Knesset. Opening a volume of Hans Christian Andersen fables, I read aloud to my colleagues the well-known story "The Emperor's New Clothes."

This fairy tale, unfortunately, reflects the status of current U.S.-Israel relations. Because both the Israeli and American governments want fervently to believe that their mutual interests are growing ever greater and that peace in the Mideast is looming ever closer, they pretend it is so, just as the emperor's subjects pretended that he was arrayed in expensive finery. But behind the outward trappings of mutual respect and goodwill—exhibited by government officials in flattering eulogies and carefully worded proclamations of optimism—*stands the all-too-naked truth: The policies of Prime Minister Begin and his Likud Party have headed Israel on a collision course not only with America but with the Arabs and the rest of the world as well.*[13] [Emphasis supplied]

Earlier in the Carter administration, a red alert had been flashed to Israel and to the Jewish community in America. Carter had been heard to say that the Palestinians had some "legitimate rights" and Brzeszinski had said that the U.S. has a direct interest in the outcome of the Middle East conflict and had a legitimate right to exercise its own leverage with Israel and the Arabs to obtain a settlement.

For the benefit of its readers, the October 11, 1977, edition of the *Jerusalem Post* explained this latest development and goes on to reassure its readers that there is no cause for concern to Israel:

But should we be all that surprised by the current tilt in U.S. policy? Maybe not, according to one respected Washington observer of the Middle East scene.

I.L. Kenen, the honorary chairman of the American-Israel Public Affairs Committee, pointed out some days ago that the first years of new administrations in Washington have usually proved to be difficult ones for Israel. Testifying before a Senate Foreign Relations Subcommittee, Kenen said that *"a review of U.S. policy in the Middle East reveals a recurrent quadrennial exercise."* [Emphasis supplied]

The *Jerusalem Post* article continues:

Behind the [U.S.] Administration's zealousness is the rosy report on Arab intentions which Vance brought back from his August trip to the

Middle East. His message was clear: The Arab states are ready to sign peace treaties with Israel in exchange for a return essentially to the pre-1967 lines and the creation of a Palestinian "entity" of one type or another on the West Bank. Thus, the U.S. has a "historic" opportunity to achieve peace—an opportunity that must not be missed.

As mentioned above, the first years of new administrations have traditionally seen new U.S. peace initiatives in the Middle East. *Re-election time is still three years away.*

The Begin Government is clearly trying to avoid such a split with Washington. But the Carter Administration at this stage may feel that it can risk some strains with Israel in order to promote the Geneva peace talks.

If historical experience is anything to go by, the President and his advisers will soon learn that the domestic price is too high to pay. An organized, articulate, and vocal interest-group operating in America's democratic system can cause the executive branch of government a lot of headaches if aroused, as happened last week after the Vance-Gromyko statement.[14] [Emphasis supplied]

During the balance of 1977, the Carter administration never ceased its efforts to reconvene a Geneva conference, including an offer to the Soviet Union to resume its former position as co-chairman. This caused an almost "hysterical" response from Israel. In the meantime, however, events in Israel were developing which would play a critical role in later peace negotiations.

The Likud victory had opened the flood gates to the extremist religious parties who had supported the Likud and claim to believe, as Begin does, that the West Bank and Gaza are "sacred territories," part of "Eretz Israel," and that not a foot of it can be bargained away. The October 17, 1977, edition of *U.S. News & World Report* contains the following report, datelined Nablus, and entitled "Israel Is in No Mood to Give Up Anything," and is quoted in part below:

Here on the West Bank of the Jordan River, President Carter faces his toughest task in mediating an Arab-Israeli peace: persuading Israel to turn over this land to the Palestinians.

Israel is in no mood to give up anything to anybody. Instead, Israelis are digging in everywhere on the West Bank and on the other Arab territories seized in the 1967 Mideast war.

From the Golan Heights, Israeli settlements march down the length of the West Bank and into the Sinai Desert. They range in size from tiny farming villages to huge apartment complexes on the Arab side of Jerusalem. *There are 46 settlements on the West Bank alone. In all, about 55,000 Jews live on* land that belonged to the Arabs before 1967.

Push by Gush Emunim. Now, an ultranationalist religious group named Gush Emunim—Bloc of the Faithful—is urging Prime Minister Menachem Begin to permit even more Israeli towns in occupied areas.

Begin shared Gush Emunim's convictions that the West Bank and Gaza Strip *are part of the biblical Jewish homeland and that Israelis should be free to settle anywhere in the regions.*

Hostility toward Israelis is evident in Arab towns. Cars with Israeli plates often are stoned, and military officials caution Jewish visitors to carry guns. It's not uncommon to see Israelis on the West Bank riding bicycles with machine guns strapped to their backs.

Despite the hostility and danger, the debate *in Israel is not over whether to settle the occupied territories but how fast to proceed with new towns.* Even into crowded Hebron itself. They say the ancient city, an important Jewish center in biblical times, should belong to Jews, not Arabs.[15] [Emphasis supplied]

A critical analysis of the then state of American Middle East diplomacy was published in the *Los Angeles Times,* written by Edward R.F. Sheehan, a research Fellow at Harvard's Center for International Affairs. His article entitled, "Is Carter Counting on a Geneva Miracle?" is quoted below:

U.S. policy in the Middle East has assumed dream-like dimensions. There exists an almost phantasmagoric contradiction between American theory and practice in the Arab-Israeli conflict.

The theory, pronounced consistently by President Carter since he took office, is commendable. He has spoken lucidly of Israeli withdrawal to the 1967 frontiers and the creation of a Palestinian "homeland"—in exchange for which the Arabs must confer full peace on Israel. Already, to an extent few of us thought possible only six months ago, the Arabs have expanded their definition of peace in keeping with Carter's wish.

Having come this far, the President is now in the process of demolishing his own policy. *Plagued by the pressures of domestic politics and the protestations of Israel's American constituency,* the President has openly contributed to Prime Minister Menachem Begin's public-relations triumph in Washington—fostering the illusion that Israel and the United States agree on goals at Geneva.

Privately, Carter made it clear to Begin that the American and Israeli positions on territory and the Palestinians are wide apart, but publicly he seemed to endorse Vice President Mondale's ecstatic declaration that Israeli-American relations have never been more harmonious, and he has cast Egyptian President Anwar Sadat and other moderates into a crisis from which they may not recover.

There is, as the result of the positions enunciated by Begin in Washington, particularly on the Palestinians, no basis for going to Geneva. And yet the President seems resolved to convene the peace conference and to persuade the Arabs to attend, in the Micawberish hope that once the parties get there some miracle will happen.

It is, however, vain to expect that Begin will bend unless he is subjected to intense American pressure. The entire history of American-Israeli relations illustrates that Israeli concessions will come only under the threat of sanctions. Carter's peace plan will become a hollow word game unless it is enforced, unless theory is linked to practice, *unless the laudable American legal position is functionally applied.*

We are in grave danger of repeating the errors that helped to produce the October war. *In the several years before that conflict we exhorted the Israelis to be reasonable and gave them guns to resist our exhortations.* Israel, the argument went, needed "confidence" to negotiate, *but it took the guns and rejected our advice. Now the president promises never to withhold military aid as a means to prevail on Israel to accept the American concept of peace.*[16] [Emphasis supplied]

CAMP DAVID

It was at this point, November 9, 1977, that Anwar Sadat, president of Egypt, made his dramatic overture to Israel and offered to negotiate peace terms. Israel responded favorably to this offer and began negotiations with Egypt.

However, by February 1978, negotiations between Sadat and Begin had ground nearly to a halt and President Sadat in desperation flew to Washington to seek President Carter's aid in breaking the deadlock with Israel. *Time* magazine, February 13, 1978, reports on the stalled Egyptian-Israeli peace talks:

THE PROBLEMS SADAT LEFT BEHIND

One of them is the settlements that block a settlement.

When Egyptian President Anwar Sadat flew to Washington last week, he left behind him a peace process that had ground very nearly to a halt. As one Egyptian official put it, "The two sides have gone as far as they can in bilateral negotiations. The time has come for the U.S. to step in and break the log-jam."

Sadat left for the U.S. at a time of rising tension between the U.S. and Israel over the establishment of new Israeli settlements in the occupied West Bank of the Jordan River. There are only about 45,000 Israelis in the West Bank (compared with 700,000 Arabs). Nonetheless, the U.S. has always opposed the settlements, *partly because they violate Article 49 of the Fourth Geneva Convention, which prohibits a country from moving its own people into occupied territories, and partly because the pioneer communities are a provocation to the Arabs.* On the other hand, Israeli Premier Menachem Begin has always insisted upon the *right of Jews to live in Judea and Samaria (the biblical lands that encompassed the West Bank) and their historical obligation to settle it.* On separate visits to Washington last year, Begin and Foreign Minister Moshe Dayan assured U.S. officials that there would be no new civilian settlements in the West Bank and that any new pioneers in the area would live within the confines of existing army camps.

Dayan insisted last week that he had made no such promise about the settlements, but a U.S. official snapped: "Our notes [from the September meeting] differ." Another Administration official was more blunt. "They're lying," he said. "There's no other way to call it."[17] [Emphasis supplied]

The February 13, 1978, edition of *Newsweek* describes the nature and purpose of Sadat's visit to Washington:

Sadat told a *Newsweek* correspondent on board that he was "disappointed and discouraged" by the slow progress toward peace in the Middle East. Now he wanted the U.S. to play a much more forceful role as an "arbiter"—and as a source of pressure on Israel.

The Middle East "peace process" had clearly stalled, and Sadat was playing one of his few remaining cards. He had come to Washington to enlist the support of Carter, Congress, and the American public.

"Truth Squad": Israeli officials admitted they were a bit anxious about the outcome of Sadat's trip, and Foreign Minister Moshe Dayan was dispatched to the U.S. to head an Israeli "truth squad." *We're not too worried about Congress, where we have many good friends, and we're convinced that Sadat will fall on his face if he tries to weaken our ties with American Jewry,"* said a policymaker in Jerusalem. "But we are apprehensive about what will come out of Sadat's meetings with Carter, who likes to please his guests by saying something they want to hear."

Israel's anxiety was heightened by the dispute with the Carter Administration over its new settlement on the West Bank at Shiloh, the site of a biblical city. When members of the militant Gush Emunim movement began erecting prefab houses there, Carter sent a blunt message to Jerusalem: "I am confident that Prime Minister Begin will honor the commitment personally made to me and thus will not permit this settlement to go forward."

Message: As Washington interpreted it, Begin's promise—conveyed by Dayan last fall—was that Israel would authorize no further settlements for a year. Speaking in the Knesset, Dayan said the promise covered only the rest of 1977. But *Newsweek* learned that *Begin recently sent Carter a message assuring the President that Shiloh was merely a temporary archaeological project* and that Israel would live up to the U.S. interpretation of the original pledge—an implied promise that the Gush Emunim settlers would be withdrawn. *The settlers themselves, however, insisted that they were not archaeologists.*[18] [Emphasis supplied]

Prime Minister Begin was scheduled to arrive in Washington for talks with President Carter on March 14 and 15 for another attempt to break the Middle East impasse.

Although the Israeli position with respect to the West Bank continued to shift between Israel's "need for security" and its "historic or religious rights" to the land, it was considered by all parties that Resolution 242, adopted by the Security Council of the United Nations on November 22, 1967, calling for Israeli withdrawal from the occupied territories, was the basic foundation for a settlement.

BEGIN REJECTS U.N. RESOLUTION 242

Suddenly, in early March 1978, Begin declared that U.N. Resolution 242 did not apply to the West Bank and Gaza because Israel had a historical biblical right to the territories, and was not committed to return them to anyone. (*U.S. News & World Report,* March 20, 1978.)

He also advanced a novel theory that the "occupied lands" referred to in

Resolution 242 were not "occupied" by Israel since she *owned* them as part of Eretz Israel.[19]

Carter was astounded at this reversal and stated in a news conference that Israel's rejection of Resolution 242 was a change in the policy of the Israeli government from what it had been for the past ten years. Furthermore, it was contrary to the interpretation of Resolution 242 by all the other governments involved.

By this time, the atmosphere surrounding the forthcoming meeting between Carter and Begin started to heat up. The political situation is described in an article appearing in the March 20, 1978, edition of *Newsweek* entitled "Carter and the Jews":

When they arrived for Friday night services last week, *1,000 members of the Stephen S. Wise Temple in an affluent district of West Los Angeles found their temple geared up for an all-out assault on the Middle East policies of President Jimmy Carter.* First, they were steered to the synagogue's social hall where a dozen tables were set up with sample letters to be copied and sent to Carter, Senators Alan Cranston and S.I. Hayakawa of California and the rest of the state's Congressional delegation. LET YOUR VOICE BE HEARD, said brightly lettered signs on the tables. When the worshipers gathered for the traditional prayers, they heard an angry sermon from Rabbi Isaiah Zeldin about Administration pressure on Israel and Carter's proposal to sell jet fighters to Saudi Arabia and Egypt. Said Robert Feldman, the temple's social-action chairman: "We are crazy about this thing, just fighting mad."

A Big Question Mark: All around the U.S. last week, in their synagogues and out among their friends and colleagues, a growing number of American Jews were saying just about the same thing. Their anxiety over Carter's policy was heightened by the resignation of White House staffer Mark Siegel, *Carter's main liaison with the Jewish community,* and by the expectation that Carter himself would be taking a tough line with Israeli Prime Minister Menachem Begin when they meet.

Not all Jews think Carter's approach is incorrect, however, and many more have their doubts about Prime Minister Begin's increasingly controversial hard-line position. Ultimately, they say, some compromise by Israel is inevitable. "Begin has not seized this really historic opportunity to do something," said millionaire Democratic contributor Max Palevsky.[20] [Emphasis supplied]

As expected, the meeting between Begin and Carter failed to resolve any of the issues. Finally, on the initiative of President Carter, a special summit conference was called to be held at Camp David. After thirteen days of intense negotiations, Carter, Begin, and Sadat reached a historic agreement, the Camp David Accords of September 1978, from which emerged the Israeli-Egyptian peace treaty under which Israel agreed to return the Sinai to Egypt.

Under the terms of the Camp David Accords, which are primarily concerned with the Sinai, the issues concerning the status of the West Bank, Gaza, and the Palestinian refugees, were not resolved—but, rather, swept aside as an insoluble problem to be dealt with in the future.

By concluding the Egyptian-Israeli peace treaty, the Likud had succeeded in securing its southern front. This enabled it to proceed to achieve its most important objective—the permanent occupation and annexation of all of Palestine.

To understand this development in terms of the highly complex Israeli political structure, we quote again from Perlmutter's book, *Israel: The Partitioned State:*

> *The fervor of fundamentalists, especially as embodied by Gush, sprang up in once-fertile but now rather sterile intellectual ground.* Historical Labor and Revisionist Zionism had become intellectually exhausted, clinging to pragmatic Zionism. Not even Begin was quite in the main-stream of the new Revisionism and in one sense could be included in the bloc of exhausted pragmatic Zionists. Small wonder then that the *new activist Zionists, the new Revisionists and the new fundamentalists flourished after 1967, turning into the most vital, aggressive realizers of Zionism's iron law: the settlement of Complete Zion.*
>
> *There is a new revival of Zionism in the land, wearing the mantle of fundamentalism, driven by a single-minded belief in Eretz Israel, thriv-ing in an emotional and intellectual vacuum left by the intellectual bankruptcy of the secularist Labor party and the Revisionist nationalists.* It is a kind of Zionism hardly envisioned by the sturdy kibbutzim leaders of years gone by, but is a fundamentalist, activist Zionism that is on the rise. There is no real opposition in sight.
>
> The rejectionist front is also representative of the Begin era. Although opposed to Begin's pragmatism, it nevertheless represents a most significant intellectual and political foundation for Begin-Herut-Likud and its ultimate aspiration—*Shlemut Ha-Moledet, the unity of*

the land—and total rejection of any sort of partition.[21] [Emphasis supplied]

SECOND BEGIN GOVERNMENT: 1981-1983

Begin's coalition government represented a new alignment of the political, social, and cultural forces replacing the Socialist Zionist Center, the old progressive and nationalist alignment composed of Jews of European and American origins (the Ashkenazim). The second Begin government was supported by an element in the electorate even more radical and militant than the government itself. It was an emerging electorate that was politically aggressive, inflexible on territorial concessions, and militant in its attitude toward the Palestinian problem.

The ten years which have elapsed since the Camp David Accords have witnessed profound changes in the Middle East, all of them dangerous and inimical to the cause of peace. Among these developments were the assassination of Anwar Sadat, the disastrous invasion of Lebanon by the Israeli hawks led by Ariel Sharon, the resignation of Prime Minister Begin, and his place taken by his even more extreme terrorist, Yitzhak Shamir.

Another highly significant change, in the past ten years, has been the emergence of Israel's Oriental Jews (Sephardim). The Oriental Jews were strongly attracted to the militant radical Zionism doctrines personified by Begin, Shamir, and Sharon. Contributing to this phenomenon has been distinct alteration of the demographics in Israel's society. The Oriental Jews now outnumber the Jews of European origin, a trend that is continuing and bodes ill for the future.

The old parties which founded Israel and the images of Ben-Gurion, Levi Eshol, and Golda Meir *no longer have the popular appeal that "Eretz Israel" and territorialism have attracted.*

In 1982 the Begin government had no serious opposition from the Labor party which was in political disarray. Likud had no internal restraining forces to exert a moderating influence on the Begin-Sharon government.

The single most important force that could have restrained the excesses of Israel's extreme right and prevented a new "March of Folly," was the government of the U.S., which, as we shall see in the discussion in the next chapters, has been paralyzed by the economic and political power of the Israeli Lobby.

In the meantime, however, in the ten years since Camp David, the West Bank situation has continued to deteriorate, and attitudes to polarize. At the urging of the Israeli government and with strong financial aid, many thousands of settlers were induced to migrate to the West Bank to fill the new settlements being constructed. As the new Israeli settlements proliferated, the hatreds and fears on both sides grew deeper. Finally, these pent-up emotions burst forth in the Palestinian uprising (Intifada) only to be met by the equally fierce emotion of the Israeli settlers and brutal repression by the Israeli army.

The position of the religious right has continued to harden. The unthinkable is not only being "thought," but loudly advocated. In the minds of the far right parties, the final solution to the Palestinian problem *is expulsion of the entire population from the West Bank and Gaza.*

Throughout the frustration of the past twenty-two years, it has been the position of the moderate Arab countries, as well as our friends and allies, that the U.S. government is the one party which is on good terms with both Israel and the Arab moderates, and only it has the power and authority to influence Israel toward a constructive solution to the Palestinian problem.

Other nations have assumed that, because the U.S. gives enormous sums to Israel, amounting to almost four billion dollars per year (equivalent to $1,000 for every man, woman, and child in Israel), and provides it with the best military equipment in the world, the U.S. should be in a position to require Israel to modify its position which is necessary if peace in the Middle East can ever be achieved.

The entire world remains incredulous that *Israel can, and does with impunity, defy or oppose American foreign policy and that America meekly continues to support and finance Israel in its adventures, even when its actions are against the best interests of the U.S. and against Israel's own best interests.*

How this paradox is explained is the subject of the following chapter on the "Israeli Lobby."

CHAPTER VI

The Israeli Lobby

T HE YEARS 1977 through 1979 marked a turning point in the prospects for peace in the Middle East.

On the positive side was the signing of the Camp David Accords between Israel and Eygpt, which settled the Sinai issue. On the negative side was the ascendancy of the Likud party to power, which effectively destroyed any further chance for an overall peace settlement.

With the Likud came an abrupt radicalization of the Israeli government and a new attitude on the part of the government of Israel toward the U.S. This new attitude has manifested itself in a variety of ways. Frequently, it has taken the form of total indifference to U.S. opinion. At other times, it can be seen as a special delight in "nose thumbing" the U.S. Recently, it has, on occasion, become an *outright and calculated defiance of the U.S. and its policies.*

This deterioration in the relationship between the U.S. and Israel's Likud government can be traced directly to the uncritical, unwavering, and often unreasoning support of what has come to be known as the "Israeli Lobby." It is the power and political influence of this Lobby that is the source of the arrogance displayed by the Likud government of Israel toward the U.S. and the rest of the world.

As will be shown in this and subsequent chapters, the activities of the Lobby have done incalculable damage to Israel, and the Israeli people, as well as to the cause of peace.

This view parallels that expressed by Yehoshafat Harkabi* in his latest book, referred to earlier, entitled *Israel's Fateful Hour.* In it, Harkabi accuses the U.S. government of failing to act as Israel's *true friend,* by not speaking out frankly and forcefully against the reckless politics of the Begin-Shamir government. He says, "That's what friends are for—to tell you when you are wrong."[1]

Harkabi explains that former Prime Minister Begin has been idolized in Israel, because the Israeli people were *misled by the U.S.* into believing that the U.S. supported and approved of the *reckless and disastrous policies of the Likud and the Gush Emunim in settling the West Bank.* He says the U.S. has been too fearful and timid in not criticizing the Israeli government and that the U.S. has failed in its duty to speak out forthrightly to make its opposition clear. As a result, he says, *the U.S. is largely responsible if Israel suffers* the calamity which he fears is on the way.[2]

The root cause of the failure of the U.S. to speak out concerning the conduct of the Likud government is not simple "fear" and "timidity," it is a matter of the political paralysis of American government. The U.S. government has no will of its own where Israel is involved. What the U.S. can and cannot do in the Middle East is determined by the Israeli government through the power and influence of the Israeli Lobby.

If the Israeli people have been betrayed, as Harkabi says, it is the Israeli Lobby in this country that bears the sole responsibility.

On July 5, 1977, on the front page of *The Wall Street Journal,* an article appeared entitled the "Potent Persuaders," a portion of which article is set forth below:

WASHINGTON—Congressman Thomas Downey, the young and liberal Democrat from Long Island, considers himself a good friend of Israel.

But last year he had doubts about a foreign-aid bill even though it contained more than $1.7 billion for the Jewish state. His mail was running strongly against foreign aid in general, and Mr. Downey was uneasy about the whole aid program.

So some concerned rabbis came to call, they wanted a positive vote on Israel's behalf. As the congressman remembers, he said he would suppress his qualms if there was a "show of support" from his own district, where only 5 percent of the voters are Jewish.

---

* Yehoshafat Harkabi is Israel's foremost authority on Arab relations, a former Chief of Military Intelligence for Israel and previously an advisor to Prime Minister Begin.

Two days later, he received 3,000 telegrams from constituents, and Congressman Downey voted "yes."

That is the so-called Israeli Lobby in action, mobilizing support whenever it thinks interests of the Jewish nation are at stake. It may well be the most effective of the many pressure groups in Washington—variously admired or feared. It zealously guards Israeli interests against the vicissitudes of U.S. presidents and legislators whose perceptions don't always square with those of Jerusalem or of the influential American Jewish community. *Its main goal is to get the maximum possible political, economic and military support for Israel.*

Achievements and Criticisms: The Lobby's achievements are numerous. *But critics contend that it sometimes undermines broader U.S. goals by its fervent backing of one side in the long-running Middle East dispute and thus hinders the cause of peace. There are also complaints that the Lobby's tactics can be abrasive, eroding sympathy for the Israeli cause.*

The debate over Israel's future will intensify this summer. That is because some basic policy differences between Washington and Jerusalem have become obvious as Mid-east negotiations grow more serious. Many Israelis and American Jews fear that President Carter is trying to impose American-made peace terms on the region—terms that they feel might be extremely dangerous to Israel. A serious confrontation looms, and this prospect has already activated the worried Lobby.

New Government in Israel: Preventing such a showdown is the Lobby's current task. The assignment seems especially urgent now that a conservative government has taken office in Israel, after 29 years of Labor Party dominance. Its ideas about peace terms differ sharply from those of Mr. Carter. Most notably, the new prime minister, Menachem Begin, considers the occupied West Bank of the Jordan River—the biblical Judea and Samaria—to be Israeli land by historical right; he calls it "liberated territory," although President Carter says most or all should be returned to Arab control. The degree of difference will be tested when Mr. Begin meets President Carter here beginning July 19.

A campaign to muffle potential disputes is underway. Leaders of American Jewish organizations, politicians friendly to Israel, Israeli diplomats and the official registered lobbying organization—the American Israel Public Affairs Committee—are all in action.

One broad goal is to convince the White House, Congress and the U.S. public that neither Mr. Begin nor his policies are really outlandish and that he is a moderate man with broad support at home. *Although he once led a violent urban guerrilla force,* Israel's friends insist that Mr. Begin isn't a bomb thrower who will sabotage peace efforts.

Bridging the Gap: Another goal of Israel's supporters is to convince President Carter to talk less and, in particular, to stop calling for major Israeli territorial withdrawals and an unspecified "homeland" for Arab Palestinians.

To a degree, it is working. Mr. Carter last week promised to "refrain from additional comments on specifics" until he meets Mr. Begin. But earlier, the administration repeated its insistence that peace terms must include major withdrawals and a Palestinian homeland.

Mr. Begin's position is that Israel won't under any conditions withdraw to the borders that existed before the 1967 war, and won't agree to the establishing of a Palestinian state on the West Bank and in Gaza.

American Jewish leaders are counseling Mr. Begin to cool it a bit. They want him to stress flexibility when discussing peace talks and avoid pinning himself down to hard and controversial positions. *Thus, he says he will discuss anything with the Arabs even though there is much he will never agree to.* Jewish leaders also want him to drop such terms as "liberated territories," which can have an adverse impact with the U.S. public.

Israel's supporters, of course, include most of this nation's six million Jews, who feel strong religious, ethnic or political ties to the tiny nation. Because of this affinity, many are willing to work for Israel's cause—by sending cables to Congressmen or making political contributions, for example.

As a group, they also have unusual political savvy. "They are plugged into the Washington-based network," a veteran congressional staffer says. "They are well-armed with the usual vehicles that lobbyists need, they are adept and intelligent—and they know how these cats meow."

Stressing Moderation: The American Israel Public Affairs Committee, led by its aggressive if not abrasive director, Morris Amitay, is cranking out a flood of press releases and statements that stress Mr. Begin's moderation.

The pro-Israel operatives here are working closely with the new government in Israel. Some met recently with Schmuel Katz, who was sent to the U.S. as Mr. Begin's personal representative. Democratic Sen. Richard Stone of Florida, one of Israel's staunchest friends, visited Mr.

Begin in Israel to counsel caution after conferring here with seven concerned Senators who regularly support Israel.

"Begin policy as enunciated so far can only lead to disorder," an influential ally of Israel worries. "It would create, for the first time, a deep schism between Israel and the American Jewish community."

Rallying Behind Begin: For now, however, Jewish leaders are rallying behind Mr. Begin, stressing—as does Rabbi Schindler—that he has been "for 29 years a responsible leader of the loyal opposition," and isn't by nature a fanatical terrorist. "There is emerging in the American Jewish community a feeling that we have to be supportive of Begin," the rabbi says. He argues that the prime minister *will prove flexible on all major peace issues—including withdrawal from West Bank territories.*

If a confrontation does come nonetheless, *much of the Israeli Lobby's efforts will be focused on Congress, where it is often possible to thwart the Executive Branch. The most conspicuous action might well occur in the Senate Foreign Relations Committee.*

This committee and its staffers can make things happen. When the Ford administration began a "reassessment" of Mideast policy in 1975, staff members got 76 Senators to sign a letter of support for Israel, effectively squelching the administration move for policy changes. When Mr. Carter's new arms-sales policy didn't specifically promise special treatment for Israel, *a Senate committee uproar caused him to revise it hurriedly. And in secret bill-writing sessions, staffers often get aid terms for Israel modified, as by lowering loan interest rates.*

Arousing Anger: All this has angered successive administrations. Aides to former Secretary of State Henry Kissinger say the Lobby's opposition forced him to drop thoughts of seeking a comprehensive Mideast peace settlement last year. Secretary of State Cyrus Vance is unhappy about Senate leaks of secret information he made available in May: two days later, it appeared in the Israeli press. And when President Carter recently planned to meet secretly with four key Senators who back Israel, the word was somehow passed to lobbyist Amitay—who called on each one to shore up his support before the meeting occurred.

Critics contend that such tactics don't always serve either American or Israeli long-term interests. Some think a confrontation between Washington and Jerusalem, possibly leading to a schism within the American Jewish community, could damage chances for Mideast peace and radicalize the Arab world. Sen. Abe Ribicoff of Connecticut, a leading supporter of Israel, has expressed this fear publicly.

Several congressional sources contend that opposition to a particular pro-Israel measure, such as a plan to send deadly concussion bombs to the Jerusalem government, *can bring suggestions that the opponents are secretly anti-Semitic. Several legislators and staffers strongly resent such suggestions. "That's the pervasive fear they strike in the hearts of members up here," one Capitol Hill aide says. "If you're in opposition, you get a big white paintbrush that says you're anti-Semitic."* As Democratic Rep. David Obey of Wisconsin sees it, "If you question their programs, they say you are for their enemies and against them. . . . I defend Israel but not irrational policies that will lead to war for both of us."

Trying to Discredit Kissinger: Israeli lobbyists have even used this line to try to discredit Mr. Kissinger, himself a Jew. They have contended that he was tough on Israel because he was ashamed of his own background and wanted to ingratiate himself with a non-Jewish establishment. But if some eloquent speeches by Mr. Kissinger about his heritage are any measure, this charge hasn't any foundation.[3] [Emphasis supplied]

It is difficult to believe that more than ten years have passed since *The Wall Street Journal* article was written—but the "Potent Persuaders" are, if anything, more potent today. The power and influence of the Israeli Lobby is as broadly based under the leadership of Yitzhak Shamir as under Menachem Begin.

JEWS AND POLITICAL ACTIVISM

To understand the Israeli Lobby and its various levels of activity it is first necessary to have some idea of the relationship of the American Jewish community to our political system and the nature and extent of its involvement in the political process. An excellent work on this subject is a book entitled *Jews and American Politics,* by Stephen Isaacs, which is the source of much of the information on the subject presented in the next several pages of this chapter.

The Jewish people wield political power in America far beyond their numbers. Historically, this power has been used to a large extent in support of liberal causes and the Democratic party, and has been in the highest tradition of American democracy. Indeed, it should be emphasized that, in the past, Jewish participation in American political life has redounded greatly to the benefit of our nation.

As a general rule, Jews in the past have been reluctant to run for political office and, as a result, there have been relatively few Jews in the Congress or in the governorships. The reasons, according to Isaacs, are twofold.

One, they have perhaps underestimated the willingness of the people to elect a Jew to high office and two, they prefer to avoid the high visibility of public office and would rather exert their influence behind the scenes. While this attitude is beginning to change and more Jews are now running for office, particularly at the state and local levels, the strong preference is still to be "kingmaker" rather than king.

Jewish political power and influence derive from a number of sources, one of which (but not necessarily the most important) is money. Jews normally donate more than half the large gifts to national Democratic campaigns. Although they are less of a financial factor in the Republican party, they are, nevertheless, of considerable significance.

Another and perhaps equally important source is political activism. Jewish political activism is found at all levels, from the ballot box to the highest councils of government and politics. It is estimated that Jews now comprise between 10 percent and 20 percent of those actively involved in the Democratic side of American politics.

They were prominent in the top management entourage of nearly all of the principal Democratic presidential contenders in 1972: Edmund S. Muskie was managed by Berl I. Bernhart; Henry S. Jackson had Ben J. Wattenberg; Hubert Humphrey used Max Kampelman; George McGovern had Frank Mankiewicz.

Of the Richard Nixon "political enemies" list, released by the Senate Watergate Committee, seven out of the first eight, and a total of twelve out of the first twenty were Jewish.

Of the three principal national public opinion surveys, two (Louis Harris and Daniel Yankelovich) are Jewish. Pollsters have discovered that an extraordinarily high percentage of people, who ask to do their interviewing, are Jewish.

One of the nation's most prominent political reporters, David S. Broder, is Jewish, as was the late Theodore White, our most popular political historian and author of *The Making of the President*. There have been innumerable Jewish speech writers for virtually all candidates and presidents, including the former Chairman of the Democratic National Committee, Robert Strauss.

It is a fact that Jews are simply more active and interested in politics than their fellow Americans. Nearly four times as many Jews as non-Jews protested American-Vietnam military policy.

Another source of power is the media. The major television networks were founded by David Sarnoff, William S. Paley, and Leonard Goldenson. These organizations are heavily Jewish, as are their reportorial staffs.[4]

The fact that no network "anchor man" is Jewish is explained by Isaacs as an effort to avoid the appearance to the viewing public of being too "Jewish." "Jews could be the 'back room' presidents of the network news divisions, while the non-Jewish anchor man could project a comforting WASP image to an overwhelmingly WASP audience."[5]

The newspaper industry, as such, is neither owned nor controlled by Jewish interests. However, the newspapers in which Jews occupy senior editorial positions are especially influential in national politics. These include the *New York Times, Washington Post, The Wall Street Journal,* and *New York Post.* The late Walter Lippman, perhaps the greatest of modern political journalists, was Jewish, as were Arthur Krock and David Lawrence. These have been succeeded today by such prominent and capable political journalists as Joseph Kraft, Max Lerner, and William Safire.[6]

A further and very effective source of political power is the presence of Jews in the government itself. While the number of Jewish office holders, at the national level, do not exceed the relative proportion of Jews to the general population, *the number of Jews in staff positions in Congress and in many of the federal administrative agencies far exceeds their proportionate representation in the population.* Many of these are key positions which can be, and are, effectively used to accomplish specific objectives.

An example of such objectives is the amendment to force the Soviet Union to ease restrictions on the emigration of Soviet Jews (The Jackson-Vanik Amendment). This was devised and drafted by Jewish activist senatorial staffers. The same holds true of the Arab boycott legislation. One staffer is quoted as saying that a certain Jewish senator, who "cares deeply about Jewish affairs," has enough seniority now to place some sixty of "his" people in key committee jobs around the Senate.[7]

Why this effort to place activist Jews in key positions is important, according to the same Jewish staffer, is that "There are only six million of 'us' [Jews] and two hundred million of 'them.' "[8]

How the "us" (Jewish minority) manages to get things done, according to the staffer, is explained by the fact that senators "have a million things to do and generally take the recommendations of their administrative assistants." If the senator does not cooperate, the next step is to call for "outside help" which means direct pressure on the senators from their Jewish constituents.

In this way, according to Stephen Isaacs, the apparatus is able to generate a flood of letters to Congress or the president, or to deluge the editorial offices of the nation's newspapers with letters to the editor giving the impression of overwhelming popular support for or against any given measure.

Another Senate staffer says, "What you have in this country is a fantastic untapped reservoir of Jews who are in influential positions . . . relatively wealthy, well-educated, professional, politically active, who when organized can get the support of three-quarters of the Senate."[9]

In an editorial in *The Wall Street Journal,* entitled "The Hired Hands," the power of these congressional staffers is discussed:

A few years ago, people who worried about making government accountable for its actions used to point to the federal bureaucracy as the major obstacle standing between hapless citizens and the elected officials they're supposed to control. These days, as Congress takes an increasingly active role in setting national policy, observers are shifting their attention and concern to another group of unelected decision-makers—congressional staffs.

In two recent articles in *The Public Interest,* Michael J. Malbin and Michael Andrew Scully have described the growing power of these staffs and the special problems that arise from this power.

Even more important than the growth in staff numbers has been the kind of jobs they have come to do for their congressmen. Mr. Scully points out that today staffers not only set the agenda for our legislation and organize the hearings and negotiations that shape it, but actually draft the laws themselves and write the reports of legislative intent that accompany them.

And when they do all these things, the staffers are not just mirroring the congressional will. For one thing, their very numbers and levels of activity change the shape of the lawmaking process; instead of merely carrying out a legislative program, they also help create one, inventing things to do where there were none before. For another, they are highly partisan: they tend to seek not dispassionate knowledge but the knowledge that brings advantage. And to add to these problems that Mr. Malbin and Mr. Scully describe, too many of these staffers seem to have been schooled to the assumption that the private sector may best be thought of as an insidious disease requiring a federal remedy.

To hear all of this it would seem congressional staffs are good candidates for the next leading example of the arrogance of irresponsible power.[10]

This means that some of the most important legislation affecting our foreign and domestic policies, our most sensitive relations with the Soviet Union, the Arab world, and even world peace itself is being devised, drafted, and promoted by the same congressional staffers who are unabashed Israeli partisans.

Finally, the ballot box itself is a source of power. Jews vote in numbers far out of proportion to their percentage of population. This is not only due to the fact that the vast majority of Jews vote, but to the fact that a far lesser percentage of non-Jews exercise their franchise.

The eight states where Jews are most concentrated—California, Maryland, Massachusetts, Pennsylvania, New York, New Jersey, Connecticut, and Florida—are big electoral vote states where the Jewish vote can be decisive in a close election.

An Israeli diplomat claims: "President Ford's defeat on November 2, 1976, can be attributed to his reassessment of U.S. policy toward the Mideast in 1975, when he squeezed us to make concessions to the Arabs. Many Jews have not forgotten that—or forgiven." The diplomat points out that a small shift to Mr. Ford in voting among the 2 million Jews in New York City would have reversed the election result in New York State and the nation.

AIPAC

The umbrella organization for lobbying for the Jewish state in this country is the American Israel Public Affairs Committee (AIPAC).

AIPAC coordinates its activities with other Jewish organizations, such as the American Jewish Committee and the Anti-Defamation League of B'nai B'rith. AIPAC works to influence Congress and the executive branch on issues of importance to Israel, such matters as the Middle East problem and economic and military aid, the Arab boycott, and Soviet Jews' emigration. A Senate staff member says that, "AIPAC has a strong grass-roots operation that can deliver letters and phone calls to members of Congress from their home states. At any given moment, it can mobilize."

Thus, we have a situation where Israel can exert almost irresistible political influence upon the Congress and executive branch of the U.S. government by mobilizing Americans, from the grass-roots to the highest levels of government, in support of its policies even when these policies are against the best interests of the U.S. and its citizens and, in fact, against the best interests of Israel itself.

The "Farm Lobby" is obviously no match for the Israeli Lobby when an American farmer's ability to sell his glut of grain to Russia depends on the number of Jews allowed to emigrate from the Soviet Union (The Jackson-Vanik Amendment). Nor is the "Business Lobby" any match for the Israeli Lobby when the proposed rules and regulations, under which an American company can carry on trade with friendly Arab countries, are being drafted by the Anti-Defamation League of the B'nai B'rith. This matter is discussed later in the chapter entitled "The Arab Boycott."

The extraordinary effectiveness of the Israeli Lobby is a classic in the use of power politics. Its performances in the election year 1976 was awesome. Throughout the campaign, both presidential candidates (Carter and Ford) desperately tried to out-promise each other in concessions to Israel.

The humiliating spectacle of the president of the U.S., within ten days of Election Day, suddenly bypassing the objections of the defense department and announcing that the U.S. would provide Israel with the ultra-modern CBU 72 anti-personnel bombs, infrared night vision devices, M60 tanks and artillery, (the approval for all of which had previously been withheld by the military) seems to be taken for granted as part of the American political scene.

Within the same week, President Ford also ignominiously abandoned the administration's position on the Arab boycott and capitulated to the Israeli Lobby, which had coerced a frightened Congress into imposing tax penalties on American companies who were honestly trying to do business with the Arab countries. It is no wonder that Israel's foreign minister, Yigal Allon, after watching the presidential debates on TV, is reported as saying, "I don't know if Carter or Ford won. All I know is that Israel won."

In the chapter entitled "Jewish Power" of his book *Jews and American Politics,* author Isaacs exults in the newfound ability of the Jewish community to influence political events in America:

With unprecedented vigor they brashly and openly spoke up for their fellow Jews in Israel, bombarding the White House and Congress with telegrams, letters and calls insisting that America continue its staunch support of Israel.

Heedless of "whether they might seem to the 'goyim' to be causing too much trouble," Isaacs goes further to say:

The Jews' new confidence in their Americanism and in their use of these tools was spelled out quite specifically, for instance, in an article in the February 1974 issue of *The National Jewish Monthly,* a publication of B'nai B'rith. The article, by Franklin R. Sibley, a congressional aide, blatantly called Jewish contributors' attention to Jews' "friends" and enemies who were up for election in 1974:

One-third of the Senate comes up for re-election this coming fall: among them are vigorous friends of Jewish causes. . . .

A few senators consistently opposed to Jewish concerns are also up for re-election. *Foremost among these is J.W. Fulbright (D-Ark.), who has lent respectability to the Arab cause and given it a voice in the Senate it never enjoyed before. A believer in détente with the Soviets to the detriment of Israel's interests,* he has labored diligently against legislation offered by Henry M. Jackson (D-Wash.), linking preferential trade terms to the relief of Soviet Jewry. Other members of the Senate seeking re-election this year who chose not to sponsor the Jackson Amendment are Henry L. Bellmon (R-Okla.), and Gaylord Nelson (D-Wis.).[11] [Emphasis supplied]

One cannot fail to be struck by the irony of this quoted statement. The new confidence of the Jews in their "Americanism" is demonstrated by an "enemies list." They call for the defeat of Senator Fulbright because he is a believer in détente with the Soviet Union to the "detriment of Israel's" interests. Nothing is said about whether détente (a creation of Henry Kissinger) might be in America's interest.

Senator Fulbright was attacked and defeated for re-election because he lent *"respectability to the Arab cause,* and a voice in the Senate it never had before."

The enormous and acknowledged influence of the Israeli Lobby is sometimes rationalized by saying that everybody in America has a "lobby," and therefore Jews have the American right to use whatever muscle they can muster toward their special interests. What is lost sight of in this argument is that we are not talking about a "Jewish" Lobby but an *Israeli Lobby.* In the past, the "Jewish" Lobby has, in fact, functioned appropriately as a lobby, i.e., in supporting civil rights causes, opposing school prayers, promoting liberal abortion laws, opposing capital punishment, and other liberal positions. In doing so, it has operated as a legitimate special interest group in American society.

However, in the past twenty or more years, the Jewish Lobby for the most part has become the *Israeli* Lobby which has become involved in matters transcending domestic issues and politics. Indeed, and we emphasize again, its principal thrust and orientation has been toward the support, by any means, of the policies of the government of Israel regardless of the best interests of the U.S., its allies, or that of world peace—or, for that matter, *the best interests of the Israeli people.*

THE TABOO

There is a second and even more crucial distinction between the Israeli Lobby and the typical lobby. If one disagrees with or opposes the Farm Lobby, for example, he is free to say so. He can write his congressman—send a letter to the editor, march on Washington, or write a book.

No such freedom exists in America so far as opposition to Israeli policy or the Israeli Lobby is concerned. It is simply "taboo." To do so, automatically exposes one to being branded "anti-Semitic," a "Fascist," a "Nazi," or part of the lunatic fringe. Prudent people simply will not take such a risk. Thus the effectiveness of the highly vocal and articulate Israeli partisans is multiplied by the fact that *they operate in a vacuum of opposition.* The following example will illustrate what is meant by this:

Assume, for instance, that a congressman has received a thousand letters on the subject of emigration restrictions on Soviet Jewry, and assume further that 975 of these letters urge the congressman to support the legislation (the Jackson-Vanik amendment) while only 25 urge non-support.

If the congressman is naive he might consider this response as an accurate reflection of the opinions of his constituency. On the other hand, in all probability, he would recognize that the 975 supporters are mostly Jewish and prompted by an organized campaign and thus not a true sample of the views of the electorate. However, the fact that only 25 non-Jews wrote at all would seem to indicate to the congressman that the vast majority of his constituents who did not write were indifferent and that only the Jews felt strongly enough to write. But in this assumption, the congressman would be dead wrong. He would have failed to take into consideration the known fact that most Americans have become so conditioned and intimidated by the "taboo" that they prefer to remain silent—rather than risk the accusation of being called "anti-Semitic," if they frankly and openly express their views.

The same holds true for letters to the editor. From a reading of letters to the editor in any metropolitan newspaper, when an issue involving Israel is in the news, one would conclude that 95 percent of the people of the U.S. passionately support the Israeli position on the issue. This again is a gross error. Most non-Jews simply do not write to the editor or say or write anything publicly which can be construed by Jewish sensitivities or the Anti-Defamation League as "anti-Semitic." As far as the greater part of the Jewish community is concerned, anything less than wholehearted support for any Israeli position, however unreasonable, is by definition "anti-Semitic." Indeed, there is a serious question whether, if such letters to the editor were written, they would even be published, because many newspaper editors are even more sensitive to the taboo than their readers.

So programmed have our leaders become that the very instant the buzz word "anti-Semitic" is heard there is an automatic "knee jerk" reaction—a hasty attempt to retract, apologize, placate—anything to avoid *the awful charge of anti-Semitism.* Thus, it is not simply the financial and political power of the Israeli Lobby that is the source of its influence—but also the pervasive, quiet, unspoken censorship of the taboo, which the Israeli Lobby exploits to the fullest.

THE ANTI-DEFAMATION LEAGUE AND THE FIRST AMENDMENT

The Anti-Defamation League was originally formed many years ago as a defense against slanderous and libelous attacks on Jews and the Jewish community. Its record over the years, in this respect, has been highly successful. However, inasmuch as there is little, if any, slander, libel, or defamation against Jews anymore, the league in recent years has extended its activities to monitoring the various media, to detect and react against any utterances which the league considers *might* be "anti-Semitic." This can be anything which is judged by the league as unfriendly, unflattering, or critical toward a Jew, Jews, Zionism or Israel, or even if a congressman or senator votes for only three billion dollars instead of four billion dollars in grants to Israel.

Needless to say, simply having the power to *define* "anti-Semitism" in any particular context (which the league freely asserts) is a highly effective method of stifling even the most legitimate criticism or comment.

Thus, all that is required to smother any objective consideration of issues involving say, for example, Israel, is simply to define any contrary position as "anti-Semitic." Since there is absolutely no defense against the charge of "anti-Semitism," most prudent people have long since preferred silence on sensitive issues to the risk of exposing themselves to the accusation of "anti-Semitism," with its inevitable "Hitler" and "Holocaust" associations.

This not too subtle form of intimidation operates as a de facto abridgment of freedom of speech. In other words, it is a highly effective form of censorship, which imposes a clear "prior restraint" on what can safely be said in this country on certain and often highly important subjects.

In an article entitled "A Certain Anxiety" appearing in the August 1971 issue of the prestigious Jewish magazine, *Commentary,* Norman Podhoretz, editor and publisher, explains the "taboo" as follows:

> Now it is perfectly true that anti-Zionism is not necessarily anti-Semitism. But it is also true, I fear, that the distinction between the two is *often invisible to the naked Jewish eye,* and that anti-Zionism has served to legitimize the other expression of a good deal of anti-Semitism which might otherwise have remained subject to the *taboo* against anti-Semitism that prevailed in American public life from the time of Hitler until, roughly, the Six-Day War, and it is more than anything else *the breaking of the taboo,* the *taboo* against the open expression of hostility to Jews, which has caused some of us to feel a certain anxiety about the Jewish population in America.... It is so long since overt hostility to Jews has been regarded as a permissible attitude in America that we cannot say what consequence, if any, might follow this inhibition.[12] [Emphasis supplied]

A similar concern was expressed in another article by Podhoretz appearing in the February 1972 issue of *Commentary,* entitled "Is It Good For The Jews?":

> During the period running from the end of the Second World War to the middle or late 60's, Jews had no need to ask whether anything was good for the Jews, for the simple and sufficient reason that in America at least almost everything was good for the Jews. Anti-Semitism still existed, mainly on the political Right, but so discredited had it become through its association with the name of Hitler *that no-one who aspired to respectable status in American public life dared voice anti-Semitic sentiments openly or dared make any use of anti-Semitism* in appealing for the support of others. For the penalty was instant banishment from the world of acceptable opinion.
>
> Whether or not, then, the actual level of anti-Semitic feeling declined in America, the sheer number of anti-Semitic statements, or indeed of statements hostile to Jews *in any way or to any degree,* most certainly did

decline in the public prints, on the airways, in political speeches, and probably *even in private conversation!!*[13] [Emphasis supplied]

The taboo, thus described, raises some disturbing questions, as well as some novel concepts, as far as our First Amendment freedoms are concerned. We have assumed that the American Civil Liberties Union (ACLU) had long ago made clear to Americans the meaning of our sacred guarantees of freedom of speech and press, as well as the evils of censorship.

True, the taboo referred to by Podhoretz is not "censorship" imposed by the government. However, if one *dares not* voice any statements *hostile* to Jews in *any way* or to *any degree,* even in *private* conversation, the operative restraint on free speech is even more insidious.

The very concept of a "taboo" is, of course, a negation of the essential spirit of our Constitution. In the language of the U.S. Supreme Court:

The command of the First Amendment is that falsehoods and fallacies must be exposed not suppressed. American Communication Assn. C.I O.U. Douds, N.Y. 70 S. CT. 674 339 U.S. 382.

Surely the ACLU, which is a champion of unpopular causes, would find enormous difficulty in reconciling its concept of civil liberties with the existence of a taboo. From any viewpoint, as has been said, it constitutes a de facto infringement upon freedom of speech and press with all of the evils inherent therein.

If in this country, one dare not make any statement that is in any way or to any degree "hostile" to Jews—what is hostile?—who is to judge? Podhoretz himself points out that the distinction between "anti-Semitism" and "anti-Zionism," to the naked Jewish eye, is often invisible.

Since the accusation of "anti-Semitism" can be made in disregard of such "invisible" distinctions, (without risk to the accuser, or defense to the accused), the power exists to deny "respectable status in American public life" to anyone who voices any opinion or expresses any view unpopular with the Jewish community or the Anti-Defamation League (ADL).

This, however, is not the only penalty to be suffered by anyone breaking the taboo. According to Podhoretz, they will suffer *instant banishment from the world of acceptable opinion.* But what is "acceptable" opinion? Acceptable to whom? Both Nazi Germany and Soviet Russia have always offered total freedom to voice "acceptable opinions."

A good example of what can happen when someone dares to express an "unacceptable opinion" is the case of General George Brown, former chairman of the U.S. Joint Chiefs of Staff. In a press interview, the text of which was released on October 17, 1976, he was asked by a reporter the following question:

> Speaking about the Middle East, are Israel and its forces more of a burden or more of a blessing to the U.S. from a purely military point of view?

General Brown's frank and honest answer was, "Well, I think it's just got to be considered a burden." He answers the question more fully by explaining that someday Israel might actually be a tremendous asset. General Brown's answer was that, from a military standpoint, Israel was a burden at that time because the vital U.S. tank reserve in Europe had been depleted to replace Israel's losses in The Yom Kippur War, leaving the U.S. with less than 50 percent of the tanks necessary for the defense of NATO. Also, that the U.S. is sending certain new weapons systems to Israel, which we have not yet supplied to our own armed forces.[14]

The Los Angeles Times *the following day, in a calm and reasoned editorial, pointed out that Brown was right.* He had merely acknowledged that U.S. military support of Israel is costing billions of dollars annually. That, the *Times* said, "clearly adds up to a burden rather than a blessing, and no good purpose would be served by pretending otherwise."[15]

Nowhere, it should be emphasized, did General Brown say or imply that we should not continue to support and supply Israel with weapons. He merely said (having been asked to express his opinion) that, from a military standpoint, Israel was not a "blessing." However, no sooner did the text of General Brown's interview reach the media than a wave of hysteria swept the country. Letters flooded the editorial offices of the nation's newspapers condemning General Brown's remarks as "anti-Semitic." President Ford hurriedly apologized for General Brown, obviously concerned that this might affect his chances for re-election.

Many voices, including such usually sensible people as Senator Howard Baker, demanded that General Brown be fired. Leaders of major Jewish organizations called on President Ford to "censure" General Brown. After a special meeting of the Conference of Presidents of major American Jewish organizations it was announced, rather ominously, that *"The Jewish community does not consider the matter of General Brown to be closed."* General Brown's heinous offense was that he failed to say that Israel was a "military blessing."

One lonely voice dared to risk the awful "banishment." Senator Barry Goldwater is quoted in the *Los Angeles Times*:

"I agree with him [General Brown]," Goldwater said in an address to the Inland Daily Press Assn.'s annual fall meeting. "We can't continue to give any country equipment from our own inventory and not deplete our own war machine." Later, in explaining his remark, he said, *"Israel has gotten everything she ever wanted [from the U.S.] ... in some categories, more than she can use."* He said that it was all right with him, but "if we give Israel $2 billion [in equipment], then let's buy $2 billion for ourselves. Unless we regain our military superiority," he said, "the only choice can be nuclear war or surrender." Goldwater said, "That was what Brown was trying to say, only he was misunderstood."[16] [Emphasis supplied]

The Wall Street Journal tried to restore some semblance of common sense into this irrational scene and offered the following editorial comment:

Various overeager New York politicians, unfortunately including Senator James Buckley, are demanding General Brown's ouster as a result. Senator Mondale, who is not supposed to be the hatchet man on his team, is likening General Brown to a "sewage commissioner."

But an honest appraisal of the drift of his remarks would have to indicate he is not suggesting Israel's abandonment and that his observations are probably clear-eyed and correct.

It looks to us as if General Brown's real sin is excessive candor, which leaves us confused, since we thought everyone agreed our leaders needed to be more candid, not less so. If Governor Carter wants to pursue the matter and set a "higher standard," he may as well announce that in a Carter administration no interviews will be granted except by officials who have been lobotomized.[17]

What must be resisted and overcome is simply this kind of covert and overt intimidation; the mischievous result of the "taboo"; the existence of a gag rule on discussing openly, and disagreeing frankly, with the Israeli partisans. There is obviously no freedom of speech on the subject of Israel when the Chief of Staff of the Armed Forces of the U.S. cannot say that Israel is not a military blessing, without causing a national uproar and suffering the threat of being fired. The intimidation has worked, as intended; General Brown has been apologizing ever since.

These successful efforts to intimidate the chairman of the Joint Chiefs of

Staff, as well as the president of the United States, clearly defeat and frustrate the very purpose of the guarantees of freedoms of speech and press. These freedoms are just as effectively curtailed by intimidation and inhibition as by outright prohibition.

In the words of the U.S. Supreme Court:

> Expression of opinion is entitled to protection no matter how unorthodox or abhorrent it may seem to others. The basis of the free speech guarantee of the First Amendment is the hypothesis that speech can rebut speech, that propaganda will answer propaganda and that free debate of ideas will result in the wisest governmental policies.
>
> The right of free speech and free press guaranteed by the Constitution extends to all subjects which affects ways of life, without limitation to any particular field of human interest, and includes in the main freedom of expression on political, sociological, religious, and economic subjects.
>
> Freedom of discussion must embrace all issues about which information is needed or appropriate to enable the members of society to cope with the exigencies of their period. Thornill vs. State of Alabama, 60, S. Ct. 736 310 U.S. 88.

Never has our society been in greater need of a full discussion of critical issues so that we can "cope" with the "exigencies of the time." There are few issues now confronting our country that do not directly or indirectly involve a solution to the Middle East problem. If freedom of speech and press have any meaning or value at all, it is here and now.

The paralyzing fear of violating the taboo, which grips the Congress as well as the executive branch of the government, is nowhere better illustrated than in the case of Senator Fulbright.

SENATOR FULBRIGHT SPEAKS OUT

On April 15, 1973, Senator J. William Fulbright appeared on the CBS "Face The Nation" program. In the nationally televised interview, he said, that the *"administration was unable to exert pressure on Israel for a Middle East settlement because the U.S. Senate was subservient to Israel."* He added that "despite the fact that the U.S. provided Israel with a major part of the wherewithal to finance or pay for everything Israel does, leverage could not be applied," he said, "because *Israel controls the Senate."*

Fulbright declared, "We should be more concerned about the U.S. interest rather than doing the bidding of Israel."[18] On May 30, at the opening of two-day hearings that his committee initiated on the energy situation, Fulbright charged that U.S. policy was to give Israel unlimited support for unlimited expansion; he urged U.S. cooperation with oil-producing countries.

In a return appearance on "Face The Nation," October 7, 1973, *Senator Fulbright repeated his assertion that the Israelis control Mid-Eastern policy in the Congress and the Senate.* When the program monitor called Fulbright's statement a "fairly serious charge," the Senate Foreign Relations Committee chairman countered, "The charge is a fact of life."[19]

Here we have the chairman of the Senate Foreign Relations Committee charging publicly, on two separate occasions, that the Senate of the U.S. was "subservient to a foreign power," a charge vastly more serious than anything involved in the Watergate scandal. Either the charge was true or Senator Fulbright (who was certainly in a position to know) was lying to the American people.

If the latter was the case, then Senator Fulbright grossly insulted and impugned the integrity of the U.S. Senate. If so, why was not an immediate investigation called for? Why was there no public outcry and a demand for censure by the Senate? Senator Joe McCarthy's charges were nothing compared with the gravity of Senator Fulbright's accusation. There is, of course, *no mystery.* There was nothing for the Senate to investigate because every senator knew full well that Senator Fulbright's charge was indeed the truth.

But Senator Fulbright paid the price for truth. He was courageous (or foolhardy) enough to violate the "taboo" and was put on the Jewish "enemies" list and was banished from public life by being defeated for re-election.

Incredible as it sounds, there is more freedom of speech and press in Israel than in the U.S. Senate or the American media. Yet the Israeli Lobby continues relentlessly to be more "Israeli" than the Israelis in Israel where there is strong opposition to the Likud policies.

In his recent work entitled *Israel's Fateful Hour,* referred to earlier in this chapter, Yehoshafat Harkabi, Israel's foremost expert in Arab relations and former chief of military intelligence and advisor to Prime Minister Begin, makes certain bitter criticisms of the U.S. which are shocking in their implication.

Harkabi complains that the U.S. government has allowed Israel to pursue policies which will inevitably be calamitous for Israel. He points out that by not speaking out against the Israeli government's policies, such as the West Bank settlements, the U.S. has misled the Israeli public into thinking that the U.S. supports the settlements.

He begs the U.S. to speak frankly and to make its position clear instead of speaking "timidly" as it always has. He emphasizes that the U.S. not only has the right—but the duty to speak out.

He is bitter that the behavior of the U.S. was such that it was interpreted by many Israelis as meaning that the annexation policy of Mr. Begin was correct, leading them to idolize, to vote for, and support the approach of the Likud and the Gush Emunim. He believes that the U.S. has not been a true friend of Israel, because "a real friend is one who does not endorse all our views," but, on the contrary, despite the anger it may incur, draws our attention to our errors and insensitivities.[20]

Finally, he expresses this lament:

> I fail to understand why they [the U.S.] are so apprehensive of speaking out and saying that the present policy of annexation will miscarry, that it is bound to fail, that it will end in national bankruptcy *or that it is suicidal*—whatever is their evaluation. By such diffidence Americans do a *disservice to Israel* and to themselves.[21] [Emphasis supplied]

Were Yehoshafat Harkabi to read this and the following two chapters he would learn that the "timidity" and "apprehension" is no mystery. He would learn that those in our government with the courage to speak frankly and as a "true friend" of Israel are no longer with the government—they have been banished.

All of Harkabi's charges and complaints are valid and true. The strange aspect of his criticisms is that they are aimed at the "puppets" (our congressmen and president), not the "puppeteer" (the Israeli Lobby).

Since a man of the stature of Harkabi is mystified at U.S. conduct in the Middle East and doesn't apparently understand why officials of the U.S. government don't speak out, don't criticize Israel, and are timid and apprehensive, there must be many more people in the dark concerning the direction and formulation of U.S. foreign policy in the Middle East. The next chapter, "The Israeli Lobby in Action," will, if nothing else, enlighten Harkabi and other well-meaning people who are baffled and confused about America's Middle East policies.

CHAPTER VII

The Israeli Lobby in Action

I N A TELECAST of the popular CBS show "60 Minutes," on October 23, 1988, a 15-minute segment of the program was devoted to the political activities and the power and influence of the Israeli Lobby.

The distinguished interviewees included: Charles Percy, former Senator and chairman of the Foreign Relations Committee; George Ball, former Under-Secretary of State and U.S. Ambassador to the U.N.; Rabbi Miller, Vice President of the American Israel Public Affairs Committee (AIPAC); and Senator Daniel Inouye.

The following excerpts are taken from the official transcript of the program:

AIPAC

MIKE WALLACE: There are few lobbies working the corridors of Capitol Hill with as much clout as AIPAC, the American Israel Public Affairs Committee. They're the people who tell the Congress which legislation affecting Israel they like, and which they don't. They are not agents of the Israeli government, but out of personal conviction as American Jews they lobby the Congress and the administration for measures that support the State of Israel. But the charge is that apart from lobbying, AIPAC also gets involved in election campaigns by setting the tone, the line for about 80 pro-Israel political action committees around the country, pro-Israel PACs that have given $6 million this year to a variety of candidates. One race they're focusing on is the senatorial contest in Rhode Island, where they say Republican Senator John Chaffee has a poor record on Israel. And they want him out.

AIPAC says it is the spearhead for support for Israel here in Washington. It is not a political action committee, it does not make campaign contributions. But the clout of AIPAC here on Capitol Hill is legendary.

GEORGE BALL: *Practically every congressman and senator says his prayers to the AIPAC lobby. Oh, they've done an enormous job of corrupting the American democratic process.* It's the most effective lobby in the United States today, and I would put that ahead of the National Rifle Association.

WALLACE: What's wrong with picking a candidate to support on the way he has voted? Isn't that the American way?

BALL: *I think it's—it's a caricature of the American way.*

RABBI ISRAEL MILLER: *The word power when it's used for AIPAC is a myth. It's baloney.* AIPAC is powerful only because the American people are behind Israel.

WALLACE: Rabbi Israel Miller is a Vice President of AIPAC. AIPAC is not anti-Chaffee?

In recent years, AIPAC and the pro-Israel PACs have helped defeat, among others, Congressmen Paul Findley and Pete McCloskey, Senators Harrison Schmidt of New Mexico, Walter Huddleston of Kentucky, and Chuck Percy of Illinois. Like Senator Chaffee, Percy, too, came out in favor of that sale of AWACs to the Saudis.

SENATOR CHARLES PERCY: I finally reached the stage where, as chairman of the Foreign Relations Committee, I saw our foreign policy totally turned around with a Moslem world—800 million people—*looking askance at the United States of America, what is happening, who is running the foreign policy. Can Israel and the prime minister have more power than the entire Senate of the United States or the President of the United States? And that to me—I simply said, enough is enough.*

WALLACE: That particular AWAC sale to Saudi Arabia did manage to pass the Congress, and in 1984, pro-Israel PACs and other individuals spent millions to unseat the powerful Senator Percy.

Let me quote to you the words of the executive director of AIPAC. After the defeat of Chuck Percy, a few years back, he said to a Jewish group in Toronto, quote, *"All the Jews in America, from coast to coast, gathered to oust Percy. And the American politicians, those who hold positions now and those who aspire, got the message."*

RABBI MILLER: It was an infelicitous expression of that which Tom felt in his enthusiasm and in his zeal. I think if he had it to say all over again he would have put it altogether differently.

WALLACE: Rabbi Miller, about a year ago, the *New York Times* wrote, *"AIPAC has become a major force in shaping U.S. policy in the Middle East. The organization has gained the power to influence a presidential candidate's choice of staff, to block practically any arms sale to an Arab country, and to serve as a catalyst for intimate military relations between the Pentagon and the Israeli army." How did AIPAC become so powerful?*

RABBI MILLER: *Again, I'll say that that's very flattering, but it's a myth. It's just not so.* The American people support Israel, and therefore Congress votes as it does.

WALLACE: One of Israel's staunchest supporters is Senator Daniel Inouye of Hawaii, who says that AIPAC has nothing to do with his feelings about Israel.

SENATOR DANIEL INOUYE: If I can help Israel—help herself, in every instance I do so. I'm also convinced it's in our national interest. I've yet to see any country in that part of the world that is as reliable, as far as our strategic requirements are concerned, as Israel is.

BALL: *I don't believe it's an ally at all. We have no alliance with it.* I mean, they insist on total freedom of action, and they insist on our subsidizing their total freedom of action.

WALLACE: The amount of that subsidy is remarkable, and a testament to AIPAC's clout on Capitol Hill. Altogether, Israel gets more than $3 billion a year in assistance from the United States.

SENATOR PERCY: *Sometimes the votes go through without a single debate. Involving billions of dollars. You couldn't spend that kind of money in this country without a huge debate going on. But a foreign government gets this money without debate because, simply, it's—it's just organized to get it.*[1] [Emphasis supplied]

The response by AIPAC to the CBS telecast was made by Morris Abram, chairman of the Conference of Presidents and Major American Jewish Organizations and reported in the *Jerusalem Post* of November 5, 1988.

Abram said that "the program was filled with distortions, innuendoes, and inaccuracies that made it a piece of shabby journalism."[2]

It is important to note that in response to two different questions Rabbi Miller, Vice President of AIPAC, made the astonishing statements that the political "power" of AIPAC is a *"myth," "it's baloney," "It's just not so."*

After hearing these remarkable statements of Rabbi Miller, the vast viewer audience of "60 Minutes" and the rest of the American people are entitled to know and determine for themselves whether Rabbi Miller is right in characterizing the political power of AIPAC as a *myth,* or shabby journalism as the Lobby calls it, or whether it is a matter with which the American public should be seriously concerned as we enter a critical period when the fate of Israel and world peace may be in the balance.

For this chapter, "The Israeli Lobby in Action," we have relied heavily upon the text and sources contained in the book entitled *They Dare to Speak Out,* by ex-Congressman Paul Findley. Having served in Congress for twenty-two years before being defeated by an AIPAC-organized campaign, Mr. Findley is in a unique position, as a former congressman, to shed light directly from the halls of Congress on the operation of the Israeli Lobby and the dangers it poses to our political process.

IS THE POLITICAL POWER OF AIPAC A MYTH?

It is generally acknowledged in Congress that AIPAC is the pre-eminent lobbying power in Washington. However, the Washington presence is only the most visible tip of the Lobby. Its effectiveness rests heavily on the foundation built nationally by U.S. Jews, who function through more than 200 national groups.

Actually, those who provide the political activism for all organizations in U.S. Jewry probably do not exceed 250,000. The Lobby's most popular newsletter, AIPAC's "Near East Report," has a distribution that the organization believes is read by most Jewish citizens who have an interest in pro-Israel political action, whether their primary interest is AIPAC, B'nai B'rith, the American Jewish Committee, the Anti-Defamation League, the Jewish National Fund, the United Jewish Appeal, or any of the other main national groups. The newsletter is sent without charge to news media, congressmen, key government officials, and other people prominent in foreign policy. AIPAC members get the newsletter as part of their annual dues.

In practice, the Lobby groups function as an informal extension of the Israeli government. This was illustrated when AIPAC helped draft the official statement defending Israel's 1981 bombing of the Iraqi nuclear reactor and then issued it at the same hour as Israel's embassy. In the past, no Jewish organization has ever publicly taken issue with positions and policies adopted by Israel.* AIPAC's charter defines its mission as legislative action, but it now also represents the interests of Israel whenever there is a perceived challenge to that country's interests. Because AIPAC's staff members are paid from contributions by American citizens, they need not register under the Foreign Agents Registration Act. *In effect, however, they serve the same function as foreign agents.*

Over the years, the Israeli Lobby has thoroughly penetrated this nation's governmental system, and the organization that has made the deepest impact is AIPAC, to whom even the President of the U.S. turns for advice on matters relating to the Arab-Israeli issue.[3] *Most congressional actions affecting Middle East policy are either approved or initiated by AIPAC.*[4]

To accomplish these feats for Israel, AIPAC director Thomas A. Dine utilizes a team of hard-driving, able professionals and keeps them working together smoothly. He keeps policy lines clear and the troops well-disciplined. AIPAC's role is to support Israel's policies, not to help formulate them, so AIPAC maintains daily telephone communications with the Israeli embassy, and Dine meets personally with embassy officials at least once a week.

Though AIPAC has a staff of less than one hundred—small in comparison to other major U.S. Jewish organizations—it taps the resources of a broad nationwide network of unpaid activists. Annual membership meetings in Washington are a major way to rally the troops. Those attending hear prominent U.S. and Israeli speakers, participate in work-shops and seminars, and contribute financially to the cause. The conferen-ces attract top political figures including the Israeli Ambassador, senior White House and State Department officials, and prominent Senators and House members.[5]

AIPAC's outreach program is buttressed by a steady stream of publica-tions. In addition to "Action Alerts" and weekly "Near East Report," it issues position papers designed to answer or often discredit critics, and advance Israel's objectives. The most controversial publication of all is an "enemies list" first issued in the spring of 1983 entitled "The Campaign to Discredit Israel," which provides a "directory of the actors": twenty-one organizations

---

* Only recently, and for a brief period of time, has there been a divergence of viewpoint as a result of the proposed revision by the Israeli Orthodox Rabbinate of the "Law of Return."

and thirty-nine individuals AIPAC identified as inimical to Israeli interests.

Included in the list are such distinguished public servants as former Under-Secretary of State George W. Ball, retired Ambassadors Talcott Seelye, Andrew Killgore, John C. West, James Akins, and former Senator James Abourezk. There are also five Jewish dissenters and several scholars on the list.

The Anti-Defamation League of B'nai B'rith also issues its own "enemies list": *Pro-Arab Propaganda in America: Vehicles and Voices* lists 31 organizations and 34 individuals. These books are nothing more than blacklists, reminiscent of the worst tactics of the McCarthy era. A similar "enemies list" is employed in AIPAC's extensive program at colleges and universities.

Through "Action Alert" mailings AIPAC keeps more than one thousand Jewish leaders throughout the U.S. informed on current issues. An "Alert" usually demands action to meet a legislative challenge on Capitol Hill, requesting a telephone call, telegram, or, if need be, a personal visit to a recalcitrant congressman. The network can have almost instantaneous effect.[6]

This activism is carried out by an elaborate system of officers, committees, and councils which give AIPAC a ready, intimate system for political activity from coast to coast. Its nineteen officers meet once a month to confer with Dine on organization and management. Each of its five vice-presidents can expect eventually to serve a term as president. A large executive committee totaling 132 members is invited to Washington every three months for briefings. A national council lists over 200 names. These subgroups include the leadership of most U.S. Jewish organizations.

The AIPAC staff is not only highly professional and highly motivated but also thoroughly experienced. Director Dine worked in several Capitol Hill jobs, first on the staff of Democratic Senator Edward Kennedy, later on the Foreign Relations Committee under Democratic Senator Frank Church of Idaho, and finally as staff director on foreign policy for the Senate budget committee. Among AIPAC's four lobbyists are or have been Douglas Bloomfield, Ralph Nurnberger, Esther Kurz, and Leslie L. Levy. All but Levy worked in foreign policy for a senator or congressman before joining AIPAC.

Bloomfield, once an intern under Democratic Senator Hubert Humphrey of Minnesota, worked for ten years for Democratic Congressman Ben Rosenthal of New York. Nurnberger worked for several years on the Senate Foreign Relations Committee and for Republican Senator James

Pearson of Kansas. Kurz worked, in succession, for Democratic Congressman Charles Wilson of Texas, and Republican Senators Jacob Javits of New York and Arlen Specter of Pennsylvania.

The four divide up the membership of the House and the Senate. Actually, only a handful of legislators are keys to success, so each of the four lobbyists needs to watch carefully only about thirty lawmakers. They concentrate on legislators from the twelve states which have a Jewish population of at least three percent: New York, New Jersey, California, Massachusetts, Ohio, Illinois, Michigan, Pennsylvania, Maryland, Delaware, Florida, and Connecticut.

The movement from congressional staff job to AIPAC also occasionally works the other way. A few veterans of AIPAC have moved to government assignments, among them Jonathan Slade, now with Democratic Congressman Larry Smith of Florida, and Marvin Feuerwerger, who was with Democratic Congressman Stephen Solarz of New York before he joined the policy planning staff at the State Department. Both Smith and Solarz are members of the Foreign Affairs Committee, and both are passionate supporters of Israel.[7]

AIPAC has convinced Congress that it represents practically all Jews who vote. Columnist Nat Hentoff reported this assessment in the New York *Village Voice* in June 1983, after a delegation of eighteen dissenting rabbis had scoured Capitol Hill trying to convince congressmen that some Jews oppose Israeli policies. The rabbis reported that several congressmen said they shared their views but were afraid to act. Hentoff concluded: "The only Jewish constituency that's real to them [congressmen] is the one that AIPAC and other spokesmen for the Jewish establishment tell them about."[8]

An Ohio congressman speaks of AIPAC with concern:

But what distresses me is the inability in American policymakers, because of the influence of AIPAC, to distinguish between our national interest and Israel's national interest. When these converge—wonderful! But they don't always converge.[9]

After the 1982 elections, Thomas A. Dine summed up the significance of AIPAC's achievements: *"Because of that, American Jews are thus able to form our own foreign policy agenda."*

Later, when he reviewed the 1984 election results, Dine credited Jewish money, not votes: "Early money, middle money, late money." He claimed credit for defeating Republican Senators Charles Percy of Illinois and Roger Jepson of Iowa, and Democratic Senator Walter Huddleston of Kentucky, all of whom incurred AIPAC wrath by voting for the sale of AWAC planes to Saudi Arabia. *Dine said these successes "defined Jewish political power for the rest of this century."*[10]

THE McCLOSKEY CASE

Real debate is almost unknown in the Congress on the subject of aid to Israel, most congressmen fearing Lobby pressure carefully avoid statements or votes that might be viewed as critical of Israel. A young congressman, Pete McCloskey, in 1980 (not fully aware of the rules), called for an end to the building of Israeli settlements in the occupied territory of the West Bank *which the U.S. and all other countries except Israel considers as illegal and contrary to international law.*

To put pressure on Israel to stop, McCloskey wanted the U.S. to cut aid by $150 million—the amount he estimated Israel was annually spending on these projects. In the end, tough realities led him to drop his plan to bring the matter to a vote. Representative James Johnson, a Republican from Colorado and one of the few to support McCloskey, was aware of the pressure other congressmen were putting on him. Johnson declared that many of his colleagues privately opposed Israel's expansion of settlements but said *Congress was "incapable" of taking action contrary to Israeli policy: "I would just like to point out the real reason that this Congress will not deal with this matter is because [it] concerns the nation of Israel."*

Most committee action, like the work of the full House, is open to the public, and none occurs on Israeli aid without the presence of at least one representative of AIPAC. His presence ensures that any criticism of Israel will be quickly reported to key constituents. The offending congressman may have a rash of angry telephone messages to answer by the time he returns to his office from the hearing room.

Lobbyists for AIPAC are experts on the personalities and procedures of the House. If Israel is mentioned, even behind closed doors, they quickly get a full report of what transpired. These lobbyists know that aid to Israel on a roll call will get overwhelming support.[11]

Still not aware of the political danger of his position, McCloskey, after a trip to the Middle East in 1979, concluded that new Israeli policies were not in America's best interests. He was alarmed over Washington's failure to halt Israel's construction of West Bank settlements—which the administration itself had labeled "illegal"—and to stop Israel's illegal use of U.S.-

supplied weapons. The congressman asked, "Why?" McCloskey had raised a provocative question: "Does America's 'Israeli Lobby' wield too much influence?" In an article for the *Los Angeles Times* he provided his answer:

"Yes, *it is an obstacle to real Mideast peace."* McCloskey cited the *risk of nuclear confrontation* in the Middle East and the fundamental differences between the interests of Israel and the U.S. He observed that members of the Jewish community demand that Congress support Israel in spite of these differences. This demand, he argued, *"coupled with the weakness of Congress in the face of any such force, can prevent the president, in his hour of both crisis and opportunity, from having the flexibility necessary to achieve a lasting Israeli-Palestinian peace."*[12] [Emphasis supplied]

On the next election day, all three of McCloskey's opponents received Jewish financial support. Stephen S. Rosenfeld, deputy editorial page editor of the *Washington Post,* drew a definite conclusion: *"Jewish political participation defeated McCloskey."*[13]

McCloskey's troubles, however, were not over. A tracking system initiated by the Anti-Defamation League (ADL) of B'nai B'rith assured that McCloskey would have no peace, even as a private citizen. The group distributed a memorandum containing details of his actions and speeches to its chapters around the country. According to the memo, it was designed to "assist" local ADL groups with "counteraction guidance" whenever McCloskey appeared in public.[14]

Trouble followed him even on the campus. McCloskey accepted an invitation from the student governing council of Stanford University to teach a course on Congress at Stanford. Howard Goldberg—a council member and also director of the Hillel Center, the campus Jewish club— told the group that inviting McCloskey was "a slap in the face of the Jewish community." [15]

THE QUINTESSENTIAL LOBBYIST

Stephen Solarz, a highly visible Congressman who represents a heavily Jewish district in Brooklyn, prides himself on accomplishing many good things for Israel. Since his first election in 1974, Solarz established a reputation as an intelligent, widely-traveled, aggressive legislator, totally committed to Israel's interests.

In a December 1980 newsletter to his constituents, he provided an *un-*

precedented insight into how Israel—despite the budgetary restraints under which the U.S. government labors—is able to get ever-increasing aid. Early that year he had started his own quest for increased aid. He reported that he persuaded Secretary of State Cyrus Vance to come to his Capitol Hill office to talk it over. There he threatened Vance with a fight for the increase on the House floor if the administration opposed it in committee. Shortly thereafter, he said Vance sent word that the administration would recommend an increase—$200 million extra in military aid—although not as much as Solarz desired.

His next goal was to convince the Foreign Affairs Committee to increase the administration's levels. Solarz felt an increase approved by the committee could be sustained on the House floor—he was right.

Solarz summed it up in his letter as follows:

Israel as a result will soon be receiving a total of $660 million more in military and economic aid than it received from the U.S. government last year. Through a combination of persistence and persuasion we were able to provide Israel with an increase in military-economic aid in one year alone which is the equivalent of almost three years of contributions by the national UJA [United Jewish Appeal]. [Emphasis supplied]

In his newsletter, Solarz explained to his constituents that he had sought membership on the Foreign Affairs Committee because *"I wanted to be in a position to be helpful to Israel."*[16]

Proof of his dedication was evidenced in September 1984 when, as a member of the House-Senate conference on Export Administration Act amendments, he demanded in a public meeting to know the legislation's implications for Israel. He asked Congressman Howard Wolpe, *"Is there anything that the Israelis want from us, or could conceivably want from us that they weren't able to get?"* Even when Wolpe responded with a clear "No," Solarz pressed, "Have you spoken to the [Israeli] embassy?" Wolpe responded, "I personally have not," he admitted, "but my office has." Then Solarz tried again, "You are giving me an absolute assurance that they [the Israelis] have no reservation at all about this?" Finally convinced that Israel was content with the legislation, Solarz relaxed. "If they have no problem with it, then there is no reason for us to," he said.[17]

To put this in perspective: If the eighty or more military bases and installations around the country (which Congress is in the process of closing for economic reasons) are in fact closed, the estimated annual savings (of six hundred million dollars) is less than the increase arranged by Congressman Solarz in military and economic aid to Israel in 1980. Adjusted for inflation the increase in Israel aid is almost twice as much.

A veteran Ohio congressman observes:

> When Solarz and others press for more money for Israel, nobody wants to say "No." You don't need many examples of intimidation for politicians to realize what the potential is. The Jewish Lobby is terrific. *Anything it wants, it gets. Jews are educated, often have a lot of money, and vote on the basis of a single issue—Israel.* They are unique in that respect.[18] [Emphasis supplied]

CONGRESSMAN DYMALLY'S DILEMMA

Democratic Congressman Mervyn W. Dymally, former lieutenant-governor of California, came to Washington in 1980 with perfect credentials as a supporter of Israel.

In his successful campaign for lieutenant-governor, he spoke up for Israel in all the statewide Democratic canvasses. He co-founded the "Black Americans in Support of Israel Committee," organized pro-Israel advertising in California newspapers, and helped to rally other black officials to the cause. In Congress, as a member of the Foreign Affairs Committee, he became a dependable vote for Israeli interests.

Nevertheless, in 1982, the pro-Israeli community withdrew its financial support, and the following year the AIPAC organization in California marked him for defeat and began seeking a credible opponent to run against him in 1984. Explaining this sudden turn of events, Dymally cites two "black marks" against his pro-Israeli record in Congress. First, he "occasionally asked challenging questions about aid to Israel in committee"; although his questions were mild and infrequent, he stood out because no one else was even that daring. Second—far more damning in the eyes of the AIPAC—he met twice with PLO leader Yasser Arafat.[19] Both meetings were unplanned and of no international significance. Nevertheless, it created an uproar in the Jewish community.

Dymally found intimidation everywhere. Whenever he complains, he says, "he receives a prompt visit from an AIPAC lobbyist, usually accompanied by a Dymally constituent." He met one day with a group of Jewish constituents, "all of them old friends," and told them that, despite his grumbling, in the end he always voted for aid to Israel. He said, "Not once, I told them, have I ever strayed from the course." One of his constituents spoke up and said, "That's not quite right. Once you abstained." "They are that good," marveled Dymally. "The man was right."

Dymally considers membership on the Foreign Affairs subcommittee on the Middle East a "no win" situation.[20] He says of many of his Jewish critics in California, *"What is tragic is that so many Jewish people misconstrue criticism of Israel as anti-Jewish or anti-Semitic." He speaks admiringly of the open criticism of Israeli policy that often occurs within Israel itself: "It is easier to criticize Israel in the Knesset [the Israeli parliament] than it is in the U.S. Congress, here in this land of free speech."*

Dymally notes that 10 out of the 37 members of the Foreign Affairs Committee are Jewish and finds it *"so stacked there is no chance" for constructive dialogue.* He names Republican Congressman Ed Zschau of California as the only member of the Subcommittee on Europe and the Middle East who "even shadow boxes."[21]

At one hearing on economic aid to foreign countries, only Dymally complained that aid to Israel was too high. "How can the United States afford to give so much money in view of our economic crisis . . . to a country that has rejected the President's peace initiatives, and stepped up its settlements in the occupied territories?" he demanded.[22]

THE CASE OF CONGRESSMAN ED ZSCHAU

At the same hearing referred to by Congressman Dymally, Ed Zschau, a freshman Republican from California, provided the only other break from the pro-Israel questioning: "Do you think," he asked, "there should be conditions [on aid to Israel] that might hasten the objectives of the peace process?" Getting no response, he pressed on: "Given that we are giving aid in order to achieve progress in peace in the area, wouldn't it make sense to associate with the aid some modest conditions like a halt in settlement policy?"[23] He received no support on his questions. *Although Congressman Zschau did not then know it, his political fate was sealed.* In 1986, Representative Edwin Zschau was defeated for the Senate by Senator Alan Cranston, financed in part by AIPAC.

According to a report in the June 24, 1987, edition of *The Wall Street Journal,* a key figure in Zschau's defeat may have been Michael Goland, a Los Angeles developer, who is one of the largest donors to AIPAC who has been active in opposing candidates he views as being unfriendly to Israel.[24] Mr. Goland recently agreed to pay a $5,000 fine for his role in running television commercials attacking former Senator Charles Percy of Illinois who was defeated in his 1984 race for re-election. According to the *Los*

Angeles Times, the commercials were illegal because the source of the financing was not disclosed.

According to *The Wall Street Journal,* at a reception held for Zschau, Goland is quoted as saying to Zschau, *"I'm going to get you just like I got Percy."*[25]

Since the establishment of modern Israel in 1948, only a handful of senators have said or done anything in opposition to the policies of the government of Israel. Those who break ranks find themselves in difficulty. The trouble can arise from a speech, an amendment, a vote, a published statement, or a combination of these. It may take the form of a challenge in the next primary or general election. Or the trouble may not surface until later—after service in the Senate has ended. Such was the unfortunate destiny of another senator.

THE ADLAI E. STEVENSON III CANDIDACY

The cover of the October 1982 edition of the monthly magazine *Jewish Chicago* featured a portrait of Adlai E. Stevenson III, Democratic candidate for governor of Illinois. In the background, over the right shoulder of a smiling Stevenson, an Arab, rifle slung over his shoulder, glared ominously through a kaffiyeh that covered his head and most of his face. The headline announcing the issue's feature article read, "Looking at Adlai Through Jewish Eyes." The illustration and article were part of an anti-Stevenson campaign conducted by some of the quarter-million people in Chicago's Jewish community who wanted Stevenson to fail in his challenge to Governor James R. Thompson, Jr.[26]

Thompson, a Republican, was attempting a feat sometimes tried but never before accomplished in Illinois history—election to a third term as governor. Normally, a Republican in Illinois can expect only minimal Jewish support at the polls. A crucial part of the anti-Stevenson campaign was a caricature of his Middle East record while he was a member of the U.S. Senate. Stevenson was presented as an enemy of Israel and an ally of the PLO.[27]

This was astonishing to Stevenson since the make-up of his campaign organization, the character of his campaign, and the support he had received in the past in Jewish neighborhoods provided little hint of trouble ahead from pro-Israel quarters.

Several of the most important members of his campaign team were Jewish: Philip Klutznick, President Emeritus of B'nai B'rith and an organizer of the Conference of Presidents of Major Jewish Organizations, agreed to organize Stevenson's main campaign dinner. Milton Fisher, prominent attorney, was chairman of his finance committee; Rick Jasulca, a public relations executive who became Stevenson's full-time press secretary. Stevenson chose Grace Mary Stern as his running mate for the position of lieutenant-governor. Her husband was prominent in Chicago Jewish affairs.

Stevenson himself had received several honors from Jewish groups in preceding years. He had been selected by the Chicago Jewish community as 1974 Israel Bonds "Man of the Year," and was honored by the government of Israel—which established the Adlai E. Stevenson III Chair at the Weizmann Institute of Science in Rehovot. Stevenson had every reason to expect that organized Illinois Jewry would overlook his occasional mild position critical of Israeli policy.

But trouble developed. A segment of the Jewish community quietly launched an attack that would cost him heavily. Stevenson's detractors were determined to defeat him in the governor's race and thus discourage a future Stevenson bid for the presidency. Their basic tool was a document provided by AIPAC in Washington. It was presented as a summary of Stevenson's Senate actions on Middle East issues—though it made no mention of his almost unblemished record of support for Israel and the tributes the Jewish community had presented to him in testimony of this support.

For example, AIPAC pulled from a 21-page report Stevenson prepared after a 1967 trip to the Middle East just one phrase: "There is no organization other than the PLO with a broadly recognized claim to represent the Palestinians." This was a simple statement of fact. But the writer of the *Jewish Chicago* article, citing the AIPAC "summary," asserted that these words had helped to give Stevenson "a reputation as one of the harshest critics of both Israeli policy and of U.S. support for the Jewish state." Stevenson's assessment of the PLO's standing in the Palestinian community was interpreted as an assault on Israel.[28] In fact, the full paragraph in the Stevenson report from which AIPAC took its brief excerpt is studied and reasonable:

The Palestinians are by general agreement the nub of the problem. Although badly divided, they have steadily increased in numbers, economic and military strength, and seriousness of purpose. They cannot be left out of any Middle East settlement. Their lack of unity is reflected in the lack of unity within the top ranks of the PLO, but there is no organization other than the PLO with a broadly recognized claim to represent the Palestinians.

The Stevenson report was critical of certain Israeli policies but hardly hostile to Israel. "The PLO," he wrote, "may be distrusted, disowned and despised, but it is a reality, if for no other reason than that it has no rival organization among Palestinians."

Stevenson went on to issue a challenge to the political leaders of America:

> A new order of statesmanship is required from both the Executive and the Legislative Branches. For too long Congress has muddled or gone along without any real understanding of Middle Eastern politics. Neither the U.S., nor Israel, nor any of the Arab states will be served by continued ignorance or the expediencies of election year politics.[29]

None of this positive comment found its way into the AIPAC report or into the *Jewish Chicago* article or into any of the anti-Stevenson literature which was distributed within the Jewish community during the 1982 campaign.

The anti-Stevenson activists noted with alarm that in 1980 Stevenson had sponsored an amendment to reduce aid to Israel and the year before had supported a similar amendment offered by Senator Mark O. Hatfield, Republican of Oregon. The Hatfield amendment proposed to cut, by 10 percent, the amount of funds available to Israel for military credits.

Stevenson's amendment focused on Israeli settlements in occupied territories, which President Carter and earlier administrations characterized as both illegal and an obstacle to peace but did nothing to discourage beyond occasional expressions of regret. Stevenson proposed withholding $150 million in aid until Israel halted both the building and planning of additional settlements. The amendment did not cut funds; it simply withheld a fraction of the $2.18 billion total aid authorized for Israel that year. In speaking for the amendment, Stevenson noted that the outlay for Israel amounted to 43 percent of all U.S. funds allocated for such purposes worldwide:

> This preference for Israel diverts funds from the support of human life and vital American interests elsewhere in an interdependent and unstable world. . . . If it could produce stability in the Middle East or

enhance Israel's security, it could be justified. *But it reflects continued U.S. acquiescence in an Israeli policy which threatens more Middle East instability, more Israeli insecurity, and a continued decline of U.S. authority in the world. Our support for Israel is not the issue here. Israel's support for the ideals of peace and justice which gave it birth are at issue.* It is, I submit, for the Israel government to recognize again that Israel's interests are in harmony with our own and, for that to happen, it is important that we do not undermine the voices of peace in Israel or justify those, like *Mr. Begin, who claim U.S. assistance from the Congress can be taken for granted.*[30] [Emphasis supplied]

The amendment was overwhelmingly defeated.

Of course, all that Senator Stevenson was trying to do was exactly what Yehoshafat Harkabi is begging America to do—he spoke up frankly as a true friend of Israel. The members of Congress who are afraid to speak out are *not* (as Harkabi says bitterly) *real friends of Israel. Obviously, their actions are not prompted by any genuine friendship for Israel, or special concern for its well-being—they are motivated simply by political cowardice.*

All that a real *enemy of Israel* needs to do is to support enthusiastically the pied pipers of the Likud and watch Israel march blindly into—as Harkabi says—catastrophe.

A flyer distributed by an unidentified "Informed Citizens Against Stevenson Committee," captioned "The Truth About Adlai Stevenson," used half-truths to brand Stevenson as anti-Israel during his Senate years and concluded: "It is vitally important that Jewish voters be fully informed about Stevenson's record. Still dazzled by the Stevenson name, many Jews are totally unaware of his antagonism to Jewish interests." The committee provided no names or addresses of sponsoring individuals. The message on the flyer concluded:

Don't forget. It is well-known that Stevenson considers the governor's chair as a stepping-stone to the presidency. Spread the word—Let the truth be told![31]

A major problem was the unprinted—but widely whispered charge of "anti-Semitism" against Stevenson—a man, who, like his father, had spent his life championing civil rights for all Americans. "I learned after election day there was that intimation throughout the campaign," recalls Stevenson.

Stevenson's running mate, Grace Mary Stern, recalls: "There was a very vigorous [anti-Stevenson] telephone campaign in the Jewish community." She says leaflets charging Stevenson with being anti-Israel were distributed widely at local Jewish temples, and adds there was much discussion of the "anti-Semitism" accusation. "There was a very vigorous campaign, man to man, friend to friend, locker room to locker room. We never really came to grips with the problem."

Campaign fund raising suffered accordingly. The Jewish community had supported Stevenson strongly in both of his campaigns for the Senate. After his remarks in the last years of his Senate career, some of the Jewish support dried up.[32] In the end, Thompson was able to outspend Stevenson by better than two to one.[33]

The only Jews who tried to counter the attack were those close to Stevenson. Philip Klutznick, prominent in Jewish affairs and chairman of the Stevenson Dinner Committee, said, "It is beneath the dignity of the Jewish community to introduce these issues into a gubernatorial campaign." Stevenson's campaign treasurer, Milton Fisher, said, *"Adlai's views are probably consistent with 40 percent* of the Knesset [Israeli parliament]."

Stevenson was ultimately defeated in the closest gubernatorial election in the state's history. The margin was 5,074 votes—one-seventh of one percent of the total 3.5 million votes cast.[34]

Thomas A. Dine, Executive Director of the American Israel Public Affairs Committee, gloated, "The memory of Adlai Stevenson's hostility toward Israel during his Senate tenure lost him the Jewish vote in Illinois— and that cost him the gubernatorial election."[35]

Stevenson too believes the effort to discredit him among Jews played a major role in his defeat: "In a race that close, it was more than enough to make the difference." Asked about the impact of the Israeli Lobby on the U.S. political scene, he responded without hesitation:

There is an intimidating, activist minority of American Jews that *supports the decisions of the Israeli government, right or wrong.* They do so very vocally and very aggressively in ways that intimidate others so that it's their voice—even though it's a minority—that is heard and felt in American politics. But it still is much louder in the U.S. than in Israel. In other words, you have a much stronger, more vocal dissent in Israel than within the Jewish community in the U.S.. *The prime minister of Israel has far more influence over American foreign policy in the Middle East than over the policies of his own government generally.*[36]

A PROFILE IN COURAGE

In 1963, Senator J. William Fulbright, of Arkansas, chaired an investigation that brought to public attention the exceptionally favorable tax treatment of contributions to Israel and thereby aroused the ire of the Jewish community.[37] The investigation was managed by Walter Pincus, a journalist Fulbright hired after reading a Pincus study of lobbying. Pincus recalls that Fulbright gave him a free hand, letting him choose the ten prime lobbying activities to be examined and backing him throughout the controversial investigation. One of the groups chosen by Pincus, himself Jewish, was the Jewish Telegraph Agency—at that time a principal instrument of the Israeli Lobby. Both Fulbright and Pincus were accused of trying to destroy the Jewish Telegraph Agency and of being "anti-Semitic." Pincus remembers, "Several senators urged that the inquiry into the Jewish operation be dropped. Senators Hubert Humphrey and Bourke Hickenlooper [then senior Republican on the Foreign Relations Committee] were among them. Fulbright refused."

The Fulbright hearings also exposed the massive funding illegally channeled into the American Zionist Council by Israel. More than five million dollars had been secretly poured into the council for spending on public relations firms and pro-Israel propaganda before Fulbright's committee closed down the operation.

Despite his concern over the Israeli Lobby, *Fulbright took the exceptional step of recommending that the U.S. guarantee Israel's borders.* In a major address in 1970, he proposed an American-Israeli treaty under which the U.S. would commit itself to intervene militarily if necessary to "guarantee the territory and independence of Israel" within the lands it held before the 1967 war. The treaty, he said, "should be a supplement to a peace settlement arranged by the United Nations." The purpose of his proposal was to destroy the arguments of those who maintained that Israel needed the captured territory for its security.

Fulbright saw Israeli withdrawal from the Arab lands it occupied in the 1967 war as the key to peace. Israel could not occupy Arab territory and have peace too. He said Israeli policy in establishing settlements on the territories "has been characterized by lack of flexibility and foresight."[38]

As referred to earlier in the previous chapter, Fulbright, on CBS television's "Face The Nation" in 1973, declared that the Senate was "subservient" to Israeli policies which were inimical to American interests. He said, "The U.S. bears a very great share of the responsibility for the continuation of Middle East violence. It's quite obvious that without the all-out support by the U.S. in money and weapons, the Israelis couldn't do what they've been doing."39 Fulbright was saying fifteen years ago what Yehoshafat Harkabi is now saying in his book *Israel's Fateful Hour*— namely, that the *U.S. is at fault for Israel's desperate situation* because the U.S. allowed Israel and the Likud to do whatever it wanted to do, and that *the U.S. is responsible for the oncoming disaster to Israel.*

Fulbright said the U.S. failed to pressure Israel for a negotiated settlement, because:

> The great majority of the Senate of the U.S.—somewhere around 80 percent—are completely in support of Israel, anything Israel wants. This has been demonstrated time and time again, and this has made it difficult for our government.

His criticism of Israeli policy caused concerns back home. Jews who had supported him in the past became restless. After years of easy election victories, trouble loomed for Fulbright for his Senate seat.40 Fulbright was defeated. He was on the "enemies list." Several Jewish organizations claimed credit for Fulbright's defeat.

Since his defeat, Fulbright has continued to speak out, decrying Israeli stubbornness and warning of the Israeli Lobby. In a speech just before the end of his Senate term, Fulbright warned, "Endlessly pressing the U.S. for money and arms—and invariably getting all and more than she asks— Israel makes bad use of a good friend." His central concern was that the Middle East conflict might flare into nuclear war. He warned somberly that "Israel's supporters in the U.S. . . . by underwriting intransigency, are encouraging a course which must lead toward her destruction—and just possibly ours as well."

Fulbright sees little hope that Capitol Hill will effectively challenge the Israeli Lobby:

> It's suicide for politicians to oppose them. The only possibility would be someone like Eisenhower who already feels secure. Eisenhower has already made his reputation. He was already a great man in the eyes of the country, and he wasn't afraid of anybody. He said what he believed.

Then he adds a somewhat more optimistic note: "I believe a president could do this. He wouldn't have to be named Eisenhower." Fulbright cites a missed opportunity:

I went to Jerry Ford after he took office in 1975. I was out of office then. I had been to the Middle East and visited with some of the leading figures. I came back and told the president, "Look, I think these Arab leaders are willing to accept Israel, but the Israelis have got to go back to the 1967 borders. The problem can be solved if you are willing to take a position on it." Ford, he said, did not take his advice.[41]

SENATOR WILLIAM HATHAWAY'S DEFEAT

In the spring of 1978, AIPAC unceremoniously abandoned another Senate Democrat with a consistent pro-Israeli record, Senator William Hathaway of Maine (who had, without exception, cast his vote in favor of Israel's interests), in favor of William S. Cohen, his Republican challenger.

Hathaway had cooperated in 1975 when AIPAC sponsored its famous "spirit of 76" letter. It bore Hathaway's name and those of 75 of his colleagues and carried this message to President Gerald R. Ford: "We urge that you reiterate our nation's long-standing commitment to Israel's security by a policy of continued military supplies, and diplomatic and economic support." Previously, Hathaway, on occasion, declined to sign certain "sense of the Senate" resolutions prepared by AIPAC.

Ford, dissatisfied with Israeli behavior, had just issued a statement calling for a "reappraisal" of U.S. policies in the Middle East. His statement did not mention Israel by name as the offending party, but his message was clear—Ford wanted better cooperation in reaching a compromise with Arab interests, and "reappraisal" meant suspension of U.S. aid until Israel improved its behavior. *It was a historic proposal, the first time since Eisenhower that a U.S. president even hinted publicly that he might suspend aid to Israel.*

Israel's response came, not from its own capital, but from the U.S. Senate. Instead of relying on a direct protest to the White House, Jerusalem activated its Lobby in the U.S., which, in turn, signed up as supporters of Israel's position more than three-fourths of the members of the U.S. Senate.

A more devastating—and intimidating—response could scarcely be conceived. The seventy-six signatures effectively told Ford he could not carry out his threatened "reappraisal." Israel's loyalists in the Senate—Democrats and Republicans alike—were sufficient in number to reject any legislative proposal displeasing to Israel that Ford might make, and perhaps even enact a pro-Israeli piece of legislation over a presidential veto.

The letter was a demonstration of impressive clout. Crafted and circulated by AIPAC, *it had been endorsed overnight by a majority of the Senate membership*. Several senators who at first had said "No" quickly changed their positions. Senator John Culver admitted candidly, "The pressure was too great. I caved." So did President Ford. He backed down and never again challenged the Lobby.

This wasn't the only time Hathaway answered AIPAC's call to oppose the White House on a major issue. Three years later, Ford's successor, Jimmy Carter, fought a similar battle with the Israeli Lobby. At issue this time was a resolution to disapprove President Carter's proposal to sell F-15 fighters to Saudi Arabia. The White House needed the support of only one chamber to defeat the resolution. White House strategists felt that the House of Representatives would overwhelmingly vote to defeat the sale, so they decided to put all their resources into the Senate.[42]

The Israeli Lobby pulled out all the stops. It coordinated a nationwide public relations campaign which revived, as never before, memories of the genocidal Nazi campaign against European Jews during World War II. In the wake of the highly publicized television series, "Holocaust," Capitol Hill was flooded with complimentary copies of the novel on which the TV series was based. The books were accompanied by a letter from AIPAC saying, "This chilling account of the extermination of six million Jews underscores Israel's concerns during the current negotiations for security without reliance on outside guarantees."

The pressure was sustained and heavy. Major personalities in the Jewish community warned the fighter aircraft would constitute a serious threat to Israel. *Nevertheless, a prominent Jewish Senator, Abraham Ribicoff of Connecticut, lined up with Carter.* This was a hard blow to Morris Amitay, then director of AIPAC, who had previously worked on Ribicoff's staff. Earlier in the year, Ribicoff, while keeping his own counsel on the Saudi arms question, *took the uncharacteristic step of sharply criticizing Israeli policies as well as the tactics of AIPAC. In an interview with* The Wall Street Journal, *Ribicoff described Israel's retention of occupied territory as "wrong" and unworthy of U.S. support. He said AIPAC does "a great disservice to the U.S., to Israel and to the Jewish community."* Ribicoff could now tell the truth, *he did not plan to seek re-election.*

The Senate approved the sale, 52 to 48, but in the process Carter was so bruised that he never again forced a showdown vote in Congress over Middle East policy.

Hathaway was one of the group who stuck with AIPAC, but this was not sufficient when election time rolled around. AIPAC wanted a senator whose signature—and vote—it could *always* count on. Searching for unswerving loyalty, the Lobby switched to Cohen. Hathaway was defeated in 1978.[43]

THE LOSS TO THE SENATE OF CHARLES PERCY

One of the leading lights of the Senate has been Senator Charles Percy of Illinois, who began his first term in 1967.

In his first election, 60 percent of Jewish votes—Illinois has the nation's fourth largest Jewish population—went to his opponent. But in the next six years, Percy supported aid for Israel, urged the Soviet Union to permit emigration of Jews, criticized PLO terrorism, and supported social causes so forcefully that Jews rallied strongly to his side when he ran for re-election. In 1972, Percy accomplished something never before achieved by carrying every county in the state and, even more remarkable for an Illinois Protestant Republican, received 70 percent of the Jewish vote.

His honeymoon with Jews was interrupted in 1975 when he returned from a trip to the Middle East to declare, "Israel and its leadership, for whom I have a high regard, cannot count on the U.S. in the future just to write a blank check." He said Israel had missed some opportunities to negotiate and he described PLO leader Yasser Arafat as "more moderate, relatively speaking, than other extremists such as George Habash." He urged Israel to talk to the PLO, if the organization would renounce terrorism and recognize Israel's right to exist behind secure, defensible borders, noting that David Ben-Gurion, Israel's first prime minister, had said that Israel must be willing to swap real estate for peace.

A week later Percy received this memorandum from his staff: "We have received 2,200 telegrams and 4,000 letters in response to your Mideast statements.... [They] run 95 percent against. As you might imagine, the majority of hostile mail comes from the Jewish community in Chicago. They threaten to withhold their votes and support for any future endeavors."

That same year Percy offended pro-Israel activists when he did not sign the famous "spirit of 76" letter through which seventy-six of his Senate colleagues effectively blocked President Gerald R. Ford's intended "reappraisal" of Middle East policy. This brought another flood of protest mail.

Despite these rumblings, the Israeli Lobby did not mount a serious campaign against Percy in 1978. With the senator's unprecedented 1972 sweep of the state fresh in mind, they did not seek out a credible opponent either in the primary or the general election.

However, the 1984 campaign was dramatically different. Pro-Israel forces targeted him for defeat early and never let up. Percy upset Jews by voting to support the Reagan administration sale of AWACS radar planes to Saudi Arabia (a sale also supported by the Carter administration). These developments provided new ammunition for the attack already under way against Percy. Percy's decision was made after his staff members who had visited Israel said they had been told by an Israeli military official that the strategic military balance would not be affected, but that they did not want the symbolism of the U.S. doing business with Saudi Arabia.

Early in 1984, AIPAC decided to mobilize the full national resources of the Israeli Lobby in a campaign against Percy. In the March primary, it encouraged the candidacy of Congressman Tom Corcoran, Percy's challenger for the nomination. One of Corcoran's chief advisers and fundraisers was Morris Amitay, former executive director of AIPAC. Corcoran's high-decibel attacks portrayed the senator as anti-Israel. His fundraising appeals to Jews cited Percy as "Israel's worst adversary in Congress." A full-page newspaper advertisement, sponsored by the Corcoran campaign, featured a picture of Arafat and headlined, "Chuck Percy says this man is a moderate." A letter to Jewish voters defending Percy and signed by fifty-eight leading Illinois Jews made almost no impact.

Although Percy overcame the primary challenge, Corcoran's attacks damaged his position with Jewish voters and provided a strong base for AIPAC's continuing assault. Thomas A. Dine, executive director of AIPAC, set the tone early in the summer by attacking Percy's record at a campaign workshop in Chicago. AIPAC encouraged fund raising for Paul Simon and mobilized its political resources heavily against Percy. It assigned several student interns full time to the task of anti-Percy research and *brought more than one hundred university students from out-of-state to campaign for Simon.*

Percy undertook vigorous countermeasures. Former Senator Jacob Javitz of New York, one of the nation's most prominent and respected Jews, and Senator Rudy Boschwitz, chairman of the Senate Foreign Relations Committee subcommittee concerning the Middle East, made personal appearances for Percy in Chicago. In addition, one hundred Illinois Jews, led by former Attorney General Edward H. Levi, sponsored a full-page advertisement which declared that Percy "has delivered for Illinois, delivered for America and delivered for Israel."[44]

This support proved futile, as did his strong legislative endeavors. His initiatives as chairman of the Senate Foreign Relations Committee brought Israel $425 million more in grant aid than Reagan had requested in 1983, and $325 million more in 1984, but these successes for Israel seemed to make no difference. A poll taken a month before the election showed a large majority of Jews supporting Simon. The Percy campaign found no way to stem the tide and was defeated. Thousands of Jews, who had voted for Percy in 1978, left him for the Democratic candidate six years later. And these votes fled to Simon mainly because Israel's Lobby worked effectively throughout the campaign year to portray the senator as basically anti-Israel. Percy's long record of support for Israel's needs amounted to a repudiation of the accusation, but too few Jews spoke up publicly in his defense. The senator found that once a candidate is labeled anti-Israel, the poison sinks so swiftly and deeply it is almost impossible to remove.

AIPAC's Dine told a Canadian audience: "All the Jews in America, from coast to coast, gathered to oust Percy. And American politicians—those who hold public positions now, and those who aspire—got the message."[45]

GEORGE BALL'S WORDS OF WISDOM

George Ball, a lifelong Democrat, twice campaigned for Adlai E. Stevenson for president. In 1959, he became a supporter of John F. Kennedy's presidential ambitions. His diplomatic experience and prestige were diverse and unmatched. He had served as number two man in the State Department under Presidents John F. Kennedy and Lyndon Johnson. In those assignments he dealt intimately with the Cuban missile crisis and most other major issues in foreign policy for six years during which he held the post of ambassador to the U.N.[46]

Ball was one of America's best-known and most admired diplomats, but he probably destroyed his prospects of becoming Carter's secretary of state when he wrote an article entitled "The Coming Crisis in Israeli-American Relations" for the winter 1976-77 issue of *Foreign Affairs* quarterly. It provoked a storm of protest from the Jewish community.

In the article, Ball cited President Eisenhower's demand that Israel withdraw from the Sinai as "the last time the U.S. ever took, and persisted in, forceful action against the strong wishes of an Israeli government." He saw the event as a watershed. "American Jewish leaders thereafter set out to build one of Washington's most effective lobbies, which now works in close cooperation with the Israeli embassy." He lamented the routine leakage of classified information:

Not only do Israel's American supporters have powerful influence with many members of Congress, but practically no actions touching Israel's interests can be taken, or even discussed, within the executive branch without it being quickly known to the Israeli government.

He considers as incredible Israel's rejection of U.S. advice at a time when Israel's dependence on U.S. aid had "reached the point of totality." Yet he was not surprised that Israel pursued an independent course:

Israelis have been so long conditioned to expect that Americans will support their country, no matter how often it disregards American advice and protests and America's own interests.[47]

Despite such sharp criticism, candidate Jimmy Carter, for a time, considered Ball his principal foreign policy advisor and a good choice for secretary of state.

A number of Jewish leaders, however, urged Carter not to name Ball to any significant role in his administration. The characteristic which made Ball unacceptable to the Israeli Lobby was his candor; he wasn't afraid to speak up and criticize Israeli policy. Carter removed Ball from consideration.

After Carter's cabinet selection process was completed, Ball continued to speak out. Early in 1977, he wrote another article in *Foreign Affairs,* "How to Save Israel in Spite of Herself," urging the new administration to take the lead in formulating a comprehensive settlement that would be fair to the Palestinians as well as Israel. For a time Carter moved in this direction, even trying to communicate with the Palestine Liberation Organization through Saudi Arabia. When this approach floundered, Carter shifted his focus on attempting to reach a settlement between Egypt and Israel at Camp David, where Ball believes Carter was double-crossed by Begin. "I talked with Carter just before Camp David. We had a long dinner together. He told me he was going to try to get a full settlement on Middle East issues, and he seemed to understand the significance of the Palestinian issue. On this I have no doubt, and I think he desperately wanted to settle it." As we have seen after Camp David, Israel frustrated Carter's goals, continuing to build settlements in occupied territory and blocking progress toward autonomy for Palestinians in the West Bank. Ball has frequently and publicly stated his position:

When leading members of the American Jewish community give [Israel's] government uncritical and unqualified approbation and encouragement for whatever it chooses to do, while striving so far as possible to overwhelm any criticism of its actions in Congress and in the public media, they are, in my view, doing neither themselves nor the U.S. a favor.[48]

They've got one great thing going for them. Most people are terribly concerned not to be accused of being anti-Semitic, and the lobby so often equates criticism of Israel with anti-Semitism. They keep pounding away at that theme, and people are deterred from speaking out.[49]

THE ARAB TRADE BOYCOTT

Perhaps the most impressive display of raw power by the Israeli Lobby was the rapid mobilization, not only of Congress, but virtually the entire federal bureaucracy in support of its attack on the Arab trade boycott. It was a great triumph for the Lobby, and lingering disaster for the American economy.

Shortly after the first Arab-Israeli war in 1948, the Arab countries imposed a trade boycott as a means of economic warfare against Israel with which they were, and have been ever since (with the exception of Egypt), in a state of belligerency. The trade boycott, which has remained in effect with certain exceptions until the present time, was, and is, intended by the Arab nations to restrict trade or business dealings between Arab countries and those foreign companies or individuals *who help Israel. In other words, the purpose of the Arab countries was simply to avoid subsidizing their enemy.*

A trade boycott, of course, is not an Arab invention. It is a hallowed and perfectly legitimate weapon of economic warfare accepted as such by all nations. The cold war was waged by the U.S. with trade boycotts of global scope as a primary weapon. For over 25 years, the U.S. boycotted Russia and all of Eastern Europe, as well as China and Cuba. It not only forbade trade with these countries—but boycotted other countries which did not observe the U.S. boycott.

The United Nations also has imposed several far-reaching trade boycotts, including one against Rhodesia (now Zimbabwe) and another against South Africa, in which the U.S. is a leading participant.

Notwithstanding this, the Arab trade boycott against Israel was vigorously attacked by Israeli partisans in the Congress as a *form of racial prejudice and religious discrimination.*

Arab spokesmen vainly tried to make their voices heard to counter the "anti-Semitic" charges by explaining that Henry Kissinger, a Jew, has been welcomed throughout the Arab world; and that the trade boycott is against the State of Israel and its allies and supporters, *not the Jewish people as such*. However, there was no way that the simple truth could break through the cordon of taboo and intimidation established by the Israeli Lobby.

The legitimacy of the Arab position was clear and unambiguous. Mohammed Mahgoub, head of the boycott office in Damascus, stated the Arab position:

> The boycott is not based on racism or religion. We only boycott whoever supports Israel militarily or economically regardless of nationality.
>
> Arab countries do deal with Jewish friends. While there are some Moslem companies that are on the blacklist, the boycott is aimed at Israel and at those companies which contribute to the promotion of Israel's aggressive economy or to its war effort. In general, the blacklist applies to companies and individuals who have invested in Israel, contributed substantially to it or sold strategic goods to it. The sale of consumer goods to Israel is not cause for blacklisting.[50]

The large and continuous infusion of money into Israel from the world Jewish community, is a great tribute to Jewish generosity, loyalty, and solidarity. However, from the Arab point of view, to trade with Jewish-controlled businesses is simply to subsidize one of the main sources of the enemy's power.

This same philosophy is behind the U.S. Code sections, entitled "Trading With The Enemy Act." For a U.S. citizen, trading with the "enemy," or an ally of the enemy, or carrying on trade which benefits an enemy, or ally of an enemy, *is a federal crime.*

The identical reasoning applies to the boycott imposed by the Arab countries on trading with Israel and is nothing more sinister than the obvious fact that one does not feed the mouth whose hand is feeding one's enemy. Certainly, nobody can deny that the Arabs have a perfect right to decide with whom *they* will do business.

However, suddenly, in 1976, the Arab boycott assumed the proportions of a major issue. Candidate Jimmy Carter, looking toward the 1976 election, called it a "disgrace." This, incidentally, is the same Jimmy Carter who, as President, led the fight to repeal the Byrd amendment and impose a total trade boycott on Rhodesia. How did the Arab boycott, which had been in effect against Israel since 1948, suddenly, in 1976, become a "disgrace"?

The answer appears to be that in the presidential election year 1976 the Israeli partisans in Congress and the Israeli Lobby decided *it was time for a political showdown*—an all-out attempt to shatter the Arab boycott by involving the U.S. government and its various agencies and depart-

.

ments in a *concerted effort* to destroy it. The tactics were simple and time-tested—call it "religious or racial discrimination" or, better still—"anti-Semitic."

Under this banner of righteousness, the campaign began. The opening barrage came from the Commerce Oversight and Investigation Subcommittee, under the chairmanship of John E. Moss (D-Cal.), which reported that inadequate steps by executive agencies in dealing with the Arab trade boycott of Israel have compromised U.S. principles of "free trade and freedom from religious discrimination."

Following this, Rep. Bella Abzug, Chairwoman of a House Government Operations Subcommittee on Information and Individual Rights, demanded that the *Securities and Exchange Commission* disclose publicly any information it had on boycott participation by U.S. companies and to formally require every company to disclose whether or not it is observing the boycott.

This disclosure requirement was a transparent attempt to involve the SEC in matters wholly extraneous to its jurisdiction, simply to harass American companies who were doing business with the Arab countries, the only apparent reason being to find out their names so that the Israeli Lobby could bring pressure on them. Nonetheless, the SEC quickly got into the spirit of things and, among other steps, sternly warned brokerage houses and financial institutions not to discriminate against any particular "ethnic groups," nor comply with boycotts in underwriting securities.

Next, the *Department of Justice* filed suit against the Bechtel Corporation and four related companies on charges of violating the federal antitrust laws by cooperating with the Arab boycott in dealing with subcontractors.

Suddenly, out of the blue, Arthur Burns, chairman of the *Federal Reserve Board,* called for diplomatic action against the boycott and urged that if that fails then to consider legislation against it. How the Arab boycott affects the Federal Reserve and why this suddenly became important was not made clear by Chairman Burns.

Under intense pressure on October 6, 1976, during the presidential debates, President Ford ordered the *Commerce Department* to release the names of American businesses that participate in the Arab trade boycott of Israel (presumably so that the Israeli Lobby could boycott them).

After the names were released, the Secretary of Commerce, Eliot Richardson, was reported by *The Wall Street Journal* as saying:

The program of disclosure has helped dispel the widespread impression that there has been some element of discrimination against American companies that have Jewish personnel or Jewish ownership.

In addition, according to the department's general counsel ... most boycott requests involve some relatively straightforward commercial certifications regarding transports and origins of goods. *A department spokesman also said that they are revising the reporting form and will bounce [the new questionnaire] off Jewish groups and such congressional critics of the boycott as Democratic Reps. John Moss of California and Benjamin Rosenthal of New York.*[51] [Emphasis supplied]

Meantime, the *Equal Employment Opportunities Commission* filed sweeping "Commissioner's Charges" against Standard Oil alleging having bias against Jews, tied to the Arab boycott.

The biggest coup, however, came with the *Treasury Department,* and the *Internal Revenue Service.* Heavy pressure was exerted on Congress by the Israeli Lobby to include *in the Tax Reform Bill of 1976* a provision *imposing a huge tax penalty upon companies doing business abroad who observe the Arab boycott of Israel.* The forces behind the amendment were led by Ze'ev Sher, economic minister of the Israeli embassy in Washington. In the course of the hearings on the Bill, *the Ford administration properly warned that the action wouldn't stop the boycott and actually could hurt the cause of peace in the Middle East.*

Other testimony at the committee hearings warned that this legislation could jeopardize the security of U.S. oil supplies in the Middle East. It was also opposed by others on the grounds that it was a *distortion and misuse of the tax laws* to carry out foreign policy.

None of this had any effect on the committee members who were admonished by Senator Abraham Ribicoff's (sponsor of the bill) *warnings that the "Arab boycott had become an important political issue in the 1976 election campaign." The Senate, in a panic and without debate, passed the bill overwhelmingly.* The Israeli Lobby had marshaled almost every important federal agency but the Post Office.

U.S. News & World Report, September 27, 1976, summarizes the situation in the House committee in these words:

What is happening, say critics of the new legislation, is that lawmakers are attempting to make *political points in an election year by portraying the boycott as a vehicle for religious discrimination against those of the*

Jewish faith. However, the House commerce subcommittee's study found that only 15 of 4,000 boycott requests examined had clauses of a religious or ethnic nature. Arab leaders justify their boycott as an economic sanction against Israel applied in the same way that the U.S. had curbed trade with Cuba.[52] [Emphasis supplied]

While it may be somewhat irrelevant, it seems only fair to ask, at this point, where did the interests of the U.S. lie in this matter of the Arab boycott? As we know, the U.S. currently imports more than half of the oil consumed in this country. Approximately one-third of our oil imports come from Arab countries. As much as 90 percent of all the oil used by some of our allies comes from Arab countries. Our bill for foreign oil has increased enormously. Historically, most of the money spent by American consumers for petroleum products found its way into the pockets of other Americans in Texas, California, Oklahoma and other oil-producing states. The money stayed in the U.S. and both the producers and the consumers of the oil were part of our domestic economy, and the money spent was simply recycled among Americans. However, as America's oil production declines and imports of foreign oil increase, and at higher prices, a whole new and unprecedented economic factor enters the picture.

The tens of billions of dollars annually paid for foreign oil imports, which continues to increase year by year, no longer stays in this country—but is drained off mostly to the OPEC nations.

This drain, unless offset by exports to the OPEC nations and others, or by foreign investments in the U.S., seriously affects the American economy and has a significant impact on the U.S. balance of trade.

That this was a matter of indifference to the Israeli partisans is evident from the following report appearing in the September 12, 1977, issue of *Business Week* magazine:

After the Commerce Department later this month proposes regulations to implement the new U.S. anti-boycott law, business finally will begin to get a picture of the impact the legislation will have on trade with the Arab world. Comments now flowing into the department not only suggest the *effects could be dramatic* but also point up the continuing division between business and Jewish groups over the politically charged issue.

Already, the shaky alliance between the Business Roundtable and the B'nai B'rith Anti-Defamation League that resulted in a joint statement of principles on how to deal with the boycott seems to have come undone. That agreement, which had collapsed during congressional hearings only to be quickly patched up, helped mute the debate in Congress and speed the passage of legislation that both sides hailed as a good compromise.

Bad faith. But now, suggested regulations submitted to Congress by the ADL and other Jewish groups have prompted DuPont Co. Chairman Irving S. Shapiro, who also chairs the Roundtable, to charge the groups, in effect, with a breach of faith. . . .

Business concerns run deeper than the tiff over the agreement. "The proposals *would seem to demonstrate a purpose of making U.S. trade with Arab countries so difficult as to be impossible,*" Shapiro wrote. "*We do not believe it to be in the national interest to choke off Arab-American trade.*" Adds the Rule of Law Committee, a group composed primarily of major U.S. banks and oil companies: "The overall result of the ADL submission, if accepted, would be the disruption or termination of U.S. business activities in the Arab world."

Although business and the Jewish groups diverge on a number of points, these issues are at the heart of the dispute.[53] [Emphasis supplied]

Yet, heedless of the consequences to the U.S. economy, the Israeli partisans were not only trying to destroy trade relationships between American businesses and the Arab countries—but they were, at the same time, doing everything in their power to discourage and oppose Arab funds from being invested in this country. As a result, the Arab nations, tired of this hostility, are channeling billions of dollars (our dollars) into investments in European and other more hospitable countries.

The Israeli Lobby has defended its actions on the grounds that it doesn't want Arab investment in this country because of the fear that Arabs would gain too much "control" of American business. The argument is a sham. The best thing for the U.S. would be to encourage large Arab investments in this country, not only because of the favorable effect on our balance of payments, but because the Arab countries would thereby have a much greater stake in American prosperity, which could have an important bearing upon the price of oil. Moreover, it would be the Arabs then who would be vulnerable to expropriation in the event of hostilities.

While the U.S. continues to insult the Arab countries, who have chosen to be friends of the U.S. rather than the Soviet Union, by spurning their investments and charging them with religious and racial discrimination, the nations of Western Europe, Germany, France, England, Italy, and also Japan have moved into the Middle East market and taken our place.

The warning was there for all to see. As Soliman A. Solaim, a Johns Hopkins graduate who served as Saudi Arabia's Minister of Commerce, said:

> Western Europe and Japan stand ready to replace the U.S. as Saudi Arabia's principal trading partner should the U.S. deny this market to itself and in certain cases this has already happened.[54]

The Arab position was summed up by Farouk Ashdar, General Director of a royal Saudi commission responsible for spending some 30 billion dollars in development funds, as follows:

> We will not allow anyone to dictate to us how we shall conduct our affairs. We must make it plain. Any interference with the Arab boycott will negatively affect the U.S. position. We will not do business with companies which substantially improve the economy of our enemy.[55]

Perhaps the most unfortunate aspect of the matter is that the anti-boycott legislation seriously hurts the U.S. *without in any way helping Israel.* There is no one in or out of government, except for the Israeli spokesman, who feels that the anti-boycott legislation has any chance whatever of affecting the Arab determination to maintain the trade boycott against Israel.

Thus, it was nothing but a reckless and irresponsible action by Congress, an ignominious yielding to political pressure and intimidation by the Israeli Lobby, *which could not help Israel* but is doing incalculable, perhaps irremediable, damage to the interests of the U.S.

Both Secretary of State Kissinger and Secretary of the Treasury Simon (neither of which, we assume, is "anti-Semitic") strongly opposed the bill and stated:

> We believe the effect of such pressure will harden Arab attitudes and potentially destroy the progress we have made.[56]

In an article appearing in *Forbes* magazine, October 1, 1976, entitled "How to Legislate a Disaster," *Forbes* states that, after sampling opinions from both business leaders and government officials, the view was confirmed that, rather than abandon the boycott, the Arabs will abandon the U.S. The article concludes:

Wrecking U.S. trade with the Arabs and diminishing U.S. credibility among the moderate Arabs would seem a strange way to help Israel.[57]

How can something so manifestly against America's interests and the cause of peace, and of doubtful value, if not contrary, to Israel's own interest, have been literally railroaded through Congress?

Again, the answer is obvious; our timid lawmakers, as always, are in mortal fear of the Israeli Lobby. In the May 24, 1976, issue of *Business Week* magazine, an item entitled "Taking Aim at the Arab Boycott," explains it simply:

> Stiff legislation to discourage U.S. companies from complying with the Arab boycott of Israel now seems certain to become law. Key reason: *Business opponents are afraid to work against it.*
>
> The outcome could be costly. A proposal by Senator Abraham A. Ribicoff (D-Conn.) to deny foreign tax credits to companies complying with the boycott is gaining support. It will pass unless it is blocked by Senate Finance Committee Chairman Russell B. Long (D-La.). At the very least, Congress will approve the package pressed by Senator Adlai E. Stevenson III (D-Ill.) requiring companies to make public any compliance with boycott demands.
>
> *Business lobbyists are staying on the sidelines.* Corporate representatives and Congressional sources say *the issue is too hot to handle. Companies are afraid they will be labeled anti-Semitic, and possibly face stockholder complaints if they fight anti-boycott bills.*[58] [Emphasis supplied]

So arrogant had this intimidation of Congress by the Israeli Lobby become, that no effort was made even to disguise it.

In reporting on the final stages of the bill's consideration, the *Los Angeles Times* said:

> Impassioned oratory by Senator Abraham Ribicoff* (D-Conn.) on behalf of this provision (the anti-boycott amendment) . . . led Senator Russell B. Long (D-La.) to warn that unless the Treasury Dept. and other opponents of the measure came up with a compromise proposal *acceptable to the [Congressional] supporters of Israel, the entire tax bill could be scuttled.*[59] [Emphasis supplied]

---

*This is the same Senator Ribicoff who, when he was about to retire and did not seek re-election, condemned the Israeli Lobby as "unworthy of the U.S. or Israel."

We have become so inured to seeing and hearing incredible things of this nature that the shock effect has worn off.

Senator Long, committee chairman, was actually saying, as quoted above, that perhaps the most important piece of legislation passed by the Congress in 1976 (The Tax Reform Act) affecting every person in the U.S. might be defeated unless a proposal *acceptable to the supporters of Israel is adopted.*

The economic impact on the U.S. balance of trade over the past twelve years by this kind of anti-Arab legislation is immeasurable.

We do know that the U.S., for various reasons including the anti-boycott legislation, has the largest trade imbalance in history and is now, by far, the world's largest debtor nation.

An *Associated Press* release, dated July 9, 1988, reports as follows:

BRITAIN, SAUDI ARABIA INK HUGE ARMS PACT

LONDON (AP)—*Britain announced Friday it had signed its biggest-ever arms deal with Saudi Arabia.*

A Defense Ministry statement gave no details, but official sources said the deal—which includes mine sweepers and some 50 Tornado fighters—*was worth more than $17 billion. That dwarfed a $7.5 billion contract won by Britain in 1986* to supply Saudi Arabia with 72 Tornado fighters and other aircraft.

The ministry statement said the deal, signed Sunday in a memorandum of understanding, was a new phase of the previous contract and involved the supply "of additional aircraft, a construction program and specialized navy vessels."

The deal, a huge boost for the British armaments industry in the next decade, followed years of British lobbying.

Unlike the U.S. administration, Prime Minister Margaret Thatcher's government is not constrained by lawmakers protesting that weapons sales to Saudi Arabia may endanger or offend Israel.[60] [Emphasis supplied]

In the July 25, 1988, edition of *Time* magazine, the following item appeared:

Congressional resistance to Arab arms sales is having an increasingly harmful effect on U.S. diplomacy in the region. In a pair of setbacks, Saudi Arabia has turned to Britain for a $12 billion purchase of Tornado's fighter-bombers and other equipment, and Kuwait has announced it will buy weapons from the Soviet Union. Both countries have lost arms battles

> in Congress because of pressure from Israel's lobbyists. Similarly, Jordan is believed close to buying France's Mirage 2000. Some Arab nations are turning to China. Even some Israeli experts think Israel's lobby has gone too far in opposing the sales, because sales of U.S. arms would at least improve some safeguards on the use of the weapons.[61]

Former Secretary of Defense Frank Carlucci estimates that the trade lost to the Arab countries because of the Israeli Lobby's actions exceeds 75 billion dollars.

THE LOBBY AND THE JACKSON-VANIK AMENDMENT

It is also impossible to estimate the full damage to the American farm economy and long-term effects on the U.S. balance of trade by the passage, in 1974, of the so-called Jackson-Vanik Amendment to the 1974 Trade Act, which was sponsored by the Israeli partisans in Congress and pushed through by the Israeli Lobby.

This law cut off the Russians from Export-Import Bank financing and denied them most favored nation tariff treatment until emigration for Russian Jews was made easier and substantially increased in numbers.

The Soviets reacted by sharply *reducing* the number of Jews allowed to leave and simply bought their wheat and other agricultural products from other countries.

Nobody explained to the American farmer why he could not sell his wheat, or why the American taxpayer had to buy his surplus from him and store it at enormous cost, or how this is related in any way to how many Jews emigrate from the Soviet Union.

CHAPTER VIII

Israel and the United States
The Special Relationship

O UT OF THE combination of the activities of the Israeli Lobby
and the effect of the "taboo," there has developed a unique
relationship between the U.S. and Israel. It is often described by Israeli
diplomats, and American politicians, as a "special relationship," and indeed
it is.

Although it appears superficially to be an *alliance* between the U.S. and
Israel, it is not. Not only is there *no treaty of alliance between the U.S. and
Israel, but Israel does not want one!* Under the special relationship, Israel
has all of the benefits of a formal alliance and none of the restraints or
responsibilities of an ally. Israel determines its own foreign policy *unilater-
ally* and makes no bones about it. Its policies may be regarded by the U.S.
and the rest of the world as dangerous, or in violation of international law
or as an "obstacle to peace"—but this does not deter Israel nor do these
circumstances, strangely enough, have any adverse effect upon the special
relationship with the U.S.

However, under the unwritten terms of the special relationship, the U.S.
gives Israel its latest, most advanced, and secret weapons (often before they
are available to our own armed forces), while Israel remains so secretive
that it has flatly refused admittance to a committee of the U.S. Senate to
visit its "peaceful" nuclear reactor installations at Dimona. Israel has also

refused to sign the Nuclear Non-Proliferation Treaty sponsored by the U.S.

Customarily, allies are required to respect each other's strongly held views in critical areas affecting international peace. Israel, however, defiantly continues to build new settlements on confiscated Arab lands on the West Bank despite pleas from the U.S. that these actions violate international law and create additional and serious obstacles to any Middle East peace settlement. Is it conceivable that the U.S. would tolerate conduct of this kind from such "allies" as Britain, Germany, or Japan?

THE MYSTERY OF THE USS LIBERTY

The first clear indication of the special nature of the relationship with Israel came with the notorious Israeli attack on the USS *Liberty*.

During the 1967 Six-Day War between Israel and Egypt, the U.S. electronic and intelligence research vessel *Liberty* was cruising in international waters in the Mediterranean and was suddenly attacked by Israeli torpedo boats and jet aircraft. The attack, which lasted *almost two hours,* killed 34 American sailors and wounded 171.[1]

A U.S. naval court of inquiry found that the *Liberty* was, without question, in international waters; the weather was clear; the ship's identity plainly marked and the U.S. flag waving in the wind.

The attack was apparently ordered by Moshe Dayan to prevent the U.S. from intercepting Israeli messages. When the circumstances of the attack became known, an elaborate conspiracy of secrecy was organized from President Johnson on down to cover up the extent of Israel's involvement and to keep from the American people the deliberate nature of the Israeli attack.

Israel, of course, protested its innocence and promised to pay for the damage to the ship. But even this small reparation was not forthcoming, despite repeated efforts and requests by the State Department over the last twenty years.

The story of the intentional attack on the USS *Liberty* and the shameful efforts of the U.S. government to cover up Israel's duplicity, is told in a book entitled *Assault on the Liberty,* by the cypher officer of the USS *Liberty,* James M. Ennes, Jr., published after his retirement from the navy in 1980.[2]

However, the U.S. has more than held up its end of the special relationship. At the beginning of the October 1973 war against Egypt, Israel had suffered severe losses in tanks and planes and was on the verge of defeat when the U.S., under Nixon and Kissinger, swiftly mounted an enormous military airlift which, according to Prime Minister Golda Meir, "saved Israel."[3]

Another well-known incident of Israel's indifference to, or defiance of, its obligations to the U.S. was reported in the April 8, 1979, edition of the *Los Angeles Times.*

According to the *Times,* a State Department spokesman announced that the circumstances, scale, and duration of Israel's incursion into Southern Lebanon, in which over one thousand (mostly civilian) casualties were inflicted, raises serious questions as to whether U.S. arms supplied to Israel *were used illegally.* Israel, in violation of its agreement with the U.S., used the latest high tech, anti-personnel (cluster) bombs which break into hundreds of fragments capable of massive killing.[4]

These bombs were received by Israel from the U.S., on the *condition* that they would be used only in an all-out *defensive* war where Israel's survival was at stake. The Lebanon incursion was totally offensive and many targets were Palestinian refugee camps.

A *Los Angeles Times* editorial appearing in the April 9, 1979, edition comments on the matter:

> . . . the basic issue, rather is Israel's violation of its agreement with the U.S. that was meant to control how and when the CBUs (cluster bombs) could be used.
>
> This goes very much to the value and enforceability of the conditions that the U.S. often attaches to its arm transfers abroad and at least *in the immediate case it goes as well to the reliability of Israel's pledges.*[5] [Emphasis supplied]

It is the irrational nature of this special relationship with Israel that our allies and the other nations of the world cannot comprehend. What they are unable to understand is that Israel decides for itself what it will and will not do in its relations with the rest of the world, and the U.S. provides and finances the military weaponry and technology necessary to support those policies, even though the U.S. may be in total opposition to them. If such Israeli policies result in war, the U.S. immediately mobilizes all available military equipment and weaponry, depleting in the process of its own critical reserves in order to give Israel whatever is necessary to achieve victory. It makes no difference that in doing so the U.S. may be severely straining the bonds between us and our allies in Western Europe and Japan and jeopardizing our relationship with the Arab world, not to mention running the grave risk of a nuclear confrontation.

After Israel's war is over, it is then the duty of the U.S., under our special relationship, to provide new billions of dollars' worth of the most sophisticated and advanced weapons available to maintain Israel's continued defiance of the rest of the world and of the U.S. To make the situation even more bizarre, Israel has copied much of the advance weapons technology given to it by the U.S. and has been marketing it around the world. In effect, the U.S. has become the research and development division of the Israeli armament industry, which is now an important international arms supplier. One of its best customers is South Africa against whom the U.S. is trying to lead a world boycott.

OUR LEAKY FORTRESS

One of the most insidious consequences of the special relationship is the demoralizing effect it has had on the personnel in our State and Defense Departments.

The Pentagon houses most of the Department of Defense and is the core of American military security. Across the Potomac is the Department of State, the nerve center of our nation's worldwide diplomatic network. These buildings are channels through which flow, each day, thousands of messages dealing with the nation's top secrets. No one can enter either building without special identification or advance clearance, and all entrances are heavily guarded.

These buildings are, in effect, fortresses where the nation's most precious secrets are carefully guarded by the most advanced security technology.

How safe are those secrets? As far as Israel is concerned, they are an open book.

According to an American ambassador, who had a long career in the Middle East: "The leaks to Israel are fantastic. If I have something I want the Secretary of State to know but don't want Israel to know, I must wait till I have a chance to see him personally.

"It is a fact of life that everyone in authority is reluctant to put anything on paper that concerns Israel, if it is to be withheld from Israel's knowledge," says the Ambassador. "Nor do such people even feel free to speak in a crowded room of such things."

The Ambassador offers an example from his own experience. He had received a call from a friend in the Jewish community who wanted to warn him, as a friend, that all details of a lengthy document on Middle East policy, that he had just dispatched overseas, were *out*. The document was classified "top secret," the diplomat recalls. "I didn't believe what he said, so my friend read me every word of it over the phone."[6]

In the view of this diplomatic source, leaks to pro-Israel activists are not only pervasive throughout the two departments but "are intimidating and very harmful to our national interests." He says that, because of the ever-present Xerox machine, diplomats proceed on the assumption that even messages they send by the most secure means will be copied and passed on to eager hands. "We just don't dare put sensitive items on paper." A factor making the pervasive insecurity even greater is the knowledge that leaks of secrets to Israel, even when noticed—which is rare—are never investigated.

Whatever intelligence the Israelis want, whether political or technical, they obtain promptly and without cost at the source. Officials, who normally would work vigilantly to protect our national interest by identifying leaks and bringing charges against the offenders, are demoralized. *In fact, they are disinclined even to question Israel's tactics for fear this activity will cause the Israeli Lobby to mark them as trouble-makers and take measures to nullify their efforts, or even harm their careers.*

The Lobby's intelligence network, having numerous volunteer "friend-lies" to tap, reaches all parts of the executive branch where matters concerning Israel are handled. Awareness of this seepage keeps officials—whatever rung of the ladder they occupy—from making or even proposing decisions that are in the U.S. interest.

If, for example, an official should indicate opposition to an Israeli request during a private interdepartmental meeting—or, worse still, put it in an intraoffice memorandum—he or she must assume that this information will soon reach the Israeli embassy, either directly or through AIPAC. Soon after, the official should expect to be mentioned by name critically when the Israeli ambassador visits the secretary of state or other prominent U.S. official.

The penetration is all the more remarkable, because much of it is carried out by U.S. citizens on behalf of a foreign government. The practical effect is to give Israel its own network of sources through which it is able to learn almost anything it wishes about decisions or resources of the U.S. government. When making procurement demands, Israel can display better knowledge of Defense Department inventories than the Pentagon itself.[7]

Richard Helms, Director of the CIA during the 1967 Arab-Israeli war, recalls an occasion when an Israeli army request had been filled with the wrong items. Israeli officials resubmitted the request complete with all the supposedly top-secret code numbers and a note to Helms that said the

Pentagon perhaps had not understood exactly which items were needed. "It was a way for them to show me that they knew exactly what they wanted," Helms said. Helms believes that during this period no important secret was kept from Israel.

Not only are the Israelis adept at getting the information they want—they are masters at the weapons procurement game. A former deputy assistant secretary of defense, who is a specialist in Middle East policy, recalls Israeli persistence:

> They would never take no for an answer. They never gave up. These emissaries of a foreign government always had a shopping list of wanted military items, some of them high technology that no other nation possessed, some of it secret devices that gave the United States an edge over any adversary. *Such items were not for sale, not even to the nations with whom we have our closest, most formal military alliance—like those linked to us through the North Atlantic Treaty Organization.* [Emphasis supplied]

He learned that military sales to Israel were not bound by the guidelines and limitations which govern U.S. arms supply policy elsewhere. He says, "Sales to Israel were different—very different."

This Department of Defense official has vivid memories of a military liaison officer from the Israeli embassy who called at the Defense Department and requested approval to purchase a military item, which was on the prohibited list because of its highly secret advanced technology. "He came to me, and I gave him the official Pentagon reply. I said, 'I'm sorry, sir, but the answer is no. We will not release that technology.'"

The Israeli officer took pains to observe the bureaucratic courtesies and not antagonize lower officials who might devise ways to block the sale. He said, "Thank you very much, if that's your official position. We understand that you are not in a position to do what we want done. Please don't feel bad, but we're going over your head." And that, of course, meant he was going to the office of the secretary of defense, or perhaps even to the White House. Yet this Department of Defense official has high respect for the efficiency of Israeli procurement officers:

> You have to understand that the Israelis operate in the Pentagon very professionally, and in an omnipresent way. They have enough of their people who understand our system well, and they have made friends at

all levels, from top to bottom. They just interact with the system in a constant, continuous way that keeps the pressure on.[8]

The Carter White House tried to establish a policy of restraint. Zbigniew Brzezinski, Carter's assistant for national security, remembers in an interview Defense Secretary Harold Brown's efforts to hold the line on technology transfer. "He was very tough with Israel on its requests for weapons and weapons systems. He often turned them down." But that was not the final word. For example, Brzezinski cites as the most notable example Brown's refusal to sell Israel the controversial anti-personnel weapon known as the cluster bomb. Despite written agreements restricting the use of these bombs, Israel used them twice against populated areas in Lebanon, causing death and injury to many civilians. Brown responded by refusing to sell the deadly replacements. But even on that request, Israel eventually prevailed. President Reagan reversed the Carter administration policy, and cluster bombs were returned to the approved list.

Others who have occupied high positions in the executive branch have been willing to speak candidly (but only with the promise of anonymity) on the astounding process through which the Israeli Lobby is able to penetrate the defenses at the Defense Department—and elsewhere.

An official recalls one day receiving a list of military equipment Israel wanted to purchase. Noting that "the Pentagon is Israel's 'stop and shop,' " he took it for granted that the Israelis had obtained clearances. So he followed usual procedure by circulating it to various Pentagon offices for routine review and evaluation:

> One office instantly returned the list to me with a note: "One of these items is so highly classified you have no right to know that it even exists." I was instructed to destroy all copies of the request and all references to the particular code numbers. I didn't know what it was. It was some kind of electronic jamming equipment, top secret. Somehow the Israelis knew about it and acquired its precise specifications, cost and top secret code number. *This meant they had penetrated our research and development labs, our most sensitive facilities.*[9] [Emphasis supplied]

Despite that worrisome revelation, no official effort was launched to discover who had revealed the sensitive information.

Israel's agents are close students of the U.S. system and work it to their advantage. Besides obtaining secret information by clandestine operations, they apply open pressure on executive branch offices thoroughly and effectively. A weapons expert says the embassy knows exactly when things are scheduled for action:

> It stays on top of things as does no other embassy in town. They know your agenda, what was on your schedule yesterday, and what's on it today and tomorrow. They know what you have been doing and saying. They know the law and regulations backwards and forwards. They know when the deadlines are.

He admires the resourcefulness of the Israelis in applying pressure:

> They may leak to Israeli newspapers details of their difficulty in getting an approval. A reporter will come in to State or Defense and ask a series of questions so detailed they could be motivated only by Israeli officials. Sometimes the pressure will come, not from reporters, but from AIPAC.
>
> If things are really hung up, it isn't long before letters or calls start coming from Capitol Hill. They'll ask, "Why is the Pentagon not approving this item?" Usually, the letter is from the Congressman in whose district the item is manufactured. *He will argue that the requested item is essential to Israel's security. He probably will also ask, "Who is this bad guy in the Pentagon—or State—who is blocking this approval? I want his name. Congress would like to know."*[10] [Emphasis supplied]

The American defense expert pauses to emphasize his point: "No bureaucrat, no military officer likes to be singled out by anybody from Congress and required to explain his professional duty." He recalls an episode involving President Carter's Secretary of Defense, Harold Brown:

> I remember once Israel requested an item on the prohibited list. Before I answered, I checked with Secretary Brown and he said, "No, absolutely no. We're not going to give in to the bastards on this one." So I said no.
>
> Lo and behold, a few days later I got a call from Brown. He said, "The Israelis are raising hell. I got a call from [Senator Henry] 'Scoop' Jackson, asking why we aren't cooperating with Israel. It isn't worth it. Let it go."[11]

This attitude sometimes causes official restrictions on sharing of information to be modified or conveniently forgotten. As one defense official puts it, the rules get "placed deeper and deeper into the file.":

> A sensitive document is picked up by an Israeli officer while his friend, a Defense Department official, deliberately looks the other way. Nothing

is said. Nothing is written. And the U.S. official probably does not feel he has done anything wrong. Meanwhile the Israelis ask for more and more.[12]

During the tenure of Atlanta Major Andrew Young, as U.S. Ambassador to the U.N. during the Carter administration, Young recalls, "I operated on the assumption that the Israelis would learn just about everything instantly. I just always assumed that everything was monitored, and that there was a pretty formal network."

Young resigned as Ambassador in August 1979, after it was revealed that he had met with Zuhdi Terzi, the PLO's U.N. observer, in violation of Kissinger's pledge to Israel not to talk to the PLO. Press reports on Young's episode said Israeli intelligence learned of the meeting and that Israeli officials then leaked the information to the press, precipitating the diplomatic wrangle which led to Young's resignation.[13]

Israel denied that its agents had learned of the Young-Terzi meeting. The press counselor at the Israeli embassy went so far as to tell the *Washington Star*, "We do not conduct any kind of intelligence activities in the U.S." This denial must have been amusing to U.S. intelligence experts, one of whom talked with *Newsweek* magazine about Mossad's (Israel's Foreign Intelligence Agency) activities here: "They have penetrations all through the U.S. government. They do better than the KGB," said the expert, whom the magazine did not identify. The *Newsweek* article continued:

> With the help of American Jews in and out of government, Mossad looks for any softening in U.S. support and tries to get any technical intelligence the administration is unwilling to give to Israel.
>
> "Mossad can go to any distinguished American Jew and ask for his help," says a former CIA agent. The appeal is a simple one: "When the call went out and no one heeded it, the Holocaust resulted."
>
> *The U.S. tolerates Mossad's operations on American soil partly because of reluctance to anger the American Jewish community.*[14] [Emphasis supplied]

Penetration by Israel continued at such a high level that a senior State Department official who has held the highest career positions related to the Middle East confides, "I urged several times that the U.S. quit trying to keep secrets from Israel. Let them have everything. They always get what they want anyway. When we try to keep secrets, it always backfires."

An analysis prepared by the CIA in 1979, entitled "Israel: Foreign Intelligence and Security Services," demonstrates how the U.S. continues to be a focus of Mossad operations:

> In carrying out its mission to collect positive intelligence, the principal function of Mossad is to conduct agent operations against the Arab nations and their official representatives and installations throughout the world, particularly in Western Europe and the United States. . . .
>
> Objectives in Western countries are equally important (as in the U.S.S.R. and East Europe) to the Israeli intelligence service. Mossad collects intelligence regarding Western, Vatican and U.N. policies toward the Near East; promotes arms deals for the benefit of the IDF, and *acquires data for silencing anti-Israel factions in the West.*[15] [Emphasis supplied]

Under "methods of operation," the CIA booklet describes the way in which Mossad makes use of domestic pro-Israeli groups. It states that "Mossad over the years has enjoyed some rapport with highly-placed persons and government offices in every country of importance to Israel." It adds, "Within Jewish communities in almost every country of the world, there are Zionists and other sympathizers who render strong support to the Israeli intelligence effort." It explains:

> Such contacts are carefully nurtured and serve as channels for information, deception material, propaganda, and other purposes. . . . Mossad activities are generally conducted through Israeli official and semiofficial establishments.
>
> The Israeli intelligence service depends heavily on the various Jewish communities and organizations abroad for recruiting agents and eliciting general information. The aggressively ideological nature of Zionism, which emphasizes that all Jews belong to Israel and must return to Israel, has had its drawbacks in enlisting support for intelligence operations, however, since there is considerable opposition to Zionism among Jews throughout the world.
>
> Aware of this fact, Israeli intelligence representatives usually operate discreetly within Jewish communities and are under instructions to handle their missions with utmost tact to avoid embarrassment to Israel. They also attempt to penetrate anti-Zionist elements in order to neutralize the opposition.[16]

The theft of scientific data is a major objective of Mossad operations, which is often attempted by trying to recruit local agents. The CIA report continues:

> In addition to the large-scale acquisition of published scientific papers and technical journals from all over the world through overt channels, the Israelis devote a considerable portion of their covert operations to obtaining scientific and technical intelligence. This had included attempts to penetrate certain classified defense projects in the U.S. and other Western nations.[17]

Leaks of classified information remain a major problem for policy-makers. One official says that during the Carter administration his col-leagues feared to speak up even in small private meetings. When Israeli requests were turned down at top secret interagency meetings, "the Israeli military attache, the political officer, or the ambassador—or all of them at once—were lodging protests within hours. They knew exactly who said what, even though nothing had been put on paper." He adds, "No one needs trouble like that."

He says that the assistant secretary of defense for international security affairs was often subjected to pressure. Frequently the Israeli embassy would demand copies of documents that were still in the draft stage and had not reached his desk.[18]

To strike back at government officials considered to be unsympathetic to Israeli needs, the Israeli Lobby singles them out for personal attack and even the wrecking of their careers. In January 1977, a broad-scale purge was attempted immediately after the inauguration of President Carter. The perpetrator was Senator Richard Stone of Florida, a Democrat, a passionate supporter of Israel. When he was newly installed as Chairman of the Senate Subcommittee on the Middle East, he brought along with him a "hit list" on a call at the White House. In his view, fifteen officials were not sufficiently supportive of Israel and its weapon needs, and he wanted them transferred to positions where their views would create no problems for Israel. Marked for removal were William Quandt, Brzezinski's assistant for Middle East matters, and Les Janka, who had served on the National Security Council under Ford. The others were career military officers, most of them colonels. Stone's demands were rejected by Brzezinski and, accord-ing to a senior White House official, "after pressing reasonably hard for several days," the senator gave up. Although unsuccessful, *his demands caused a stir. One officer says, "I find it very ironic that a U.S. Senator goes to a U.S. President's National Security Advisor and tells him to fire Americans for insufficient loyalty to another country."*[19]

Admiral Thomas Moorer recalls a dramatic example of Israeli Lobby power from his days as chairman of the Joint Chiefs of Staff. At the time of the 1973 Arab-Israeli war, Modecai Gur, the defense attache at the Israeli embassy, who later became commander-in-chief of Israeli forces, came to Moorer demanding that the U.S. provide Israel with aircraft equipped with a high technology air-to-surface anti-tank missile called the Maverick. At the time, the U.S. had only one squadron so equipped. Moorer recalls telling Gur:

> I can't let you have those aircraft. We have just one squadron. Besides, we've been testifying before the Congress convincing them we need this equipment. If we gave you our only squadron, Congress would raise hell with us.

"Do you know what he said? *Gur told me, 'You get us the planes; I'll take care of Congress.'*" Moorer pauses, then adds, "And he did." America's only squadron equipped with Mavericks went to Israel.

Moorer, now a senior counselor at the Georgetown University Center for Strategic and International Studies, says he strongly opposed the transfer—but was overruled by "political expediency at the presidential level." He notes President Richard Nixon was then in the throes of Watergate. But, he adds:

> I've never seen a President—I don't care who he is—stand up to them [the Israelis]. It just boggles your mind.
>
> They always get what they want. The Israelis know what is going on all the time. I got to the point where I wasn't writing anything down.
>
> *If the American people understood what a grip those people have got on our government, they would rise up in arms.* Our citizens don't have any idea what goes on.[20] [Emphasis supplied]

Jewish groups in the U.S. are often pressed into service to soften up the Secretary of State and other officials, especially in advance of a visit to the U.S. by the Israeli prime minister. A senior defense official explains, "Israel would always have a long shopping list for the prime minister to take up.

We would decide which items were worth making into an issue and which were not. We would try to work things out in advance." There was the constant concern that the prime minister might take an arms issue straight to the President, and the tendency was to clear the agenda of everything possible.

On one such occasion, Ed Sanders, President Carter's adviser on Jewish affairs, brought a complaint to the National Security Council offices: "I'm getting a lot of flack from Jewish congressmen on the ALQ 95-J. What is this thing? And why are we being so nasty about it? Shouldn't we let Israel have it? The President is getting a lot of abuse because the Pentagon won't turn it loose." It was a high technology radar jamming device, and soon it was approved for shipment to Israel.

In advance of Carter's decisions to provide a high technology missile to Israel, a procession of Jewish groups came, one after another to say:

Please explain to us why the Pentagon is refusing to sell AIM 9-L missiles to Israel. Don't you know what this means? This missile is necessary so the Israelis will be able to shoot down the counterpart missile on the Mig 21 which carries the Eight Ball 935.

A former high-ranking official in security affairs cites the intimidating effect of this procession on career specialists:

When you have to explain your position day after day, week after week, to American Jewish groups—first, say, from Kansas City, then Chicago, then East Overshoe—you see what you are up against. These are people from different parts of the country, but they come in with the very same information, the same set of questions, the same criticism.

They know what you have done even in private meetings. They will say, *"Mr. Smith, we understand that in interagency meetings, you frequently take a hard line against technology transfers to Israel. We'd like you to explain yourself."* [Emphasis supplied]

Jewish groups in turn press Capitol Hill into action:

We'll get letters from Congressmen: "We need an explanation. We're hearing from constituents that Israel's security is threatened by the refusal of the Pentagon to release the AIM 9-L missile. Please, Mr. Secretary, can you give me your rationale for the refusal?"[21]

Every official of prominence in the State and Defense departments proceeds on the assumption—and certainty—that at least once a week he will have to deal with a group from the Jewish community. One of them summarizes:

One has to keep in mind the constant character of this pressure. *The public affairs staff of the Near East bureau in the State Department figures it will spend about 75 percent of its time dealing with Jewish groups.* Hundreds of such groups get appointments in the executive branch each year. [Emphasis supplied]

In acting to influence U.S. policy in the Middle East, the Israeli Lobby has the field virtually to itself. Other interest groups and individuals who might provide some measure of counterbalancing pressure have only begun to get organized.[22]

THE POLLARD SPY CASE

For many years, the penetration of our Defense and State Departments' secrets by the Israelis has been denied vigorously and dismissed as preposterous, until the sensational Pollard spy case was broken.

Pollard, a Jewish American citizen, was caught in 1987 after a long record of espionage activities on behalf of Israel. He was captured just as he was entering the Israeli embassy in Washington seeking refuge. He and his wife were convicted of espionage and he was sentenced to life in prison.

The American Jewish community's reaction was of horror and embarrassment. The Israeli government passed it off as a *"rogue operation" which the Israeli government, they swore, did not know anything about.* This was too much for almost anyone in the U.S. Jewish community to swallow.

Henry Siegman, the Executive Director of the American Jewish Congress, summed up his reaction in these words, published in the *Los Angeles Times:*

The Pollard spy scandal has played itself out as a tragedy in three acts: stupidity, arrogance and cover-up.

When the information about Israeli spying against the U.S. first came to light it was seen as unbelievably stupid. It was difficult to imagine what conceivable gain would justify jeopardizing the massive economic and military support that Israel receives from the U.S.

Then came Act 2 as we watched in disbelief the rewarding of those responsible for what Israel has insisted was an illicit operation. *Nothing but arrogance could account for what appeared as Israel's nose thumbing at America's sense of a friend betrayed. One of the spymasters received a fat job as head of a major government enterprise, the other was promoted to the command of Israel's second largest air force base, since in the real world rogues are not rewarded.*[23] [Emphasis supplied]

Joseph Jaffee, who is the foreign editor and columnist of the *Suddeutsche Zeitung* in Munich, in an article reprinted in the *Los Angeles Times,* explains his reactions:

Many American Jews have given vent to anxieties thought to be safely buried. We've had it so good in America and now there is Jonathan Pollard (like the Rosenbergs decades ago) to provide the goyim with their best ammunition against us—"the dual loyalty" smear. *In Israel, on the other hand, widespread shame and anger directed at the government has been mixed with defiance toward the American Jewish Community....* [Emphasis supplied]

He adds that, instead of cringing, American Jews should draw comfort from the fact that they will not be held accountable for the stupidities of Israel's government, which has added cowardice to *chutzpah,* in the handling of Pollard and the aftermath.[24]

Hyman Bookbinder, special representative in Washington for the American Jewish Committee, and other Jewish leaders have called the Pollard case the most serious breach ever between Israel and America and its six million Jews.[25] The following are excerpts from an article appearing in the *Los Angeles Times* by Richard B. Straus datelined Washington:

Some call it the Teflon country, but Israel, like the U.S. President associated with the term, finds the going sticky these days.

First came the Iran arms scandal. Although the Tower Commission went to great lengths to differentiate between Israeli involvement and ultimate American responsibility for decision-making, *the impression lingers that Israelis pushed and prodded the Reagan Administration into disaster. As Vice President George Bush was quoted as saying to the commission, "We were in the grips of the Israelis."* Even an Administration official considerably more sympathetic to Israel than Bush, Secretary of State George P. Shultz, expressed concern about Israel promoting interests not coincidental with the U.S.

But now the Israelis find themselves on the receiving end of some of the harshest criticism in recent years from those very same congressional friends—and the issue is not Iran-related. The trouble is the notorious spy case involving Jonathan Jay Pollard. When the former U.S. Navy Department analyst with high-level security clearance was nabbed last year passing classified information to Israel, the Israeli government disclaimed all responsibility, claiming that Pollard's activities were part of a "rogue operation."

Things have not turned out that way. First, the smuggled intelligence data turned out to be extremely sensitive. Second, *two Israelis behind this "rogue operation" were promoted rather than punished by the Israeli government.*

Most important, Pollard-related events have ignited a growing storm of outrage from Israel's most important backers—Congress and the American Jewish community.

If, as one congressman complained, *the promotion of Pollard's Israeli handlers "rubbed our noses into it,"* American Jewish leaders were in an even less enviable position. A group of them visiting Israel last week made their displeasure unmistakably clear and unexpectedly public.

But instead of chastening their Israeli hosts, the American Jewish leaders' remarks only prompted more tough talk from Jerusalem. Said one well-connected official, "It is very wrong for the American Jewish community to go as far as it did. You don't put Israel on trial because a few people have been accused." Other Israelis went even further, accusing American Jews of responding harshly because of their fears of being accused of dual loyalty. The respected Israeli political theorist Shlomo Avinieri told an Israeli newspaper that "American Jews, despite their material success and intellectual achievements, fear they may not be seen by non-Jews as being truly American."

As the internecine battle raged, American Jews, who within the last decade have attained important posts in the U.S. foreign-policy bureaucracy, have begun to join the angry chorus. They charge that their views, not their identities, were being compromised. Said one Jewish State Department official, "What Pollard shows is not that Jews, but Israel is disloyal."[26] [Emphasis supplied]

In many ways, the Israeli government's arrogance is the human response to the years of blind support by a highly activist part of the American

Jewish community for anything Israel does, even if it ultimately hurts Israel. Israel "right or wrong," is wrong for everybody.

Alexander Cockburn, columnist for *Nation,* in the March 18, 1987, edition of *The Wall Street Journal* expresses his views of the matter:

> American Jews nervously ponder the fact that other spies for Israel may be brought to book and fear the revival of the old charges of "dual loyalty."
>
> They have sent a high-level delegation to Israel to impress upon that country's government the delicacy of the situation and the damage inflicted on U.S.-Israeli relations. They and others have asked how it is that the Israeli government could have acted with such careless arrogance, first to enter into such a relationship with Pollard and finally *to promote the two men identified as Pollard's senior Israeli handlers,* Messrs. Eitan and Sella.
>
> The answer is simple enough. *Israel as represented by its recent governments, has acted with careless arrogance because it had every reason to believe that its carelessness would be unchecked and its arrogance unchallenged.*
>
> So it had nothing to do with the loaded phrase "dual loyalty" to say that the *furious resistance among many of Israel's admirers in this country to any criticism or any act of any Israeli government in recent times has inevitably fostered in the minds of many Israeli officials the notion that they can get away with anything.*
>
> Fortified by their "yes men" here, Israeli officials no doubt conceived that they would remain *immune from sanctions concerning such activities as the bombing of the U.S. intelligence ship, Liberty,* continued occupation of the territories, illegal settlements, sabotage of any realistic peace process, invasion of Lebanon, bombing of Tunis, and so forth.[27] [Emphasis supplied]

The lesson, however, is never learned. Some Israelis are lashing out bitterly at U.S. Jews for failing to stand up for the Pollards and have started a "Citizens for Pollard" fund to free them. A strongly-worded letter from an American Jewish physician was published in the September 8, 1987, edition of the *Jerusalem Post,* which is critical of American secular Jews. The letter ends with the following words:

> Legal opinion offers no hope for the Pollards. The answer has to be political. Jewish citizens of the U.S., must impress upon their political

leaders the need for an independent, impartial tribunal to re-evaluate the case without resort to secret briefs and frenzied appearances by State Department representatives. It is just possible that without the hysteria, an independent court will see the truth of the case and *finally free these two individuals whose main crime was Jewish patriotism.*[28]

Hyman Bookbinder, in the March 30, 1988, edition of *Time* magazine, has replied bluntly, "Pollard is a criminal found guilty in our system of justice, it's as simple as that. If it was perceived in America that we had come to the defense of Pollard our credibility as a Jewish community would be down to zero overnight and Israel would be the loser."[29]

In Washington, the staunchly pro-Israel *New Republic* called the Jerusalem government behavior, in the Pollard affair, "morally unworthy and politically stupid"—adding that "if the smart asses in the *corridors of Israeli power think that Israel is a 'Teflon nation,' they may be in for a shock."*[30]

As we have said, the fault does not lie entirely with the Israelis. For many years they *have* led a teflon existence. *The political cowardice* of the U.S. government, in the face of provocation after provocation, has emboldened the Israeli government to think that they could do what they pleased and the "special relationship" and the Israeli Lobby would protect them from any accounting for their actions. *They have become addicted to teflon.* The Likud government's attitude toward the U.S. and the Jewish community in this country is best described as a "patronizing contempt."

THE ISRAELI LOBBY AND "DUAL LOYALTY"

So-called "dual loyalty" is not an issue here. Whether or not it exists and, if so, to what extent, is extraneous to the purposes of this book.

If a charge is to be made against the Israeli Lobby in this respect, it is better expressed as dual *"disloyalty."*

If Harkabi and others are right when they say that the "Friends of Israel" (a term which AIPAC uses when referring to its constituents) are not true friends of the Israeli people; that they have failed in their duty to speak out against the abuses of the Likud government; that they have misled the Israeli people and caused them to believe that America supported the disastrous policies of the Likud with respect to the occupied territories; and that these false friends are responsible for the catastrophe which Harkabi feels may overcome Israel, to whom, then, is the Israeli Lobby's loyalty directed?[31]

George Ball does not exaggerate when he said on the "60 Minutes" interview (see Chapter VII) that the Israeli Lobby has "done an enormous job of corrupting the American democratic process."[32]

This is not to say that the *motives* which prompted and underlay the activities of the Lobby are "corrupt," or that there is anything inherently wrong in these activities as they view them.

There are many rationalizations for the zeal with which the Israeli Lobby pursues its objectives—"the end justifies the means"—"there are only six million of *us* and 200 million of *them*," and the ever-present spectre of the Holocaust. Jewish fears (often to the point of paranoia) must be recognized and can only be regarded with empathy.

However, the concern, which is central to the thesis of this book, is that these fears are being *exploited* and tragically *misdirected* by the Israeli Lobby, which is responsible for the strange attitude of the American Jewish community of "non-involvement in Israel's internal affairs." In the meantime, the *real dangers* are being ignored.

As will be discussed in subsequent chapters, the Lobby's activities and its blind and uncritical attitude toward the Likud government has brought Israel to the brink of disaster.

It is often said that Israel is the earthly embodiment of the spirit of the Jewish people; and that the fate of the Diaspora is bound up with the fate of Israel. How, then, can the Jewish establishment in America take the attitude that it is "not our concern how Israel is governed?"

American Jewry not only have the right but the *obligation* to become involved with the fate of Israel before it is too late. While there is still time, the Lobby ought to use its power and influence to lobby *the Knesset*. Let it use its abundant campaign funds to support and elect candidates to defeat the Likud government. Never before has the need been so great for the moral support of the American Jewish community on behalf of the voices for peace in Israel.

In an article appearing in the *Jerusalem Post*, December 31, 1988, edition, "The Diaspora's Right to Intervene," Henry Siegman, Executive Vice President of the American Jewish Congress, provides the answer to the mystery of the strange reluctance of American Jews to become actively involved in Israel's fate—*they are intimidated by the political ploy of the Likud government* which shouts down any attempt by American Jews to offer constructive criticism by accusing them of *"collaboration with Israel's enemies."* Any bona fide efforts for peace coming from the Diaspora are rejected as *"outrageous interference in the internal affairs of Israel."*

This Likud technique is as effective in silencing Jewish criticism from the

Diaspora as the "anti-Semitic" charge is in stifling Gentile expressions of opinion. Since everybody is either a Jew or a Gentile, the Likud cleverly makes itself immune to *any* outside criticism.

The Israeli Lobby's party line, that there should be no criticism of Israel from American Jews, is no surprise since the Likud is the Lobby's client, to which the Lobby's loyalty is obviously pledged.

Siegman claims that, were the Labor government in power and negotiating to exchange land for peace, the Likud would "not hesitate for a fraction of a moment to seek Diaspora Jewry *intervention* including appeals to U.S. Congressmen":

They would do so despite their insistence *today* that to invoke such outside intervention constitutes outrageous interference in the internal affairs of Israel. And I would understand and accept their actions in those circumstances, for they would be acting out of a genuine conviction that they are preventing Israel's dissolution. What I do not accept is *their unwillingness to grant to those who disagree with them as to where Israel's real security lies the Jewish legitimacy that they arrogantly claim only for themselves.*[33] [Emphasis supplied]

The revelation that the survival of Israel is being held hostage to the political hypocrisy of the Likud is frightening.

In the same article, Siegman points out that the time has now come for the Diaspora to play a new and vital role and that the responsibilities of American Jewry have now changed dramatically in the face of the new challenges. These, he says, are of a quite different nature for American Jews:

Now, however, a new situation has been created, for the goal is no longer outlasting the Arabs. At least half of Israel—half its government, half its people and considerably more than half its military experts—has concluded that to do nothing may invite disaster. *Israel's security and survival, according to this view, now depend not on maintaining the status quo but on changing it. Maintaining American Jewish unity in support of the status quo has thus become a politically irrelevant goal insofar as Israel's security and survival are concerned*—if those who see the status quo as Israel's deadliest enemy are correct.

American Jewry has thus entered a new and terribly unsettling phase in which the old slogans have become irrelevant. Unity is hardly an end in itself. *Inevitably, American Jews who care passionately about Israel's survival must deal with the substance of the issues, and cannot satisfy themselves with "maintaining Jewish unity" if that unity serves to perpetuate the status quo.* If the status quo were, in fact, to lead to Israel's undoing, it would be scant comfort for *American Jews to point out that at least they preserved Jewish unity—while Israel went down the tube!*

There are some who maintain that despite these changes American Jews—for a variety of reasons—have no moral right to interfere in questions that affect Israel's security. In real life, however, Jews who care passionately about Israel will seek to *influence what happens there precisely on issues that affect its existence,* because their conscience and guts will not permit them not to. They will not stop to ask whether there exists theoretical justification for their intervention; their deep caring is, for them, sufficient cause.

American Jews no longer enjoy the luxury that they once had of avoiding policy debates on Israel which might detract from their central preoccupation with the maintenance of a united political front in the U.S. Given the new realities in Israel, it could hardly be otherwise. If Israelis are deeply divided over what policies serve their country's well-being and, indeed, its very survival, those divisions will inevitably be reflected in the life of *American Jewry as well.*[34] [Emphasis supplied]

CHAPTER IX

American Jewry and Free Speech

F ROM THE foregoing chapters, the reader would be justified in
assuming that the extensive and superbly organized Israeli Lobby,
jointly with AIPAC, speak for the entire American Jewish community.

Fortunately, this is not true but, nevertheless, they pretend to so speak
and succeed in this pretension only because open dissent in the American
Jewish community is not allowed. Any breaking ranks or public disagreement with the policies of the Likud government is considered equivalent to
"treason."

The government of Israel gives high priority to maintaining a show of
unity among U.S. Jews. This unity is regarded as a main line of Israel's
defense—second in importance only to the Israeli army—and essential to
retaining the support Israel must have from the U.S. government.

It is scarcely believable, but the average American Jew is subject to more
restraints on what opinions he can express publicly about the Israeli
government's policies than a non-Jew. More importantly, the penalties for
violating these rules are drastic. The Gentile may have to endure the
consequences of the charge of "anti-Semitism," but the Jewish dissenter in
America is "exiled." An Israeli Jew is free to write or say things for which
an American Jew would be ostracized. Few Jews are foolhardy enough to
break ranks, no matter how strong their opinions.

The Jewish community is, of course, united in their support of the State of Israel but this does not mean that the Israeli government's actions or policies are approved by all, or even most, Jews. However, the Jewish establishment insists that what must be avoided, at all costs, is the appearance of "disunity." In its efforts to quell criticism, the Israeli Lobby's first goal is to still Jewish critics. In this quest it receives strong support from the Israeli government.

Therefore, for an individual Jew to speak out against the Israeli government is unthinkable—the Jewish version of hara-kiri. The Jewish community, as is true of many ethnic groups, is socially and businesswise relatively close and cohesive. There are many interwoven and interdependent relationships which must be maintained and Israel has served, for many years, as a great unifier of the Jewish people and a focal point for Jewish solidarity and generosity.

Many major social events revolve around fund-raising campaigns for various Israeli causes. Exclusive social gatherings are often held to meet some special dignitary from Israel. Jewish clubs are demanding on the allegiance of their membership to the Jewish establishment. An ill-chosen or too frank a remark can cause a total loss of status in the community.

This artificial unity, however, has been self-defeating and has caused great damage to Israel. As Harkabi says, the Likud has stayed in power only by convincing the Israeli people that American Jewry *is behind them 100 percent*. This has created the bizarre situation where it appears that approximately 50 percent of Jews in Israel support the Likud, while nearly 100 percent of the Jews in America do.[1]

This, of course, can only happen because the Likud cannot control free speech in Israel, but it *can* in America.

In his courageous book entitled *They Dare To Speak Out,* former Congressman Paul Findley recalls an event involving his friend, Phil Klutznick, from which we quote:

The world was horrified when it learned of the massacre of hundreds of civilians in the Sabra and Shatila Palestinian camps at Beirut. After four months of silence, Klutznick spoke at a luncheon in New York in February 1983. He launched a new crusade, pleading for the right of Jews to dissent:

We cannot be one in our need for each other, and be separated in our ability to speak or write the truth as each of us sees it. The real strength of Jewish life has been its sense of commitment and willingness to fight for the right [to dissent] even among ourselves.

In November, Klutznick took his crusade to Jerusalem, attending, along with forty other Jews from the U.S. and fifteen other countries, a four-day meeting of the International Center for Peace in the Middle East. Klutznick drew applause when he told his audience, which included several Israelis: "If you listen to us when we speak good of Israel, then you must listen to us when we speak ill. Otherwise we will lose our credibility, and the American government will not listen to us at all."

Despite his proven commitment to Israel, his leadership in the Jewish community, and his unquestioned integrity, Philip Klutznick was rejected or scorned by many of his establishment contemporaries. Two professionals in the Jewish Lobby community, for example, say simply that Klutznick is not listened to any longer. One of them adds sadly, "I admire Phil Klutznick, but he is virtually a non-person in the Jewish community." The other is harsh and bitter, linking Klutznick with other critics of the Israeli government as "an enemy of the Jewish people."[2]

Charles Fishbein, for 11 years a fundraiser and executive of the Jewish National Fund, provides a partial explanation for the treatment Klutznick has received:

When you speak up in the Jewish community without a proper forum, you are shunted aside. You are dismissed as one who has been "gotten to." It's nonsense, but it is effective. The Jewish leaders you hear about tend to be very very wealthy givers. Some give to Jewish causes primarily as an investment, to establish a good business and social relationship. Such people will not speak up for a non-conformist like Klutznick for fear of jeopardizing their investment.

These thoughts echo that of Klutznick himself: "Try to understand. See it from their standpoint. Why should they go public? They don't want any trouble. They are part of the community. They have neighbors. They help out. They contribute." He pauses, purses his lips a bit, then adds, "They have standing. And they want to keep it."

Klutznick smiles. "They say to me, 'You are absolutely right in what you say and do, but I can't. I can't stand up as you do.'"[3]

In private, however, many American Jews hold positions in sharp disagreement with official Israeli policies. A 1983 survey by the American Jewish Committee revealed that about half of the U.S. Jews favor a homeland for the Palestinians on the West Bank and Gaza, and recommend that Israel stop the expansion of settlements in order to encourage peace negotiations. Three-fourths want Israel to talk to the Palestine Liberation Organization, if it recognizes Israel and renounces terrorism. Only 21 percent want Israel to maintain permanent control over the West Bank. On each of these propositions, the plurality of American Jews takes issue with the policies and declarations of the Israeli government.

A plurality also holds that American Jews individually, as well as in organized groups, should feel free to criticize Israeli policy publicly. Of those surveyed, 70 percent say U.S. Jewish organizations should feel free to criticize. On this question, even Jewish leaders say they welcome criticism; 40 percent say organizations should feel free to criticize; 37 percent disagree. This means that only one-third of the leaders say they want to stifle organizational criticism of Israel. The vote by individual Jews for free and open debate is even stronger. Only 31 percent declare that American Jews individually should not criticize Israeli policy publicly; 57 percent disagree. On this question, leaders and non-leaders vote exactly alike. While American Jews say they strongly oppose some Israeli policies and believe that organizations and individuals should feel free to criticize these policies openly, the simple fact is that public criticism is almost non-existent.[4]

The explanation for this seeming contradiction is that publicly Jews must speak unanimously, but privately they can speak anonymously. Indeed, the premise upon which this book is written is that there is a large Jewish constituency in this country, as well as in Israel, which will support a peace plan which both ensures Israel's security and is acceptable to its enemies.

In the past, all attempts to break the grip of AIPAC have failed. Of the more than 200 principal Jewish organizations functioning on a national scale, only the *Jewish Agenda* and its predecessor, *Breira,* have challenged any stated policy of the Israeli government.

In return for their occasional criticism of Israel's policies, the two organizations were ostracized and kept out of the organized Jewish community. *Breira* lasted only five years. Organized in 1973, its peak national membership was about 1,000. Named for the Hebrew word meaning "alternative," it called on Jewish institutions to be "open to serious debate," and proposed "a comprehensive peace between Israel, the Arab states, and a Palestinian homeland that is ready to live in peace alongside

Israel." Prominent in its leadership were Rabbis Arnold Jacob Wolf, David Wolf Silverman, Max Ticktin, David Saperstein, and Balfour Brickner.

The counterattack was harsh. *The National Journal* reports that *Breira* was "bitterly attacked by many leaders of the Jewish establishment" and that a *Breira* meeting was "invaded and ransacked" by members of the militant Jewish Defense League. Some members of *Breira* came under intense pressure to quit either the organization or their jobs. Jewish leaders were warned to avoid *Breira*, or fund-raising would be hurt.[5]

Israeli officials joined rabbis in denouncing the organization. Carolyn Toll, a reporter for the *Chicago Tribune* and formerly on the board of directors of *Breira*, quotes a rabbi: "My bridges are burned. Once you take a position like this [challenging Israeli positions], the organized Jewish community closes you out." Officials from the Israeli consulates in Boston and Philadelphia warned Jews against attending a *Breira* conference.

It was soon barred from associating with other Jewish groups. In June 1983, its Washington, D.C. chapter was refused membership in the Jewish Community Council, a group which included 260 religious, educational, fraternal, and social service organizations.[6]

Toll laments the "suppression of free speech in American Jewish institutions—the pressures that prevent dovish or dissident Jews from organizing in synagogues, the Jewish community centers, and meetings of major national Jewish organizations" and denunciations of American Friends Service Committee representatives as "anti-Semitics" and "dupes of the Palestine Liberation Organization" for insisting that "any true peace must include a viable state for the Palestinians."[7]

Journalism is the occupation in which Jews most often and most consistently voice criticism of Israel. Richard Cohen of the *Washington Post* is a notable example.

During Israel's 1982 invasion of Lebanon, Cohen warned: "The administration can send Begin a message that he does not have an infinite line of credit in America—that we will not, for instance, approve the bombing of innocent civilians."[8]

In a later column, Cohen summarized the reaction to his criticism of Israeli policy: "My phone these days is an instrument of torture. Merely to answer it runs the risk of being insulted. The mail is equally bad. The letters are vicious, some of them quite personal." *He noted that U.S. Jews are held to a different standard than Israelis when they question Israel's policies.*[9]

Mark Bruzonsky, a persistent journalistic critic of these Israeli excesses, writes, "There's no way in the world that a Jew can avoid a savage and personal vendetta if his intent is to write a truthful and meaningful account of what he has experienced."[10]

Similar questions are raised by Nat Hentoff, a Jewish columnist who frequently criticizes Israel and challenges the conscience of his fellow Jews in his column for the *Village Voice*. During the Israeli invasion of Lebanon in 1982, he lamented:

> At no time during his visit here [in the U.S.] was Prime Minister Begin given any indication that there are some of us who fear that he and Ariel Sharon are destroying Israel from within. Forget the Conference of Presidents of Major American Jewish Organizations and the groups they represent. They have long since decided to say nothing in public that is critical of Israel.

Hentoff deplored the intimidation that silences most Jewish critics:

> I know staff workers for the American Jewish Congress and the American Jewish Committee who agonize about their failure to speak out, even on their own time, against Israeli injustice. They don't, because they figure they'll get fired if they do.[11]

Peer pressure does not always muffle Jewish voices, especially if the voice is "peerless." Such a man was Nahum Goldmann, who pioneered in establishing the State of Israel and helped to organize its crucial underpinnings of support in the U.S. and who later became a frequent critic of Israeli policy. He played a crucial role in the founding of Israel, meeting its early financial problems, influencing its leaders, and organizing a powerful constituency for it in the U.S. His service to Zionism spanned nearly fifty years. During World War I, when Palestine was still part of the Ottoman Empire, Goldmann tried to persuade Turkish authorities to allow Jewish immigration. In the 1930s, he advocated the Zionist cause at the League of Nations. During the Truman administration, he lobbied for the United Nations resolution calling for partition of Palestine and the establishment of Israel.[12]

When Israel was struggling to build its economy, Goldmann negotiated with West German Chancellor Konrad Adenauer the agreement under which the Germans paid $30 billion in compensation and restitution to Israel and individual Jews.

Goldmann's disagreement with Israeli policy toward the Arabs was his central concern. To those who criticized his advocacy of a Palestinian state, he responded:

If they do not believe that Arab hostility can some day be alleviated, then we might just as well liquidate Israel at once, so as to save the millions of Jews who live there. . . . There is no hope for a Jewish state which has to face another 50 years of struggle against Arab enemies.

In 1980 he warned:

Blind support of the Begin government may be more menacing for Israel than any danger of Arab attack. American Jewry is more generous than any other group in American life and is doing great things. . . . But by misusing its political influence, by exaggerating the aggressiveness of the Jewish Lobby in Washington, by giving the Begin regime the impression that the Jews are strong enough to force the American administration and Congress to follow every Israeli desire, they lead Israel on a ruinous path which, if continued, may lead to dire consequences.

He blamed the Israeli Lobby for U.S. failures to bring about a comprehensive settlement in the Middle East. "It was to a very large degree because of electoral considerations, fear of the pro-Israeli Lobby, and of the Jewish vote."

He warned of trouble ahead if the Lobby continued its present course. "It is now slowly becoming something of a negative factor. Not only does it distort the expectations and political calculations of Israel, but the time may not be far off when American public opinion will be sick and tired of the demands of Israel and the aggressiveness of American Jewry."

In 1978, two years before he wrote his alarmed evaluation of the Israeli Lobby, *New York* magazine reported that Goldmann had privately urged officials of the Carter administration "to break the back" of the Lobby: "Goldmann pleaded with the administration to stand firm and not back off from confrontations with the organized Jewish community as other administrations had done." Unless this was done, he argued, "President Carter's plans for a Middle East settlement would die in stillbirth." His words were prophetic. The comprehensive settlement Carter sought was frustrated by the intransigence of Israel and its U.S. Lobby.[13]

There are, however, voices in Israel and the U.S. which are trying to change these attitudes. Indicative of this is an article appearing in *The Wall Street Journal*, January 7, 1987, edition, entitled "American Jews are Increasingly Divided in Stance Toward Israel," from which the following is excerpted:

Twenty years ago, Israel's stunning victory in the June 1967 Six-Day War united American Jews behind the tiny Mideast nation as never before. But today, a younger generation has begun openly to criticize Israeli society and its leaders, signaling the end of the era of unquestioning devotion to Israel by U.S. Jews.

"Once, there was a kind of uneasiness on the part of American Jews about interfering in the internal affairs of Israel," says Rabbi Wolfe Kelman, the executive vice president of Conservative Judaism's Rabbinical Assembly. *"But now there's a growing readiness to say, 'Hey, wait a minute, what's going on over there?' "*

What's going on is that Israel is changing. It is increasingly dominated by religiously fundamentalist and politically militant Jewish immigrants from Arab countries, rather than the European Holocaust survivors who built the Israel most American Jews identify with.

A Telling Survey

"In the past, American Jews had an undifferentiated, passionate, idealized, romanticized view of Israeli society. But that has broken down as they have become more aware of Israel's conflicts between left and right, religious and secular, Jew and Arab, rich and poor," says Steven Cohen, a sociologist at New York's Queens College. A nationwide survey he took last year found that only 63 percent of U.S. Jews say that caring deeply about Israel is an important part of their Jewishness, down from 78 percent in his 1983 survey.

Attitudes began to change noticeably after Israel's 1982 invasion deep into Lebanon; many U.S. Jews complained that the push to the outskirts of Beirut went far beyond Israel's need to defend itself. Recently, American Jews have been disturbed by disclosures that Jerusalem recruited an American spy, Jonathan Pollard. Israel's reaction to the spy case, generally perceived as uncooperative, and its reluctance to cooperate with investigations of its role in the Iran-Contra scandal also rankled many American supporters.

Indeed, anger and disappointment with Israel have been so intense that some worry that these feelings could eventually translate into a gradual weakening of Jerusalem's political influence in Congress. To be sure, it is generally agreed that any effort to cut the $3 billion a year in U.S. aid to Israel would be resoundingly defeated by legislators. And support for Israel's survival and national security remains rocksolid within the Jewish community.[14]

However, the excesses and incompetence of the Likud government, and the recognition among many Jews that Israel is in grave peril, has caused several new organizations to speak out. A recent report appearing in the *Jerusalem Post,* by Charles Hoffman, mentions one of them under the heading "Left Wing Jews in U.S. Hit at Shamir Policy":

Woody Allen, Arthur Miller, Philip Roth, Betty Friedan and a group of other prominent American Jewish intellectuals have published a full-page advertisement in the *New York Times* denouncing the policies of Prime Minister Shamir as "immoral, contrary to what is best in our Jewish tradition and destructive to the best interests of Israel and American Jewry."

"No Mr. Shamir," the ad, which appears today, reads, "don't assume that American Jews support your policies toward the Palestinians." The statement calls on Shamir to start negotiations with the PLO and not to rule out the possibility that these talks might lead to the establishment of a Palestinian state.

The ad is the first public act of the Committee for Judaism and Social Justice, a national group organized during the past few months by *Tikkun* magazine. The committee, which plans to open an office in Washington, describes itself as a liberal, progressive alternative to AIPAC and the Conference of Presidents of Major American Jewish Organizations.

Other signatories to the statement include scholar Michael Walzer, journalist Carl Bernstein, *Tikkun* editor Michael Lerner, former "Yippie" leader Abbie Hoffman, novelist Marge Piercy, producer Norman Lear, Rabbi Marshall Meyer, Rabbi Arthur Waskow, and scholar Irving Howe. The list also incudes Stanley Sheinbaum of Los Angeles, who was one of the five American Jews to meet last year with Yasser Arafat in Stockholm; and Prof. Jerome Segal of the University of Maryland, who drafted a plan for Palestinian statehood last year.[15]

The *Jerusalem Post* of June 4, 1988, contains the following report, datelined New York, and entitled "Aloni Blasts Jewish Leaders in U.S. for 'Keep Quiet' Policy."

Citizens Rights Movement MK Shulamit Aloni has blasted the Conference of Presidents of Major American Jewish Organizations as "rich and fat people . . . who go to Israel to rub shoulders with important people at nice dinners, and then come back to the U.S. and rub shoulders with more important people."

Aloni, who has just completed a two-week North American speaking tour, said *she was convinced by the warm reception she had received that most American Jews opposed the positions of Prime Minister Shamir.* She said they are also turning against the view of Morris Abram, chairman of the Presidents' Conference, that American Jews should not take a public stand on issues relating to the Middle East peace process.

Discussing the American Jewish leadership, Aloni said, "I never respected Abram and the rest of these rich and fat people, because I don't know who they represent. . . . *They say that [American] Jews should keep quiet about what is happening in Israel and take a position of 'My country right or wrong.'* But they never tell the right wing to keep quiet. It is only the liberals who are told to shut up."

Aloni said that she had received warm receptions from synagogue audiences and UJA-Federation groups in cities like New York, Miami, Montreal, and Toronto. "The Federation people in Miami, Toronto and Montreal were against me when I came. But as I spoke, the whole atmosphere changed. People came up to me afterwards and thanked me for giving them back their dignity and pride in being Jewish."

Aloni told Jewish audiences: "If you have the right to speak out on human rights in countries all around the world—including Jews in the Soviet Union—*you certainly have the right to speak out on human rights in Israel. How wrong does Israel have to be before you speak up?*"[16]

We have previously referred to, and quoted from, an article written by Henry Siegman, Executive Vice President of the American Jewish Congress, appearing in the December 31, 1988, edition of the *Jerusalem Post.* The article is entitled "The Diaspora's Right to Intervene," in which Siegman points out that Jewish "unity" is pointless if the result is that "Israel goes down the tube."[17]

The unanswered question is whether enough voices will be raised loudly enough and soon enough to deal with the crisis at hand.

CHAPTER X

Israel in Crisis

THE WAR IN Lebanon differed from other Israeli wars in that it was, without any doubt, an offensive war, fought less for the benefit of Israel than for the personal aggrandizement of certain of its leaders, Menachem Begin and Ariel Sharon.

THE LEBANESE WAR: 1982-1983

Perlmutter, in his book entitled *Israel: The Partitioned State,* discusses it under the caption "Sharon's War in Lebanon," from which the following is quoted:

> The start of the war was planned with measured debate by a government which set itself a limited and specific goal in response to what it perceived as an intolerable and continued threat to its national security. The man whose responsibility it was to conduct that war, in order to accomplish his own plans set about *to manipulate his own prime minister, the cabinet, and the armed forces,* thus extending the scope and duration of the war and its tremendous potential for larger tragedy, political fiasco, and disaster. *Just as important, he misled Israel's American allies.*
>
> The blame for the Lebanese war does not rest solely with former Israeli Defense Minister Ariel Sharon; understanding the situation and events defies that kind of simplicity. But *if there is a single person who*

bears the lion's share of the responsibility for the war's steady descent into disaster, it is Sharon. His plans led directly to the involvement of Syria in the war, to the tragedy at Sabra and Shatila, to the diplomatic and military entry of the United States into the swamplike arena of Lebanon, and to the final collapse of Menachem Begin. *Indirectly his actions led to the disaster that befell the contingent-without-a-mission of U.S. Marines who died in a bomb attack on their barracks in Beirut.*[1] [Emphasis supplied]

Perlmutter points out that Begin's motives fitted Sharon's ambitions:

Sharon was helped in his ambitions by Begin's vision of fulfilling the old Revisionist-Jabotinsky dream of Eretz Israel. Begin saw the Lebanon operation as his crowning achievement, and he therefore did not need much persuading. Begin probably envisioned the strike as ensuring that he could be the prime minister who, by destroying the PLO, created a secure and united Eretz Israel. *Sharon probably saw himself riding in triumph like some Roman praetor entering Jerusalem, the next king of Israel.*[2] [Emphasis supplied]

Harkabi's judgment is even harsher. In his book, *Israel's Fateful Hour,* under the heading of "The Wages of Deception," Harkabi writes:

The Lebanon War was accompanied by lies and deceit at the highest political levels. Defense Minister Sharon has been repeatedly accused of having misled Begin and the cabinet. This explanation was disseminated not by the opposition but by sources within the Likud who are close to Mr. Begin. The accuracy of official announcements by Israel's military spokesmen, which had always been considered trustworthy, now became suspect. The Israeli Army is a people's army, and the home front soon became aware that army and government communiques contradicted what the public learned from first-hand observers.

To provide a justification for the war the Likud government also lied to the public by grossly exaggerating the terrorist acts conducted from Lebanon. Responding to a question in the Knesset, Defense Minister Rabin said that during the eleven months of the cease-fire that preceded the war the northern settlements were attacked only twice, *and that during this period Israel had suffered a total of two killed and six wounded from terrorist attacks. Moreover these attacks were preceded by Israeli air force strikes* in response to the planting of a bomb on a bus and the attack on the Israeli ambassador in London, Shlomo Argov. It was distortion at the highest political level *to present terrorism as Israel's chief problem, when the major threats are in fact the demographic balance and the menace of war. Even the official pretext for the war.*

The attack on Ambassador Argov was at bottom a lie, since it was not carried out by the PLO, but by the secessionist faction of Abu Nidal that had also assassinated PLO leaders.[3] [Emphasis supplied]

Harkabi repeats what he has said elsewhere in his book, namely, that calls for a war against "terrorism" are often used by demagogues to distract attention from the real issues. In Harkabi's words:

Terrorism is grist for the demagogue's mill, the perfect topic for inciting public opinion, arousing popular fury, acquiring popularity. It is all too easy to harp on motifs like "the right of Israelis to live in peace," and "we must use strong-arm tactics against terrorism," and so on. As I have already said, the problem is that there is no quick fix for terrorism; no military operation can put an end to it.

The most damning indictment of Begin's motives in starting the war in Lebanon is found in these words from Harkabi's account of the war.

Begin's principal motive in launching the war was his fear of the momentum of the peace process—that he might yet be called upon to honor his signature to the Camp David Accords and withdraw from the territories. Calling the Lebanon War "The War for the Peace of Galilee" is more than a misnomer. It would have been more honest to call it "The War to Safeguard the Occupation of the West Bank."[4] [Emphasis supplied]

The disastrous war in Lebanon accelerated the decline in Israeli society from the zenith it had reached at the end of the 1967 war. Prior to the November 1988 elections, the moderates in Israel had expected, or at least hoped, that the fierce emotional fires that had been fueled by the preachings of the religious radicals and the demagoguery of the Likud, would die down and be brought under control. As the November 1988 elections proved, it was a vain hope. The election results came as a shock to many people because of the significant political gains made by the religious nationalist extremist factions in the Likud party.

[173]

Earlier, Amos Perlmutter had made a pre-election forecast, which appeared in the *Los Angeles Times* edition of September 28, 1988. In it, Perlmutter offers some profound observations concerning the political scene in Israel and expresses his feelings of nostalgia for the Israel of the past and his sense of foreboding for the Israel of the future.

Perlmutter's article is entitled " 'Beautiful Israel' Wanes, Youthful Dream is Shed in a Hard Shift to Right." His observations are, in part, as follows:

The 1988 Israeli elections, and their aftermath, will be a thunderous sea change in the 40-year history of Israeli politics.

Even though the early polls seem to show a virtual deadlock, very much reflective of the American election, the end result will be the culmination of a trend that will mark a solid turnabout in Israeli politics and society.

The era of the "beautiful Israel"—dominated by such symbols as the Kibbutzim, the pioneer spirit, the leading political and philosophical tenets of socialist Zionism—is on the wane, if not over altogether.

That era reached its apogee with the 1967 war, but it was the results of the war that also laid the seeds of its decline—a decline that began in the wake of the 1973 war, continued into 1977 with Menachem Begin's startling electoral victory and remains on a steady downward pace to this day. The values of socialist Zionism are no longer dominant. Instead, one can find in Israel today the new values—a spirit of *continued territorial expansionism, shrill patriotism, an exaggerated confidence in the military might of the Israeli Defense Force, a rigid fundamentalist belief in Israeli moral righteousness and a deep suspicion that amounts to a denial of the peace process, especially after Camp David and the disastrous invasion of Lebanon. "Complete Israel," not peace with the Arabs, is the determining political issue.*

The outright cynicism that prevails about the peace process seems to be justified by ongoing events. . . .

The uprising has also had the result of offering ripe ground for political opportunists who are very much to the right of Likud, which is basically *a right-of-center party. They have gone so far as to advocate the transfer of Arabs from the West Bank.*

The difference between the extremes in the Labor and Likud parties is that the Laborites want to somehow extricate themselves from the West Bank and the Palestinians, while the *Likudites want to transfer the Palestinians bodily out of the occupied Territories and move them to*

Lebanon's Bekaa Valley. There is no love held for the Arabs in Israel. The suspicion is growing about the loyalty of Israeli Arabs who themselves, in the uprising's wake, have undergone a Palestinianization process.

The uprising, the bankruptcy of the peace process, the daily atrocities and violence have helped accelerate the change of direction in Israeli politics. Israel's electorate *appears to be moving to the right of center,* and the 1988 election may institutionalize that change, taking the last giant leap—begun in 1981 and continued in 1984—*of establishing a Likud hegemony for the next three decades.*

A huge shift—demographic, intellectual, political and ideological—is taking place as a new Israeli generation—different in leaders, ideas, orientation and action—takes over.[5] [Emphasis supplied]

Israel's crisis is deeply rooted in the moral, economic, political, and international chaos created by twelve years of Likud misrule. Among the multiplicity of ills, from which Israel is suffering, are the following:

1. Israel's economy continues to deteriorate. At best, it survives only on a life support system which requires enormous annual transfusions from the U.S. and the American Jewish community.
2. The Intifada, and the government's attempts at repression, are destroying the esprit de corps of the Israeli army and are a continuing drain on Israel's resources, estimated at two and a half million dollars per day. Israel's military leaders (with the exception of Ariel Sharon) know, and have said, that the battle against the Palestinian uprising is unwinnable.
3. There has been a significant defection and disillusionment among the intellectuals, both in Israel and the Diaspora, and support among them for the Likud government has largely eroded away.
4. Immigration to Israel has slowed to a trickle as most Soviet Jews have spurned Israel in favor of other countries.
5. The emigration of educated and talented Israelis to the U.S., and a disproportionate increase of the Oriental Jewish population (Sephardim), are changing the demographic composition of the population of Israel in favor of the less educated and more radical Sephardim.
6. The Likud years have seen a rapid increase in corruption at all levels of government, as well as in the private sector.
7. The brutality of the Likud's "iron fist" policy in the West Bank and Gaza has strained, perhaps irretrievably, the loyalty of the Arab populations of Israel proper and has shocked most of the civilized world.

The international situation is even more grim.

Menachem Begin, during his regime, earned the distinction of being perhaps the most hated head of government in the world. The world leaders recently have expressed their feelings toward the Likud government of Israel, and its arrogance, by inflicting the worst humiliation ever suffered by a member nation, when they voted (150-2) to move the U.N. session from New York to Geneva just to hear Yassar Arafat speak. Much of the sympathy of the world for the Jewish people, generated by the tragedy of the Holocaust, has been dissipated by the Likud leadership of Israel and its treatment of the Palestinians who now have the moral support of most of mankind.

None of Israel's desperate problems, internal and external, can be solved without peace. With peace can come solutions—without it, Israel's situation is hopeless.

In its hour of peril, its leadership, the Likud party, is bankrupt, dominated by a clique of religious nationalist extremists who are destroying Israel from within and isolating it from without. The Israeli ship of state is a rudderless, storm-tossed vessel with a battery of loose cannons crashing about the deck, while Captain Yitzhak Shamir and Steersman Ariel Sharon are shouting conflicting and incomprehensible orders.

Yehoshafat Harkabi, in his book *Israel's Fateful Hour*, expresses his views as follows:

> *In recent years Israel has experienced massive decline: a worsening of the public mood*, the vulgarization of political thought and language, a degeneration of norms of public conduct, permissiveness in state affairs, *demagoguery*—the good of the country shunted aside in the pursuit of short-term party gains—the domination of mediocrity, *the proliferation of falsehoods and rampant deception of the people by their rule, a magnification of domestic tensions. The responsibility for this decline belongs to a great extent to the Likud government.* This is the most serious result of the Likud's misrule, much more serious than either the economic crisis or the Lebanon War. . . .
>
> Israel was never perfect, but nevertheless it earned a reputation as a symbol of cultural and social innovation; even its military excellence was attributed to its citizens' public-spiritedness.
>
> *Today, however, unethical conduct in public life arouses no surprise in Israel: it has become the normal state of affairs.* Brutal criticisms of government activities in the press makes no stir in the public, as the

written word has been greatly devalued, along with everything else. *When a responsible newspaper like* Ha'aretz *can open its editorial column with the statement "The fraudulent acts of Ariel Sharon and Menachem Begin dragged the country into Lebanon on the basis of a false claim" [May 27, 1985] without a political earthquake's ensuing, the national conscience is clearly deadened, and perhaps dead.*[6] [Emphasis supplied]

None of Israel's crises compares in gravity with the crisis of leadership from which all else flows. The State of Israel, the earthly symbol of the Jewish people, has fallen into the hands of demagogues and fanatics who, in the name of religion, are leading the people of Israel headlong toward catastrophe.

Since support for the above-stated position is found in facts and circumstances, which both Jews (Reformed and Conservative) and non-Jews will find difficult to believe, it is necessary to rely upon sources whose credibility and authority are beyond question.

In an article appearing in the *Jerusalem Post,* December 3, 1988, entitled "The Threats Are from Within," Abba Eban, one of the few statesmen left in Israel, summarizes his views in this respect:

The existential threats to Israel and Zionism arise from within. They flow from disintegrative tendencies in Israeli society, illustrated by the spread of religious intolerance, chauvinism, fundamentalism, the eclipse of Enlightenment values, the retreat from scientific rationalism and, above all, by the incongruous and untenable structure dictated by the exercise of coercive rule over a foreign nation which inflicts more harm on Israel than upon its adversaries.

The first two years of the national unity government opened horizons of potential peace which the last two years have blocked. The solitary hope is that the Israeli public and the Jewish world may have been shocked by the atmosphere of the past few months into the realization that Israel's body has grown stronger while its soul has been undermined.[7]

RELIGIOUS FANATICISM

In his book entitled *Israel's Fateful Hour,* to which we have several times earlier referred, Yehoshafat Harkabi discusses the awakening of Nationalistic Religious Extremism *and the coming crisis in the occupied territories.* Harkabi quotes many sources to support his theses:

Many in the religious camp find justification for an annexation of the occupied territories, or at least a prohibition against withdrawal, in Nachmanides's (1194-1270) commentary on Maimonides's (1135-1204) *Book of Commandments:* "We are commanded to inherit the land that God gave to Abraham, Isaac and Jacob and must not leave it in the hands of any other nation. . . . We must not leave the Land in the hands of the [seven Canaanite nations] or of any other people in any generation." Rabbi Zvi Yehudah Kook, the mentor of Gush Emunim, commented as follows: *"These are explicit words of halakha. . . . The main thrust of the commandment is conquest by the state, Jewish national rule in this holy territory."*

Nachmanides's words, then, are the starting point for the politico-religious conceptions of a broad stratum of Orthodox Jews. For them, halakha is binding, except in rare cases where life is threatened. *Religious ordinances have absolute validity; historical circumstances cannot contradict the Creator of the Universe. The very existence of such a law is a guarantee that reality will not contravene it, and so there is no need to trouble oneself with calculations of feasibility.*[8]

The awakening of a nationalistic Judaism was a slow, evolving process, following the victory in *the Six Day War, which was interpreted as a manifestation of God's intervention.* For religious Jews, the conquest of parts of the historic land of Israel in this war cast a brilliant light on the Zionist enterprise. Taken together with the victory of 1967, the achievements of Zionism were now seen as the harbinger of a new age of great religious and national eminence. *Significant sectors of Israeli Judaism adopted Herut's position of entitlement to the occupied lands, which were now referred to by their biblical names, Judea and Samaria. The religious Gush Emunim* movement assumed the principal role in pioneering settlement activities in the occupied territories. The bond between religious Judaism and the state was changing. Whereas in its old borders the state had been merely a secular refuge, for many religious circles its new boundaries, which included the holy places in Jerusalem, Hebron, and elsewhere, endowed it with a theological significance. The Yom Kippur War and withdrawal from territory on the Egyptian and Syrian borders did not controvert the notion that a new age had begun— the "beginning of the Redemption."

Thus, within the Jewish state, *Orthodox Judaism has changed its stance in recent years: instead of being content to be a follower it has demanded a role of leadership, insisting that both domestic and foreign policy be derived from religious law.* Where Herut opposes conceding and withdrawing from the West Bank for nationalist reasons (with security considerations as a secondary factor), many religious circles offer religious arguments against withdrawal. *For them, the security problems associated with withdrawal are secondary to the religious behests:* because of the achievements of the Six Day War in recovering holy places, militant Jewish nationalism has become a significant factor in bringing closer the ultimate expression of Judaism—Redemption. The relationship between religion and policy has become more intimate; religion in the service of national policy and national policy as the implementation of religious right from a position of relative influence.[9] [Emphasis supplied]

Harkabi quotes a public statement by the prominent Rabbi Zvi Yehudah Kook:

I tell you explicitly that *the Torah forbids us to surrender even one inch of our liberated land.* There are no conquests here and we are not occupying foreign lands; we are returning to our home, to the inheritance of our ancestors. *There is no Arab land here, only the inheritance of our God*—and the more the world gets used to this thought the better it will be for them and for all of us ("Year by Year," 1968). [Emphasis supplied]

Harkabi continues:

In this view, violating the prohibition against withdrawal will hurt not only the Jews but the whole world.

In generations past, the fundamental concept of being the Chosen People served the Jews as a shield against persecution and a consolation in distress. Since 1967 it has taken on an aggressive significance *as a license to act in contradiction to accepted political norms.* The idea of being "a people that dwells apart, not reckoned among the nations" (Numbers 23:9) *has become sanctioned for deviant behavior in the international arena. International law, public opinion, the United Nations, the superpowers—for the religious extremists none of these matter.* In the world at large, religion cannot provide legal title to a territory. But for those religious extremists who believe it does, the biblical promise of the Land of Israel for the people of Israel is transformed from a religious and spiritual matter into a necessity that requires immediate implementation.... *In the world view of the relig-*

ious extremists ... as they see it, the Arabs lived in the land throughout the centuries in contravention of the Law, and their assertion of a right of residence is no better than that of a squatter.[10] [Emphasis supplied]

As typical of this viewpoint, Harkabi quotes Rabbi Shlomo Aviner, the former rabbi of Bet El (the Jewish settlement established in Samaria), and today the rabbi of the Ateret Kohanim Yeshiva:

> Let me draw you an analogy. It's as if a man goes into his neighbor's house without permission and stays there for many years. When the original owner returns the invader claims: "It's my house, I've been living here for years!" All of these years he's been nothing but a thief! Now he should make himself scarce and pay rent on top of it. Some people might say that there's a difference between living in a place for thirty years and living in a place for 2,000 years. Let us ask them: *Is there a statute of limitations* that gives a thief the right to his plunder? ...
>
> Everyone who settled here knew very well that he was living in a land that belongs to the people of Israel, so the ethnic group that settled in this place has no title to the land. Perhaps an Arab who was born here doesn't know this, but nevertheless the fact that a man settles on land does not make it his. Under the law, possession serves only as a proof of a claim of ownership; it does not create ownership. The Arabs' possession of the land is therefore a possession that asserts no rights. It is the possession of territory when it is absolutely clear that they are not its legal owners, and this possession has no juridical or moral validity (Artzi, p. 10). [Emphasis supplied]

Harkabi continues:

> For Rabbi Aviner and his followers, then, the first Arabs to settle *in the Holy Land were thieves, and the crime has been bequeathed from father to son down to the present generation.* Perhaps he is referring to collective ownership of the land and not to the ownership by each individual Arab of his own small plot. *But he says that all the title deeds for land recorded in government registers have "no juridical and moral" force.* [Emphasis supplied]

Harkabi then asks—Is there a court in the world who would endorse such an argument?[11]

The better answer to this question is that, not only would no court endorse this argument—no court would listen to it. Rabbi Aviner, however learned, is out of his depth on his "analogy." The applicable law is not the "statute of limitations" but the law of "adverse possession." Under English common law, the foundation of American jurisprudence, and under the law of most jurisdictions, a party in possession can acquire title to unoccupied land if his "possession" (for the stipulated period established by statute) is open, adverse, notorious and hostile to any other claim of title.

A "thief" *could* get title to vacant land by occupying it for the statutory prescriptive period. Nor would he have to possess it for two or three thousand years. Five years of adverse possession would suffice to confer title in California, and not more than twenty-one in most other jurisdictions.

Harkabi continues by quoting Rabbi Zvi Yehudah Kook:

We find ourselves here by virtue of the legacy of our ancestors, the basis of the Bible and history, and no one can change this fact. What does it resemble? A man left his house and others came and invaded it. This is exactly what happened to us. Some argue that there are Arab lands here. *It is all a lie and a fraud! There are absolutely no Arab lands here....* [12] [Emphasis supplied]

Under the subtitle, "From Expulsion to Annihilation," Harkabi continues:

If Jews see the Arabs' residence in the land of Israel as making them criminals, the conclusion that they should be expelled is quick to follow. Knesset member Rabbi Meir Kahane has given widespread publicity to this idea, but he did not invent it. It is based on ancient sources, and first and foremost the biblical verse *"You shall dispossess all the inhabitants of the land"* (Numbers 33:53) and the interpretations of it given by classical commentators. The eleventh-century scholar Rashi, for example, explained: "You shall drive out the land and you shall dispossess it of its inhabitants, and then you will dwell in it, i.e., you will be able to remain in it [if you dispossess it of its inhabitants], but if not, you will not be able to remain in it." *Thus the biblical verse was interpreted not as a commandment directed to the Jews in the past,* when they came out of Egypt, but as a standing order binding for the future.[13] [Emphasis supplied]

Harkabi quotes Rabbi Yisrael Ariel as explicitly demanding expulsion of the Arabs as entailed by Jewish religious law:

On the one hand there is a commandment to settle Eretz Israel, defined by our sages also as the commandment of "inheritance and residence"— a commandment mentioned many times in the Torah. Even the new student understands that "inheritance and residence" means conquering and settling the land. The Torah repeats the commandment—"You shall dispossess all the inhabitants of the land"—many times, and Rashi *explains that this means to expel them. The Torah itself uses the term expulsion a number of times.... The substance of this commandment is to expel the inhabitants of the land whoever they may be....* This is also how Rashi understands the commandment. In the Talmudic passage that mentions the commandment to settle the land Rashi explains: "Because of the commandment to settle Eretz Yisrael—to expel idol worshipers and settle Jews there." *Thus according to Rashi the commandment to settle the land means to expel the non-Jew from Eretz Yisrael and settle it with Jews.* ("Zeffiyya.")[14] [Emphasis supplied]

Harkabi continues:

Note the association of idol worshipers and non-Jews. This identification has a basis in Jewish tradition.

In Rabbi Kahane's version, expulsion of the Arabs would fulfill two functions: *The first is political, preventing the Arabs from becoming the majority* and thereby undermining Israel from within; the second is religious—*it would provide a proven means to hasten the Redemption and the coming of the Messiah.* [Emphasis supplied]

Harkabi quotes Rabbi Kahane:

The Arabs of Israel are a desecration of God's name. Their non-acceptance of Jewish sovereignty over the Land of Israel is a rejection of the kingdom. *Removing them from the land is therefore more than a political matter. It is a religious matter, a religious obligation to wipe out the desecration of God's name.* Instead of worrying about the reactions of the Gentiles if we act, we should tremble at the thought of God's wrath if we do not act. *Tragedy will befall us if we do not remove the Arabs from the land, since redemption can come at once in its full glory if we do, as God commands us....* Let us remove the Arabs from Israel and hasten the Redemption ("Thorns in Your Eyes," pp. 244-245).[15] [Emphasis supplied]

Harkabi cites Rabbi S.D. Wolpe for the following:

According to halakha it is forbidden for a non-Jew to live in Jerusalem, and in accordance with the ruling by Maimonides it is forbidden to permit even a resident alien in Jerusalem.... *True, this applies when Israel has the upper hand,* but today too, although it is not possible to expel them by force, this does not mean that we have to encourage them to live there![16] [Emphasis supplied]

Harkabi also quotes Rabbi Eliezer Waldenberg, winner of the 1976 Israel Prize (given for outstanding achievement):

It is forbidden for gentiles to live in Jerusalem. I, for example, favor upholding the halakhic prohibition on a gentile's living in Jerusalem. If we would uphold this halakha as we should, we would have to expel all non-Jews from Jerusalem and purify it absolutely (cited in "The Zionist Dream Revisited," p. 117).[17] [Emphasis supplied]

According to this interpretation of divine law, the failure to expel the Palestinians from their homeland, and all non-Jews from Jerusalem, is a transgression of religious law.

The tragic irony of this situation is pointed out by John K. Roth* in an article appearing in the *Los Angeles Times,* November 12, 1988, entitled "Kristallnacht Formula Haunts Today's Unwanted." In the article, Roth describes the situation in Germany in 1938 regarding the "Jewish problem." Strenuous efforts were being made by Eichmann to expel the Jews from Germany. At the same time, because of Hitler's conquests in Austria and Czechoslovakia, more Jews came under Nazi control.

The following are excerpts from Roth's article:

Meanwhile the presence of nearly 70,000 Polish Jews in German territory remained an embarrassment for the Nazis' promise of "Judenrein" (a state "cleansed" of Jews). By late October these Jews, rounded up by the Gestapo, were being deported to the Polish frontier. The Poles, however, were not ready to accept them. Blocked from Poland, unable to

---

*John K. Roth, the 1988 Professor of the Year for the United States and Canada, teaches philosophy and Holocaust studies at Claremont McKenna College.

return to Germany, detained in hideous conditions, these unwanted Jews found themselves in a hapless no-man's land.

When policies of forced emigration proved insufficient to solve the Jewish question, those same experts would move on to organize the Final Solution. Thus, the ultimate significance of "Kristallnacht" was that it hastened the approaches to Auschwitz.

"Kristallnacht"—the event itself, the conditions that brought it on and, even more important, the results it produced—should provoke reflection 50 years later. For early November, 1988, it has portents, too. *Some of them can be seen in Israel's election returns, which signify a turn to the right, religiously and politically.*

Peace for Israel in exchange for land, the hope of a viable Palestinian state on soil voluntarily relinquished by Israel—such possibilities are less likely now that Israel has voted. *Instead, Israeli voices advocating a purely Jewish state are going to be more determined and strident than ever. Among them are those of the Moledet (Homeland) Party, which advocated the "transfer" of Palestinian Arabs from the occupied territories.*

"Kristallnacht" happened because a political state decided to get rid of people unwanted within its borders. It seems increasingly clear that Israel would prefer to rid itself of Palestinians if it could do so. Their presence in Gaza and the West Bank is a liability and a threat to many Israeli intentions. Thus, the voice of Moledet, euphemistic and muted though it may be, is not to be taken lightly. This is particularly true when it seems equally clear that not many other nations in the world want the Palestinians either. *As much as any other people today, they are being forced into a tragic part too much like the one played by the European Jews fifty years ago.*

The anniversary of "Kristallnacht" has become an occasion for re-asserting "Never again!" That cry signals commitment to ensure the safety of Jews wherever they may be. At its best, "Never again!" signified that and much more. It is a cry to *forestall tragedy wherever people are unwanted. As a Holocaust scholar, as one who has lived and taught in Israel and who loves that country deeply, during this year's remembrance of "Kristallnacht" my thoughts are on Palestinian plight at least as much as on Israeli security.*[18] [Emphasis supplied]

Hitler failed in efforts to solve the "Jewish problem" by expulsion. He then decided on the "final solution" which was extermination.

Incredible as it may seem, this is the same "final solution" which the religious extremists are suggesting as far as the Palestinians are concerned.

GENOCIDE AND THE PALESTINIAN PROBLEM

Harkabi is deeply disturbed by what he sees as an ominous movement among the religious extremists:

> *Some nationalistic religious extremists frequently identify the Arabs with Amalek, whom the Jews are commanded to annihilate totally* (Deuteronomy 25:17-19). As children, we were taught that this was a relic of a bygone and primitive era, a commandment that had lapsed because Sennacherib the Assyrian king had mixed up all the nations so it was no longer possible to know who comes of the seed of Amalek. *Yet some rabbis insist on injecting a contemporary significance into the commandment to blot out Amalek.*

Rabbi Yisrael Hess, formerly the campus rabbi of Bar-Ilan University, published an article in the student newspaper, *Bat Koll* (February 26, 1988) entitled "The Commandment of Genocide in the Torah," which ended as follows: *"The day will yet come when we will all be called to fulfill the commandment of the divinely ordained to destroy Amalek."*

Knesset member Amnon Rubinstein citing this article adds: "Rabbi Hess explains the commandment to blot out the memory of Amalek and says that there is no mercy in this commandment: the commandment is to kill and *destroy even children and infants.* Amalek is whoever declares war against the people of God." [Emphasis supplied] In the same article quoted by Rubinstein, Hess writes:

> Against this holy war God declares a counter jihad. . . . *In order to emphasize that this is the background for the annihilation and that this is what the war is all about, that it is not merely a conflict between two peoples. . . . God does not rest content that we destroy Amalek—* "blot out the memory of Amalek"—he also mobilizes personally for this war . . . because, as has been said, he has a personal interest in the matter, it is a prime goal for us as well. [Emphasis supplied]

Harkabi continues with an alarming statement:

> *Hess implies that those who have a quarrel with the Jews instantly become Amalek and ought to be destroyed, children and all.* Amalek is identified with the Arabs: the use of the term jihad (holy war) is but one

allusion to this meaning. *Amalek is not an ancient extinct tribe but a generic enemy that each generation may identify for itself.*

Rabbi Yisrael Ariel, in a collection of articles intended to justify the religious terrorist Underground that emerged in Israel in the mid-1980s, *explained that the killing of a non-Jew is not considered murder.*[19] [Emphasis supplied]

Harkabi continues his quote from Rabbi Yisrael Ariel:

Anyone who looks through the code of Maimonides, which is the pillar of halakha in the Jewish world, and searches for the concept "thou shalt not murder" or the concept "holy blood" with regard to the killing of a non-Jew will search in vain, because he will not find it.... *It follows from Maimonides' words that a Jew who killed a non-Jew was exempt from human judgment, and has not violated the prohibition on murder.* As Maimonides writes in the Laws of Murderers: "A Jew who killed a resident alien is not sentenced to death by a court of law" ("Zeffiyya").[20] [Emphasis supplied]

If the "annihilation" and destruction of "Amalek," including his children and infants, is carried out "without mercy," will there be a "Nuremberg" trial of Rabbi Hess, Rabbi Yisrael Ariel, and Rabbi Meir Kahane on charges of *genocide?* If they should escape, will there be a Simon Wiesenthal to track them down and bring them to justice? What have all the Holocaust studies and Holocaust memorials and pilgrimages to Auschwitz accomplished? Has mankind learned nothing?

THE RACIAL SUPERIORITY OF THE JEWS

The fate of the Palestinians and other non-Jews under Jewish rule is described in detail by Harkabi and others cited:

A reasoned analysis of the status of non-Jews in a Jewish state can be found in an article entitled "A New Approach to Israeli-Arab Peace" published in *Kivvunim 24* (August 1984), an official publication of the *World Zionist Organization.* The author is Mordechai Nisan, a lecturer on the Middle East at Hebrew University in Jerusalem. *According to Dr. Nisan, Jews are permitted to discriminate against foreigners in a way that Jews would angrily denounce were it done to them. What is permissible to us is forbidden to others.* [Emphasis supplied]

Harkabi quotes from Nisan:

> *While it is true that the Jews are a particular people, they nonetheless are*
> *designated as a "light unto the nations."* This function is imposed on the
> Jews who strive to be a living aristocracy among the nations, a nation
> that has deeper historical roots, greater spiritual obligations, *higher*
> *moral standards,* and more powerful intellectual capacities than others.
> This vision, which diverges from the widely accepted egalitarian
> approach, is not at all based on an arbitrary hostility towards non-Jews,
> but rather on a fundamental existential understanding of the quality of
> Jewish peoplehood. [Emphasis supplied]

Harkabi continues:

> *Thus the concept of the "Chosen People" as an aristocracy provides*
> *sanction for the unequal and discriminatory treatment of non-Jews, who*
> *are inferior.* Nisan does not consider the possibility that other nations
> might also claim aristocratic status for themselves.[21]

One can only wonder whether the "light unto the nations," referred to
by Nisan is being held in Shamir's iron fist. Abba Eban, in an article
appearing in the *Jerusalem Post* of November 19, 1988, entitled "The
Issues That Won't Go Away," comments on the rise of Kahanism:

> To unfreeze the diplomatic deadlock is a more urgent task than to form
> a united front against the dangers of religious fundamentalism. In point
> of fact, the two issues are linked to each other. Ruling a foreign nation
> without according total equality or rights is a policy that can only be
> defended by attitudes of self-assertion and exclusivism which are incom-
> patible with prophetic Judaism and classical Zionism.
> *It is the maintenance of a non-democratic structure for over 20 years*
> *which enabled Kahanism to flourish and which has now given birth to*
> *the obscene heresy of "transfer."*
> Thousands of Jewish voters have given their mandate to the idea of
> making the lives of thousands of people in their own homes so intoler-
> able that they will "agree" to leave. Transfer is a euphemism for the kind
> of enforced or induced uprootings of which Jews were the main victims
> in history. This idea enters the Israeli bloodstream two centuries after
> Jews in Europe fought successfully to defend the principle of equal rights
> for all who live under any jurisdiction. That was the principle which

enabled Jews to become emancipated from their previous humiliation.[22]
[Emphasis supplied]

Nisan *continues in a passage that Harkabi says must be presented in its
entirety* to register the tribalism of this mindset:

The Land was the special divinely granted territorial promise to Abraham and his seed. . . . Non-Jews, without a role on the highest plane of
religious endeavor, are thus without a role on the plane of public activity.
The linkage of politics and religion in the Jewish experience is supported
by the equally tight connection between kinship and politics. Those of
"the tribe" are the sole bearers of authority to determine national affairs
in the Land of Israel.[23]

Harkabi comments:

. . . *The laws that grant equal rights to all citizens of Israel were passed
by the Knesset with no opposition.*

Today, in contrast, the demand is voiced that all non-Jewish residents
of the Jewish state be dealt with according to halakhic regulations—
which, not incidentally, *support the nationalist aim of decreasing the
number of Arabs living in the country by making their lives difficult.
Supporters of this view willfully ignore international norms, having to
do with racial non-discrimination and with civil, economic, and social
rights as formulated in international conventions, even where Israel has
formally ratified them.* [Emphasis supplied]

What is in store for the Palestinians under Israeli rule becomes clear.
Harkabi points out:

Rabbi Meir Kahane . . . asserts that: "A non-Jew who lives in the Land
of Israel can obtain only the status of 'resident alien' (*Ha'aretz*, August
13, 1983). Citizenship, political status . . . the right to vote and hold
office, all of these are reserved exclusively for Jews." Again, these ideas
are not without foundation in traditional sources. *Maimonides himself is
a major source on the treatment of non-Jews who have been conquered
and have come under Jewish rule, a category that is clearly applicable to
the Arabs of Israel proper, Judea, Samaria, and the Gaza Strip.* [Empha-
sis supplied]

Rabbi Meir Kahane is quoted by Harkabi as follows:

If the inhabitants make peace and accept the Seven Commandments

[188]

enjoined upon the descendants of Noah, none of them is slain, but they become tributary, as it is said: "They shall become tributary unto thee, and shall serve thee" (Deut. 20:11). If they agree to pay the tribute levied on them but refuse to submit to servitude, or if they yield to servitude but refuse to pay the tribute levied on them, their overtures are rejected. They must accept both terms of peace. *The servitude imposed on them is that they are given an inferior status, that they lift not up their heads in Israel but be subjected to them,* but they be not appointed to any office that will put them in charge of Israel. The terms of the levy are that they be prepared to serve the king with their body and their money (Hilkhot Melakhim, ch. 6:1).[24] [Emphasis supplied]

Nisan is quoted as stating:

The category of ben-noah [son of Noah] defines the non-Jew who has accepted the seven Noachide laws. In return for being permitted to live in the country of sacred history and religious purpose, the ben-noah must accept to pay a tax and *to suffer the humiliation of servitude* (see Deut. 20:11). *Maimonides, in his legal code on the Laws of Kings, states explicitly that he be "held down and not to raise his head against Jews." Non-Jews must not be appointed to any office or position of power over Jews. If they refuse to live a life of inferiority, then this will signal rebellion and the unavoidable necessity of Jewish warfare against their very presence in the Land of Israel....* [25] [Emphasis supplied]

Harkabi discusses the implication of this view, if applied to the Arab population of Palestine:

Nisan is not presenting merely a theoretical analysis: he offers practical suggestions as well. A non-Jew must not be appointed to any public post in Israel. With regard to the "autonomy" concept of letting the Arabs have self-rule only under Israeli supervision, he writes: "This political solution is thus in the spirit of the traditional Jewish approach, both with regard to the land of Israel and with regard to non-Jewish minorities within it."

If Canada, of which he was formerly a citizen, treated Dr. Nisan as a ben-noah, a member of the servant class with restricted rights, he would have protested it as deplorable discrimination, but *he sees no contradiction in the Jews, as the chosen people, having a license to treat non-Jews in just this way. This is tribal morality given theological justification. I do not know how many Jews share his belief, but the publication of the*

article in a leading Zionist periodical is cause for great concern.[26]
[Emphasis supplied]

Israel frequently prides itself on being the only democracy in the Middle East. Rabbi Kahane plans to change that, says Harkabi:

Meir Kahane does not mince words. *"There is an absolute and irresoluble contradiction between the State of Israel . . . and the modern nation-state that sees all of its citizens as possessing equal rights. . . .* There is a potential confrontation . . . between the Zionist Jewish state . . . and modern ideas of democracy and citizenship" (p. 109). Can we as Jews confront the world with such an assertion? Certainly there is much discrimination and repression in the world, but *few openly proclaim the right to treat others as inferior and laud themselves for doing so. The claim can now be made that Khomeinism has appeared among us.*[27] [Emphasis supplied]

Harkabi acknowledges that he may be inviting criticism by exposing the beliefs and intentions of the religious extremists. He feels strongly that the conspiracy of silence among Jews must be broken, so that these positions can be challenged openly:

A case can be made against me that by revealing these tendencies of the Jews and Israel I am providing ammunition to enemies. I find myself in a painful conflict. There is no escape from it, though there is comfort in knowing that I am not alone and am not divulging any secrets. Much of what I have written here has been aired elsewhere, including the problem of the identification of Amalek with the Arabs. Amnon Rubinstein's book, from which I have taken a number of citations, has appeared in English (though we should not pretend that non-Jews do not read Hebrew and follow what is published in the Israeli press). The article by Rabbi Yisrael Hess, "The Commandment of Genocide in the Torah," received widespread publicity and was even discussed in an English-language publication of the University of Cape Town. The burning of the New Testament was discussed in the Foreign Affairs Committee of the Knesset (Ma'ariv, July 5, 1985) and debated on Israeli television. Meir Kahane publishes his views in English. *A conspiracy of silence about these beliefs and this use of the tradition allows them to go unchallenged and encourages those who propagate them.* There can be no remedy without first identifying the problem. By hiding our shame from outsiders we hide it from ourselves as well. The Torah says many times, "You shall sweep out the evil from your midst." At the very least we must cry out against it.

The apologists who claim that non-Jews understand that Jews, like every human society, have lunatic fringes who should not be taken seriously are being irresponsible. *Kahane won election to the Knesset, and support for his position in Israel has been rising.* The same applies to other religious extremists; they are not a negligible element.[28] [Emphasis supplied]

IDOLATRY AND THE FATE OF THE CHRISTIAN ARABS

According to the religious extremists, Christians are classed as idolators. Harkabi explains:

The classification of Christians as idolators has apparently become widespread and accepted in religious literature. This is not merely a theoretical matter, since practical conclusions flow from it. *For example, in 1979 Rabbi Yosef issued a ruling that copies of the New Testament should be torn out of any edition of a Bible owned by a Jew and destroyed* (*Ha'aretz,* October 23, 1979). This ruling did not remain a dead letter. An item in the newspaper *Ma'ariv* (June 14, 1985) reported the burning of a copy of the New Testament found in the library at the base of a chief educational officer of the Israeli army.

These manifestations of hostility—the designation of Christians as idolators, the demand to invoke "resident alien" ordinances, and the burning of the New Testament—are distressing. *Outside the Land of Israel Jews never dared behave in this fashion. Has independence made the Jews take leave of their senses?*[29] [Emphasis supplied]

Harkabi continues by quoting Maimonides on the two different legal systems—one when the Gentiles are predominant and another when the Jews are in control:

It is forbidden to show them mercy, as it was said, "nor show mercy unto them" (Deut. 7:2). Hence, *if one sees one of them who worships idols perishing or drowning, one is not to save him....* Hence you learn that it is forbidden to heal idolators even for a fee. But if one is afraid of them or apprehends that refusal might cause ill will, medical treatment may be given for a fee but not gratuitously.... The foregoing rules apply to the time when the people of Israel live exiled among the nations, or when the Gentiles' power is predominant. *But when Israel is predominant over the nations of the world, we are forbidden to permit a Gentile who is an idolater to dwell among us.* He must not enter our land, even as a temporary resident; or even as a traveler, journeying with merchandise from place to place, until he has undertaken to keep the seven precepts which the Noachides were commanded to observe (Hilkhot Avodah Zara, ch. 10:8).[30] [Emphasis supplied]

Clearly, the soul of Israel is being corroded from within. The crisis of leadership infects the entire society. As quoted, Harkabi says that there is a *conspiracy of silence* to keep the knowledge of the intentions of the religious extremists from the rest of the world.

The only solution, Harkabi emphasizes, is to expose and challenge the religious fanatics because "by hiding our shame from outsiders we hide it from ourselves as well."

CHAPTER XI

Saving Israel from Suicide

T HERE ARE MANY THINGS in the relationship between
   American Jews and Israel that have very little to do with Israel's
best interests.

THE ISRAELI MYSTIQUE

The unquestioning devotion of American Jews to anything and everything "Israeli," including the fallible human beings who make up its
government at any given time, did not always exist.

Prior to World War II, there was a deep division among Jews as to the
feasibility, or even the desirability of Zionism. After the war, the weight of
opinion shifted dramatically toward the Zionist cause and support for the
State of Israel. The Holocaust, and the subsequent founding of the State of
Israel in 1948, understandably brought about many changes in the attitude
of world Jewry toward Zionism. With each succeeding Arab-Israeli war, the
Jewish world rallied, with greater and greater will and determination, to the
side of Israel. The survival of Israel, and its development into a military
power, became an obsession with the Jewish people throughout the world.
All other divisions and differences were forgotten.

Financial support from the Jews in the U.S. continued to flow in ever-
increasing volume and the resources of the American Jewish community in
political and economic power and influence were marshaled to the service
of Israel.

[193]

The spectacular victory of the Israeli army in the 1967 Six Day War was followed by great joy and jubilation and the belief by many Israelis that they were invincible.

Out of this emotional crucible the "Israeli mystique" emerged. The American Jewish community became, by stages, captivated, seduced and, finally, blinded by the mystique.

The non-Jewish population of the U.S. was, and still is, arbitrarily and simplistically classified by Jews as *for* or *against* Israel, completely ignoring the fact that there are at least 17 political parties in Israel. Some want peace, some want war, some want to expel the Arabs and resettle all of ancient Israel; others are willing to give up all occupied Arab territories for peace. Some are "hawks" and some are "doves." *American Jewry, however, became more militant than the Israelis themselves.* On some issues, when the Prime Minister of Israel could muster the support of a bare majority of the Knesset, the Israeli Lobby could deliver almost the entire Senate and President of the U.S.

A number of reasons have been suggested by Jewish writers for the consuming passion which has characterized the attitude of many American Jews toward the Israelis. One of the most challenging is that suggested by James Yafee in his book, *The American Jews.* Yafee points out that it is often said all Jews are cowards, that no Jew has the guts to fight. However, he writes:

> The Jew today can invoke Israel to convince the world that this stereotype is false. This is why even the most un-warlike American Jews delight in stories about the impact of Israel's military prowess ... it is Israel's power, its guts, which impress American Jews. The implied, and sometimes spoken, conclusion is "That'll show the gentiles what kind of stuff we're made of." He sees Israel as a vicarious extension of himself. By identifying with those bronzed invincible heroes, he somehow takes on some of the bravery, some of the strength, that he feels he could never possess unaided. "There is a strong strain of magic in this—the superstitious magic of primitive people who believe that by drinking the tiger's blood or wearing his skin they can assume the characteristics of the tiger."[1]

Of course, if either the Jew, or the Gentile (he supposedly is trying to impress), knew anything about Jewish history (some of which appears in the first chapter of this book), they would know that the Hebrew tribes were among the most warlike people in the ancient world. As we have seen, even after they were occupied by the Romans, the Jews of Judea, as well as those in the Diaspora, became the most belligerent, rebellious, intractable people in the entire Roman Empire. Throughout most of history, the Jews have been an indomitable, determined and aggressive people. Today's Israeli army, with the advantage of some of the finest weaponry in the world, is no more "heroic," and their exploits no more remarkable, than those of the Maccabees, who fought and won a guerrilla war against the Syrian armies with simple weapons and abundant courage. Viewed over the immense span of Jewish history, it becomes clear that the "ghetto Jew" (particularly as caricatured in 18th and 19th century Russia and Poland) is a historic anomaly.

Unfortunately in the past, the American Jewish community has not limited its relationships with Israel simply to a supporting role. It has often been openly militant—to the point of inciting and provoking even a harder line by the Israeli hawks in the government. *Past efforts to convince American Jews of their important role in the search for peace have been rebuffed, and labeled as "anti-Semitic."*

Such an effort was made by the Quakers who, after an exhaustive analysis of the Middle East situation, made the following plea:

> We appeal to the leaders of the powerful American Jewish community, whose hard work and generous financial support have been so important to the building and sustaining of Israel, to reassess the character of their support and the nature of their role in American politics. Our impression ... is that there is a tendency for the American Jewish establishment to identify themselves with the more hard-line elements inside the Israeli cabinet, "to out-hawk the hawks," and to ignore or discount the dissident elements in and out of the Israeli Government that are searching for more creative ways to solve the Middle East problems.[2]

This appeal by the Quakers was quoted in the book, *The New Anti-Semitism,* by Forster and Epstein, as an example of an "anti-Semitic" attitude by the Quakers.

In the same book, Forster and Epstein describe the feeling of Jews toward Israel in these words:

> For, excepting the Jewish religion itself, Israel represents the greatest hope and the deepest commitment embraced by world Jewry in two

millennia. Just as Israel's survival depends in substantial measure on support from Jews in the United States and elsewhere, Jews in the Diaspora have come to feel that their own security and the only hope for their survival as a people, in a world from which anti-Semitism has never disappeared, *depends in large measure on the survival of Israel.*[3] [Emphasis supplied]

In view of the enormous stake which world Jewry has in the survival of Israel, is it not too important a matter to be left entirely in the hands of whatever politicians happen to be in power when Israel's fate may be decided?

Fortunately, in recent years, there has been a change in viewpoint on the part of many Israeli intellectuals and some prominent members of the American Jewish community. They are urging and, indeed, pleading with American Jewry to use its influence to reverse the course that the Likud government is taking which they firmly believe can only lead to disaster. These include Abba Eban, Simha Flapan, Amos Perlmutter, Yehoshafat Harkabi, etc., and many other thoughtful and loyal Israelis who are appealing to the American Jewish community to act as *true* friends of Israel.

Many concerned Jews in America recognize that the survival of Israel cannot be taken for granted, if the present policies of the Likud government are allowed to continue. Yet, as we have seen, they are intimidated by the Likud from speaking out for fear of being charged with "collaborating with the enemy."

The consternation and anger of the American Jewish establishment, in response to the recent attempt of the Orthodox Rabbis to change the Law of Return (the "Who is a Jew?" issue), is rooted in the fear that Israel might not be a haven or refuge to the Reformed and Conservative Jews of America, if there should be a revival of "anti-Semitism" and persecution in the Diaspora. There is no doubt that the searing trauma of the Holocaust experience has left an indelible mark on every Jewish soul, often to the point where calm thinking gives way to irrational fears. This is the only explanation, it seems, that could account for the actions of Jewish leaders in rushing to Israel in a panic for fear that the Orthodox Rabbis in Israel might change the Law of Return in a manner that could deny American Jews, or their descendants, entry into Israel some day.

But, clearly, that is not where the danger lies. The Right of Return is a false promise *if there is no place to return to.*

The American Jewish community is divided on the question of exerting its influence on the Israeli government toward peace. Unfortunately, it seems that a substantial number of Jews in America prefer to leave the matter to Israel, "because Israel knows best what is best for Israel." *Nothing could be further from the truth.* Leaving it to Israel is to leave it to the Likud government and its irrational and irresponsible leadership.

The great lesson of the Holocaust is that Jews cannot afford to sit idly by until a threat to their survival gets out of control, and that fanatics and demagogues ought to be feared, not ignored—are being lost in an attitude of *dangerous complacency.* It is well and good to say "never again," but, unless prompt action is taken by responsible elements of the Jewish community in the U.S. and in Israel, "never" will soon be *here.* If it is true, as Santayana is so often quoted as saying, "that those who do not learn from history are doomed to repeat it," Israel, under the Likud, is doomed.

Abba Eban, in an article in the *Jerusalem Post* of November 9, 1988, states the case eloquently. He is quoted in part:

There is no need of many words to explain why the 1,500,000 Palestinians under military rule have an interest in a different condition. They do not have a single one of the conditions that give fulfillment or dignity to a nation's life.

It should now be equally apparent that Israeli rule over that vast and growing population weighs no less heavily on the rulers than on the ruled. The present situation endangers our national and individual security, our economy, our international relations, our democratic principles, our Jewish majority, our image in the eyes of the world, our prospect of attaining peace, our probability of avoiding war, our universal Jewish unity, our national consensus, and above all, our most cherished values.

It would be reasonable for Diaspora Jewish leaders to be longing more passionately and audibly for a Jewish state that will embrace the values which enabled Diaspora Jews to flourish in freedom.

When Diaspora Jewish leaders proclaim that "American Jews do not care" by whom Israel is governed, *they sacrifice Jewish principles in behalf of an institutionalized docility that comes close to moral apathy.*

It is incongruous to imply—correctly—that Diaspora Jews are entitled to combat the attempt to disqualify a majority of the Jewish congregations, rabbis, temples and ceremonials from the pride of their Jewish identity—and then declare indifference about Israel's government.[4]

The reluctance on the part of many American Jews to assert their influence upon the Likud government, even though the survival of Israel is at stake, is even more incredible when one considers the character of the Likud leadership. It should be asked: who are these leaders that the "non-interventionist" Jews are entrusting with the fate of Israel? What credentials do they have for such an awesome responsibility? What wisdom have they shown that they should be elevated above the criticism, advice or influence of the Jews of the Diaspora whose fate is bound up with that of Israel? What justifies this trust and confidence in the Likud that they are left to make these life or death decisions for Israel? Simply stated, *who are these modern day Solomons?*

Harkabi, former Chief of Israeli Military Intelligence and advisor to Prime Minister Menachem Begin, says that most of the desperate problems which face Israel today are the result of the Begin-Jabotinsky ethos, which has determined Israel's domestic and foreign policies since the Likud assumed power in 1977. He thinks that *Begin was incompetent to lead a government and blames the U.S. "Friends of Israel" for pushing Begin down the throats of the Israeli people.*

Harkabi blames Israel's misfortunes directly on the Likud government, and Prime Minister Begin particularly as leader of the Herut (the center party in the Likud coalition):

The Likud government presided over a series of great failures: the peace treaty with Egypt, which loomed initially as a great achievement; the Lebanon War, which turned into a fiasco; which has become a quagmire; de facto annexation; Israel's economy, which nearly collapsed; the conduct of politics that degenerated into demagoguery; the worsening in the relations between various segments of the population—those of North African and Middle Eastern origin (the Sephardim) against those of European backgrounds (the Ashkenazim), as well as religionists against secularists. Generally, the national confidence was undermined by this widespread deterioration of Israel's situation. What caused all these failures? Were they purely accidental and unrelated, or were they all of a piece? Were they the result of unforeseen problems and bad luck, or were they built in? Did they have a common denominator in some erroneous policy? Were the failures rooted in the personalities of the leaders, in their lack of ability or unsuitability for office? Or did they result from a political philosophy, aspects of these leaders' mentality and basic concepts that influenced both their personalities and their policies?

My answer is that there was a common denominator: a misperception of reality or an insufficient regard for it. The accumulation of failures cannot be explained in isolation from the Jabotinsky-Begin ethos. They all stemmed from a pattern of thought that was influenced by this ethos: a superficial approach that searched for shortcuts to great accomplishments by means of a single dramatic event or policy, a focusing on intentions instead of outcomes and an exaggerated belief in the power of the will.

Taken in the aggregate, these failures constituted a veritable national tragedy, since they critically worsened Israel's condition and weakened the basis of its existence. Many Israelis have begun to wonder whether their country can endure, whether the nation can climb down safely from the slippery cliff face to which successive Likud governments have led them. This will depend on recognition by both the public at large—and not only by a minority within it—of both the severity of the situation and its causes. Recognition that Israel's problems were intensified by its leaders' errors and not by unavoidable circumstances will bring energy for change. *On the other hand, refusing to recognize the severity of the situation will encourage the mindset that brought these calamities upon Israel and pave the way for further disasters.*[5] [Emphasis supplied]

At a symposium of the National Unity Government held at Hebrew University of Jerusalem in May 1985, Professor Shlomo Avineri noted that Begin had become hated throughout the world (despite his having received the Nobel Peace Prize),[6] implying that Israel's status throughout the world has declined because of foreign reaction to the arrogance and insufferability of Begin and the Likud government.

Aside from earning the hatred of much of the world and grossly mismanaging the affairs of Israel, what has Menachem Begin accomplished that he has been so revered a leader?

In Teddy Preuss's book, *Begin, His Regime,* he compares Begin with Ben-Gurion:

Ben-Gurion stood with his face to the future, looked ahead and was ready to pay with earnings from the past. Begin behaved quite the opposite: he stood with his face towards the past, looked backward, and was ready to mortgage the future for it.

Preuss cites a prophecy by Ben-Gurion:

Ben-Gurion's apocalyptic prophecy, found in a letter he wrote to Moshe Sharett on May 31, 1963, resounds today like a heavenly voice from beyond the mountains of darkness: *"I have no doubt that Begin's rule (Mapai is bringing his rule of Israel closer) will lead to the destruction of the state. In any case his rule will turn Israel into a monster." After six and a quarter years of his rule, Ben-Gurion's warning is not far from realization.* The peace treaty with Egypt—his one and great accomplishment—was emptied by Begin of all content and squandered through settlement activities and the Lebanon War. With the erasure of this accomplishment from the balance sheet, Prime Minister *Begin's resignation remains the sole service that he performed for his country.*[7] [Emphasis supplied]

As discussed in Chapter III of this book, Begin's successor, Yitzhak Shamir, has even less credentials except that he had a bloodier terrorist career than Begin. How much confidence can be placed in the leadership of such a man? As discussed in the chapter on Zionism, Shamir succeeded Stern as the head of the "Stern Gang," or "Lehi."

Harkabi has this to say about Lehi:

In Israel's historical self-reckoning there is nothing bleaker than Lehi's attempts to establish relations with the Nazis. At the end of 1941, seven years after Hitler had come to power and more than two years after the outbreak of the Second World War, *when the anti-Semitic atrocities of the Nazis were well-known, Lehi sought an alliance with Nazi Germany.* The memorandum transmitted from Lehi to the Germans asserted that "according to its world view and structure [Lehi] is very close to the totalitarian movements of Europe." Not only did it claim to share with Germany "common interests for a new order in Europe and the authentic aspirations of the Jewish people," but it also claimed to be close in ideology.

This attempt to make a deal with the Nazis was no isolated incident: it continued a political line that began with attempts to make contacts with the Italian Fascist government. Words of praise to Hitler appeared in the Revisionist press, provoking a sharp rebuke from Jabotinsky himself. The Germans' response was negative but *Lehi was not deterred: a few months later, it sent Nathan Yellin-Mor to the Balkans to arrange a meeting with the Germans and persuade them of the benefit to them of an alliance with the Jews against Britain.*

When this affair became known, after the German diplomat von Hantig published his memoirs in 1974, Eldad and Yellin-Mor had to defend their actions. Eldad described them as a far-sighted scheme to rescue the Jews of Europe, since at the time the Final Solution had yet to be adopted. Yellin-Mor reported that Abraham Stern, the leader of Lehi, had anticipated a German defeat and feared that Britain would dominate the entire Middle East. Did Stern and his colleagues truly believe that assistance from Lehi could tip the scales in favor of Germany, and that it was better for the Jews that Germany win the war?

It is doubtful whether the long history of the Jews, full as it is of oddities and cruel ironies, has ever known such an attempt to make a deal with rabid enemies—of course, ostensibly for reasons of higher political wisdom. But how could cooperation with the Nazis have furthered the establishment of the "Kingdom of Israel"? What could have induced the Nazis to cooperate with the Jews and so radically change their entire ideology to the point of intimate partnership with them?

Perhaps, for peace of mind, we ought to see this affair as an aberrant episode in Jewish history. *Nevertheless, it should alert us to how far extremists may go in a time of distress, and where their manias may lead.*[8] [Emphasis supplied]

Harkabi's admonition that we should be *alert* to how far extremists may go and where their "manias may lead" must be taken seriously.

To be alert is to recognize that the "manias" of the extremists are leading Israel—which is leading the Israeli Lobby—which is leading the government of the United States—which will lead, if not stopped, to a war of unthinkable consequences. The possibility that Ariel Sharon may realize his ambition to succeed Shamir is too appalling to contemplate.

The reckless and irrational policies of the Likud are alienating the nations of the world, and destroying any chance for peace. Moreover, the alliance between the Likud and the religious extremists, with their religious and ethnic hatreds, threatens to undermine a century of amity and friendship with the Gentile population of the West. *From this, the Jews of the Diaspora cannot afford to remain aloof.* Harkabi writes:

For many Jews, Israel has become the prime focus and symbol of Jewish identity.

Jews, especially in the United States, are disposed to liberalism. When liberal public opinion is critical of Israel, they experience a cognitive dissonance, and this gnaws at their Jewish identity. The future of the reputation of the Jewish people throughout the world now *depends on Israel's good name and international stature.* More than any other state, Israel is a hostage to world public opinion. Israelis must remember this. We Israelis must be careful lest we *become not a source of pride for Jews but a distressing burden.*

Moreover, Israel is the *criterion according to which all Jews will tend to be judged. Israel as a Jewish state is an example of the Jewish character,* which finds free and concentrated expression within it.[9] [Emphasis supplied]

If Israel today is the example of the "Jewish character which finds free and concentrated expression in it," *the religious extremists and fanatics are making a mockery of World Jewry.*

Harkabi asks why the Jews allow the religious extremists in Israel to spread religious and racial hatred without protest:

> *Religious Jews seem unaware how much explosive material is latent in the assertion that Halakha takes precedence over the law of the land.*
>
> If, as Meir Kahane and many others assert, Jews have the right to expel Arabs and aliens from the Land of Israel, why do the nations of the world have to allow Jews to live in their countries? *The same reasoning applied to Rabbi Yosef's ruling that the New Testament should be burned and the unfortunate case of the actual burning of a copy thereof: it provides retroactive legitimacy to the burning of Jewish holy books by Christians.*
>
> The most revolting manifestations of this trend—even if it involves only a tiny minority in Israel—is the revival of the command to blot out the memory of Amalek and the identification of Amalek with the Arabs. *How can a rabbi's assertion that the killing of a non-Jew is not murder be justified?* Christians might say that killing Jews isn't murder, thereby providing sanction for all the pogroms of history. *How can Jews hold up their heads when they hear such claims and not actively combat them?*[10] [Emphasis supplied]

More important, how can the Anti-Defamation League sit idly by and allow this defamatory and calumnious attack on Jewish principles and ethics? This is *real* "anti-Semitism."

IS ZIONISM RACISM?

As indicated in the previous chapter, Revisionist Zionism, championed by Menachem Begin and Yitzhak Shamir, and the central philosophy of the Likud party, is not reticent on the subject of the superiority of the Jewish race as compared with the rest of mankind.

Harkabi describes the ideology of the Likud: "It attributes supreme value to the concept of nation or race. Its natural extension is the idea that the 'whole world is against us.' In its most extreme form it presents nonsegregation and openness toward strangers as 'treason against Judaism.' This view of a unique essence also breeds the belief that the Jews are allowed what is forbidden to others.

"On a political level, the idea that the *greatness of the Jews stems from their essence is translated into self-righteousness:* Israel is not responsible for untoward development in the Arab-Israeli conflict and indeed cannot be. It is no accident that Begin promoted this attitude and found immediate support for it, and himself, among religious circles."

Harkabi continues with a summary of the religious extremists' concept of the Chosen People:

> *The Jews as the Chosen People are superior in their essence to all other human beings.* Their divine election is a fact, an absolute fact. *The difference between Jews and non-Jews is thus part of the very nature of things.* "[God] separated between the profane and the holy, between the light and the darkness, between Israel and the nations." The sages have provided us with passages in this spirit too: "Israel is dear, having been called sons of the holy one"; anyone who preserves a single life of Israel is considered to have preserved an entire world; "all Israel has a share in the world to come" (not only as a reward for fulfilling the commandments); *"no non-Jew has a share in the world to come." In this view, Jews and non-Jews were molded from different matter.* True, a non-Jew can convert to Judaism, but by doing so he changes his essence. The attitude toward the non-Jew is closed, and the emphasis is on strict segregation. *The greatness expressed by chosenness is embodied in the Jewish collective essence.*[11] [Emphasis supplied]

Statements by Israeli government officials condemning apartheid in South Africa as "completely contrary to the very foundations in which Jewish life is based," are the ultimate in hypocrisy.

Mark A. Bruzonsky,* in an article entitled "Israel Is Too Much Like South Africa," appearing in the *Los Angeles Times,* August 20, 1985, makes the point convincingly:

I first encountered the charge that Zionist racism makes Israel comparable to South Africa in the early 1970s, while I was chief representative of the International Student Movement for the United Nations. I protested vehemently in a long personal letter to an assistant of the U.N. secretary-general, Kurt Waldheim. Officials of the American Zionist Youth Foundation sent copies of that letter to Jewish university students in the United States and Israel, and then commissioned me to write monthly articles on Zionism for their newsletter.

I next confronted the Israel/South Africa comparison at Princeton University while obtaining a master's degree in international affairs. Prof. Richard Falk, himself Jewish, repeatedly linked the situations of the two countries in his course on international law. I remember sharing the outrage of my Israeli student colleagues. Once again I protested vehemently.

I provide my own history on the issue to make it clear that for many years I aggressively challenged comparisons of South Africa and Israel. Now I have come to conclude that the similarities between the two outweigh the differences.

Tragically, Israel today has become precisely what many of its liberal founders feared—a besieged, divided, polarizing country whose methods of repression against the Palestinians parallel those of white South Africa against the blacks.

Here are what I view as the important points of similarity:
—In both cases, self-determination is being sought by a mistreated, oppressed, abused ethnic group—the blacks of South Africa, the Palestinians in the territories occupied by Israel since the 1967 war.
—Both governments are engaged in escalating militarism, intimidation and brutality.
—Both oppressed groups have resorted to open challenge and increasing violence.
—In both cases the potential for escalating conflict is growing.
  ... the Israeli government has further stepped up a campaign against

---

*Mark A. Bruzonsky was Washington associate of the World Jewish Congress during 1977-1983. He is co-editor of "Security in the Middle East," being published for the Woodrow Wilson International Center for Scholars at the Smithsonian Institution.

its Palestinian subjects that over the years has included deportation, imprisonment, collective punishment and, occasionally, documented torture. Emergency regulations left over from British Mandate days in what used to be called Palestine, similar to those imposed in South Africa, are enforced by Israel in the occupied territories.

Looked at historically rather than through the obscuring lens of day-to-day headlines, the white minority of South Africa and the Jewish minority in the Middle East *are both coming up against their own inescapable contradictions. In an era of non-discrimination and secularism they are ideologically wedded to principles that many in the world term racist.*

The situation is more confused in the case of historic Palestine, a land that the world community voted to partition in 1947 between the same two nationalist *movements that are in conflict today. Jewish ethnicity and chauvinism in combination with Zionist nationalism have created a mix that is discriminatory in spirit if not in actual laws.*

The greatest distinction between Israel and South Africa is that Zionism is legally non-discriminatory while apartheid is legally racist. And yet, if we are to be honest, in practice the results are comparable.

The most hopeful difference between the two may be that an acceptable solution is still conceivable for Israel and the Palestinians—peaceful coexistence and mutual recognition of both peoples' national rights. However, increasing attacks of Jewish settlers on the West Bank *and rising Israeli support for extremists are signs that time may also be running out in the Middle East.*

More recently the Israeli government said that it "unconditionally objects to the policy of apartheid in South Africa," although it took no steps to alter the substantial trade, arms and security relationship that exists between the two countries. *Prime Minister Shimon Peres condemned apartheid as "completely contrary to the very foundations on which Jewish life is based."*

But around the world today people who speak in one way and act in another have little credibility. *Vigorous protest of apartheid while acquiescing in Israel's continuing campaign to intimidate the Palestinian people into submission is hypocrisy.*[12] [Emphasis supplied]

In the *Los Angeles Times,* June 5, 1989, edition, the following news item appeared, datelined Jerusalem:

Jewish settlers yesterday attacked and beat Israeli peace activists trying to deliver food and medicine to Palestinian children in Gaza Strip refugee camps. In the West Bank, soldiers reportedly shot and killed a Palestinian teen-ager.

The developments followed a raid Monday by Jewish settlers on a Palestinian refugee camp. A 13-year-old girl was shot to death in the rampage.

An Israeli court in Kfar Saba, near Tel Aviv, yesterday ordered five Jewish seminary students suspected in the rampage jailed pending further investigation. *The seminary's spiritual leader, Rabbi Yitzhak Ginsburg, justified the slaying and said the blood of Jews and non-Jews cannot be equated.*[13] [Emphasis supplied]

Is this from *Mein Kampf?*

Unless the moderate Jews in Israel and the Diaspora speak out against this arrogant perversion in the name of religion, they should remain silent when the United Nations equates *Zionism with racism.*

Old Jewish doctrines that were thought dead and buried are being revived by the religious extremists. The pernicious doctrine that there are two standards of morality—one when the Jews are weak and another when the Jews are dominant—is being raised again in the name of Maimonides (the great Jewish philosopher of the late Middle Ages). Harkabi explains:

The victory of 1967 led certain extremists to the belief that the age had in fact come when Israel was stronger than the nations of the world, or nearly so. Maimonides explained that the restrictions on idolaters *(identified with non-Jews in general)* are applicable only in such a period: "The foregoing rules applied to the time when the people of Israel lived reviled among the nations, or when the gentiles' power is predominant. But when Israel is predominant over the nations of the world, we are forbidden to permit a gentile who is an idolater to dwell among us" (Avoda Zara, 10:6). *Thus Maimonides distinguished between two periods: when "the nations of the world are stronger than Israel," and their wrath is to be feared, and when "Israel is stronger than the nations of the world," and may treat them in a high-handed manner.*[14] [Emphasis supplied]

Harkabi continues:

Jewish religious extremism has been associated with a startling deterioration in the quality of theological thought. Its leaders usurp God's role and decide what his position should be, claiming that . . . *they "know" that God has signed up to back the Israel cause, is angry with gentiles, can no longer restrain his wrath, and is about to explode against them.* Meir Kahane has explained that the establishment of the State of Israel was "the beginning of God's wrath, *his vengeance on the gentiles who ignored his existence."*

The pattern of thinking implied by Rabbi Zvi Yehudah Kook's statement that the *entire world* will have to get accustomed to the idea that Israel will not yield a single inch of the occupied territories, and it will be better for them when they do so, is also distressing. *The statement implies a threat that if the world does not accept annexation it will be punished.*[15] [Emphasis supplied]

THE RISE OF XENOPHOBIA

Harkabi cites Mordechai Nisan's *The Jewish State and the Arab Problem* as indicating an alarming increase in hostility to the Gentile world:

There is no need for compensation in case an ox owned by a Jew gores an ox owned by a gentile, whereas there is need for compensation in the opposite case (Hilkhot Nizkei Mammon, ch. 8:5). An article lost by a Jew should be returned but not one lost by a gentile (Hilkhot Gzeilah VeAvedah, ch. 11). Dr. Nisan justifies these discriminations on the grounds of "cultural differences" (ibid.) *These discriminatory laws can now be transposed from the private to the political domain.* Thus, Israeli Jewish claims to Eretz Yisrael are superior, and the Palestinian claims can be summarily rejected, thus there is no need for a compromise with them. The West Bank should be annexed by Israel forthwith, and the ensuing demographic problem be solved by a "transfer" of the Arabs to other countries (p. 124).[16]

Judaism has been radicalized in two ways: politically, in supporting extreme nationalism and annexation of the West Bank; socially, *in fostering hostility to gentiles in general and Arabs in particular.* We find ourselves in a grave predicament. True, expressions of hostility and discriminatory enactments existed earlier, but until now they were moot. Since 1967, they are no longer so and the possibility has been breathed into them by the demand that such laws should be applied *here and now.* Thus, they have been actualized and made plausible. *We can no longer shrug our shoulders at the hostile material on the pretext that it is a very minor as well as extinct part of the Judaic tradition. Indeed, I suspect that the new developments in the Jewish religion constitute transmutation of great significance.* As these changes occur before our eyes we may fail to appreciate how revolutionary they are. *What has surfaced cannot again be routinely submerged.*[17] [Emphasis supplied]

The argument that "Kahanism" is an aberration is disposed of by Harkabi in these words:

After Rabbi Meir Kahane's election to the Knesset, many religious Jews began to describe him as an anomaly, an aberrant weed that had grown in the garden of Judaism. It seems to me that this explanation is simplistic and evasive. First, Kahane is not alone in holding these views. *Focusing exclusively on him distorts the true picture: significant parts of his platform are shared by many others, including important rabbis and heads of yeshivas. The Kahanist phenomenon extends far beyond the narrow confines of his declared supporters,* even if most religious Jews have grave doubts about many of his positions. Second, Kahane and other religious extremists certainly do not represent all of Judaism (who does?) but they do represent certain elements found within it. They mark the extreme of traditional Jewish concepts. As has been said, their stand is based on texts drawn from the greatest sages of our tradition. Citing "good" texts for humane attitudes toward "the stranger" does not refute or erase the "bad" texts.

Kahane's use of the tradition hinders the religious moderates' campaign against the extremists, for fear that opposition to him will be taken as an attack on the great sages upon whom he relies, which would disqualify the moderates in the eyes of the religious public. *If Kahane is twisting and distorting the texts and the meaning of halakha, the rabbis ought to prove it. The assertion that Kahane and his ilk are perverting the spirit of Judaism is rather far-fetched.* It is hard to say what the true spirit of Judaism is; ultimately this is a matter of subjective impressions.[18] [Emphasis supplied]

David Shipler, in his masterwork and Pulitzer Prize-winning book entitled *Arab and Jew: Wounded Spirits in a Promised Land,* also points out the tendency of the religious extremists to cite only scriptural texts that support their position:

Gush Emunim activists take what they wish from the contradictory sources. As the eleven- and twelve-year-old boys in Kiryat Arba explained, they are learning in their yeshivas that the Arab is Amalek, the enemy tribe that God instructed the Jews to fight eternally and destroy: "Amalek was the first of the nations; but his latter end shall be that he perish for ever." (Numbers 24:20.) Hagai Segal, a settler from Ofra, was quoted in the settlers' paper *Nekuda* as declaring, "The Torah of Israel has nothing to do with modern humanistic atheism. The Torah yearns for revenge. Such a Torah is not humanistic."

Expressions of bellicose intolerance are given religious sanction and rationalization, which then filter into some segments of the lay population. *Some rabbis, such as Eliezer Waldenberg, winner of the 1976 Israel Prize, declared that Halakha, Jewish law, required strict separation of Jews from Arabs, preferably an apartheid system or, better yet, the expulsion of the "goyim," all non-Jews, from Jerusalem.* An American correspondent and his family became targets of some of this chauvinism in the Jerusalem neighborhood where they lived; the word "goy" was scratched into the paint of their car, and the children were hassled by Israeli youngsters on the street. Zohar Endrawos, an Arab in the mostly Christian Galilee town of Tarshiha, remembered Jewish youngsters in neighboring Maalot making crosses with their fingers and spitting on them. Another rabbi, writing in the student newspaper of Bar-Ilan University, near Tel Aviv, argued that the Torah prescribed genocide against the modern Amalek. At the Gush Emunim settlement of Elon Moreh, when security men went to investigate the murder of an eleven-year-old Arab girl by settlers, they were met with signs reading "Ishmaeli Police."[19] [Emphasis supplied]

Shipler also sees Kahanism as a serious threat:

In the year after his Kach movement's election to the Knesset with one seat, Kahane's popularity soared to the point where, by the autumn of 1985, the public-opinion polls recorded enough support for him to win ten or eleven seats in a new election. Even allowing for Israelis' propensity to vent their frustration and anger more extensively on questionnaires than at the ballot box, the Kahane phenomenon alarmed the liberal-minded establishment enough to prompt President Chaim Herzog to tell a group of high-school students in a Tel Aviv suburb, "I think it is a disgrace to the Jewish people—and that is how it looks to the whole world—that a person could rise in the Jewish state and present a program that is very similar to the Nuremberg laws"—the measures promulgated by Nazi Germany in 1935 to strip Jews of their rights.

Kahane satisfied the lust for simplicity that is fed by rage. He offered order as an antidote to uncertainty, complexity.[20]

It is clear that a malignancy is growing within the body politic of Israel. The Israeli people cannot be fully alerted to the seriousness of this threat if they are lulled into the belief that the powerful and influential American Jewish community either supports the policies of the Likud and the religious extremists, or is indifferent to them. Begin clung to office on the strength of the boast that he "could handle the Americans." Shamir is playing the same game.

An article appearing in the *Los Angeles Times* February 2, 1989, edition, entitled "Jewish Doves See Need to Criticize Israel," again calls attention to the critical need for Diaspora Jews to speak out:

THE HAGUE—Dovish members of the international Jewish community agreed here Wednesday that there *is a need to speak out against Israeli policy in dealing with the Palestinian uprising in the occupied territories.*

Drora Kass, director of the New York office of the International Center for Peace in the Middle East, was a member of the American Jewish delegation that met last December in Stockholm with leaders of the Palestine Liberation Organization. She recalled the criticism she received at the time from fellow American Jews, but she said the meeting may have encouraged PLO Chairman Yasser Arafat to take a more moderate line in a speech to a meeting of the U.N. General Assembly later that month in Geneva.

Kass said she believes that concerned Jews have not only a right but also a duty to speak out for peace in the occupied territories—the West Bank of the Jordan River and the Gaza Strip.

And she argued that American Jews should articulate their disagreement with Israel's tactics in suppressing the nearly 14-month-old Palestinian uprising. Otherwise, she said, Israeli leaders will not get an accurate impression of the anti-violence sentiments held by most American Jews.

Kass said it was the failure of American Jews to object to Israeli policy, out of what she called a misguided desire to maintain Jewish unity, that led Israeli Prime Minister *Yitzhak Shamir to say on returning from visiting the United States that "all American Jews are behind me."*[21] [Emphasis supplied]

Harkabi emphasizes the seriousness of the failure of the moderates in Israel and the U.S. to take action:

The absence of a strong opposition to religious extremism by recognized Jewish religious and lay leaders abroad and by the chief rabbis and the political leadership in Israel is apt to be considered a tacit tolerance of its views. So far the *reaction of moderate religious circles has been weak.* Stronger reactions will come only if the matter becomes urgent, if public debate embarrasses the religious and lay leadership. It will not move of its own accord, because of the roots that the extremist positions have in the tradition. It is not the call for a discussion of the problem that is damaging but rather the reluctance to grapple with it.

Let us remember that what is at stake is not some secondary question, or a problem that will go away if it is ignored. The struggle is for the soul of Judaism and its status in the world, and for the moral and political status of the State of Israel.[22] [Emphasis supplied]

THE UNTOUCHABLES

In addition to the racial discrimination which is rooted in the religious concept of "The Chosen People," there is virulent and widespread racial antagonism which pervades the Israeli population, both religious and non-religious, which is "sociological." This has been discussed briefly in Bruzonsky's comparison of Israel to South Africa cited earlier.

The Palestinian Arabs comprise a distinct underclass politically, socially, and economically. India has its "untouchables"—the Israelis have the Palestinians. They do the menial work, jobs that Jews will not stoop to— garbage collectors, janitors, dishwashers, construction workers, fruit pickers, etc. The word "Arab" has come to have a pejorative connotation: "Arab work" is menial work;[23] "Don't act like an Arab," can mean any number of unattractive attributes. The prevailing attitude among most Israelis toward the Palestinians is one of fear but mostly *contempt.* They believe that Arabs must be treated brutally because "force is the only language they understand."[24]

For many Palestinians, daily life is one of harassment, humiliation and intimidation. Palestinians of the professional and educated classes who don't fit the untouchable mode are systematically deported or imprisoned.

Shipler quotes one Palestinian's description of the situation:

We have over one thousand two hundred leaders of the community who have been deported. These were leaders who were not involved in any kind of activities that even subjectively you can call terrorist. These are church leaders, university presidents, union leaders—they threw them out. You have a thousand two hundred laws that have been implemented, arbitrarily controlling every aspect of life in a very racist and apartheid way. You need a permit to plant tomatoes and to plant eggplants and to plant vines. You have to get a permit if you want to plant a plum tree in front of your house. If you lose your ID [card], you are in vital trouble. If you do not follow all this trickery in paperwork you are out and the border is sealed.

Shipler points out that little is done by Israeli police to protect the Palestinians:

For most of the six years that Menachem Begin was Prime Minister, Jews could kill Arabs on the West Bank with impunity. Arrests were sometimes made, prosecutions sometimes begun. But somehow the cases rarely came to trial. The pattern of leniency was documented by an Assistant Attorney General, Judith Karp, who studied seventy instances of Jewish violence against Arabs during a year beginning in the spring of 1981. She found that even in cases of murder, the army, which administered the West Bank under Defense Minister Ariel Sharon, intervened to thwart police investigations or, at the very least, failed to press for vigorous police action. Settlers came to see themselves as living amid lawlessness. In murder cases, the report said, "the appropriate energy and required efficiency for investigations of this kind were not evident." Describing two incidents in which settlers killed Arab boys, Karp wrote, "The suspects received a summons to present themselves to the police station. They announced that they would not appear and that they would speak only with the military authorities. The police did not do anything to bring the suspects to the police station despite the grave suspicion." Where soldiers had shot Arabs, she said, "the soldiers' version was believed even though it did not seem reasonable, and the circumstances of the incident supported the complainant's version." Karp's findings produced no action by the Justice Ministry, the police, or the army, and she therefore resigned as head of a committee examining the problem. The report was suppressed for a year by the Justice Ministry. It was released only after Yitzhak Shamir became Prime Minister and a round of Jewish terrorism broke out.

Many Palestinians believed the Jewish settlers were laying the psycho-logical groundwork for the Arabs to panic and flee should warfare erupt, just as the massacre of Arabs at Deir Yassin led many to flee during the 1948 war for fear that the Jews would massacre them as well. Indeed, the germ of this idea could even be found occasionally in the utterances of Jewish settlers. In 1980 *Nekuda* quoted a resident of the settlement of Ofra, Aharon Halamish, as telling a symposium on Arab-Jewish rela-tions, *"We have to make an effort so that the Arab people have a hard time in this country. If we employ them and develop them, we are undermining ourselves. We don't need to throw grenades in the casbah or to kick out the Arabs, but there is nothing wrong with our giving them a hard time and hoping they get killed."*[25] [Emphasis supplied]

It is not difficult to understand the killings and brutalities committed by Israeli soldiers in the occupation forces. Shipler quotes a Hebrew University faculty member:

A Hebrew University faculty member, Shlomo Ariel, writes to *Ha'aretz* about disturbing attitudes in discussions with young Jews *who are about to enter the army*:

I met with about ten groups of fifty young people each, which *represents to a certain extent a random and representative sample of the Jewish population of Israel of this age level, with all its strata and ethnic origins*.... The young participants, almost unanimously, expressed full identification with the racist positions of Finkielshtein toward Arabs. To the claim that the latter are Israeli citizens with equal rights according to the law, the typical reaction was that Israeli citizenship should be denied them. In each discussion group there were a few who proposed physically liquidating the Arabs, right down to the elderly, women, and children. They received the comparison between Sabra and Shatila [the Beirut refugee camps] and the Nazi destruction favorably, and said with full candor that they would carry out such destruction with their own hands with no inhibitions or pangs of conscience. Not one expressed shock or reservations about these declarations, but there were those who said that there was no need for physical liquidation; it would be enough to exile them across the border. Many supported apartheid on the model of South Africa. The idea that to the Arabs of Israel this country is their country and birthland was received with amazement and mockery. Any moral claim was rejected with scorn. In each group there were not more than two or three holders of humanitarian, anti-racist views on this question, but it could be seen that they were afraid to express themselves publicly, and indeed those few who dared to express their unpopular opinions were immediately silenced by a chorus of shouts.[26] [Emphasis supplied]

If this is, as said, a representative sample of Israeli youth, the future of Israel is grim indeed. Human rights organizations, and the U.S. State Department, have condemned Israel's oppressive occupation tactics and brutalities as inexcusable. Today, in civilized Israel, the only *capital offense* is rock throwing.

Shipler recounts an incident which makes especially chilling reading, because the Israeli commander was a woman:

Troops and policemen have, on occasion, been prosecuted for brutality, but only half-heartedly after much public uproar, and their sentences have usually been light. Strict guidelines on opening fire during demonstrations have been promulgated, but little or no training has been given in crowd control, leaving every inexperienced soldier at the mercy of his fears with only a deadly rifle as his protection from angry stone-throwers. A grinding guilt works at the bowels of Israeli consciousness. Or, worse, a callous frustration numbs the young Jew and carries over into his own open democracy. He has grown up thinking the Arabs are good for beating.

The infectious brutality festered and then broke into an open sore in the Tel Aviv civilian guard, which patrols streets and watches for suspicious characters who might be planting bombs. Jewish high-school students from Herzliya, north of Tel Aviv, were shocked at what they witnessed when they volunteered for night duty in 1984. Under the supervision of Sarah Rahamim, the chief of their base, bands of volunteers from Tel Aviv schools drove through the city, spotted Arabs, pushed them into stairwells, slapped and punched them. "We were driving in the area of the central bus station," one girl told *Ha'aretz*. "Suddenly we saw three Arabs in front of us. One of the volunteers asked them what they were doing here and where they worked. He instructed them to enter a stairwell in a nearby house and to wait there. . . . I told Sarah that I had heard that they were beating them, and I wanted to know what was going on. Sarah said to me: 'Go look. When my daughter sees it, she gets a good laugh.' I got out of the patrol car and went to the building door. The three Arabs were facing the wall with their arms raised. One of the volunteers asked one of the Arabs: 'Where do you live?' The Arab answers, and he yells at him: 'Why are you lying?' and hits him. Another question and another shout: 'You're lying!' And a blow." During another patrol, she said, "We saw an Arab running. We didn't know if he was running because of us or because of the rain. We all got out of the patrol car and stopped him. Everyone was armed even though we had not passed the firing range [test] and it's forbidden. . . . I came to the door of the apartment house. . . . The student leader was holding the Arab's identity card. In front of him stood the Arab with his hands up, and behind him stood a volunteer with drawn rifle with the cartridge in. I heard the student leader say to the Arab: 'If we see you again, that will be the end of you.' And he slapped him. They make a real thing out of the beatings. They talk about this experience to everyone. One guy broke an Arab's tooth, the second forced another Arab to crawl. Another boasted that he broke two of an Arab's teeth."

Another student, a boy, told the paper, "The guys on the base prepared me by saying that you have to beat Arabs because Arabs rape girls and are a criminal nuisance. When you beat them, they go away. When we drove in an area without Arabs, what's called a 'clean area,' the volunteers explained to us that it was clean because they were beaten and they fled." The volunteers mocked Arabs for their accents and tried to make them cry. The commander, Sarah Rahamin, was forced to resign, but no criminal action was taken.

The conscience of the country is always there, yet wrongs are done as a matter of routine. A system of military courts hears security and political cases in the occupied territories, and many of the judges are attorneys and law professors, not career military men, who preside during their month of reserve duty each year. But the ostensible judicial protections are easily foiled by the latitude of the Shin Beth to force confessions, by the fear of Arabs to charge publicly that they have been tortured, by the reluctance of the courts to throw out confessions that are challenged, by the inability of many Arab families to afford defense lawyers, by the fact that laws on the West Bank and Gaza Strip are made by military decree with no legislative input.[27]

How common this callous and extreme cruelty may be is difficult to say, but from the reports of human rights agencies it is not, by any means, rare.

Moreover, it has official sanction since it furthers the government's policy of harassing and terrorizing the Arab population in the West Bank and Gaza, to the point where their lives become so intolerable that they will be forced to leave their homes and lands.

Whether they are forced to leave or not, the well of fear and hatred between Israelis and Palestinians is bottomless. It is no exaggeration to say that more rancor and bitterness have been engendered in Palestine in the past forty years than the British in North Ireland were able to create in four hundred years.

Shipler summarizes his conclusions which end on a note of hopelessness that any reconciliation between the two peoples is possible:

> I found it less easy to draw the lines of cause and effect. It may be, as those involved think, that the racism, anti-Semitism and class prejudice are just corollaries to the main proposition, appendages of attitude attached to the essential confrontation of two peoples over one tract of territory. *But now, after decades, just as war and terrorism have evolved into origins themselves, so have prejudices and stereotypes worked their way so thoroughly into literature, education, history, language and social mores on both sides that they seem to govern the conflict as much as they are created by it. Disease and symptoms intertwined.*[28] [Emphasis supplied]

The horrifying details of the Tel Aviv incident, as well as Shipler's final conclusion, are quoted primarily to show that so-called "peace plans" that talk about "autonomy" for the Palestinians under Israeli rule, or suggesting a trial period, during which Israelis and Palestinians "get to know each other better," are hoaxes. The problem is not that they don't know each other, but that they *do* know each other.

Abba Eban has made a valiant effort to appeal to Israel's youth, without much impact.

In an article appearing in the November 19, 1988, edition of the *Jerusalem Post*, entitled "The Issues That Won't Go Away," he writes:

> Likud representatives *especially the younger generation* will have to ask themselves whether they can serve the national and Jewish interests permanently if they make the territorial indivisibility of Eretz Israel a matter of rigid dogma *against the historic and demographic realities,*

against the opinion of all mankind and against at least half of the Israeli nation.[29] [Emphasis supplied]

Up to this point we have focused our attention primarily upon Israel's internal problem and its relationship with the Palestinians in the West Bank and Gaza.

In the balance of this chapter, we will discuss the international situation as it affects Israel and its security.

THE ARAB NATIONS AND ISRAELI EXPANSIONISM

Much of the attitude of the Arab nations in the Middle East toward Israel is rooted in the Arab perception that Israel is a predatory power, continually seeking to expand its borders at the expense of the Arab countries.

Our purpose here is to seek and determine whether this perception has any basis in fact and what can be done to allay Arab fears. In this effort we will discuss some of the reasons why Israel's Arab neighbors are fearful of, and therefore hostile to, Israel.

In Chapter III we have traced the development of Zionism from Theodor Herzl's concept of a Jewish homeland (not necessarily in Palestine) up to the founding of the State of Israel in 1948.

The following is a brief chronological summary of the important events leading up to the establishment of the Jewish state. Except where sources are otherwise indicated, all source references are found in Chapter III.

It has been shown that following Herzl's death, the leaders of the Zionist movement, Ben-Gurion, Weitzman, and Jabotinsky, were united in one purpose only—the establishing of a Jewish state in *all* of Palestine. The Arab inhabitants were to be replaced or overwhelmed by Jewish immigration and dealt with in a manner as to deprive them of any political rights in Palestine.

The first official endorsement of the concept of a Jewish "homeland" is found in the British government's famous Balfour Declaration made in 1917. This short note from Anthony Balfour, British Foreign Minister, to Lord Rothschild "expressed sympathy with Jewish Zionist aspirations"— "it being clearly understood that nothing shall be done which may prejudice the civil and religious rights of the existing non-Jewish communities in Palestine."

The Zionists promptly seized upon the Balfour Declaration as justification for its intent to establish a completely Jewish state in Palestine. Among other claims it announced that "Palestine is to become as Jewish as England is English."

This distortion of the intent and meaning of the Balfour Declaration caused the British to issue its "White Paper" in the spring of 1939 in which it stated emphatically and unequivocally that the Balfour Declaration was *not* intended and could not be used by the Zionists to justify a Jewish National Home in *all of Palestine or the subordination of the Arab population.*

The Zionists rejected the "White Paper" and, in 1942, began an all-out terrorist campaign intended to drive the British out of Palestine. As we have seen, the terrorist campaign succeeded and caused the British to surrender its "League of Nations Mandate" over Palestine to the newly created "United Nations."

After a lengthy study of the Palestine problem, the U.N. decided that the only possible solution was to "partition" Palestine into two independent sovereign states, one Jewish, and one Palestinian. The Jewish state, with a population of 650,000, was allotted approximately 55 percent of the land and the Palestinian state, with a population of 1,300,000, was allotted 45 percent of the land.

The U.N. Partition Resolution enacted in 1947, to be effective in 1948, makes a specific point that the Partition *solves* the Jewish-Palestinian problem because the solution definitely *fixes* the extent of the territory to be allotted to the Jews. It goes further, and says that the solution carries the *sanction of the United Nations* which involves a *finality which should allay Arab fears of further expansion of the Jewish state.*

At the time that the skeptical Palestinians were being told by the U.N. not to worry, since the boundaries of the Jewish state, which was being created, were "fixed," the Zionists had no intention whatsoever of abiding by these fixed boundaries.

To the Zionists, the Jewish state was only a first step—a springboard to the goal of taking over all of Palestine. Thus, the Zionist strategy never wavered from its basic position that *all* of Palestine was to be Jewish and that no Palestinian state would be allowed, *regardless of the U.N. Partition Resolution.* On May 14, 1948, Ben-Gurion declared the establishment of the State of Israel.

Immediately following this declaration, certain of the adjoining Arab states (but not the Palestinians) attacked Israel which repelled the Arab attack and, in the resulting "War of Independence," the Israeli army overran large areas of land that had been allotted to the Palestinians under the U.N. Partition plan.

By means of military action, propaganda and another campaign of terrorism led by Menachem Begin and Yitzhak Shamir, seven hundred thousand peaceful Palestinian inhabitants were driven from their homes and lands into refugee camps where they and their descendants live to this day.

Israel confiscated the Palestinian homes and lands and incorporated them into the State of Israel.

The *myth* that the Palestinians would have had their Palestinian state, had they not attacked Israel in 1948, has been exposed by Simha Flapan and other prominent Israeli historians *as Israeli government propaganda.*

In Israel's Six-Day War in 1967 with Egypt, Jordan and Syria, the Israelis achieved another quick victory as a result of which they invaded and occupied the remaining land inhabited by the Palestinians on the West Bank and Gaza. They also invaded and occupied the Egyptian Sinai and the Syrian Golan Heights, as well as all of Jerusalem.

Following the Six-Day War, the U.N., in 1967, adopted Resolution 242 which requires Israel to return the occupied lands on the West Bank and Gaza to its Palestinian inhabitants. Israel accepted U.N. Resolution 242.

In 1977, the newly-elected Prime Minister of Israel, Menachem Begin, rejected U.N. Resolution 242 on the grounds that it does not apply to the West Bank and Gaza because they are sacred lands given by God to Abraham and are the property of the Jewish people.

Israel thus has developed from the concept of a Jewish "homeland" to a military (including nuclear) power, *technologically equal* to any nation on earth including the NATO countries and the Soviet Union.

As might be expected, this inexorable expansion has been watched by the Arab countries with deepening anxiety. What the Arabs see is a relentless drive by Israel to invade and conquer the Arab lands from the Nile to the Euphrates, which includes Jordan, Lebanon, Syria and Iraq. This is the announced purpose of Israel's powerful Gush Emunim movement.

After seeing their worst fears come to pass and the U.N., which was supposed to protect them, shown to be helpless, how can the Arab countries *not* be fearful of Israel? Harkabi finds ample reasons for Arab concern:

> The call to expel the Arabs, however, is tantamount to calling for the de-Arabization of territories that are today Arab, and this makes the conflict symmetrical. For the Arabs, fighting Israel then becomes an existential imperative: the Arabs of the neighboring countries cannot remain

apathetic in the face of a possible expulsion of Arabs from the West Bank, if only to prevent their countries from being flooded by Palestinians. The mere beginning of expulsion would cause Israel's peace with Egypt to collapse overnight. The conflict would become a matter of life or death, and this would impel the Arabs to unite despite all their divisions. Any attempt to expel the Arabs *would result in international repercussions of unprecedented scope, and in all-out war on the part of the Arab states.*

This trend toward making the conflict symmetrical is to be found not only in overt statements about "transferring" the Arabs, *but also in threatening remarks about Israeli intentions to expand into the territory of Arab countries. Such utterances have appeared in Israeli publications. In a similar vein are expressions of Israeli intentions to impose a Pax Israelica on the Middle East, to dominate the Arab countries and treat them harshly. A gross example of this is an article entitled "A Strategy for Israel in the 1980s," by Oded Yinon,* which appeared in *Kivvunim,* a journal published by the information department of the World Zionist Organization in February 1982. It is not surprising, given the auspices under which it is published, that Arabs attributed great importance to its content and assumed that it expressed the views of official circles with regard to Israeli policy and goals. The article had wide repercussions in the Arab world, a fact that testifies to Arab feelings of vulnerability.[30] [Emphasis supplied]

Are the Arab nations being unreasonable in not wanting a "Pax Israelica" in the Middle East? The question which deserves a serious answer is "who is threatening whom?" Harkabi discusses further the impact of Yinon's book:

Yinon goes on to describe in detail *how to partition every Arab country,* according to geographical and ethnic consideration. One wonders at the temerity of the editors who published an article in the organ of the World Zionist Organization *describing how Israel will partition the Arab countries.* Perhaps the failed Israeli attempt to impose a new order in the weakest Arab state—Lebanon—will disabuse people of similar ambitions in other territories.

Be that as it may, a symmetry has been created in the ideas of the two parties to the conflict. *The organ of the World Zionist Organization presents a detailed plan for the destruction of the Arab states,* albeit in an elegant fashion, and presents this as *a prime strategic goal for Israel.*

In doing so, it provides the Arabs *with retroactive legitimation for their goal of destroying Israel, presenting their struggle against it as a life-or-death conflict.*[31] [Emphasis supplied]

Anything more provocative, or calculated to create fear and anxiety in the Arab countries, can scarcely be imagined. Moreover, there is nothing that the Arab nations hear from Israel that is in any way reassuring. They know that the Arabs are identified as Amalek, an enemy to be destroyed, and its memory to be blotted out. The article entitled "The Commandment of Genocide in the Torah," referred to in the previous chapter, was not something found in the "Dead Sea Scrolls," but in an article written by Rabbi Hess *for Israeli university students in 1988.*[32] Spokesmen for the religious extremists are condemning the Israeli government for being too timid in asserting its military power. They boast that Israel is stronger than all the nations of the Middle East (which the Arabs do not deny); that Israel should be afraid of nobody (including Russia); and that Israel's problems could be solved in one swift blow against its enemies if the government would just *do it.* The Arab nations are not exaggerating their vulnerability. They see themselves defenseless against the Israeli juggernaut. They can expect no help from the U.S. which is rendered powerless by the Israeli Lobby.

The Arabs have the moral support of the world, which, however, is small consolation. They see the U.N. helpless to implement its resolutions. They see human rights violations flaunted by Israel with impunity. In 1948, and again in 1967, the Arabs could see clearly that the promise of the U.N., to the effect that Israel's boundaries would be fixed and guaranteed by the U.N., was false. The assurances made by the U.N. to the Palestinians that they had nothing to fear from Israeli expansionism were meaningless. It became apparent that Israel had never intended to abide by the boundaries established by the U.N. Partition Resolution.

It is obvious to the Arabs that Israel has accomplished exactly what the Zionists had said all along that they *would* accomplish, namely, the conquest of all of Palestine.

The Arabs see the religious extremists (encouraged by the Likud) openly claiming the biblical right to all the Arab lands from the Nile to the Euphrates. The rabbis and the Likud have made no secret of the fate of the Arabs under Israeli rule. They are to be subject peoples ruled by an iron hand, not fit to associate with Jews.

Israeli children are being taught all about the Holocaust and their *duty* to wipe out Amalek. Thus, this poison is being dispensed at all levels of Israeli society from the synagogues and universities, to the kindergartens. The mind of a child (or of anyone else for that matter) cannot absorb the horrors of the Holocaust without finding someone to hate. Since there are no Nazis around against whom vengeance can be sought, Begin, Shamir and Sharon have solved this problem by calling the Arabs *the Nazis of today* and a proper target for retribution. If there is any doubt in anyone's mind that this poison has become systemic, the survey of the opinion of Israeli youth quoted earlier should remove it.

As we have seen, the World Zionist Organization has presented a detailed plan for the destruction of the Arab states *"as a prime strategic goal for Israel."* It may be that Israel is already preparing for this.

The Israeli government announced on September 9, 1989, a new five-year military budget which included a half billion shekels per year for the cost of suppressing the Intifada. The government report went on to say that the reason that a "multi-year" budget is being submitted, rather than an annual one, is that it is necessary in order *"to counter growing threats from the Arab world on an increasingly high tech battlefield."*

ISRAEL AND THE UNITED STATES VERSUS THE WORLD

Very little has been said, or written, about one of the most remarkable incidents in the field of international relations in recent history.

In December 1988, the U.S. refused to grant a visa to Yasser Arafat to allow him to address the U.N. General Assembly convened in New York City.

The U.N. General Assembly responded by voting 150 to 2 (U.S. and Israel) to adjourn its session and reconvene in Geneva, Switzerland, for the sole purpose of hearing Arafat. This decision involved moving the representatives of nearly all the peoples of the earth more than three thousand miles to hear a speech by the leader of the Palestine Liberation Organization on the Israeli-Palestinian problem. Yet the Israelis and Palestinians together number less than two-tenths of one percent of the more than five billion inhabitants of the globe.

Who is this Arafat person? Is he a spellbinding Demosthenes or a Cicero that the world is so eager to hear his voice? Not at all! He is, in fact, just a little bald man, half-shaven, said by the Israeli government to be a terrorist, rather inarticulate in English, and wearing a sort of napkin on his head. There is none of the charm or poise of a Sheik Yamani. He has, however, certain distinctions. Ariel Sharon has asked to have him assassinated and recently one Israeli peace activist was jailed for six months for having talked to him.

How is this extraordinary, almost bizarre, phenomenon to be explained? Is it possible that "anti-Semitism" has now infected a billion Chinese, eight hundred million Hindus, and all the multitudes of the other peoples of the earth who have never heard of Abraham, Moses, Jesus Christ, the Nazis or the Holocaust? Why this unanimous repudiation of Israel and deliberate humiliation of the U.S.? Can it be that "the cliché" (as David Shipler calls it) that "everyone is against us" has become a self-fulfilling prophecy?

If this is really true, some person in Israel ought to have the common sense to ask why.

Some reasons are, of course, evident. Although Israel owes its existence to the U.N., it has been a somewhat ungrateful child.

A few examples come to mind.

Israel has, as have all the members of the U.N., subscribed to the foundation principle of the U.N.—*the inadmissibility of acquiring territories by war,* yet Israel has virtually doubled its size by conquest.

Israel accepted the Partition Resolution of the U.N., which provided for two independent sovereign states in Palestine—one Jewish and the other Palestinian—but Israel had no intention of remaining within the borders established by the U.N. or ever permitting a Palestinian state.

Israel originally accepted U.N. Resolution 242 calling for a return of the occupied territories on the West Bank and Gaza, but the Likud government has rejected it.

Israel is in continuous violation of international law in establishing Israeli settlements in the occupied territories of the West Bank and Gaza.

In 1982, Israel launched an unprovoked war of aggression in Lebanon resulting in thousands of civilian casualties (mostly Palestinian refugees). This was the final blow which destroyed Lebanon.

Israel is also the unrepentant recipient of the condemnation of most human rights organizations in the world.

Not only did the U.N. vote represent an unprecedented rebuke to Israel and the U.S., but it is reported to have been one of the most enthusiastic votes on record in the General Assembly of the U.N.

Yet one suspects a deeper reason for this enthusiasm than simply the U.N.'s disgust and disappointment over Israel's conduct. It may indeed be the world's reaction to the righteous hypocrisies of the Likud leaders; the spectacle of terrorists condemning terrorism; racists ranting about racism and blaming the whole world for the Holocaust[33] while preaching the genocide of "Amalek with his women and children."

Even these, however, may not account for the emotional nature of the U.N. vote. Perhaps it was the mournful sight of the United States of America, the standard bearer for the Free World, sitting in the U.N., head bent, alone and shackled to Israel.

RELIGIOUS FANATICISM IN THE NUCLEAR AGE

While the world's attention, over the past decades of the cold war, has been focused upon the super power rivalry and the danger of a nuclear war, a far greater threat to the peace of the world has been growing almost without notice.

Most people have taken comfort in the belief that neither the U.S. nor the Soviet Union would be "crazy" enough to actually start a nuclear war. Mutual Assured Destruction (MAD) was the essence of the deterrent. Most of the concern has been that one or the other of the nuclear powers might *accidentally* fire a nuclear missile. Therefore, elaborate steps have been taken by both governments to prevent such an occurrence.

But what kind of nightmares would the world be having if Khadafi possessed a large nuclear arsenal; one of the finest air forces in the world; the highest level of military technology existing and boasted that he could strike his enemies anywhere on earth and would do so if, in his judgment, any nation threatened his security.

Yet, this is precisely what the fanatics in the Likud government are in a position to do, have threatened to do, and have in fact done, in the strike against the Iraqi nuclear reactor.

It is abundantly clear that the Likud government is dominated by a dangerous group of religious fanatics, whose primary "intent and purpose," according to Harkabi, is to amass political power and hold completely the reins of the government of Israel.

This is in preparation for the final triumph of Jewish history—"Redemption and Messianism"—which Harkabi says threaten Israel's survival:

> The explicit assertion that a certain period is the beginning of the Redemption arouses a hope that can only be destructive. Paradoxically, no idea poses a greater menace to the survival of the State of Israel *than that which links Zionism with Redemption and Messianism.*[34] [Emphasis supplied]

Harkabi believes that the ideas of Redemption and Messianism are *portents of disaster* because the disappointment caused by a failure of the Messiah to appear may be so unbearable that the consequences cannot be predicted. Harkabi explains:

> *The ideas of Redemption and Messianism are a portent of disaster in two respects.* In the short term, the *Messianic idea is a distraction from the need to consider reality and encourages unrealistic and rash policies.* What is the benefit of a Messianism whose practical result is that through the annexation of territories Israel becomes an Arab country or nearly so? Some would defend the new Messianism by presenting Zionism as a manifestation of a natural, historical Redemption. But what is the benefit of a Messianism without a Messiah? *The disappointment caused by disasters not mitigated by heavenly salvation can have serious consequences. A widespread obsession with Messianism is liable to end in grief.*
>
> Meir Kahane is certain that disaster is not on the cards: *"The State of Israel is not a political creature; it is a religious creature.* No power in the world could have prevented its establishment, and *no force can destroy it"* (p. 244). For him, "History is not a sequence of detached and chance events. There is a plan for history; the Jew is coming home for the third and final time. . . . 'The first redemption was the redemption from Egypt; the second was that of Ezra; and the third redemption has no end.' " The verses from *Midrash* are guarantee enough for him.[35] [Emphasis supplied]

It is highly doubtful that the Jewish community in the U.S. is at all aware of the intensity of the feelings of the religious extremists and the danger they pose to Israel, if their plans are carried out.

Harkabi doubts that even most Israelis are fully aware of the situation:

> Even many Jews fail to grasp the strength of the faith in the imminent arrival of the Messiah among some religious extremists, including members of Gush Emunim. Most Israelis are simply unaware that these circles deny any possibility that the Messiah might yet be long in coming, may even not come, *and the extent to which this faith supports them through hardships, prepares them for catastrophes, and encourages their adventures. They scorn all who doubt that the Messiah is coming soon and see tangible signs of his coming in every Zionist success and military victory.*

This faith also has a functional significance. *Without it, there is little sense to the settlement movement.* In addition, the more circumstances contradict their political ideas—the more it becomes evident that the territories cannot be held, that the Arabs are multiplying and will attain a majority, that the Arabs cannot be expelled and are rebelling—*the more tenacious their belief that the Messiah's coming is imminent.*

Placing the ideas of Redemption and Messianism at the center radically changes the Zionist ideology and the goal of the establishment of the Jewish state. The goal of Zionism ceases to be the solution for the historical vulnerability of the Jews and becomes the establishment of a state that will serve as a means to bring on the Redemption.[36]

The fact that there were Jews who plotted to blow up the Dome of the Rock should be a source of grave concern. It cannot be assumed that those who were brought to trial were alone. *Might a group opposed to eventual negotiations for resolving the Arab-Israeli conflict plant a bomb in the mosques as a means to derail them? Given the psychosis prevalent in some circles in the country, the chance that something like this will happen is not negligible.* In this context we cannot dismiss the significance of the widely disseminated aerial photograph of the Old City in which the mosques were airbrushed out of existence and replaced by a model of the Second Temple. Such a picture is apt to inspire yearnings for its realization. *Jewish extremists call the mosques an abomination, and this designation itself seemingly requires action to remove them.* In a yeshiva adjacent to the Temple Mount, garments for the Temple priests are already being woven in anticipation that they will be needed in the near future. *In other yeshivot, the detailed laws of animal sacrifices have become a popular topic of study, as if they will soon have contemporary relevance. Before, the Messiah was a hope, now he has become a necessity.*[37] [Emphasis supplied]

Messianic expectations have added a whole new politico-religious element to the Middle East powder keg. Irrationality is now, more than ever, the norm in the camp of the religious extremists.

Harkabi sees it as one of the greatest threats to peace:

One belief in the religious outlook goes far beyond the evaluation of the Jabotinsky ethos *that reality permits the Jews to behave as they wish: the belief that the Messiah's arrival is imminent.* If the Messiah is on his way there is nothing to fear; he will bail us out of all misfortunes and grant

Israel the final victory. The Messianic idea serves as a sort of insurance policy against all complications, countering all fears that reality might be a stumbling block on the road to desired goals. To many religious Jews, the successes of Zionism are signs that the Redemption has begun.[38]

Proponents of this view hold that Israel need have no fear of future wars, and can even provoke them at will. Rabbi Shlomo Aviner has written: "We must live in this land even at the price of war. Moreover, even if there is peace, *we must instigate wars of liberation in order to conquer it" (Arzi, p. 11). He does not specify what additional territory* should be conquered, but his words are clearly based on the assumption that everything is possible and all is permitted. It does not occur to him that going to war is a dangerous gamble.

One can understand *why soldiers and other young Israelis like Meir Kahane's thesis that Israel is indeed a mighty power but its leadership is too hesitant to make proper use of its forces to solve all Israel's problems with one blow, eliminating terrorism and expelling the Arabs. All of this comes close to the spirit of* the Jabotinsky-Begin ethos—the solution in a single energetic event.[39] [Emphasis supplied]

The important thing that must be kept in mind is that these are not the rantings and ravings of a Khomeini. These are people who boast of the power to strike any target on earth. They can start a war against anybody, at any time, for any reason and they want the world to know it.

It must be recognized that a new phenomenon has appeared, unprecedented in the history of the world, the consequences of which are incalculable—fanaticism and nuclear missiles.

An example of the emotional frenzy of religious fanatics, when the Messiah is believed to be at hand, may be seen in the account given by Abram Sachar of the Bar-Kokba rebellion, which appears in the first chapter of this book.

Bar-Kokba had the will, if not the power, to blow up the world—Israel has the power. Harkabi quotes Rabbi Kahane:

"We have it in our power to bring the Messiah" (Ha'aretz, August 8, 1984). The desires of the Almighty are merely a technical detail; *the decisive factor is the Jews' own will. If the Jews' own will can bring the Messiah, who can stand against them? The Arabs? The Americans? The Russians?*

Only those with an unshakable faith in the imminent arrival of the

Messiah could have begun to plot the demolition of the mosques on the Temple Mount, as the members of the so-called "Jewish Underground" did, without worrying about the consequences of such an act. *How else could they ignore the strong possibility that some or all of the forty Muslim states, from Indonesia and Pakistan to Morocco and Mauritania, would retaliate by declaring a holy war against Israel, that the superpowers would intervene to prevent a general conflagration,* and might even demand that Jerusalem be placed under international rule? Perhaps those who planned this deed hoped that God, confronted by the danger to Israel's existence from a Muslim Jihad, would be "compelled to send the Messiah in order to prevent the destruction of the third temple."[40] [Emphasis supplied]

There is a mindset among Israelis which most non-Jews (particularly those who lived through World War II) would find incredible. The vast majority of Israelis apparently believe that the Allies in World War II knew all about the Holocaust while it was in progress and could have stopped, or at least interfered with, the Nazi death camps. The Jewish response to this strange belief is, of course, a belligerent paranoia.

In May of 1983, the Israeli polling firm of Smith Research Center conducted an exhaustive survey of Israeli attitudes toward the Holocaust.

The survey revealed that the overwhelming majority of Israelis (83 percent) saw it as a major factor in how they saw the world. The report states that the "trauma of the Holocaust is very much on the minds of Israelis even in the second and third generations." An overwhelming majority (91 percent) believed that Western leaders knew of the mass killings and did little to save the Jews; only slightly fewer (87 percent) agreed with the following proposition:

"From the Holocaust we learn that Jews can not rely on non-Jews."[41]

Shipler says that this creates a "reverence for power which grows out of history's powerlessness and reverberates through Israeli-Jewish society." He quotes Rabbi David Spritzer in a letter to the *Jerusalem Post*:

One of the most important gains consequent to the establishment of the State of Israel has been the change in the traditional image of the Jew from the passive weakling who could be kicked about, robbed and murdered almost at will. Jewish blood has been cheap for hundreds of years. . . . Not any longer. If someone hits us in the stomach we will smash his head, perhaps those of his abettors too. . . . *I am not altogether displeased that the Jew is viewed as actually dangerous, that even a small provocation will engender a massive reaction.* We need the luxury of that image *for at least a generation.*[42] [Emphasis supplied]

Thus, we have all the elements necessary for achieving "critical mass;" a paranoia which extends to most of the population (not just religious extremists), a majority of which feel the world is against them;[43] an attitude nourished by constant reminders of the Holocaust; a deep suspicion that, underneath, the whole world is "anti-Semitic"; that non-Jews are not to be trusted.[44] Behind them is a God who is "mobilizing" against the Gentiles, and urging that Israelis defy any efforts to take away their "sacred lands" and who will punish them if they do allow it—a God who has chosen them as the select of mankind and expects them to live up to that responsibility—a Messiah who is *waiting for them to act*—a God who will guarantee victory.

What happens if the Messiah does not come and Israel becomes more isolated from the rest of the world and the dangerous reality of Israel's position becomes clear, even to the religious extremists? As Harkabi says, no one can say what will happen but it "portends disaster."

What if the nations of the world do not permit the Israelis to expel the Palestinians and the Arab states do not sit idly by waiting for Israel's army to reach the Nile and the Euphrates?

Israeli cities are already within the range of missiles from Egypt, Saudi Arabia, Syria and Iraq.

THE SAMSON COMPLEX

As long ago as October 9, 1977, shortly after the Likud government came to power, a report from Dial Torgenson, the Jerusalem correspondent for the *Los Angeles Times,* entitled "Israel Thinks The Unthinkable," was filed. The following is a portion of that report:

Since 1973, Israel has built up its arms-producing industrial base. It now makes not only its own artillery shells but its own jet fighters and tanks. The lessons of 1973 have not been lost upon this country. There has been a tremendous stockpiling of food, oil and ammunition for "the next time"—always, in Israel, whose people have fought four wars since 1948, there is talk of "the next time." Now, with hopes for Geneva peace talks shifting like the fitful Hamsin wind from the deserts of Jordan, there is talk everywhere of "the next time."

War in the Middle East could be disastrous for the Western world. Israeli military men have hinted darkly of taking the next war to the Arabs, Entebbe-style, and even the brief war Israel can afford could cause a disruption in oil supplies from which the industrial nations would find it hard to recover. The worldwide recession resulting from the 1973 Yom Kippur War *is just now fading. Next time it may be harder. Suppose, for example, that the next war left the oil fields of Israel's Arab foes in smoking ruins?*[245] [Emphasis supplied]

Several months earlier Torgenson had written an article for the *Los Angeles Times* entitled "Begin: How Explosive Are His Policies?"

The article from which the following is quoted provides an important insight into some Israeli thinking. Torgenson emphasizes the potential for global disaster:

JERUSALEM—The Zealots of Masada chose suicide over slavery, and died on their mountaintop fortress as the Romans prepared to conquer them. They gave a name to national suicide: The Masada Complex.

Samson, betrayed by Delilah, blinded and brought before the Philistines in their temple of Gaza, was a different type of zealot. *As the Philistines mocked him, he threw his might against the central columns of the temple and brought it down, killing all those in it—and himself. His was the suicide which took his tormentors with him: call it the Samson Complex.*

Israel stands today in as much danger as it once faced from the Romans and the Philistines. It is a nation that stands alone—except for its links, perhaps emanating to utter dependence, with the United States.

Israelis, to whom history has bequeathed millennia of disaster, calmly face their options—options which have been increased by Entebbe and the secrets of Dimona, Israel's atomic research center.

Some of these options have been only vaguely hinted at, but they are terrifying to the men who guide the other nations of the world.

"If there is another war," said Israel's chief of staff, Mordechai Gur, "there is no guarantee it will be fought exclusively on the Golan Heights and the Sinai Peninsula." *Israel learned at Entebbe that it could mount ground-air strikes over huge distances, a lesson not lost upon the Arabs. The Saudi Arabian government cited Gur's statement as a threat by the Israelis to blow up its oilfields.*

It has also been widely hinted that Israel would not let countries like

Libya and Saudi Arabia finance a war against them and escape punishment. From Tel Aviv, it is 1,280 miles to Tripoli, 960 to Riyadh, and 2,200 to Entebbe. *The possibility of a strike against the Arab oilfields is part of the balance of terror of the Middle East. Israel, according to many foreign sources, has developed atomic weapons at its Dimona facility and Israel has planes capable, with aerial refueling, of delivering such weapons across vast distances. Is it any wonder world powers view the threat of another Middle East war with dismay?*

"If the Arabs did not destroy Israel in their first strike," said a highly placed Israeli government official, "the Israeli counterstrike would set the Arabs back 50 years. *The possibility terrifies the Europeans. If Israel destroys the oilfields, the wheels of Western Europe would soon grind to a halt.* The Russians could just get on their tanks and drive right over—there would be nobody to stop them. And Japan would falter and halt, too.

"This is no longer an Israeli-Arab war we're talking about. It's a global matter."

But there is the history of the Jewish people to consider and what will happen in the Middle East may be affected by the events of the past.

"Jews will never be led away to be killed again," said a young sabra woman whose mother and father, almost alone out of their families, survived World War II Poland. "If they leave us no choice, it will not be Masada—*it will be Samson.*"

What if Israel takes Europe with it when it goes?

"When I'm gone, and Israel is gone, I couldn't care less," she said.

And Western Civilization, as we know it?

"I couldn't care less." [Emphasis supplied]

The article concludes with the observation that, unless the occupied territories are returned, Israel and the Palestinians "will live with a balance of terror while the threat of disaster hangs poised in the air, a disaster in which Israel would be Samson, and the temple *so vast that few nations would be unaffected by its fall.*"[46] [Emphasis supplied]

Time magazine's issue of July 4, 1988, contains an article entitled "A Deadly New Missile Game," which reports on the escalating arms race in the Middle East:

Now that the superpowers have agreed to eliminate medium-range missiles from their arsenals, these weapons are fast turning into the most sought-after items in the Middle East. In the process, they are changing the nature of warfare in one of the world's most volatile regions. True, the missiles being stockpiled by seven Middle Eastern nations (Egypt, Iran, Iraq, Israel, Libya, Saudi Arabia and Syria) are not yet nuclear—with the highly probable exception of Israel's. But the conventionally armed weapons have figured prominently in the eight-year-old gulf war between Iraq and Iran, and they threaten to make future conflicts in the region bloodier and more intractable than ever before. Writes W. Seth Carus of the Washington Institute for Near East Policy: "It is only a matter of time before these countries acquire significant inventories of accurate missiles armed with highly lethal warheads."

What helped touch off the current Middle East arms race, beginning about three years ago, was the "war of the cities," in which Iran showered missiles on Baghdad and Iraq later reciprocated against Tehran. To reach Iran's capital, which was beyond the flight capacity of their Soviet-made Scud-B missiles, the Iraqis managed to double the weapon's range to 360 miles. During the latest outbreak of this war-within-a-war last winter, the two sides fired more than 200 missiles at each other, claiming at least 2,000 lives. The casualties would be much greater if Middle Eastern nations had equipped the missiles with chemical warheads, as many experts predict they eventually will.

Curbing the region's missile arsenals has proved to be a difficult if not impossible task. U.S. officials were stunned last March by intelligence reports that Saudi Arabia had secretly purchased at least ten Chinese CSS-2 missiles, each with a range of 1,550 miles. Last week, in an attempt to head off yet another missile deal, the U.S. expressed "deep concern" at the prospect of China's selling the Syrians its M9 missiles (estimated range: 500 miles).

Also last week, in an incident that could damage Washington's relations with Cairo, federal officials accused five people, including two Egyptian army colonels, of seeking to smuggle from the U.S. a tightly controlled chemical used in the manufacture of missiles. Cairo apparently wants the material, called carbon-carbon, to enhance the accuracy of a new missile, code-named Bader-2000, that Egyptian and Argentinian scientists are developing with Iraqi money.

Israel, which produces two classes of Jericho missiles, has grown increasingly alarmed as one hostile neighbor after another has begun collecting weapons that could reach population centers inside the Jewish state. When asked about the rumored Syrian-Chinese deal, Prime Minister Yitzhak Shamir replied cryptically, "We shall not sit by idly." His words suggested *a possible pre-emptive strike against a future Syrian missile cache.*

The U.S. has lately moved to the forefront of efforts to put a lid on further proliferation. Last year Washington helped form the Missile Technology Control Regime, an agreement with six other Western nations that severely restricts the export of missile-related hardware and technology. Speaking at June's special session on disarmament at the United Nations, Secretary of State George Shultz warned that "we are already seeing signs of a dangerous new arms race which will put at risk countries far removed from the gulf region itself." The irony is that both the U.S. and the Soviet Union, even as they seek to reduce their own arsenals, appear unable to contain the spread of missiles among their Middle East clients.[47] [Emphasis supplied]

On May 6, 1989, an article was published in the *Los Angeles Times* entitled: "Arming the Middle East: An Ominous List Expands," written by Enrico Jacchia, Director of Strategic Studies at the Free University of Rome. The article is set forth in full:

The quickening arms race in the Middle East is raising concerns among nations bordering the Mediterranean. Libya, Israel, Syria, Iraq and Egypt have acquired new and dangerous military technology, dramatically increasing the dangers of local confrontations.

Europeans, who welcomed the elimination of the SS-20, cruise and Pershing 2 missiles, are dismayed by the prospect of a proliferation of new mass-destruction weapons at their southern doorstep.

The list of hardware creating ominous risks gets longer every month: chemical weapons, missiles, nuclear arsenals and sophisticated bombers.

As for Col. Moammar Kadafi's chemical plant, strong U.S. pressures have not prevented the continuing transfer of technology and basic materials from industrialized countries to Libya, according to European sources. The Western World will soon have to decide what to do about it, but in the meantime a new dimension has been added to the Libyan threat: the Soviet supply to Tripoli of high-performance bombers and an airborne refueler.

Allies on the southern flank of the North Atlantic Treaty Organization have been puzzled by the Soviet move, which contradicts the

Kremlin's claim that Moscow wants to play a more conciliatory role in the Arab-Israeli conflict, seeking to increase its influence in the region through policies that bolster stability, rather than undermine it.

The international press has focused its attention on the threat that an enhanced Libyan capability might imply for Israel. However, William H. Webster, director of the U.S. Central Intelligence Agency, recently told a congressional committee that if Libya extended the range and performances of its warplanes, the entire balance of power in the region could be altered.

All the more so, given Kadafi's unpredictability. A couple of years ago he substantiated his threats against Italy by ordering two Scud missiles—which fortunately missed—to be fired at the Italian island of Lampedusa. Kadafi claimed a U.S. Coast Guard station on Lampedusa had guided American planes on their April, 1986, raid on Libya. The Italian Ministry of Defense has pointedly announced that new radar systems will be installed in the Southern part of the peninsula, acknowledging that the Soviet SU-24 bombers recently sold to Libya could, if refueled in the air, reach all of Italy—as well as parts of France and West Germany.

While the chemical weapons situation is not encouraging, recent developments concerning missiles and their potential payloads are no brighter. These weapons appear to be more freely available in the international arms market than was intended by the Seven industrial nations (the United States, Britain, Canada, France, Italy, Japan and West Germany) when they agreed to restrict access to missile technology in April, 1987, with the Missile Technology Control Regime. And now there is a growing risk that surface-to-surface medium-range missiles will be armed with nuclear warheads and spread throughout the Middle East.

Israeli officials have alleged that Iraq is secretly engaged in a crash program to build nuclear warheads for a medium-range missile under development with technical and financial assistance from Argentina and Egypt. While the missile project (called Condor 2 by the Argentines) has been confirmed, the allegations about the Iraqi nuclear program have raised doubts. Both the news and the unconfirmed allegations, nevertheless, offer Israel a good reason—or a good pretext—for proceeding with its crash program on nuclear arms, missiles and other sophisticated weapons.

Estimates on the number of atomic warheads Israel possesses vary considerably, depending on interpretations given to data that Israeli technician Mordecai Vanunu disclosed in his Oct. 5, 1986, interview with the *London Sunday Times.* Israel might have an arsenal of 100 or 200 nuclear devices, according to several specialists who analyzed the data and examined the photographs supplied by Vanunu. Accepting the authenticity of his technical data, Theodore Taylor, a former U.S. weapons designer, and Frank Barnaby, a British nuclear scientist who debriefed Vanunu extensively, also believes Israel has produced weapons that use nuclear fusion: H-bombs.

The consensus among U.S. officials who have access to the information provided by intelligence sources is that Israel's nuclear arsenal contains no more than 50 to 70 devices. Yet even an arsenal of this size is much bigger than all previous estimates and could enable Israel to develop a nuclear strategy based on a panoply of tactical, medium range and strategic atomic weapons.

This is a distinct change in the Middle East scenario. France has been until now the only medium-size power to have a totally independent nuclear deterrent, the *force de frappé*—striking force—and an original doctrine for its employment. Has the *force de frappé* concept proliferated? *Israel is apparently developing a missile that can reach the Soviet Union.* Should we conclude that Israel has a nuclear defense strategy?

If this is a plausible conclusion, then Gen. Charles de Gaulle's predictions have been proved right. De Gaulle was utterly skeptical about the possibility of preventing the spread of atomic weapons through international constraints. His nuclear doctrine was based on the assumption that every industrial nation would, in time, possess its own nuclear arsenal composed of a panoply of weapons adapted to its specific situation and needs—its own *force de frappé.*

The importance of Israel's nuclear development has increased to a point that it might constitute an Israeli *force de frappé* doctrine—a doctrine playing a vital role in Israeli defense and strategic thinking. This, in turn, gives a powerful impetus to the arms buildup of the Arab and Muslim states in the region. *Something must be done to arrest this calamitous spiral.*[48] [Emphasis supplied]

The September 25, 1989 issue of *U.S. News & World Report* contains an article on Iraq's current military buildup upon which Israel's defense minister comments:

Israeli Defense Minister Yitzhak Rabin warns that Iraq is "potentially the most dangerous nation in the Middle East." "Let's not even talk about Iraqi chemical weapons, nuclear development and missiles," says a senior intelligence office in Tel Aviv. "They have more tanks than the French and enough troops to maintain security on their 1,000-mile border with Iran and still send 10 divisions across Jordan to attack us."[49]

If any further proof is needed that the Middle East situation is completely out of control, the report appearing in the *Jerusalem Post* of September 23, 1989, entitled, "Israeli Missile Capability Causes Concern in Moscow," should suffice:

Soviet Foreign Minister Eduard Shevardnadze is expected to take up the question of Israel's ballistic missile capability with Foreign Minister Moshe Arens when they meet in New York this month.

The Israel foreign and defense ministries have both denied knowledge of the firing of a 1,300 km-range ballistic missile into the Mediterranean between Libya and Greece last week. The Soviet news agency Tass, quoting "Soviet Defense Ministry data," reported such a firing from the region of Jerusalem. (The *Washington Post* has quoted U.S. officials as saying the Soviet report was accurate.)

In the past, Moscow has shown great sensitivity to and expressed concern about Israel's ballistic capabilities and reports of the "Jericho-II" missile. The matter has been raised in bi-lateral meetings at the highest level, with Israel consistently trying to reassure the Kremlin on this point.

In July 1987, Radio Moscow's Hebrew-language service accused Israel of developing a nuclear-capable missile, reportedly called the Jericho-II. The Soviets reacted angrily to the reported launching calling the missile a threat to its security and warned Israel not to continue developing a weapon that is said was capable of reaching its southern border.

The Geneva-based International Defense Review reported at the same time that Israel had successfully fired the missile into the Mediterranean and that it covered 820 kilometres on the test. According to Tass, Israel launched a ballistic missile in January 1988.

According to *Jane's Defense Weekly,* Israel conducted a second secret test of its Jericho-II surface-to-surface tactical nuclear missile in September 1988. *Jane's* said the missile's projected maximum range is about 1,500 kms. The magazine pointed out that in that case it would be capable of hitting the capitals of all of Israel's potential enemies, including Baghdad.

Israel, which launched its first satellite on September 19 last year, has always refused to comment on whether it is developing missiles, let alone nuclear weapons.

Strategic expert Dore Gold, told the *Jerusalem Post* that over the last two years the Soviets have been "increasingly sensitive to the proliferation of missile technology along a belt of countries from Libya to India close to their southern border."

"The Soviets have been seeking areas of policy coordination on the Middle East with the U.S.," said Gold. "The missile proliferation issue could become as useful to them for this purpose as the Palestinian issue."[50]

In the following final chapters of this book we will attempt to define the crucial issues, discuss a way out of this onrushing nightmare, and propose a solution to the Israeli-Palestinian conflict.

CHAPTER XII

The Issues

IN DISCUSSING THE major issues between Israel and the Palestinians, an attempt will be made to clear away the accumulated diplomatic debris which has piled up over the years and to dispel the clouds of rhetoric which have obscured the facts to the point where the issues have been made difficult to identify and, hence, impossible to solve.

In this, we will follow a loose format consisting of a summary statement of the issue and, where appropriate, the position of each party with respect thereto, and a brief analysis of the merits of the arguments on both sides. Roman numerals are used simply to identify the issues, not to indicate relative priority or importance.

As stated earlier, this book is concerned only with the primary and fundamental issues dividing Israel and the Palestinians, i.e., the status of the West Bank and Gaza and the Palestinian refugee question.

These are the explosive issues—the Middle East time bomb on which time is fast running out. The question of the future status of Jerusalem, however important, does not have the same urgency and should be left for future negotiations. Similarly, the status of the Golan Heights is a separate question involving Syria and should also be left for future negotiations between the parties.

The Issues

ISSUE I: THE PROBLEM OF THE PALESTINIAN REFUGEES

THE PALESTINIAN POSITION ON THE REFUGEES

In 1948, during Israel's War of Independence, some 700,000 men, women and children were driven from their homes in Palestine by a combination of Israeli military forces, roving bands of terrorists led by Menachem Begin and Yitzhak Shamir, combined with an orchestrated propaganda campaign by the Israeli government to frighten the Palestinians into fleeing their homes.

These refugees have never been allowed to return to their homes and lands, which were promptly confiscated by the Israeli army, and are now within the boundaries of Israel proper—not the West Bank. Today, these refugees, with their descendants, number in excess of one million, many of which have been living in settlements and camps under wretched conditions over the past 40 years. The refugees seek to return to their lands *in Israel* or to receive just compensation.

THE ISRAELI POSITION ON THE REFUGEE PROBLEM

The Israelis contend that the Palestinian refugees left their homes and lands *voluntarily,* trusting the promises of the Arab states that they could return with the "victorious" Arab armies.

Israel argues that the refugees "abandoned" their lands which were then confiscated by Israel. The Israeli justification for this summary confiscation and for not allowing the refugees to return after hostilities ceased, is: "They lost the war—they lose the land."

ANALYSIS

1. The facts pertaining to this issue are fully discussed and detailed in Chapter IV entitled "The Arab-Israeli Wars." In summary, the Palestinian position *is completely justified* by Simha Flapan. The Israeli position, according to Flapan, *is a myth and pure propaganda.* Flapan's position is also supported by other prominent Israeli historians.

2. In further support of the Palestinian position, the United Nations Charter (under which the State of Israel came into being) *prohibits the acquisition of land by conquest.*

U.N. Resolution 242 also calls for a "just settlement" of the Palestinian refugee question.

ISSUE II: THE RETURN BY ISRAEL OF THE OCCUPIED TERRITORIES ON THE WEST BANK AND GAZA

THE PALESTINIAN POSITION ON THE RETURN OF THE OCCUPIED TERRITORIES

Israel should withdraw all of its forces from the occupied lands on the West Bank and Gaza and return to its 1967 borders.

JUSTIFICATION FOR THE PALESTINIAN POSITION

U.N. Resolution 242 promulgated by the Security Council on November 22, 1967, after the conclusion of the Six Day War, reads in part as follows:

> *Emphasizing the inadmissibility of acquiring territory by war* and the need to work for a just and lasting peace in which every state in the area can live in security.
>
> *Emphasizing* further that the member states in accepting the Charter of the United Nations have undertaken *a commitment to act in accordance with Article 2 of the Charter.*
>
> 1. *Affirms* that the fulfillment of the charter principles requires the establishment of a just and lasting peace in the Middle East, which should include the application of both the following principles:
>   (i) *Withdrawal of Israeli armed forces from territories occupied in the recent conflict* (the 1967 Six Day War).
>   (ii) Termination of all claims or state of belligerency and respect for, and acknowledgment of, the sovereignty of territorial integrity and political independence of every state in the area and their right to live in peace with secure and recognized boundaries free from threats or acts of force. [Emphasis supplied]

U.N. Resolution 338, enacted October 22, 1973 (following the October 1973 war), calls upon the parties concerned to start immediately after the cease fire to implement the Security Council's *Resolution 242 in all its parts.* Israel has done nothing to implement U.N. Resolution 242 or 338.

ISSUE III: THE ESTABLISHMENT OF A PALESTINIAN STATE

THE PALESTINIAN POSITION ON A PALESTINIAN STATE

The Palestinian people have an undeniable legal right to self-determination and to a sovereign state to be established on the West Bank and Gaza.

JUSTIFICATION FOR THE PALESTINIAN POSITION

The *Plan of Partition* adopted by the United Nations on November 29, 1947, *which divided Palestine into separate Jewish and Arab states,* is the juridical basis upon which the State of Israel was declared and came into existence, and the basis upon which the Palestinian state has been declared. If the U.N. Partition Resolution is not valid for the Palestinians, *Israel has no legal foundation.*

The United Nations' Partition Plan adopted on November 29, 1947, states in part as follows:

1. The basic premise underlying the partition proposal is that the claims to Palestine of the Arabs and Jews, both possessing validity, are irreconcilable, and that among all of the solutions advanced, *partitions will provide the most realistic and practicable settlement,* and is the most likely to afford a workable basis for meeting in part the claims and national aspirations of both parties.

2. *It is a fact that both of these peoples have their historic roots in Palestine,* and that both make vital contributions to the economic and cultural life of the country. *The partition solution takes these considerations fully into account.*

3. *The basic conflict in Palestine is a clash of two intense nationalisms.* Regardless of the historical origins of the conflict, the rights and wrongs of the promises and counter-promises, and the international intervention incident to the Mandate, there are now in Palestine some 650,000 Jews and some 1,200,000 Arabs who are dissimilar in their ways of living and, for the time being, separated by political interests which render difficult full and effective political co-operation among them, whether voluntary or induced by constitutional arrangements.

4. Only by means of partition can these conflicting national aspirations find substantial expression and *qualify both peoples to take their places as independent nations in the international community and in the United Nations.*

5. *The partition solution provides that finality which is a most urgent need in the solution.* Every other proposed solution would tend to induce the two parties to seek modification in their favor by means of persistent pressure. *The grant of independence to both States, however, would remove the basis for such efforts.* [Emphasis supplied]

Thus, a Palestinian state is not something thought up recently by the PLO and Yasser Arafat.

The right to an independent Palestinian state was granted to the Palestinians in 1947 in the same document in which the right to a State of Israel was granted to the Jewish Agency.

Israel's responses to the Palestinian Positions on Issues II and III are based on three alternative arguments.

ARGUMENT 1

It is necessary for Israel to occupy (and annex) the West Bank and Gaza in order to give Israel *defensible borders,* otherwise Israel would be too vulnerable to attack from its Arab neighbors. Israel's *security* cannot be jeopardized. A Palestinian state next to Israel would destroy Israel's security.

ARGUMENT 2

The so-called "occupied lands" of the West Bank and Gaza are part of ancient Eretz Israel given by God to Abraham in perpetuity and, as such, are "sacred" lands which must not be returned. Therefore, they cannot properly be called "occupied lands" because Israel *owns* them. They should be called "Judea" and "Samaria," and not the "West Bank." Israel has not conquered them, it has "liberated" them. That is why Israel has rejected the application of U.N. Resolution 242, because it doesn't apply to lands that are already owned.

ARGUMENT 3

Israel has a *"historic right"* to all of Palestine and ancient Eretz Israel.

ANALYSIS

On a legal basis, the Palestinian case is completely valid and incontestable. Israel's case is based on non-legal arguments, which it contends overrides legalities.

ISRAEL'S ARGUMENT 1—SECURITY

Obviously, no nation on planet Earth has "defensible borders," including the United States. The idea that a few (or many) miles of added territory will provide security for *any* nation is a primitive concept more appropriate to the days of castles, moats and city walls. It is "Maginot Line" thinking. In an age of supersonic bombers, ballistic and guided missiles, chemical and biological weapons and nuclear bombs and artillery, security for Israel, or any nation, can only come with a just and durable peace. All else is a fatal delusion.

Today, Israel has little to fear from the Palestinians or other Arab countries over which it has undisputed military superiority. Essentially, what is at issue is *Israel's permanent security needs*.

Security is the critical issue involved in any plan for peace so far as Israel is concerned and must be viewed on the basis of a "worst case" scenario. Israel's security is an *absolute prerequisite* to any successful peace plan.

Since we are stipulating that Israel's security is a *sine qua non*, discussion of the matter of *how* Israel's security can be assured will be deferred until we examine and analyze the details of the Plan for Peace itself.

ISRAEL'S ARGUMENT 2—DIVINE RIGHT: ANALYSIS

Israel's claim to the West Bank and Gaza, based on "Divine right," has many facets to it. Admittedly, a land title issue where God is the putative grantor, leaves little in the way of legal precedent for guidance.

The Divine right justification for Israel's refusal to abide by U.N. Resolution 242 and 338 was only raised as a serious issue when the Likud government took power in the spring of 1977 and it dumfounded President Carter in his first meeting with Prime Minister Begin. This is the reason why Carter gave up trying to discuss with Begin the West Bank and Gaza (which Sadat called the "Mother Issue" of the Middle East) and concentrated upon the Sinai question, which Begin did not claim was sacred land or part of Eretz Israel.

There is a question whether this mystical claim of Divine right should be seriously addressed at all. It has been decided to do so for two reasons.

First. It is the ostensible ideological or religious reason behind the Likud's West Bank and Gaza settlement policy—the most bitter and emotional issue of all. Since the beginning of the Intifada, the Likud (on behalf of the Israeli settlers) has been putting increasing emphasis on the biblical claim. As far as the West Bank settlers are concerned, the biblical claim is paramount, and security is secondary.

Second. If Israel's *security* problem is satisfactorily resolved, the "Divine right" and "historic right" arguments are all that the Likud has to fall back on in its efforts to justify holding on to and annexing the West Bank and Gaza. This means that these issues must be addressed at some point and this is the proper place.

Preliminarily, and before proceeding to more important considerations, the following general observations with respect to the Divine right position are appropriate:

1. The scriptural basis for the Divine right argument is one on which biblical scholars are in hopeless disagreement, and there are a myriad of interpretations, most of them contradictory.
2. Most Jews in Israel and elsewhere are secular, non-observing Jews who do not interpret the Old Testament literally and would not support the Divine right argument. The evidence is overwhelming that the American Jewish community's dedication to Israel has been, and is, based upon a perpetual fear that the State of Israel might be destroyed by its enemies, and not upon any Divine mission to restore Eretz Israel. What a majority of the Israeli people want is *peace with security.*
3. Even the relatively small minority of Jews who are "Orthodox" are divided concerning Zionism and whether the modern State of Israel is the fulfillment of biblical prophecy and the beginning of the Messianic Age.
4. While it must be conceded that God works in mysterious ways, the fact is that the founding fathers of Zionism were European socialists who, for the most part, were non-religious Jews (some of them atheists) whose guiding principles were to create an agrarian society based on social justice related in no way to a fulfillment of Judaism. Historian Paul Johnson, in his highly regarded (and pro-Israel) *History of the Jews,* states what is undisputed:

   Zionism had no place for God as such. For Zionists, Judaism was just a convenient source of national energy and culture, the Bible no more than a State Book. That was why from the start most religious Jews regarded Zionism with suspicion or outright hostility and some (as we have noted) believed it was the work of Satan.[1]

The Likud government insists that the media not refer to the West Bank as the "West Bank" but, rather as "Judea" and "Samaria." As we have seen in the first chapter, "Samaria" *as such* was inhabited, *not by Jews,* but by

Samaritans who, at the time of the destruction of Jerusalem by the Romans (A.D. 70), had been living in Samaria for 800 years. This is a small matter but, since this subject is engaging the world's attention, efforts should be made to eliminate even small historical inaccuracies.

Nevertheless, the implications of the Divine right argument are intriguing and, before leaving the mystical aspects of this subject, we are compelled to ask several hypothetical questions.

It is commonly known that one of the fundamental and underlying causes of the war with Japan was the ultimatum issued to Japan by the U.S. and other Western powers, to abandon its conquest of China and withdraw its armies or suffer a trade embargo. Japan had a clear choice of getting out of China, or facing economic strangulation. Since she would not, or could not, get out of China, the embargo was imposed on Japan and Pearl Harbor followed.

What if the Japanese, in 1941, had responded to our ultimatum by claiming that a Shinto god had *promised* China to the Japanese people 2,500 years ago (China being the original homeland of the Japanese)?

Suppose, for example, the Japanese argued, as does the Likud, that they were not "occupying" China but were "liberating" it to make room for Japanese settlers, and it was necessary to torture and kill trouble-making Chinese to keep order.

These hypothetical questions are not as fanciful as the Likud Divine right argument. Indeed, the Japanese would have a better case for China than the Likud does for the West Bank and Gaza.

The validity of the Japanese claim to its "ancient homeland" would be supported by a hundred million devoutly believing Japanese, vastly more than the number of Orthodox Jews in the world. The Japanese also had a living, breathing god-Emperor with lineage going back 2,500 years, who could confirm, if necessary, that China *had* been promised to the Japanese people. The emperor was officially "divine" until 1945; and many Japanese believe he continued to be divine until his death.

What would be the response of the U.S. to the Japanese position? This is more than an interesting speculation; it puts the Likud's Divine right argument into a rational perspective.

This brings us to the final and decisive response to the Likud's Divine right argument.

Assuming that such a right ever existed and, over the last 3,000 years, it had not been abandoned; extinguished by "adverse possession"; revoked by "Yahve" (God) because of the transgressions of the Israelites; and was, in the eyes of the Zionists, a valid and subsisting right in 1947, it nevertheless cannot be raised today and recognized as a legal or moral right of Israel to the West Bank and Gaza for the simple reason that it was clearly and indisputably *forfeited* when Israel accepted the Partition of Palestine in 1947.

Having never raised or asserted it at the time that Israel's statehood and the Partition Resolution was being debated and voted on in the U.N., Israel is "estopped" from doing so now. The only appropriate remedy for Israel might be a request by Prime Minister Shamir for a rehearing on the matter by the General Assembly of the United Nations.

However, the Divine right claim is a *dangerous* argument which Israel should not in any event pursue. It plays directly into the hands of the so-called hard-line Arab countries who believe, for some reason or another, that Israel is an expansionist-minded and predatory power and that *even keeping the West Bank and Gaza would not satisfy its territorial ambitions.*

President Assad of Syria makes a special point that, if the Likud and the Gush Emunim biblical positions are accepted as far as Eretz Israel is concerned, then all of the land between the "Nile and Euphrates," which includes *Syria, as well as Lebanon, Iraq, and Jordan, would belong to Israel.*

The so-called "hard-line" Arab countries have good reason to be suspicious of Israel's real intentions, if the religious extremists are controlling Israel's foreign policy. Harkabi writes:

Jewish religious circles also promote the expansionist tendencies of the State of Israel. An item in *Ha'aretz* (August 24, 1985) reported on the distribution of information sheets for school excursions to sixty principals. The author of the document explained:

We're talking about the most convenient method for expansion. . . . *From the political perspective, we have to reach the Tigris and Euphrates. It's written in the halakha.* There's no argument about this, the only argument is over applying it in practice—whether it needs to be done by force or not. As for the boundaries of the Land of Israel, there are no arguments; they are clear axioms.[2]

The Arab states can conclude from this that there is no point in making peace with Israel because there is no limit to the territorial claims of the religious extremists.

ISRAEL'S ARGUMENT 3: ISRAEL HAS A HISTORIC RIGHT TO ALL OF PALESTINE

It is not clear whether this "historic right" is independent of Divine sponsorship, or whether it is claimed by the Likud only when the Divine right argument is not, for some reason, persuasive. In any event, its chief defect as an argument is that it is utterly meaningless.

However, since it regularly appears in print and on television, and the prime minister of Israel solemnly speaks of it for all the world to hear, it cannot simply be ignored. Being an argument devoid of meaning, it is only with some embarrassment that an attempt is made here to answer it, since it is *logically* impossible to do so.

Since no help is offered from the advocates of this nebulous right as to its origin, nature or significance, or how, when and by whom it can be invoked, acquired or lost, one must necessarily improvise and imagine what a "historic right" *could* mean, and what the consequences would be if it were incorporated into international jurisprudence and applied as a rule of law.

If it is intended to mean that there is some inherent historic right of a people to return to lands held by their ancestors, no matter how long ago, and to dispossess or expel the peoples now in possession, then there is little land on earth, except Antarctica, the title to which is not impaired or subject to challenge. If, however, it means that only the *Jewish people* have this historic right, then we come full circle back to "God."

On the other hand, if this same principle of historic right applies to mankind *as a species,* a goodly portion of the population of the U.S. are squatters.

THE CASE OF THE CHEROKEE NATION

The Cherokee Indian nation less than two hundred years ago occupied, and had occupied, from time immemorial, approximately 40,000 square miles of fertile land located, for the most part, in Virginia, North and South Carolina, and Georgia. Their right to retain these historically-held lands was confirmed by a treaty with the U.S. government.

The Cherokees were a highly intelligent, civilized and peaceful people. They were agricultural, not nomadic and, during the early part of the nineteenth century, were a prosperous and successful society. The Cherokees had developed a thriving lumber industry, had established numerous schools and built an extensive network of roads. Alone among North

American Indians, they had a written language and had always maintained peaceful relations with their white neighbors.

However, by the year 1838, a huge influx of settlers, prospectors, and miners had begun encroaching on their territory, all of whom coveted the Cherokee lands. It was then decided, by the government of the United States under Andrew Jackson, that the Cherokees would really be happier in Oklahoma.

The Cherokees did not see it that way but did not go on the warpath. They simply complained bitterly about this injustice and took their case to the U.S. Supreme Court, where the great Justice, John Marshall, confirmed the title of the Cherokees to their lands. Justice Marshall did not have an army but Andrew Jackson did and it was then that Jackson uttered his famous statement—"John Marshall made his decision, let him enforce it."

Jackson dispatched the army to round up the Cherokees, all 18,000 of them. Not being warlike, many tried to escape into hiding but, eventually, nearly all were captured. The army corralled the Cherokees in military camps throughout a stifling summer, during which many died and many more fell ill. In the fall and winter, the Cherokees were moved west, some in flatboats, some in wagons, others on foot.

American Heritage "History of the Cherokees" describes this sad event in these poignant words:

A young private who watched one wagon train pull out wrote that "in the chill of a drizzling rain on an October morning I saw them loaded like cattle or sheep into six hundred and forty-five wagons and started toward the west. . . . When the bugle sounded and the wagons started rolling many of the children . . . waved their little hands good-bye to their mountain homes."

The Cherokees had twelve hundred miles to go before they reached eastern Oklahoma at the end of the trek they would forever after remember as the Trail of Tears. As their homeland disappeared behind them the cold autumn rains continued to fall, bringing disease and death. Four thousand shallow graves marked the trail. Marauding parties of white men appeared, seized Cherokee horses in payment for imaginary debts, and rode off. The Indians pressed on, the sullen troopers riding beside them.

They came at last to the Mississippi, gray and swollen under the huge unfamiliar sky. The ragged Indians stared across the river at the lands they had never seen and never wished to see. Behind them lay the East, the graves of their ancestors, places of their birth, the land that they—and all the other tribes—had loved well, and had struggled to hold, and had lost forever.[3]

If there is such a thing as a "historic right," can there be any question that the Cherokees have a right to return and repossess their historic homelands? The history is fresh—the facts thoroughly documented—their rights adjudicated by the U.S. Supreme Court. Certainly, the God of Justice must be on their side. What further is needed to invoke and enforce their "historic right" to North and South Carolina, Georgia, and parts of Virginia?

Would the present inhabitants of those states, living on formerly Cherokee lands, accept being called thieves, as Rabbi Aviner calls the Palestinians? Would they agree to be "transferred out," in order to make room for returning Cherokees? How would they respond if the Cherokees adopted the Likud policy of making their lives so miserable they would want to leave? Would they agree that the Cherokees were simply liberating their ancient lands?

The injustice being done in the case of the Palestinians is compounded. The whites *did* steal the land; the Palestinians are innocent.

It would be a great boon to some of the oppressed of mankind if the Likud scholars would deign to explain and define this right of the historically dispossessed. It may be, given the opportunity, that the Australian aborigines, who have a history and prehistory going back *40,000 years,* would prefer the climate of Sydney to the Outback.

THE CASE OF IRELAND

The Irish people, north and south, had lived on their lands for thousands of years. Beginning with Elizabeth I of England and extending through Cromwell's misrule, the Irish of the north were driven from their lands at the point of the sword to a rocky, barren, windswept county in Western Ireland, "Connaught." The British battle cry to the Irish was—"To Hell or Connaught." The Irish mistakenly thought they were being given a choice—the British gave them *both* for four centuries.

The British used the confiscated land of Ulster (North Ireland) to settle colonies of alien Scotch Presbyterians, who became the ruling class of Northern Ireland, while the real Irish were forced into living a subclass marginal existence, where they were persecuted religiously, economically and politically, a situation which persists to this day. The Northern Ireland problem is not (despite common belief) a *religious* one—it is a *civil right issue* almost as bad as the blacks in South Africa and much like the Palestinians.

The Southern Irish, however, were not banished to Connaught but were simply dispossessed of their lands and made serfs. Serfs, of course, were necessary to work the large new estates being set up in Ireland by the British gentry and the land confiscators.

Do the Irish have a "historic right" to their ancient lands?

Of course, the Cherokees and the Irish are only two small peoples among what must be hundreds of millions of dispossessed and resettled populations all over the world since the year 700 B.C., *the last time the Israelites lived in what became Samaria.*

What is puzzling about all this is that, in a world full of lawyers, the Likud can, without challenge, conjure up something called a "historic right" which is recognized by no code of law or system of justice from Hammurabi to the Charter of the United Nations, and is not part of any body of jurisprudence anywhere. If the "historic right" claim were pleaded in any cause in any court or tribunal, national or international, it would be summarily dismissed, on motion, as "frivolous." Yet it commands the enforced attention of the governments of the world, and "rights" are invented *ad hoc* by the Likud government without reason or rationale, heedless of the consequences to the lives of millions of unfortunate people clinging to a small piece of land, home to their ancestors, in mortal fear of being driven out.

"Historic right" is a mischievous, as well as meaningless, claim. It fires the passions of the Israeli settlers on the West Bank, where little Jewish boys, fresh from Minsk, tell little Palestinian boys, whose families have lived there for centuries, to "get out of our Jewish land."

Finally, Israel should be aware that both the Divine right claim and the historic right claim are hazardous and can have serious political ramifications, because *they effectively rip the lid off Pandora's box* (as Flapan calls it) and bring into question the very *bona fides of the foundation of Israel itself.*

Earlier in this chapter, the view was expressed that any rights to the West Bank and Gaza, which may have existed 3,000 years ago and were not abandoned or negated since, were *forfeited* when Israel accepted the U.N. Partition Plan in 1947. However, that is by no means the whole story.

It is important to read what Simha Flapan has to say on this point in his book, *The Birth of Israel: Myths and Realities:*

Israel's legendary willingness to *compromise* and sacrifice with regard to the *scope of the Jewish state was the foundation on which its entire mythology was built during the crucial period of the U.N. deliberations in 1947 and 1948. The myth was invoked by all of Israel's representatives*—Moshe Sharett, Abba Eban, Eliyahu (Eliat) Epstein, Gideon Raphael, and Michael Comay—*in their conversations with U.N. delegates, foreign ministers, and foreign diplomats.* Typical was the argument made by Sharett, who was Israel's first foreign minister and second prime minister, to the U.N. Palestine Commission on January 15, 1948:[4] [Emphasis supplied]

Sharett is quoted as saying:

The Jewish people, as represented by the Jewish Agency, have declared themselves *willing to cooperate* in the implementation of the *compromise solution* [Partition] because they made an effort to approach the problem in a realistic spirit, to understand and *admit the legitimate rights and interests of the other section of the population of Palestine, namely, the Arabs of Palestine.* [Emphasis supplied]

Flapan continues:

Israel's *ostensible acceptance* of the resolution remained *its most important propaganda weapon, even as it violated one section of that document after another.* Today, with Israel controlling the West Bank, the Golan Heights, and southern Lebanon, the myth lingers on, engraved in Israel's national consciousness and in its schoolbooks. Yet throughout the hundred-year history of the Zionist movement and the Yishuv (the Jewish community in Palestine), the vision of the great majority *was always one of a homogeneous Jewish state in the whole or at least in the greater part of Palestine.*[5] [Emphasis supplied]

What Flapan says in his thesis is that the representatives of the Jewish Agency to the United Nations, during its deliberations on creating the State of Israel, *deceived* the U.N. delegates, foreign ministers and foreign diplomats as to *Israel's future territorial intentions after it acquired statehood,* in order to get the necessary votes of the delegates to establish a Jewish state.

Thus, not only did the Jewish Agency representatives at the U.N. *fail to raise any claim of right, Divine or historic,* to the portion of Palestine allocated to the Palestinians in the partition—but they *made positive disclaimers* of such a right.

Had the truth been brought out *when truth was called for,* Israel would never have come into existence. The U.N. would never have countenanced a claim to *all* of Palestine, or an intent by Israel to absorb all of it.

Simha Flapan died on April 13, 1987, as his book went to press. The final two paragraphs of the book stand as a fitting last testament:

> At the same time, it must be recognized that the support of the Israeli peace camp for Palestinian self-determination, mutual recognition, and coexistence is not enough. *Diaspora Jewry and friends of Israel abroad must realize that present Israeli policy is doomed* to reproduce over and over again the cycle of violence that shocks our sensibilities every time we read or hear of wanton murder and bloodshed, whether the hand that perpetrates it detonates a bomb or fires a pistol. *The collective revenge of an army is no more righteous or admirable than the individual revenge of a desperate youth for the murder of one of his people. It is only propaganda and distorted vision that labels one "terrorism" and the other "national defense."*
>
> It is, then, in the hope of clarifying the distorted vision on our side of the conflict—that is, on the Jewish, Israeli side—that I have written this book.[6] [Emphasis supplied]

CHAPTER XIII

Israel's Dilemma

AS A CONSEQUENCE of the Likud policies over the past thirteen years, Israel finds itself in a position where it seems that whatever course is followed it will lead either to failure or disaster.

It is a multi-horned dilemma. These are the apparent alternatives:

1. If Israel attempts to maintain the status quo, it will continue to have more than two million enemies within its jurisdiction (including the Israeli Arabs) and the Palestinian uprising will eventually escalate into a guerrilla war.

2. If it annexes the West Bank and Gaza into Israel proper, the Palestinians will, in the not-too-distant future, outnumber the Jewish population and it will no longer be a Jewish state.

3. If Israel withdraws from the West Bank and Gaza and permits a Palestinian state to come into existence, it is concerned that its boundaries will be indefensible and that it will eventually be vulnerable to attack from the Palestinian state and neighboring Arab nations.

4. If it expels the Palestinians of the West Bank and Gaza, Harkabi fears an all-out war in which Israel will still have 500,000 Israeli Palestinians within its borders as enemies, and face a coalition of Arab and Moslem countries from Mauritania to Indonesia.

5. Finally, it can continue its military occupation of the territories under martial law and harass, brutalize and kill the Palestinians in the hope that they will find life to be so intolerable that they will be forced to

abandon their homes and leave Palestine. This is the Israeli policy currently being pursued by the Likud government.

HOW DID ISRAEL GET INTO THIS EXCRUCIATING DILEMMA?

As mentioned several times, Harkabi believes that Israel is facing a calamity that could have been prevented if the U.S. government and the "Friends of Israel" in America (AIPAC) had spoken out against "Beginism" and the Likud's settlement policies in the West Bank and Gaza.

There can be no question that the Israeli Lobby and their collaborators in the U.S. Congress and the executive branch of the U.S. government bear a major share of the responsibility for the desperate dilemma facing Israel today. In fact, Israel's misfortunes can be traced directly to a fateful decision made by the American Jewish establishment in the early part of 1977.

As mentioned earlier, in the spring of 1977, the Likud party (led by Menachem Begin) scored an upset victory over the Labor party which had been in power for the previous 29 years, ever since the founding of the State of Israel.

A "summit" meeting between the new Prime Minister Begin and the recently elected President Carter was scheduled for July 19, 1977. At that time, Begin was not particularly well known to the Jewish community in this country and the upcoming meeting was the source of some anxiety within the Jewish leadership.

It was then that a crucial decision was made by the Israeli Lobby, which was to have a profound effect upon the course of events in the Middle East for the next decade. These events have culminated in the current crisis which threatens Israel's survival and world peace.

On July 5, 1977, *The Wall Street Journal,* in a front page article entitled "The Potent Persuaders," discusses in detail the power and influence of the Israeli Lobby and the Lobby's strategy for the upcoming meeting between the heads of state. The article has previously been quoted at length in the first several pages of Chapter VI of this book.[1]

Prime Minister Begin's views regarding the occupied territories of the West Bank and Gaza were no secret. He had long maintained the position that these were "sacred" Jewish lands which could never be returned, nor would a Palestinian "homeland" ever be considered.

The problem was that Begin's position was contrary to longstanding U.S. policy in the Middle East and to U.N. Resolution 242, that Israel had ostensibly accepted, and which had recently been publicly confirmed by President Carter and Secretary of State Cyrus Vance.

The primary objective of the American Jewish leadership was to prevent, if possible, a showdown between Carter and Begin but, in the event that a confrontation did occur, to have the plans ready to put the Israeli Lobby into immediate action.

However, Begin's career and his reputation in the Jewish community left something to be desired. He was clearly not another Abba Eban and, if the Jewish community were to be asked to rally around him, his image needed some polishing, which is what the establishment set about to do. This was not an easy task. According to *The Wall Street Journal* article previously referred to:

> The American Israel Public Affairs Committee, led by its aggressive if not abrasive director, Morris Amitay, is cranking out a flood of press releases and statements that *stress Mr. Begin's moderation.*
>
> The pro-Israel operatives here are working closely with the new government in Israel. Some met recently with Schmuel Katz, who was sent to the U.S. as Mr. Begin's personal representative. Democratic Sen. Richard Stone of Florida, one of Israel's staunchest friends, visited Mr. Begin in Israel to counsel caution after conferring here with seven concerned Senators who regularly support Israel.
>
> "Begin policy as enunciated so far *can only lead to disorder,*" an *influential ally of Israel worries.* "It would create, for the first time, a deep schism between Israel and the American Jewish community."[2] [Emphasis supplied]

In the process of repackaging Mr. Begin, he was carefully coached "to cool it," and not to "appear inflexible" and to avoid being "pinned down on specific issues." He was also requested for the time being not to refer to the West Bank as "liberated" territories rather than occupied territories.

Begin's promoters assured everyone that Begin had given up "bomb-throwing." However, it is clear from the text of *The Wall Street Journal* article that the "new" Begin was not such an easy sell and that considerable skepticism still existed in the Jewish community. Therefore, it seems to have required an all-out effort, including some extravagant promises by Begin's image-makers, to overcome some of the misgivings of the Jewish community concerning Begin.

HOLOCAUST II?

THE DIE IS CAST

The Wall Street Journal reported:

> *For now,* however, Jewish leaders are rallying behind Mr. Begin, stressing—as does Rabbi Schindler—that he has been "for 29 years a responsible leader of the loyal opposition," *and isn't by nature a fanatical terrorist.* "There is *emerging* in the American Jewish community a feeling *that we have to be supportive of Begin,"* the rabbi says. He argues that the prime minister *will prove flexible on all major peace issues— including withdrawal from West Bank territories.*
>
> If a confrontation does come nonetheless, *much of the Israeli Lobby's efforts will be focused on Congress, where it is often possible to thwart the Executive Branch.* The most conspicuous might well occur in the Senate Foreign Relations Committee.[3] [Emphasis supplied]

In the meantime, representatives of the Israeli Lobby were meeting with Carter to explain to the new president the facts of life as the Israeli Lobby saw them.

Not surprisingly, at the meeting with Begin, Carter did not mention "returning the occupied lands for peace." No reference was made by him concerning a "Palestinian homeland." Yet, these were two of the most important matters which Carter had announced publicly he would push for at the meeting with Begin.

Begin took the advice of his handlers and followed the script. His was a stellar performance of sweet reasonableness.

In order to follow the advice of his coaches not to get "pinned down," he developed a special language which would, in ordinary parlance, be called "double talk"—but which will be referred to here as—"Beginspeak."

Thus, he was able to cheerfully assure everyone that he was willing to negotiate anything with the Palestinians but there was *much* (not specified) he would never agree to. (This concession was later qualified by adding the condition that he would have to pick the Palestinians that he would be willing to negotiate with.)

Whether or not Begin invented the felicitous but meaningless expression "the peace process" at this first meeting, or later, is not clear—but it became a key part of his vocabulary as long as he held office.

Time magazine of August 1, 1977, reporting on the Carter-Begin meeting, asked rhetorically what happened to Carter's previously announced position on the West Bank and Gaza and a Palestinian homeland? *Time* supplied its own answer by stating that, since his meeting with a group of prominent Jews, Carter had "softened his attitude toward Israel," and decided to play the role of "pussy cat" and for "some unknown reason," according to *Time,* did not choose to press "his earlier prescriptions for Israeli concessions, including withdrawal from the occupied territories and a Palestinian homeland." *Time* reported that Begin "side-stepped the issue." It was clear to the world that, in the face-off, it was Carter who *blinked.*[4]

For Begin, it had been a *tour de force.* Carter had publicly backed down on raising the key issues.

Begin became an instant hero to Jews in the U.S. and in Israel. It was considered a major diplomatic triumph and Begin made the most of it. The "Potent Persuaders," whose victory it really was, were content to let Begin take the credit.

It was also a great propaganda coup for Begin. He showed the Jews in Israel that he could stand up to Washington. After this, no one would doubt his boast that "he knew how to handle the Americans." Arrogance became his trademark. The Israeli Lobby unwittingly created its own "Frankenstein monster."

When the die was cast for Begin, the Israeli Lobby and Israel had passed the point of no return. From then on, Begin would do the lecturing and the scolding and the American Jews would listen. He was the star and the script didn't call for any director.

The irony of this is that it really wasn't all Begin's fault. He had wanted to say, as he has said many times since, that "he would never agree to giving up a single foot of the West Bank and Gaza." It was the image makers of the Israeli Lobby, not Begin, who insisted on projecting Begin as a "moderate" and "flexible, even on the West Bank and Gaza."

Begin was not ashamed of having been a terrorist. He bragged about it and wrote a book about his experiences. Furthermore, Begin was right, he did learn how to handle the Americans. He quickly realized that the U.S. government was crippled; that those in the government did not want to hear, or deal with, the truth and he shrewdly decided that, if the people in the U.S. government wanted double talk—double talk they would get. He recognized that the U.S. government was in mortal fear of the Israeli Lobby and, as long as he gave them a few crumbs that they could seize upon, such as "everything's negotiable," or "we will talk to anyone" (except there is nobody to talk to); "I believe in the peace process," or "America is 100% behind Israel and relations have never been better,"—they went away happy! He wasn't really trying to deceive people—he was just shoving pacifiers in their mouths.

Any time that Begin might slip and inadvertently tell the plain truth, the press and the U.S. government were quick to interpret it as only a bargaining position. Nobody in this country wanted to think, or would let himself believe, that Begin (and later Shamir) meant exactly what he said back home.

1. There would never be a Palestinian homeland, much less a Palestinian state.
2. That Israel did not want "autonomy" for the Palestinians—it wanted to get rid of them by any means necessary.
3. That the Israeli settlements on the West Bank and Gaza would *never* stop, but would continue to be established as fast as the U.S. supplied the money to build them.

In other words, nothing had changed since the early Zionists said, after the Balfour Declaration, "Palestine is going to be as Jewish as England is English."

Since nobody in the U.S. government had the courage to be the first to say "the emperor has no clothes on," our Middle East policy lapsed into schizophrenia—a major factor in creating the dangerous deadlock underlying the Israeli-Palestinian crisis. For thirteen years, the U.S. has meekly participated in this charade. Our presidents and diplomats have developed a special vocabulary to be used in reporting on the results of meetings between representatives of Israel and the U.S.

Samples of post-meeting announcements by U.S. officials with accompanying translations are:

The meeting was "useful."	*We agreed on nothing.*
The meeting was "frank."	*We disagreed on everything.*
The meeting was "constructive."	*We're not sure what we agreed on.*

Harkabi says that the U.S. has occasionally been known to muster up enough courage to describe Israeli defiance as "unhelpful," or an "obstacle to peace."

This diplomatic cowardice on the part of the U.S. is not only responsible for Israel's perilous predicament but it has cost the U.S. dearly in the respect of its friends and allies. Never has the United Nations been more *united*—never has Israel been so *alone*—as on the day the U.N. voted, 150-2, to go to Geneva to hear Yasser Arafat.

FACING THE REALITIES

The frustrations and disappointments which the U.S. has experienced over the past thirteen years in trying to resolve the Israeli-Palestinian conflict are the consequences of our failure to recognize two fundamental truths:

1. The Likud government of Israel is contemptuous of the U.S. and has no respect, either for the U.S. government or the American people.
2. The leaders of the Likud government do not want, and never have wanted, peace—they dread it. Their only interest is power and personal aggrandizement.

The evidence which supports these conclusions is extensive and is set forth in detail in previous chapters.

THE FIRST REALITY

The contempt which the Likud has for the U.S. is obvious and it is richly deserved. They know better than anybody that Israel can make or break U.S. presidents, senators, congressmen and diplomats. How could the Likud leadership be expected to feel otherwise than contemptuous, when every representative of the U.S. government wears a collar around his neck and they know the leash is held by their friends and colleagues in the Israeli Lobby.

The most recent examples of the humiliating condescension with which the Likud leadership treats the U.S. are found in two articles in the *Jerusalem Post* by Abba Eban having to do with Secretary of State George Shultz' visit to Israel in the latter part of 1988 to discuss a peace initiative.

In the first article entitled, "The Threats Are From Within," Eban writes:

Nothing in our region is too improbable to be true. Israeli leaders, the Israeli press, American Jewish supporters of Israel, and some celebrated columnists are justly castigating the Palestinian leadership for not being sufficiently emphatic in supporting Resolution 242. All of them have overlooked the awkward fact that the Israeli government does not support it at all. We are recommending strong medicine for others while refusing to swallow any of it ourselves.

Mr. Shamir has never allowed any mention of 242 to pass his lips except in tones of rejection. Compared with Mr. Shamir, the Palestine National Council is almost a devotee of 242. Resolutions 242 and 338 are at least mentioned in the PNC statement; there is no trace of them whatever in the Israeli coalition agreement because the Likud negotiators in 1984 resisted the Labour proposal to include 242 as one of the sources of Israeli governmental policy.

During Secretary of State Shultz's visit to this area last September, Mr. Shamir told him that 242 is not applicable to a negotiation with the Jordanians and Palestinians, because the resolution was "exhausted" by the withdrawal from Sinai (which also would never have taken place if Mr. Shamir had been prime minister in 1977). This prime ministerial rejection of 242 led to the collapse of the Shultz initiative and contributed to the disengagement of King Hussein from the peace process. *While some governments have not explicitly endorsed 242, Mr. Shamir is the only prime minister in the world who has actually turned it down.*[5] [Emphasis supplied]

In a follow-up article in the *Jerusalem Post,* Eban blames Shamir for destroying the American peace proposals:

Jordan's role became additionally impossible when Mr. Shamir told Secretary Shultz that *he stood both for Resolution 242 and for permanent Israel retention of all of the territory under Israel's control.*

It is intellectually respectable to be for *one of these but to invoke both is sheer frivolity.* Moreover, in the Camp David framework agreement, the Israel government, then under Likud control, declared that "the future status of the West Bank and Gaza and Israel's negotiation of a peace treaty with Jordan must be governed by *all* the principles and provisions of 242," one of which is withdrawal of forces.

To be for Camp David and also for total Israeli control of the entire West Bank and Gaza is thus *just as absurd* as to be for 242 and to be in favour of West Bank settlements.

To interpret a legal document against its legislative history and against the intention of all of its sponsors *"mocks intellectual integrity,"* and is a *bizarre* doctrine.[6] [Emphasis supplied]

Perhaps the only surprise in this is that Eban was surprised. The U.S. experience proved long ago that dealing in "absurdity," "frivolity" and "mocking intellectual integrity" is what the Likud does best. Shamir is merely indulging in a little "Beginspeak" in which he has become very fluent.

THE SECOND REALITY

The record of the past thirteen years demonstrates that no one has worked harder than Menachem Begin to save Israel from peace. As Harkabi states, "Begin's primary motivation in starting the disastrous war in Lebanon was fear of the momentum of the peace movement, and that he might be called upon to honor his signature on the Camp David Accords." As previously noted, Harkabi called the Lebanon war the "War to Safeguard the Occupation of the West Bank."[7]

Ariel Sharon, hero of the battles of the refugee camps, was the other instigator of the Lebanon war, which was based on lies and deceit at the highest level. Sharon saw himself, Amos Perlmutter says, "as the King of Israel."[8]

While all the nations of the world understand and recognize the hypocrisy of the Likud's "peace process," the Likud continues to make a mockery out of U.S. peace efforts and a game out of fooling Washington. There is no question that Shamir also knows "how to handle the Americans."

In an article in the *Jerusalem Post* of March 6, 1989, entitled "The Illusion of Shamir's Peace Plan," Israeli journalist Uri Avery writes:

The new Israeli "peace ideas," revealed last month by Prime Minister Yitzhak Shamir, bring to mind the stage routine in which the illusion of walking and even sprinting is created without the pantomimist advancing a single inch. Shamir's intention was to generate feverish diplomatic activity, giving the illusion of movement without actually advancing even an inch closer to peace.[9]

In the July 17, 1989, issue of *Time* magazine, an article was published entitled "Power, Not Peace."

A portion of the article is quoted below:

Extremism was in the ascendancy again last week in the Middle East. Capitulating to the hard-line right of his Likud bloc, Israeli Prime Minister Yitzhak Shamir fettered his own plan for elections in the occupied territories *with stiff conditions that seem to doom the peace initiative.*

Shamir's initiative was never more than a tentative move toward starting a dialogue between the Israelis and the Palestinians. It offered Arabs in the occupied territories the chance to elect representatives to negotiate with Israel a transitional period of self-rule—a possible beginning if Palestinians were willing to take it. But under the terms of the initiative, the Palestinian representatives could have no overt connection with the Palestine Liberation Organization. Not surprisingly, no Palestinians rushed to embrace the scheme. Still, coaxed by the U.S., the P.L.O. was giving the plan serious consideration.

Last week those hopes lay in rubble. Rather than risk losing power, Shamir chose to scuttle his peace diplomacy. He sidestepped a challenge to his leadership by embracing four conditions laid down by hard-line Industry and Trade Minister Ariel Sharon and his allies and plainly designed to be unacceptable to the Palestinians. Most indigestible was a restriction barring the 140,000 Arab residents of East Jerusalem from participating in the proposed elections. Shamir also agreed that Israel would not return any of the occupied territories to "foreign sovereignty," that the construction of Jewish settlements in the West Bank and Gaza would continue and that the proposed elections could not take place until the nineteen-month-old intifadeh ended. Ironically, Shamir has espoused these same positions many times. But he had hoped to keep them in the background while he maneuvered to *keep on top of the pressures for peace.*[10] [Emphasis supplied]

In addition to Abba Eban, other Israelis are finally beginning to recognize that the Likud has been deluding them all along about its desire for peace. In an article in the *Jerusalem Post* of October 28, 1989, entitled "Moment of Truth," David Landau, a member of the editorial staff of the *Post,* complains that "Shamir is still wrapping his true intent in a tissue of disingenuousness. The words 'peace,' 'Camp David' and 'two-phase solution' studded his policy statements, but they do not mean what they say."

Landau writes:

Thus, when Shamir asserted to the *Jerusalem Post* last week that he is confident the Palestinians of Judea, Samaria and Gaza will eventually ditch the PLO and talk to Israel on Israel's terms, he didn't mean it. He isn't confident. *What he means is that as far as he is concerned the present situation can continue indefinitely. Intifada? Isolation? Brutalization? Prolonged stalemate and eventual threat of war? If these are the price for retaining Judea, Samaria and Gaza, then they are an acceptable price.*

But he does not say that either. Rather, he speaks of the "government's peace initiative"—pretending that he has not just emptied that term of any vestige of meaning. He speaks of "Camp David" ignoring his own and Foreign Minister Arens's opposition to that agreement. He speaks of his "commitment" to the "two-phase solution," concealing his determination that the first phase (carefully circumscribed autonomy for the Palestinians) remain in force indefinitely (unless the Arabs accept the Likud's ideas for a permanent settlement).

He formerly disqualified the PLO because it was terrorist and committed to Israel's destruction. Now, having (at least formally) renounced those two characteristics, the organization is still disqualified. In the premier's words, "Because we oppose a Palestinian state in Eretz Yisrael, we cannot negotiate with the PLO."

But since Shamir opposes any withdrawal from the territories, he cannot in truth negotiate with anyone—because he has nothing to negotiate about. But that truth is unpalatable; Shamir therefore obfuscates it with words and concepts castrated of their original meaning.[11] [Emphasis supplied]

This, of course, is "Beginspeak" at its finest. It may be news, and also disillusioning, to the *Jerusalem Post,* but it's been going on non-stop for thirteen years.

But why should anyone be surprised that demagogues like Shamir and Sharon do not want peace? If peace broke out, what would become of them? What are the job opportunities for someone with Shamir's experience? What can a "hero" like General Sharon look forward to as a finish to his illustrious career? As of now, Sharon is riding on top of the world promoting his book, the title of which is not "Shalom" but "Warrior." He appears on American television talk shows as a celebrity. He is being wined and dined everywhere. If peace comes, who would buy his book or even buy his lunch?

SHARON AND HIS "FINAL SOLUTION"

Regardless of which Likud leader holds power, Israel's dilemma remains unchanged and she will continue as she is, bleeding to death. However, if Sharon's ambition to become Prime Minister is achieved, a new and far more ominous development is in prospect. The question then arises—how would Sharon solve Israel's dilemma and why does Sharon appear so confident that he has a solution? The answer may be that he *does.* His solution has nothing to do with "peace," other than avoiding it at all costs. From Sharon's standpoint, it has everything going for it and made to order for a would-be "King of Israel."

Sharon's power base consists of the following:

1. The Religious Nationalist Extremists who are clamoring for a solution to Israel's dilemma by one great military strike to *expel* the Palestinians (Amalek) from the West Bank and Gaza using any means necessary, which will pave the way for the coming of the Messiah.
2. The Gush Emunim and other West Bank settlers who, for personal or religious reasons, are determined *to get rid* of the Palestinians.
3. Those in Israel who, regardless of religious conviction, believe that the Palestinians must be "transferred" (expelled) in order to preserve the Jewishness of the Jewish State.
4. Those Israelis who are not religious zealots and who are not disposed to war for war's sake, but who are exhausted psychologically with Israel's continuing dilemma and feel that *some* solution is better than *no* solution. They will follow a leader (even Sharon) if he promises an end to the debilitating internal strife which is destroying Israel.

What is Sharon's solution? As discussed earlier, present Likud policy is designed and intended to bring about emigration from the West Bank and Gaza by making life in the occupied territories intolerable for its Palestinian inhabitants. Some highly-placed individuals in the Israeli military have considered accelerating this process by shipping the Arabs to Jordan in lorries.

However, this is obviously too slow a process to solve problems which must be solved now. Sharon has boasted that he could put down the Intifada in 48 hours if he was in charge of the Israeli army. But simply putting down the uprising still leaves the Palestinians in possession of their lands, and nothing is *solved.* On the other hand, even Sharon cannot simply load 1,500,000 or more Palestinians on trucks and dump them into Jordan. That process would also be too slow. Long before it could be carried to completion, the United Nations, with the support of the major powers, would no doubt intervene. This would be the worst of all possible worlds. All of Israel's present problems would be exacerbated and the hostility of the world community would be raised to such a pitch that a peace might be *imposed* on Israel. However, these are risks that Sharon need not take. There is a safer and proven alternative. It can be summarized as follows:

1. Israel would continue to stall, delay and confuse any peace efforts by using the same tried and true methods which the Likud has successfully employed for the past thirteen years.
2. It will not be long before the peacemakers are thoroughly discouraged and have given up in frustration.
3. It will be at this point that Arafat's probationary period will be at an end and the extremists in the PLO will say "we told you so" and will take over a newly radicalized PLO.
4. The Intifada will escalate into *real* terrorism in the occupied territories verging on guerrilla warfare. Everything will be done by Sharon to provoke the PLO into committing terrorist acts.
5. The West Bank settlers will demand that the government mobilize the Israeli army to stop these "atrocities."
6. Sharon will then announce to the world that "I told you so—the PLO has always been nothing but a bunch of terrorists and could never be trusted."
7. Sharon will declare an "insurrection" in the occupied territories and mobilize the Israeli army to put down the "revolt" and restore order. The battle plan will be the same used in 1948 by the Haganah under Ben-Gurion, the Irgun terrorists under Begin, and the Lehi under Shamir. The elements of this war plan are set forth in detail in Chapter IV, taken from Israeli declassified military archives and the Ben-Gurion diaries.[12]
8. The Israeli army, together with its West Bank settler "vigilantes," will launch a surprise attack and will sweep across the West Bank and Gaza. Hundreds of Palestinian villages will be destroyed, and homes and lands devastated. A few massacres, like Deir Yassin in 1948, will be carried out to make sure the Palestinians get the message of what will happen to them if they don't leave.

Slowly at first, and then in a tidal wave of humanity, more than 1,500,000 terrified Palestinian men, women and children will stream in a panic across the border into Jordan.

This efficient plan for expelling the Palestinians presents no serious problem to the Israeli army. In 1948, a much smaller Israeli army, far less well-equipped than the present one, by using these same tactics successfully drove 700,000 innocent unarmed Palestinian refugees into exile.

Notwithstanding the bloodthirsty demands of the religious fanatics, that Amalek be "wiped out with his women and children," we can safely assume that Sharon's plan will not call for mass murder and that the killing that will be involved will only be that which is necessary to terrify and force the Palestinians to flee.

LOGIC, NOT PROPHECY

Does it require some special expertise, secret sources or prophetic powers to justify projecting the scenario just described? Not at all. It is simply a logical progression from the known facts.

Among the facts that are well-known are these:

Israel's dilemma must be solved soon and Sharon knows it. He is no procrastinator. Sharon also knows that simply putting down the Intifada solves nothing because the 1,500,000 Palestinians still remain in the West Bank and Gaza. If Sharon (or anyone in the Likud with his philosophy) comes to power, it will be on the promise of a final solution to the "Palestinian problem."

Sharon is on record that the Palestinians belong in Jordan, not on the West Bank and Gaza and that Jordan should be their "homeland." He has also stated emphatically that the U.S. should not get involved—the Palestinian problem is for Israel to handle. His supporters among the religious extremists are condemning the present Israeli government as too timid in solving the Palestinian problem and have demanded that the Palestinians (Amalek) be driven out of the sacred occupied lands or God will not allow the Israelis to continue living in Israel and will not send the Messiah.

The West Bank settlers are bitterly critical of the Israeli government for not sending enough troops into the occupied territories to protect them from the stone-throwing Palestinians.

Sharon's supporters are agreed that with Israel's military power, they have nothing to fear from anyone and that Israel's Palestinian problem can be solved with one bold stroke. All that is needed is a leader with the courage to do it.

The only reason for the present delay in expelling the Palestinians is that the Sharon faction is not yet in full control of the Israeli government.

But have we been imputing to Sharon, intentions and motivations that are too extreme to be taken seriously? The answer is—only if Sharon has never meant anything he has ever said or done. Moreover, Sharon is by no means alone, among the highest levels of the Israeli military, in his attitude toward the Palestinians.

General Eitan, Israel's chief of staff during the Lebanon war, testified before the Knesset foreign relations and defense committee just before his retirement in April 1983. Shipler, in his book *Arab and Jew,* writes:

> He [Eitan] told the legislators that many more Jewish settlements had to be built on the West Bank; that if there were 100 settlements between Jerusalem and Nablus, Arabs would not be able to throw stones. "When we have settled the land, *all the Arabs will be able to do about it will be to scurry around like drugged roaches in a bottle,*" declared Israel's highest military officer. The remark triggered a storm of outrage among many Israeli Jews, but it also prompted expressions of admiration for Eitan, who showed up in public opinion polls a month later as the country's leading choice for chief of staff. In 1984 he was elected to the Knesset.[13]

An outraged Israeli writer said that Eitan's remarks were intended to dehumanize the Palestinians so that the military's job becomes easier—"cockroaches are not killed—*they are exterminated.*"[14]

A HOLY WAR

The religious extremists have a worshipful attitude toward the militant generals in the Israeli army command.

Harkabi explains that:

> For the extremists, Israel's *might* is a guarantee that no harm will befall them. According to Rabbi Z.Y. Kook, *the IDF is "holy" and even its weapons are "holy"* (for all that some of them are manufactured abroad by non-Jews and "idolaters"). *Generals who openly violate religious precepts are venerated like saintly rabbis.* A phenomenon which is perhaps related is the creeping militarization of religious language, and perhaps even of religious thought. Maimonides would be dumbfounded to hear a rabbi like Rabbi Hess speak of the "personal interest" of a God who "mobilizes" himself.
>
> The faith in Israel's military capacity becomes a functional, psychological, and cognitive need, because without this faith the entire theological structure, including the idea that we are living at the beginning of the Redemption, would collapse. Little wonder that this faith is in full flower, Israel is stronger than all the forces in the Middle East, they believe, *and not even the Soviets dare raise a finger.* In this view, setbacks are caused not by intrinsic limitations of Israeli might, *but by a leadership that is too timorous* to exploit the means at its disposal.

Such a faith is a vital part of the world view of the extremists who have settled in the occupied territories because it seems to offer an insurance policy against the collapse of their entire enterprise.[15] [Emphasis supplied]

Thus an analysis of the evidence almost compels the conclusion reached here regarding Sharon's intentions in pursuing his final solution. Indeed, the logic is inescapable:

1. Sharon has no doubt as to what *should* be done about the Palestinians.
2. His fiery and highly vocal supporters are crying that it *must* be done.
3. Sharon knows the only way that it *can* be done.
4. If he is elected Prime Minister, he will have the *power* to do it.
Conclusion: That is what Sharon will do.

But what about Israel herself? Is the "final solution of the Palestinian problem" the final solution for Israel's dilemma or the final chapter for Israel?

Of course, no one can predict for certain what the fate of Israel would be under the circumstances described and we do not presume to do so. Although a number of thoughtful minds in Israel have expressed the fear of another "Holocaust" or an "Armageddon" or a Moslem "Jihad," we refrain from *predicting* any of these, our purpose being satisfied by pointing out and analyzing the danger of such a catastrophe happening. Proceeding, therefore, on the assumption that the Palestinian expulsion will become a fait accompli without provoking military action against Israel from any source.

What would the reaction be from the world community? We can, of course, only speculate. But it can be said with some degree of certainty that the United Nations cannot remain indifferent.

Let us assume then, the mildest response that can be expected or imagined from the world community. It is inconceivable that the U.N. sanctions against Israel would not be more severe than those imposed on South Africa. In the eyes of the world, nothing that South Africa has done would begin to compare with Israel's crime if it expelled the Palestinians.

The following would in all likelihood be among the penalties incurred:

1. A severance of diplomatic relations with Israel by most nations.
2. The expulsion of Israel from the U.N. (this has almost happened on a number of past occasions when the provocation was far less).

3. A trade embargo and boycott against Israel in which most all nations would participate (except South Africa).

As far as the U.S. is concerned it is impossible to say what it would do. But regardless of the U.S. reaction the sweeping economic sanctions of the rest of the world would be ruinous for Israel.

The price that Israel might have to pay to lift economic sanctions could well be an imposed peace on the basis of the U.N. Partition resolution and its 1948 boundaries as well as nuclear disarmament.

It is hard to imagine Israel accepting these conditions, particularly nuclear disarmament, when its paranoia regarding the rest of the world would then be confirmed by reality. What then would Israel's response be?

Can Israel retaliate against economic isolation and eventual strangulation by a nuclear strike? If so, against whom? When and how does Israel play its nuclear card? Japan responded to economic isolation in 1941 by the Pearl Harbor attack (the 1941 version of a nuclear strike) and began a war it knew it could never "win."

In Chapter XI, we cited the great concern expressed from many quarters, including the Soviet Union, about the escalating nuclear missile race in the Middle East.

It is ironic that the U.S. and the Soviet Union have, after 40 years, begun to engage seriously in reducing their nuclear weapons stockpiles while, at the same time, the Middle East is rushing toward Armageddon with Israel building the same type nuclear missile that Washington and Moscow have agreed to eliminate.

An article published in the November 6, 1989, issue of *Newsweek* entitled "Israel's Deal with the Devil?" reports on recent disclosures in the Middle East nuclear missile race. The following is an excerpt from the article:

> For years now, it has been a more or less open secret in defense circles that Israel is engaged in military collaboration with the apartheid government of South Africa. Israel is thought to be South Africa's largest arms supplier. Some Israelis say the relationship is necessary for their survival. Other people see it as a deal with the Devil—which explains last week's fuss over a pair of reports on NBC News.
>
> The network charged that Jerusalem was involved in a "full-blown partnership with Pretoria to produce a nuclear-tipped missile for South Africa." It said South Africa's Overberg testing range, near the town of Arniston, was built to Israeli specifications. Citing "a CIA document," it

said "the first missile flight of the Jerusalem-Pretoria alliance was on July 5th," when a rocket flew 900 miles toward Antarctica. In exchange for the technology, NBC said, Israel gets the use of test facilities there and "a continuous supply of enriched uranium for its nuclear warheads."

"It's all lies," said Israeli Prime Minister Yitzhak Shamir. But both countries are known to have nuclear-weapons capabilities. And a U.S. official with intimate knowledge of the subject told *Newsweek* that: the Israel-South Africa missile partnership couldn't be closer." The official said: "We know everything—names, dates, everything."

The missile project involves technology from Israel's Jericho-2B missile, an intermediate-range weapon of the type that Washington and Moscow have agreed to eliminate. Israel used a Jericho as the first two stages of a rocket called Shavit (Comet), which launched a satellite into orbit last year. American experts estimate that the Jericho-2B could hurl a one-ton warhead more than 1,700 miles.

The timing is further complicated by friction between Washington and Jerusalem. The two allies are at loggerheads on a number of issues, notably Shamir's reluctance to implement his own proposal for elections on the occupied West Bank. Having pushed and cajoled the Arabs into agreement, the administration now discovers, in the words of one senior U.S. official, that Shamir "can't say yes to his own plan." The implied threat to Israel's military aid from the U.S., which amounts to a vital $1.8 billion a year, may have been designed to put new pressure on Israel.[16]

Despite Prime Minister Shamir's statement that the report above quoted "was all lies," the Pentagon on November 15, 1989, confirmed it as true.

If, and when, another war comes to the Middle East, there are few things that can be predicted. One thing, however, we can be assured of—Israel will never accept defeat. When the Israelis say that "never again" will they be the *only* victim, they mean it. The end will come not as with the zealots of Masada, but as with Samson pulling down the pillars of the temple.

When the Arab oil fields are in ruins; when enough cities have been vaporized; when the casualties are in the millions, the Jews of Israel will not be among the survivors—they will fight hopelessly to the death.

CHAPTER XIV

A Plan for Peace

FOR THOSE WHO HAVE tried to find the "road to peace" in the Middle East, it has been a treacherous journey, inevitably ending in bitter disappointment.

THE PERILOUS ROAD

As a result of these failures in the many good faith efforts to bring peace to the Middle East, the idea has gained credence that the Israeli-Palestinian deadlock defies solution much like North Ireland. As a result, a certain attitude of hopelessness has begun to pervade any discussion of the Middle East crisis.

To adopt this attitude, however, is to fall victim to the Likud's strategy, which is to convince the world that there *is no solution* except Israel's status quo. Under the guise of seeking peace, the Likud has spent most of its time and effort during the past thirteen years planting land mines and booby traps along the road to peace. They have cleverly led peace seekers up blind alleys and into Israeli Lobby ambushes. Most of the problems encountered in the search for peace have *not been real*, they have been *contrived*. The biggest obstacle to peace has simply been relentless Likud *sabotage*.

To divert attention from itself, as the main roadblock to peace, and to further discourage genuine peace efforts, the Likud has fostered the view that the issues involved in the Palestinian situation are enormously "complex," the strategy being that if they can discourage and frustrate peace efforts to the point where everyone "gives up," they have won their primary objective.

At this writing, this strategy is becoming dangerously close to success. It would be well, of course, if the Israeli-Palestinian crisis could be locked away and forgotten about. Unfortunately, long before the conflict reaches the North Ireland stage, it is more likely to have exploded in fire balls and mushroom clouds, perhaps taking a sizable part of the Middle East with it.

THE BUSH ADMINISTRATION

After Secretary of State Baker's initial strong and courageous grasp of the situation, and his forceful comments on the "Greater Israel" theme, many people took heart. Recently, however, it has been rumored that the administration is already wearying of the challenge.

In an article published in the *Jerusalem Post* of September 23, 1989, the Bush administration's Middle East policy is discussed.

It is pointed out in the article, entitled "Why Bush Is in No Hurry to Take the Plunge," that President Bush and Secretary Baker are politicians and, therefore, *"appreciate the special place that Israel has carved out for itself in the American political scene."*

The following are further excerpts from the article:

For the most part, Bush, Baker and their colleagues regard it as a very risky, even no-win situation.

Thus, those people in Israel and the Arab world who are hoping for an active and high-level American mediatory role are in for a sorry disappointment.

Defense Minister Yitzhak Rabin and Jordan's Crown Prince Hassan both emerged from meetings with Bush, Baker and other U.S. officials in recent weeks reportedly upset by the administration's reluctance to get too deeply involved in the peace process.

Barring some major development, Egyptian President Hosni Mubarak and Finance Minister Shimon Peres—among other Middle Eastern leaders due to visit Washington—*will similarly be disappointed by the administration's passivity.*

Beyond the widespread sense in Washington that the Middle East is hopeless, there are also other more pressing problems right now on the American agenda, including the war against drugs, the economy, and the superpower relationship.

Most observers here agree that there are only two ways that the U.S.

is going to get deeply involved in the Middle East. The first will be if there is some sort of urgent crisis—involving either hostages or actual hostilities. Short of that kind of emergency, the president and the *secretary of state will want to wait on the sidelines.*

Administration officials, despite this gloomy assessment, will continue to go through the diplomatic motions. They will continue to explore Israel's plan for Palestinian elections in the West Bank and Gaza Strip. They will focus on Egypt's 10-point proposal to implement those elections. There will be numerous meetings with Arab and Israeli leaders.

But right now, this administration has no real stomach for undertaking the tough kind of decisions, the dogged hard work, and the political risks necessary to achieve progress.[1] [Emphasis supplied]

In essence, the *Jerusalem Post* is telling us that President Bush and Secretary Baker have already been intimidated by the Israeli Lobby which *they now understand* has carved out a "special place" in the American political scene.

As a result, the *Post* is almost gleeful in reporting "the widespread sense in Washington is that, the Middle East situation is hopeless." The president and secretary of state want to "wait on the sidelines"; they do not want to get "too deeply involved in the peace process."

The fact that the Israeli Lobby has already discouraged Secretary Baker (within a few months of his maiden speech on the Middle East) is more than a cause for alarm, it is a warning of disaster. If the *Jerusalem Post* article is even close to the truth, it is a Likud triumph, a major victory for the Israeli Lobby and a great loss for the Israeli people.

As we have seen, the chief goals of the Israeli Lobby and its client, the Likud, are:

1. To stifle and block any efforts by American Jews to exert any influence on Likud policies.
2. To keep the U.S. from doing anything in the Middle East that the Likud doesn't approve of.

For the U.S. to be "passive" or "stand by" or "not want to get involved" (as just quoted from the *Jerusalem Post*), is a Likud prayer answered.

In Chapter XII, we have made an effort to identify and deal with the issues which lie at the root of the Israeli-Palestinian conflict. It is apparent that the *issues* are quite clear. The problem is that the positions of the parties *with respect to the issues are irreconcilable.*

Just how "complex" is the issue of the future of the West Bank and Gaza? A single bone tossed at two hungry pit bulls does not create a "complex" issue. The solution may be painful to the dogs but the issue is clear and non-negotiable. Even Shamir, in a lucid moment, states it plainly—"What's to negotiate?—They think the land is theirs, we think its ours."

There is nothing at issue in the Middle East that remotely compares in complexity with the problems that must be solved in, for example, negotiating a "Reduction of Conventional Forces in Europe," or in the "Strategic Arms Talks."

These involve matters so technical and esoteric that only a relatively few people in the world can understand them in all of their ramifications. The problems are so involved and convoluted that, with the best of intentions, they take years to negotiate.

The "complexity" argument is simply another Likud smokescreen. The Likud's success lies in the fact that rational minds have difficulty dealing with irrational concepts. This is what dumbfounded and exasperated Abba Eban in Shamir's explanation of the Likud's position on U.N. Resolution 242 (quoted earlier). The whole purpose of "Beginspeak" has been to confuse and befuddle people into thinking that something logical or sensible is actually being said.

When Begin and Shamir have announced their willingness to negotiate with the Palestinians (but not about the future of the West Bank and Gaza), it is equivalent to Gorbachev announcing at the beginning of strategic arms talks that he was ready to negotiate everything but *intercontinental ballistic missiles.*

THE OPPORTUNITY

Although the current situation in the Middle East is near flashpoint and the threat to world peace has never been greater, paradoxically the *opportunity* for genuine peace has never been more promising.

The events of the past 18 months have opened up possibilities which have heretofore been non-existent. In a sense, it can be compared to a planetary alignment in the solar system. If acted upon quickly, it can achieve remarkable results as we have seen in the Voyager II space probe. But, as in the solar system, such alignments are rare and transitory.

Included among the comparatively recent developments are the following:

1. The Bush administration has expressed a willingness to take a fresh look at the Israeli-Palestinian deadlock.
2. The United Nations is increasingly more willing to assert itself and to assume a more positive role in attempting to resolve the Middle East conflict.
3. The acceptance by the PLO of Israel's right to exist and its agreement to suspend terrorist activities so long as bona fide peace efforts are in progress.
4. The willingness of representatives of the U.S. to talk directly to members of the PLO.
5. The determination of the Palestinians to continue the Intifada until Israel removes its occupation troops.
6. Numerous indications on the part of the American Jewish community that, while continuing its strong loyalties to Israel, it is becoming increasingly skeptical and disillusioned with the policies of the Likud government.

Taken together these new circumstances have opened an unprecedented opportunity for a real peace movement which, if undertaken without delay and pursued vigorously and wisely, has a high prospect of success.

The great danger is that this historic opportunity will slip from our grasp and be lost forever either because the parties do not see it for what it is, or do not have the courage and will to pursue it. In the Israeli-Palestinian crisis there are time imperatives which are beyond the power of anyone to change.

There is another obstacle inherent in the nature of the issues which also makes many good faith attempts at achieving peace doomed from the outset.

The sincere efforts of many well-meaning people to break the Middle East deadlock by trying *to persuade Shamir to "talk to the PLO,"* even if it were to succeed, unfortunately does not bring peace any closer. Indeed, it is counter productive because it not only wastes precious time in what would certainly be interminable negotiations, but what is more important, it wastes a priceless opportunity.

Elections, with or without representatives of the PLO, are meaningless. At best, after endless haggling, all that could possibly be accomplished would be to determine *who would represent the Palestinians in negotiations with Israel on an issue which cannot be negotiated.*

THE FUTILITY OF NEGOTIATIONS BETWEEN ISRAEL AND THE PALESTINIANS

There is a belief, unsupported by history, but commonly accepted in even the highest diplomatic circles, that the secret for reaching a settlement between nations on dangerous unresolved issues is to convene a peace conference and coax or drag the parties to the "bargaining table" whereby some alchemy, and with enough time, the parties will negotiate a proper settlement of their differences. Negotiations are somehow considered to have magical properties so that, instead of being a process they tend to become an end in themselves. They become rituals rather than mechanisms for reaching solutions.

What must be understood and accepted, if any progress toward peace is to be made, is that the future status of the West Bank and Gaza is a *non-negotiable issue.*

There is much to be learned from the bitter experience of the Paris Peace Talks in which the U.S. tried to end the Vietnam War by "negotiating" a "peace with honor" and failed disastrously.

In 1968, the Vietnam War had been in progress for approximately three years during which President Johnson had vainly tried to arrange a truce with North Vietnam as a prelude to peace negotiations. Despite his desperate efforts to get the North Vietnamese to the bargaining table, he failed. On March 31, 1968, Johnson publicly announced his intention not to seek re-election.

The North Vietnamese then agreed to negotiate provided there would be no cessation or reduction in the fighting, which proceeded full scale. The U.S. sent a negotiating team headed by Averell Harriman to Paris to meet with the Vietnamese representative, Xuan Thuy. The peace conference opened in Paris on May 10, 1968, on a note of euphoria (in the U.S. delegation).

The U.S. position was clear and unchangeable. It wanted South Vietnam to be free to choose its own government. The North Vietnamese position was equally clear and unchangeable; it wanted all of Vietnam under Communist rule.

The positions of the parties were, of course, irreconcilable and not subject to compromise. This did not, however, deter or discourage the negotiators. They diligently tried every day to negotiate the non-negotiable.

The negotiations continued all through the remainder of 1968, with each side simply repeating their respective positions without any progress except that the fighting continued to get worse.

When the Nixon administration took office in January, 1969, a new negotiating team, led by Henry Kissinger, took over the negotiations. The North Vietnamese delegation was then headed by Le Duc Tho.

The frustrating and fruitless negotiations dragged on for four more years, through the Nixon administration and almost into the Ford administration. Kissinger tried every conceivable tactic to extract concessions or compromises from the North Vietnamese. He alternately threatened and cajoled with no result.

After each session, which consisted of repeating what they had said in the previous session, the negotiators would appear before the press and solemnly announce that the talks had been "helpful," or some other innocuous and meaningless bit of diplomatic jargon.

After many fine Parisian dinners and champagne toasts, the negotiators, out of exhaustion or boredom, finally signed a truce agreement which pretended to guarantee South Vietnam's independence. Finally, it was "peace with honor."

As we know, after the U.S. forces were withdrawn and the South Vietnamese took over, the North Vietnamese armies simply rolled over South Vietnam just as they had always planned to do. Saigon's name was changed to Ho Chi Minh City, a name that doubtless had been picked out before the war began.

Tragically, more American soldiers were killed *after* the peace talks than had died before. The cost to the nation in blood, pain, death and resources of the failure of our diplomats to recognize the impossibility that the *negotiations* could succeed, is immeasurable. A non-negotiable issue can be won or lost but simply cannot be *compromised.*

After the battles of Lexington and Concord, American *independence* was "non-negotiable" even though the British tried hard to open negotiations with Washington, which included an offer of autonomy for the colonies if Washington would only disband his unconventional forces, who persisted in firing at the British from behind stone walls.

George W. Ball, former Undersecretary of State in the Johnson and Carter administrations and Ambassador to the United Nations, shares this view as to the *futility of direct negotiations* between the parties in the Israeli-Palestinian conflict.

In a brilliant article appearing in *Foreign Affairs,* April 1977, issue entitled "How to Save Israel in Spite of Herself," he argued for the U.S. to step in and set the terms of settlement:

> Nonetheless it is the conventional wisdom to reject any suggestions that the United States set the proposed terms of a settlement. Instead we must let the parties find their way by palaver to some common meeting ground somewhere near the center of a no-man's land studded with land mines of hatred, religion, vested interests, rigid dogmas of military necessity. For those who believe such a feat of diplomatic navigation is feasible will believe anything.

Later in his article Ball writes:

> Many who oppose the injection of an American plan of settlement appear to regard negotiation as a mystical process that automatically grinds out solutions. Yet experience has shown again and again that effective negotiation requires at least four preconditions, none of which now exists with respect to the Arab-Israeli struggle. First, there must be a desire on each side to find a solution. Second, both sides must be convinced that negotiation is not a zero-sum game—that, in other words, the offer of a concession is not merely an advantage to the other side but a benefit to both. Third, the leaders of the negotiating nations must be sufficiently secure in their personal political positions to risk making the concessions needed for a settlement. Finally, the parties must start from positions sufficiently close if they are, by their own efforts, to find the middle ground.

One of the most difficult problems to be overcome in peace negotiations is the weakness of the negotiators in relation to their constituencies. The extent to which either side has the *power* to make unpopular concessions is extremely limited. This is where George Ball thinks that an American role is crucial:

> Finally, America's indispensable role is to provide the means of *relieving the political leaders on both sides of the need to make politically unpalatable decisions, by furnishing them the escape route of yielding reluctantly under the relentless pressure of outside forces.* This means that our President must take the political heat from powerful and articulate pro-Israeli domestic groups. It means that as a nation we must be prepared to accept abuse and blame from both sides, permitting local

politicians to save their own skins by attacking American arrogance and imperialism.[2] [Emphasis supplied]

After Ball's article was published in *Foreign Affairs,* Philip M. Klutznick, his friend and prominent member of the Jewish community, wrote a letter to the editor of *Foreign Affairs* commenting on Ball's article. Ball's reply deserves quoting in full:

> I have such high regard for Philip Klutznick as a man of integrity and perception that I am extremely reluctant to disagree with him.
>
> It would obviously be preferable for the Arabs and Israelis to negotiate a final settlement between themselves. But I cannot believe that such a procedure would succeed. In my article I pointed out that the requisite conditions to an effective negotiation in the classical mode simply do not exist between the Arabs and Israelis and, if that was true before the May elections, the victory of the Likud Party has powerfully reinforced my dubiety. *Can anyone seriously believe that a government headed by a leader who categorically asserts that he will never yield an inch of West Bank territory will be persuaded to make the requisite concessions if the United States merely plays a sideline role,* "helping to provide a framework for negotiating and submitting concrete proposals from time to time?"
>
> *In some international disputes there is wide latitude for negotiation since a settlement is often possible with any of several combinations of mutually balancing concessions. But in the Arab-Israeli dispute each side has explicitly formulated its minimal requirements and passionately asserts that it will not settle unless those requirements are met.* Thus the Israelis insist—and with good reason—on a real peace and will not be content with some vague declaration of non-belligerency. The frontline Arab states, on their part, are never going to agree to a full peace unless Israel commits herself to withdraw from substantially all territories she seized in 1967 and accepts the creation of a Palestinian homeland. Unlike many other situations, there is little room for bargaining within the context of a comprehensive settlement and, as Mr. Klutznick himself points out, " . . . piecemeal steps seem to have outlived their usefulness."
>
> No amount of pushing and prodding is likely to force either side to grant the minimal requirement demanded by the other. That can occur, it seems to me, only if the United States says in effect: "These are the

terms of a settlement based on the principles propounded by the U.N. Security Council which should satisfy each side's minimal requirements. They include powerful enforcement and security measures such as buffer zones with neutral forces, demilitarized areas, and superpower guarantees."

If the Arabs reject the U.S. proposals and refuse a full peace, even on the promise of an Israeli withdrawal, we should recognize that another war is inevitable. *But if the Arab states do agree to a full peace—as I believe they are likely to do—and the Israelis refuse to accept withdrawal essentially to pre-1967 boundaries, then the United States must face a hard national decision: Can we in good conscience continue to provide huge subsidies to enable Israeli obduracy to perpetuate a stalemate that will sooner or later lead to catastrophe for all?* Do we really want our Middle East policies to be made in Jerusalem or should we try to stave off disaster by taking a positive position of our own?[3] [Emphasis supplied]

George Ball's thoughtful and wise approach to Middle East peace was doomed for two principal reasons:

1. It called for a peaceful solution to be imposed on the parties by the United States. The concept of an "imposed" solution is anathema to the Israeli Lobby because they interpret it to mean that Israel will inevitably be the "sacrificial lamb."
2. At the time that Ball wrote the *Foreign Affairs* article, the Likud party led by Menachem Begin had just come to power and peace was the last thing they were interested in.

Much has changed in the Middle East since 1977, when Ball's *Foreign Affairs* article was written. For the most part, the changes have been for the worse.

On the positive side, however, was the settlement of the Sinai issue with Anwar Sadat at Camp David in 1979. Another positive development has been the PLO's statements regarding terrorism and the recognition of Israel. However, this is only a temporary reprieve pending Arafat's success or failure in his efforts to bring about a peaceful settlement of the West Bank and Gaza issue. The understanding reached between Arafat and the radical wing of the PLO is that Arafat must soon produce tangible results in his "moderate" approach or all bets are off.

A third, and perhaps the most important, potentially positive factor is that Jewish and Israeli intellectuals have, by and large, abandoned the Likud and its West Bank policies. This, however, must be translated into positive steps by the intellectuals to exert their influence. Unless the peace activists organize to provide leadership for the Jewish community in America and the electorate in Israel, their impact unfortunately will be minimal.

On the negative side is the fact that the Likud, which first came to power in 1977, is now fully entrenched. Furthermore, the Likud continues to gain a greater share of the electorate with each succeeding election. This is due, in large part, to a lack of alternatives for the Israeli voters. The leaders of the Likud, as is the case with all demagogues, have simple and emotionally powerful *answers* to Israel's problems. In contrast, the Labor party appears weak and indecisive.

There is good reason to believe that the Likud's hold on the government could be reduced dramatically if a peace party with a dynamic leadership would challenge the Likud with a plan for peace and security that the Israeli people could believe in.

Another very negative development has been the Likud's settlement policies in the occupied territories. In 1977, there were few Israeli settlements in the West Bank and Gaza. Since then, the Likud has launched an aggressive settlement program to get as many new settlers as possible to implement Begin's "facts on the ground" policy. Many of these new settlements are in close proximity to Palestinian villages which have been there for centuries. A large number of the settlers are religious zealots who consider the *Palestinians* as the intruders. The result has been a bitter confrontation in which the settlers carry guns and the Palestinians throw rocks. This is the emotional crucible out of which the Intifada was forged.

The West Bank settlers, which now number in excess of 70,000, are ideologically the core of the Likud's constituency.

CUTTING THE GORDIAN KNOT

As a nation, we are often so obsessed with our failures that we neglect to recognize or take credit for our successes. One of the most outstanding of these has been the North Atlantic Treaty Organization (NATO).

At the end of World War II, there were only two significant military powers in the world, the U.S. and the Soviet Union. When Winston Churchill, in his historic speech in Fulton, Missouri, announced to the world that the hopes for a peaceful post-war Europe had been betrayed and that an "iron curtain" had descended from "Stettin, in the Baltic, to Trieste, in the Adriatic," the ruined and ravaged nations of Western Europe were huddled around the U.S. like chicks to a mother hen. The Russian bear, still panting after swallowing Eastern Europe, looked to the West and saw a berry patch.

NATO was born as a brave mutual defense pact, comprising most of the nations of Western Europe, as protection against an insatiable Soviet Union and its satellites.

The unique aspect of the NATO alliance was that the U.S. did not simply make a paper commitment to come to the defense of any NATO member under attack, but pledged as security for that commitment to deploy military forces of the U.S., both land and air, *on the frontiers of the NATO countries.* This is sometimes called the "trip wire." In essence, it acts as a trigger which, when violated, automatically puts into effect a pre-planned and self-executing military response of which all parties, friend and foe, are fully aware.

The deployment of battle-ready units of the U.S. Army and Air Force on European soil as a deterrent to aggression *has been the most successful peace-keeping device in history.*

The presence of approximately 300,000 American troops in the NATO countries, of course, did not guarantee that the Soviet Union could not successfully overrun Western Europe. But it made unmistakably clear to the Soviets that, if they attempted to do so, the full military and industrial might of the United States would be engaged *from day one.* The real strength of NATO has, of course, not been the American military presence *as such*—but the *unambiguous nature of the U.S. commitment.*

If the United States had merely signed the NATO pact and then gone home, there is no doubt that the history of Western Europe and the world, for the past thirty or forty years, would have been radically different.

Once the Soviet Union reached nuclear parity with the U.S. in the year 1949, and had American troops *not* been an integral part of the defense of NATO, Russia could easily have overrun Western Europe by using only its massive conventional forces after which it could have sat back and dared the U.S. to start a nuclear war over a *fait accompli.* This seems fanciful today but in those days the threat was *real.*

The American military presence, symbolic of the U.S. commitment, was the only reason that Europe had the courage to withstand the military and psychological pressures of the Cold War.

It is doubtful that either Hitler or the Kaiser would ever have started the World Wars had they known *for certain* that America would become involved as their chief enemy.

The wisdom of the NATO alliance has borne fruit beyond what anyone could have dreamed. West Germany, the remnant of a nation destroyed, has in a few decades become the number one economic power in Europe with a standard of living equal to or exceeding that of its American conquerors. As this is written, the supreme accomplishment of NATO in addition to keeping the peace for 40 years, has been the incredible events occurring in the Soviet Union and the Warsaw Pact nations. Germany's economic renaissance, the shining example which has caused the disaffection in the Soviet bloc, is due not only to the quality of its people but the fact that the energies and vitality of the West Germans were not expended in debilitating fear of the Soviets but were channeled in a positive direction—the welfare and prosperity of its people.

OUR JAPANESE ALLY

An even more spectacular example of the success of the U.S. policy of mutual defense treaties is the case of Japan.

Militarily naked, only minutes away from Soviet bases, Japan has had the assurance of a total commitment of the U.S. to her defense backed up by U.S. armed forces, air, ground and naval, deployed in Japan. Having no worries about her security, Japan has not only beaten her samurai "swords into plowshares," but also into Toyotas, Sonys, etc., and an endless list of electronic wonders. The speed with which Japan has achieved this transformation has been breathtaking. Not too many years ago a "Mitsubishi" was not an automobile built by a joint venture with Chrysler but the most fearsome fighter plane in the Pacific, the Japanese "Zero."

From a nation in ashes in 1945, Japan has built perhaps the most successful commercial and industrial society in the world. This is not primarily because she spends a relatively small portion of her GNP on defense—but because the talents of her people are unfettered and not disrupted by fears and anxieties about her security. Her creative energies are not stifled under a blanket of fear—but are given free rein to pursue the paths of progress and prosperity. Japan's youth are in laboratories, classrooms and universities, immersed in their new computerized and electronic world, not skulking around the back alleys of West Bank villages.

THE REMARKABLE CASE OF SOUTH KOREA

Following World War II, the Korean peninsula, by agreement with the Soviet Union, was divided at the 38th Parallel into North Korea and South Korea. By 1950, Russia and Communist China were rapidly converting

North Korea into a communist satellite while the U.S. was hopeful that a republic would emerge, western style, in South Korea.

The U.S. was still in the process of sorting out just where, and to what extent, our military commitments should be made in the fluid situation which followed the global dislocations of World War II. It so happens that a highly-placed official in the Truman administration was explaining to the press, with the aid of a map, the extent of the U.S. defense perimeter in East Asia. For some reason, deliberate or accidental, the defense perimeter did not include South Korea. This was interpreted in Moscow and Peking to mean that the U.S. was indifferent to South Korean security. Not long after, the North Koreans launched a surprise attack in force on South Korea.

The U.S., realizing too late that a Communist South Korea would place the Russians and Chinese on the doorstep of Japan, hurriedly convened a meeting of the Security Council of the U.N. to meet the emergency. The Russian delegation walked out—thus foolishly missing their chance to veto the Security Council resolution to defend South Korea and repel the invasion from the North.

Thus began the Korean War, almost forgotten by many people but which resulted in American casualties nearly equal to those suffered in Vietnam. The U.S. misled the North Koreans and the Chinese with its ambiguous position and the North Koreans, in turn, misjudged the U.S. Neither the U.S. nor North Korea wanted a war. Before it was over, the U.S. had experienced spectacular victories over the North Koreans and crushing defeats at the hands of the Red Chinese. The bloody war, that nobody had wanted or intended and in which both sides were trapped, ended in a stalemate and the creation of a demilitarized zone (DMZ) on the 38th Parallel.

Under a mutual defense treaty with South Korea dated October 1, 1953, the U.S. deployed approximately 40,000 troops to guard the DMZ against any new threat from North Korea. This U.S. force is still in place and continues as it has for 35 years in a war-ready state.

At the end of the Korean War, South Korea, which together with North Korea, had been an undeveloped backward peasant society and a pre-war colony of Japan, began to build a new nation. The threatening attitude of North Korea toward South Korea never ceased and has lasted to the present day, although somewhat mellowed.

The South Korean army trained and equipped by the U.S., and the physical presence of 30,000 to 40,000 battle-ready American troops on the

DMZ, have stood guard while the energetic and ambitious South Korean people created a modern miracle. The result was a transformation of a primitive medieval society into a modern, aggressive and dynamic nation, an economic powerhouse, able to compete in the world markets on even terms with the most advanced industrial countries.

It is another example of the unique peacekeeping effectiveness of a deterrent that is clear to all potential aggressors. When there are no surprises—when predatory powers know in advance the consequences of initiating a war—the will to war usually subsides and ultimately vanishes.

ISRAEL'S SECURITY—A SOLUTION

In Chapter XII, it was stipulated that Israel's security is an absolute precondition to any acceptable peace proposal. The discussion of this all important topic was deferred to this chapter where it more properly belongs.

The matter of Israel's security is, of course, not a new question but one that has been raised and considered many times before and solutions for which have frequently been proposed.

In order for the reader to gain a quick insight into how Israel itself views the problem of its security and why it has rejected various other proposals, we have outlined a short and hypothetical dialogue which incorporates security proposals which have actually been made to Israel at various times, together with the usual responses made by spokesmen for the Israeli government.

SECURITY PROPOSAL 1

"Don't worry, Israel's security will be *guaranteed* by the United Nations."

ISRAEL'S RESPONSE

"We can't trust the U.N. After all, it was Egypt's Nasser, ordering the U.N. peacekeeping force out of the Sinai, that precipitated the 1967 War."

SECURITY PROPOSAL 2

"Israel's security will be guaranteed *by the United States* and the *Soviet Union.*"

ISRAEL'S RESPONSE

"You don't really expect us to put our lives in the hands of the Russians, do you?"

SECURITY PROPOSAL 3

"Very well, then, *the United States* will guarantee Israel's borders and its security."

HOLOCAUST II?

"We appreciate your kind gesture but you must realize that we would not even have time to dial Washington before we were overrun by an Arab army—they would be only ten miles away. Not only that, but Congress would have to convene to declare war, and besides that, any real military help is still 4,000 miles away. *We can depend only on ourselves.*"

This raises a perplexing question. Why is the U.S. committed, under solemn treaties, to expend unlimited military resources and, if necessary, to sacrifice the lives of an unforeseeable number of American soldiers to defend our NATO ally, West Germany (historically not our best friend), or Spain, or Greece, to which we have no special ties, *and not to Israel which does not even have a defense treaty with the U.S. and is not a formal ally of the U.S.? Why is Israel forced to depend on herself alone?*

Do we not owe Israel, to which we have many ties, as much security as we give, for example, to Turkey? Are the Japanese and Koreans more deserving of our defense commitments than Israel?

While peace and unbounded prosperity are enjoyed by Japanese, Germans, Koreans, and many other countries, under the American defense umbrella, Israel is paralyzed, obsessed and consumed with fears of the future. Her economy survives only with the aid of a life support system provided by the U.S. Treasury and the charity of World Jewry. Israel is a nation in siege. The best of her talented people are being drained off to the U.S. and other countries. She is wracked by internal dissension, involved in a hopeless attempt to beat and shoot the Palestinians into submission. Eastern Jewry is avoiding Israel like the plague. Israel is led by a clique of rabble-rousing demagogues, whole sole purpose is not the welfare of Israel, but is to stay in office by constantly whipping up the emotions of the Israeli people into a high state of paranoia. We ask again—*why is Israel forced to rely only on itself alone?*

When the Israelis say that they cannot depend upon "promises" or "guarantees" for their security, they are right. When they say that they could "some day" be overrun by Arab enemies before the U.S. (being 4,000 miles away) could respond—they are right. In fact, this is *exactly* the same argument used by the NATO countries to convince the U.S. to deploy and maintain its military forces on the NATO frontiers.

There is nothing new about Israel's security problem or the solution to it.

If the U.S. entered into a mutual defense treaty with Israel, as we have done with South Korea, under the terms of which the U.S. would deploy ground, air and naval forces to safeguard Israel's borders, then Israel's security is no more in doubt than that of Japan, West Germany, South Korea, or other countries which the U.S. is committed to defend and has backed up that commitment with our armed forces already in place.

If those countries have not been afraid of the Soviet Union or China or North Korea because of the U.S. military presence on their soil, can Israel say she is afraid of a Palestinian state or any Arab nation or nations?

Is the solution to Israel's security concerns, which we have just proposed, a difficult one to put into effect? Are there diplomatic or international problems which would interfere with the ability of the U.S. to proceed immediately to implement this proposed solution to Israel's security needs?

The answer is, of course, no! The U.S. can enter into a mutual defense treaty with any nation at any time without the consent of anybody, allied or otherwise.

The proposed treaty, in its essentials, is identical with the mutual defense treaty entered into with South Korea in 1953. A copy of this treaty can be found in the Appendix. The consent (ratification) of the U.S. Senate, however, is required for all treaties. Senate approval should not be difficult. Israel has many friends in the U.S. Senate so ratification should be quick and easy.

There may be some Americans who would not support a proposal to station U.S. troops in Israel, presumably because they might be exposed to terrorist attacks. If so, it may be the result of a failure to understand the plan as proposed.

The proposal to station U.S. military units within Israel's borders is made only in the context of a comprehensive peace plan in which the Palestinians would have their own independent state. Thus, the reason for PLO terrorism and the Intifada in the West Bank would no longer exist.

The American people have consistently supported the policy of Mutual Defense Treaties that involved American peacekeeping forces all over the world.

Can it be seriously argued that it is better to wait until an uncontrolled conflagration breaks out in the Middle East and for the U.S. to then desperately try to save Israel with a rescue effort from thousands of miles away, rather than to establish a just peace and rely on a credible deterrent to preserve it?

In a future war there will be no victor. The great lesson of the past forty years is that peace and security are attainable not by "winning" wars, but by preventing them.

The most authoritative and comprehensive statement of Israel's position on its security needs is set forth in an article published in the *Jerusalem Post* of February 18, 1989, by the internationally prominent publisher, Robert Maxwell.

Maxwell was a member of the Steering Committee for Prime Minister Shamir's solidarity conference held early in 1989, to demonstrate the solidarity of the Jews within and outside Israel regarding Israel's defense policies. In his article Maxwell persuasively sets forth Israel's position with respect to its security concerns. The article is quoted below in part:

I have the honor to be a member of the steering committee for Prime Minister Shamir's conference of leading Jews, whose purpose is to show the solidarity of the Jews who live and work outside Israel with the people of Israel and the initiative its government is taking for peace and security in the Middle East.

The lessons of this century, of the Holocaust, of the history of the Jewish people, are that peace and security cannot be assured by promises, by United Nations resolutions, or by professions of good intent, whether they emanate from Washington, London, Moscow or wherever Yasser Arafat's caravan has rested.

Israel requires deeds, not words. It does not need paper assurances. It needs guarantees made of steel. Since the civilized world cannot produce such guarantees, Israel must look after its own defense. In the final event, the only people the Jews can trust for their survival are the Jews themselves.

Those who are intolerant of the Jewish obsession about security must understand that it is impossible for Israel's leaders to compromise with this imperative. Compromise which threatens the existence of the Jewish state is not compromise but betrayal.

In the early years of Hitler, there were Jewish leaders who thought that the democracies would protect them. They were wrong. It has taken nearly 2,000 years to rebuild the State of Israel. It is the bounden duty of the Jewish people within and without the borders of Israel to ensure that never again will it be destroyed, to make certain that it will be maintained at almost any cost, because the final cost is the very existence of the Jewish people.

That is the price we are not prepared to pay. We have been let down too often to trust blindly again. We cannot rely upon others for our salvation, however solemn the pledges, however sincere the intent. The road to the Holocaust was paved with good intentions on the part of those democrats who were not Jews.

Israel wants peace and needs peace, but peace with security. Unlike other nations, it cannot afford to lose even one single war, because that would mean instant annihilation. And four wars have been imposed on it since 1948.

It cannot trust its whole existence to promises which may not be kept, which may not be intended to be kept and, even if they were so intended, may be incapable of being kept.

While Israel is ready to negotiate a settlement with its neighbors directly and without preconditions, it cannot accept an armed, terrorist-dominated Palestinian state adjoining it—a state, moreover, of unremitting hostility, only waiting for its revenge, not for the events of the past year or two, but for the establishment of Israel itself.

It is impossible to divorce the events of today from what has gone before. The six million dead are part of today's living history.

I am not advocating intransigence. What I am saying is that we cannot betray those who died by risking the lives of those who survived and descended from them. That is the overwhelming reality of Israel today. History only repeats itself when those in command of our nations forget the past.

Israel needs peace just as its Arab neighbors need peace. Deep down, both peoples are impatient to return to the ageless aspirations of their forefathers, to be respected for the high ethical ideals, the intellectual excellence, the ability to invent and to create that which they have demonstrated so often and so brilliantly in the past.

I believe that these aspirations are indeed within their grasp. But real peace, with real security, is the unalterable condition of this process, imposed on us by the blood-stained lessons of history, and the catastrophic experience of our own generation.[4] [Emphasis supplied]

We are impressed and greatly encouraged by the remarkable similarity between the views expressed by Maxwell in his article in the *Jerusalem Post,* and those presented in this chapter. Indeed, his article eloquently summarizes one of the principal theses of this book:

"It is the bounden duty of the Jewish people within and without the borders of Israel to ensure that never again will it be destroyed, to make certain that it will be maintained at almost any cost, because the final cost is the very existence of the Jewish people."

We have repeatedly emphasized and cited the opinion of many prominent Israelis on the importance of the involvement of Jews outside Israel with its survival.

Maxwell says that "those who are intolerant of the Jewish obsession about security must understand that it is impossible for Israel to compromise this imperative." This is the position that has been consistently taken in this book in discussing Israel's security. We have stated clearly that Israel's security is a *sine qua non,* an indispensable prerequisite to any peace proposal.

We have gone even further than Maxwell in urging Jews outside Israel to become involved with Israel's fate. We not only understand the Jewish "obsession with security," but in company with many concerned Israelis, have stressed the point that the Diaspora is not "concerned" enough with it; that there is too much passivity in the Diaspora which, as Abba Eban says, "borders on indifference."

Maxwell calls attention to the fact that the lessons of this century, of the Holocaust, of the history of the Jewish people, are that peace and security cannot be assured by promises, by United Nations resolutions, or by professions of good intent, whether they emanate from Washington, London, Moscow, or anywhere.

Israel, he says, *"requires deeds not words. It needs guarantees of steel."*

We are in total agreement with this position. The Jews in Israel are entitled to the same "guarantees of steel" that the Jews in America have; that the South Koreans, Japanese and Germans have—the armed forces of the United States.

Maxwell rightly points out that Israel cannot trust its whole existence to promises which may not be kept, which may not be intended to be kept or are incapable of being kept.

This is the crux of the matter—*promises* are simply not enough! Obviously, Japan would never have staked its nationhood on U.S. promises alone; neither would the people of West Germany or South Korea; *nor should Israel be expected to do so.* Maxwell confirms what we have assumed Israel's position to be—*Israel wants peace—but peace with security.*

In an article appearing in the *Jerusalem Post* dated June 3, 1989, entitled "Rabin Praises Military Alliance," Defense Minister Yitzhak Rabin announced that the U.S. and Israel have conducted at least twenty-seven combined military exercises in recent years. The article goes on to report:

Rabin, who met earlier with Defense Secretary Richard Cheney and other high Pentagon military and civilian officials, recalled a conversation he had had earlier this year in Tel Aviv with the commander of the Mediterranean Sixth Fleet and the U.S. ambassador to Israel.

"They came to my office and said they have reached the point where it's not enough to train in Israel U.S. Marine Corps units up to the level of company," Rabin said. "What they would like to do is to do it on battalion-level size with the use of U.S. artillery and attack helicopters."

The defense minister said he was glad to report that "a month ago, the first U.S. Marine battalion completed its exercise" in Israel, including the use of live ammunition, artillery, and attack helicopters. "And I know that the demand is to have more and more of this kind of training in Israel," he added.[5]

What is the point of this? If U.S. forces were in Israel merely to conduct maneuvers or training exercises, it accomplishes nothing for Israel's security any more than a *temporary* presence of U.S. military forces in Korea, Japan or Germany would provide security for those countries.

If the intent of the U.S. military is only to familiarize U.S. forces with the local terrain and other factors in order to be in a position to assist Israel in an emergency, it makes little sense, because there is no reason to suppose that the U.S. forces would *be there* in an emergency. If the U.S. has simply *promised to be there* in a military crisis, it could be one that the U.S. might not be able to keep in time. Moreover, as the Israelis say, any *real* help would be 4,000 miles away.

Unless U.S. forces in Israel are *stationed* and *deployed in Israel* and their presence is intended as a guarantee of Israel's security as part of an overall peace plan, the training exercises are a wasteful and unnecessary provocation to the other nations in the Middle East, and endanger U.S. military personnel for no purpose.

A mutual defense treaty with Israel is the first step in a plan for peace and the crucial step.

A PLAN FOR PEACE

The plan presented here is based upon these conclusions:

1. That peace by *negotiation* between Israel and the Palestinians is impossible, not only because of the irreconcilable nature of the issues, but because time is running out in the Middle East crisis.

2. That, after many years of discussions, conferences and failed negotiations, the respective positions of most of the principal parties in interest are sufficiently well known and understood, that a peace by *consensus* is now feasible.

This hoped-for "consensus," however, is fragile and fleeting. Therefore, if the plan proposed here is to achieve success, it must be pursued expeditiously.

The following, for our purposes, are considered to be the "principal parties in interest" in the Israeli-Palestinian conflict. They are listed, not necessarily in the order of importance.

1. The United States.
2. Israel.
3. The Palestinian inhabitants of the West Bank and Gaza.
4. The Palestinian refugees.
5. The United Nations.
6. The Soviet Union.
7. The American Jewish Community.
8. The allies of the United States.
9. The "friendly" Arab countries.
10. The "hard-line" Arab nations.

It is contemplated that the proposed plan would be sponsored by the United States and organized and implemented under its leadership.

The following is an outline of the basic elements and provisions of the plan as proposed:

I. The United States would immediately enter into a Mutual Defense Treaty with Israel, essentially the same as that presently in force between the U.S. and the Republic of South Korea, dated October 1, 1953.

While the provisions of this Mutual Defense Treaty with South Korea are more than adequate to defend Israel from attack or aggression, it is, nevertheless, recommended that certain additional provisions be included in the text of the treaty to provide Israel with further assurances:

(a) As part of the U.S. commitment under the Mutual Defense Treaty, the U.S. agrees to deploy and station military forces—air, ground and naval—at such strategic points along the borders of Israel or elsewhere as shall be mutually determined.

(b) The U.S. forces deployed pursuant to the Treaty shall be fully equipped, battle-ready units and contingents of the U.S. Armed Forces sufficient to defend Israel from attack or invasion from any source whatsoever.

(c) The number and composition of the U.S. forces shall be agreed upon between the U.S. and Israel.

II. Simultaneously with the effective date of the U.S.-Israel Mutual Defense Treaty, Israel will withdraw all of its occupation forces from the West Bank and the Gaza Strip and re-establish its frontier boundaries as they existed immediately prior to the 1967 war, pursuant to United Nations Resolutions 242 and 338.

III. The United States and Israel will recognize an independent Palestinian State as provided for in the Partition Resolution of the General Assembly of the United Nations enacted on November 29, 1947, effective May 14, 1948, to which Resolution the United States is a signatory.

IV. The borders of the said Palestinian state shall encompass the so-called West Bank and Gaza, and shall be congruent with the borders of Israel as they existed immediately prior to the 1967 war.

All Israeli settlers presently owning land in the occupied territories shall have the choice of remaining and becoming citizens of the Palestinian State or disposing of their property as hereinafter provided.

V. That a Non-Aggression Pact be entered into between the State of Israel and the Palestinian State.

VI. That a demilitarized zone (DMZ) between Israel and the Palestinian State be established, the location and extent of which shall be determined by a mutual agreement.

VII. That a commission of the United Nations be established for the following purposes:

(a) To determine the just compensation due to the Palestinian refugees for lands and property taken by Israel in the 1948 War of Independence and now incorporated into the State of Israel. It is understood and agreed that all such compensation paid by the Government of Israel in satisfaction of the claims of the said refugees shall *not* be considered "indemnification" or "restitution," but in the nature of payment for properties acquired under the sovereign right of Eminent Domain.

(b) To determine the just compensation due to Israeli settlers in the occupied territories of the West Bank and the Gaza for lands and property held by them which they may desire to dispose of.

VIII. That the city of Jerusalem remain in status quo until such time as Israel and the United Nations agree that it is propitious to convene a conference to determine the permanent status of Jerusalem.

It shall be understood and agreed that consent by any party to the continuance of the status quo shall not be construed as acquiescence to the status quo *permanently* nor as prejudicial to any right, or claim of right, presently existing.

COMMENTS AND ANALYSIS

The recommendation with respect to the status of Jerusalem is in no sense sweeping the matter under the rug—the rug is afire. The first imperative is to smother the flames. Sufficient time, perhaps decades, must be allowed to pass in order for the fears, hatreds and religious passions involved to subside.

With the coming of peace, the incitement to fear and hatred will gradually diminish and disappear. Harmony and the recognition of mutual interests *can* replace hostility. We have witnessed the Berlin Wall coming down almost overnight. The movement toward freedom, independence and self-determination is suddenly epidemic in the world. No one can say what may evolve in Jerusalem. It is even possible that some day Christians, Jews, and Moslems may discover that they share the same God.

The greatest enemy of peace in the Middle East is *delay*. One important aspect of the proposed plan is the fact that, in its critical elements, it can be activated and executed quickly to defuse the time bombs ticking away in the Middle East and already approaching the point of explosion. Among the most critical are these:

THE RADICAL "PLO" DANGER

Yasser Arafat is in a race against time. In April, 1989, Arafat was elected "President of Palestine" by the Central Council of the PLO. This was pursuant to a deal with the extreme elements of the PLO, headed by George Habash and other rejectionist and Moslem fundamentalist leaders.

Arafat convinced the radicals to allow him and the moderates one more chance to make peace with the Israelis through diplomacy, with the understanding that if he failed in his efforts, he would yield to a take-over of the PLO by the radicals, who have been urging terrorism and guerrilla warfare as the only solution.

How long this probationary period will last is anyone's guess. Habash has been quoted as saying "six months." No doubt it depends on the degree of progress being made, if any. Once convinced that Arafat is being stalled or that real progress toward peace is unlikely or impossible, Arafat's efforts and career will be over.

The Palestinians can hardly be charged with impatience. The General Assembly of the United Nations, *including the United States, voted for an independent Palestinian state more than forty years ago.*

THE INTIFADA

If history tells us anything it is that the Intifada can never be suppressed. "Restoring order," which is the euphemism used to describe the Likud's policy of beating, torturing and shooting the Palestinians, is a hopeless effort. Israel's military leadership (except Ariel Sharon) have all declared that a military solution to the Intifada is impossible.

"Restoring order," of course, was what the German army of occupation was trying to do as it hunted down, tortured and killed the members of the Maquis (French underground).

"Restoring order" is what the French were trying to do in Algeria and Vietnam; it's what the British were trying to do in Palestine when they captured and shot Jewish terrorists; it's what the Russians were trying to do in Afghanistan; it's what King George III was trying to do when he sent his Redcoats to Boston to restore order after a "disorderly" Tea Party in Boston Harbor.

THE THREAT FROM RELIGIOUS FANATICS

Most major events that have shaped the world's history have been unanticipated and ones over which governments have had little control. At this writing, the Warsaw Pact is suddenly in a state of disintegration.

In 1914, during one of the most stable periods of European history, *one* homemade bomb, thrown by a Serbian political fanatic at Sarajevo, exploded into World War I, ultimately costing the lives of twenty-five million people and changing the world for all time.

A little more than ten years ago, a plot by Jewish religious fanatics to blow up the Moslem sacred shrine—Dome of the Rock—almost succeeded. If it had, Harkabi says, it could easily have provoked a "Jihad" against Israel by perhaps forty Moslem nations from Mauritania to Indonesia. This is what the Jewish fanatics hoped would happen so that it would stop the "Sinai land for peace deal" between Egypt and Israel.

The plotters were captured but there are still hundreds of thousands of Orthodox zealots who still consider the Dome of the Rock (which sits conspicuously in the middle of Jerusalem) as an "abomination" that must be wiped out.[6]

The *Jerusalem Post* of October 18, 1989, reported on the following incident entitled "Group Lays Cornerstone of Third Temple":

Led by a cohen in priestly robes, and equipped with special vessels for the Temple ritual, two rams' horns, a clarinet and an accordion, members of the Faithful of the Temple Mount marched last week from the Western Wall to the Pool of Siloam to consecrate what they have designed as the cornerstone of the Third Temple.

An outraged Mayor Teddy Kollek described the FTM as "dwarfs walking in the footsteps of Shabtai Zvi"—a reference to the false messiah of the 17th century. Kollek said he hoped the group would not bring catastrophe to the Jewish people as other false messiahs had done, and added that although few Jews considered the acts of the FTM important, many *Arabs regarded them in a different light.*[7] [Emphasis supplied]

One rabbi is quoted as calling them "dangerous lunatics." The following is taken from an editorial in the same edition of the *Post* entitled "Engineers of Armageddon":

Acting in the exercise of its claim of sovereign right to all Jerusalem, the government left the administration of the Temple Mount to the Moslem authorities.

The government's policy has not, however, been uniformly endorsed by the citizenry. *To the messianic wing of Israeli ultra-nationalism, the status quo on the Temple Mount has been an insufferable offense calling for quick remedy.* The quickest remedy yet has been offered by the group that sought to blow up the Dome of the Rock a decade ago. The ensuing Armageddon was expected by its engineers to have the particularly beneficial result to killing the then mooted land-for-peace deal between Israel and Egypt over Sinai.

What that now-extinct underground group tried to secure, by violent clandestine means, the Temple Mount Faithful, an offshoot of the

Greater Israel Movement, has been hoping to achieve through public pressure and propaganda.

Yesterday, the second day of Hol Hamoed Succot, their leader, Gershon Salomon, laid what he described as the cornerstone of the Third Temple, at a site about a mile away from the Western Wall. That was not quite the ground he had originally had in mind.

But a fact had, as it were, been established which, by merely helping fan the Arab riot at the Old City's Herod's Gate, showed its effectiveness.

So much for the Temple Mount Faithful. The group is smallish and can easily be dismissed as inconsequential. *But it is not. If, to ordinary Jews, the group's political mangling of religion is merely an abomination, to ordinary Moslems its actions are a serious provocation. Unless it puts these unfunny oddballs in their places, the government will have to bear responsibility for their words and deeds.*[8] [Emphasis supplied]

If the Moslems consider it a "serious provocation," and if, by chance, it starts a chain reaction among the fanatics on both sides which escalates into "Armageddon"—how does the Israeli government "bear the responsibility" as suggested in the editorial? Did anyone care who bore the responsibility for the assassination of Archduke Ferdinand? The obligation is not to fix the responsibility for Armageddon, if it comes, but to stop it from coming. Yet every day, hundreds of Jews and Moslem *fanatics* and hundreds of thousands of fearful, hate-filled people are thrown together in this seething cauldron and see no way out. *On any morning we may awake to see a headline that removes the Middle East crisis from anyone's control.*

THE CONSENSUS

The question remains as to how the proposed peace plan would be received by the "principal parties in interest."

There is, naturally, no way of predicting with absolute certainty how anyone or any nation would react to the plan as proposed.

However, it is perfectly possible, in fact highly probable, that the response of most of the principal parties in interest can be ascertained in advance, based upon positions previously taken and public statements made with respect to the issues involved.

It is, of course, possible that previous publicly stated attitudes and expressions of views by a party in interest may not be an accurate reflection of a party's true position on the issues which are addressed in the plan. In such cases, the proposed plan would at least serve a valuable purpose in exposing heretofore concealed attitudes and disguised intentions.

The following are what, it is assumed, would be the positions of the respective parties in interest with regard to the proposed plan.

A. THE UNITED STATES

The U.S., as previously indicated, would necessarily have to approve of the plan and act as sponsor and coordinator in its implementation.

The plan should receive strong support from the U.S. for the following reasons:

1. The U.S., under President Truman, was the principal sponsor and advocate for the Partition Resolution passed by the United Nations in 1947, which calls for the establishment of two independent sovereign states in Palestine, one Jewish and the other Palestinian.
2. The U.S. has consistently supported United Nations Resolutions 242 and 338, which call for Israel to return the occupied lands on the West Bank and Gaza to the Palestinians and also calls for a just settlement of the claims of the Palestinian refugees.
3. It would immediately remove the concern that Israel might be attacked, defeated and destroyed if war should break out in the Middle East.
4. It would reduce the enmities and hostile attitudes in the Middle East growing out of the Israeli-Palestinian conflict, which often forces the U.S. to choose between friendly Arab states, our European allies, and Israel.

B. ISRAEL

A large majority of the Israeli people should welcome the plan. Public opinion polls have shown that all segments of Israeli society (with the exception of the religious extremists and nationalists) have strongly expressed a desire for peace *with security*. Retaining the occupied lands except for defensive purposes is not important to most Israelis. Since under the proposed plan "defensive borders" are irrelevant, this concern is eliminated. Robert Maxwell confirms that the principal concern of Israelis is *security*. David Shipler, in his Pulitzer Prize winning book quoted earlier, says:

> The biblical arguments for holding the West Bank excite very few outside the ranks of the militant movement of settlers; most Israeli reluc-

tance to relinquish the occupied territory rests on worries about security, not on God's deed to Abraham.[9]

A large majority of the Israeli people have always been willing to trade land for peace. Their concern has been that they might find themselves exchanging land merely *for the hope of peace.*

The proposed plan offers Israel assured peace and security.

Furthermore, the plan should afford great relief to the Israeli people who would no longer need to be preoccupied with such futile debate as to "whether or not we can trust Arafat."

Under a mutual defense treaty with the U.S., such useless speculation is no more relevant than a debate in West Germany after the NATO pact as to whether *Stalin could be trusted.*

The same is true of the mutual defense pact with South Korea. The South Koreans did not have to convince themselves that North Korea or China could be trusted—they trusted the United States. It was *assumed* that the North Koreans and the Chinese could not be trusted—which, of course, is the reason for the mutual defense treaty.

While we believe as stated earlier that, if Arafat can succeed in having a Palestinian state recognized, both Arafat and the PLO can be trusted to act in their own best interests. But under the proposed plan the question is moot—it doesn't make any difference whether Arafat can be trusted or not.

C. THE UNITED NATIONS

The plan would, no doubt, be approved by an overwhelming majority of the United Nations for the following reasons:

1. It would be a final implementation of the Partition Resolution passed in 1947 calling for the creation of a Jewish and a Palestinian state in Palestine.
2. It would carry out the provisions of Resolutions 242 and 338 which have been a constant source of controversy over the past 22 years.
3. It would comply with the Resolutions 242 and 338 on the need for a just solution to the Palestinian refugee problem.
4. It would remove from the annual U.N. agenda the Israeli-Palestinian conflict which has been the source of more contention, acrimony and divisiveness than any other issue in the history of the U.N.
5. It would abolish the ever-present threat of a nuclear war in the Middle East, an important duty of the U.N. in fulfilling its primary responsibility for keeping the peace of the world.

D. THE PALESTINIANS OF THE WEST BANK AND GAZA

The plan would, at last, satisfy the Palestinian nationalist movement for self-determination and give the Palestinian people the homeland and state promised to them by the U.N. Partition Resolution in 1947.

E. THE "FRIENDLY" ARAB COUNTRIES

Egypt, Saudi Arabia, the Arab Emirates, Kuwait and Jordan should provide strong support for the plan since it would remove their greatest fear, a new war in the Middle East, which might not only destroy all of the progress they have achieved in the past twenty-five years but reduce their nations to ruins.

F. OUR EUROPEAN AND ASIAN ALLIES

The plan should receive near unanimous approval. It eliminates one of the few, and perhaps only, major issues which separates the U.S. from its allies. It would restore respect for the U.S. where it has been lost and enhance the U.S. role of leadership that our allies can only applaud.

It would also eliminate one of the greatest fears of our allies, the interruption or loss of critical oil supplies from the Middle East which would inevitably result from a Middle East war.

G. THE PALESTINIAN LIBERATION ORGANIZATION

By electing Yasser Arafat "President of the State of Palestine" and according him an opportunity by diplomatic means to have the State of Palestine accepted, the radical element in the PLO have already decided to follow Arafat if he succeeds in making peace and the recognition of a Palestinian state.

The adoption of the plan would be a clear success and should receive the wholehearted support of all elements of the PLO.

H. THE AMERICAN JEWISH COMMUNITY

The response should be highly favorable to the plan. The great sacrifices made by American Jews to keep Israel alive in the face of the ever-present fears and anxieties that Israel may not survive another war, or a war after that, will have been justified.

The assurance that Israel *will* survive and be given an opportunity to fulfill its destiny, should be a source of great satisfaction to the American Jewish Community and the Jewish people worldwide.

The American Jewish Community for the first time is experiencing serious divisions and open dissension on the question of supporting the Likud's policies in the occupied territories.

A news item published in the November 25, 1989, issue of the *Jerusalem Post* reports that "U.S. community leaders are now ready to oppose Israeli policies openly":

> Political differences in Israel have spilled over into the American Jewish community, resulting in a much greater readiness on the part of American Jewry to oppose Israeli policies publicly.
>
> This was evident in the mood among the 3,000 local and national Jewish leaders attending the General Assembly of the Council of Jewish Federations here last week. Prime Minister Yitzhak Shamir received a polite but restrained reception when he addressed the conference.
>
> The Jewish leaders here were clearly divided over Shamir's refusal to exchange land for peace, and they did not accord him prolonged outbursts of applause.
>
> They certainly gave him the appropriate standing ovations and interrupted his speech a dozen times with applause. But there was widespread disappointment in what was regarded as a very hard-line speech.
>
> Shamir spoke shortly after he received a letter from 41 prominent American Jewish leaders asking him not to misread the polite applause of the audience as evidence that American Jewry supports his determination to hold on to the territories and to resist efforts by the Bush administration to bring about Israeli-Palestinian negotiations.
>
> Among those signing the letter were Hyman Bookbinder of the American Jewish Committee; Edward Sanders of the American Israel Public Affairs Committee; Ted Mann, a former chairman of the Conference of Presidents of Major American Jewish Organizations; Morton Mandel, former president of the Council of Jewish Federations; and Peggy Tishman, immediate past president of the UJA Federation of New York.
>
> But Seymour Reich, the current chairman of the Presidents' Conference, strongly disagreed with those signing the letter.
>
> "I've been traveling around the U.S.," he told the *Jerusalem Post*, "and the American Jewish community is solidly behind the prime minister. We want to give him a chance to wage peace his way. There's no break in organizational ranks."
>
> Reich dismissed the letter as the work of "a few individuals who are out of sync with the Jewish mainstream."[10]

Another letter received by Shamir during his visit was from 213 leading Reform and Conservative rabbis calling on him to "accept the principle of exchanging land for peace." Several hundred Jews also signed an open letter to the premier written by Michael Lerner, editor of *Tikkun* magazine, urging talks with the PLO, and recognition of Palestinian self-determination.

Since these divisions in the American Jewish Community are based primarily on differing views as to the best way to protect Israel's security, the proposed plan should be welcomed by both factions, since it *assures* Israel's security. With this source of contention removed, the plan would act to re-unite American Jews in the service of Israel.

I. THE SOVIET UNION

In the present international climate, where the Soviet Union is struggling with serious internal problems and the Warsaw Pact nations are in a state of turmoil, the last thing the Soviets should be interested in is undertaking destabilizing activities in the Middle East, or fomenting any problems in the area. In the process of expanding its diplomacy toward developing better relations with all nations of the world, particularly the U.S., the proposed plan should receive at least mild approval.

As earlier noted, the Soviet Union has complained of Israel's long-range nuclear missile capability. It is, therefore, possible that the proposed plan might well be received enthusiastically.

J. THE PALESTINIAN REFUGEES

It is impossible, from a practical standpoint, to restore to the Palestinian refugees the homes and lands from which they fled in 1948 and have now been incorporated into Israel proper.

While the emotional and physical suffering of the refugees cannot be compensated for, the United Nations Resolutions 242 and 338 imply that justice is required only in the form of monetary compensation. Most realistic refugees recognize that this is their only hope and have indicated a willingness to accept just compensation in lieu of the right to return to their homes and lands in Israel.

K. THE "HARD-LINE" ARAB COUNTRIES

Although Syria, Iraq and Libya can be considered parties in interest, what their responses would be is conjectural and is not significant in determining whether or not the proposed plan should be adopted. However, it would not be surprising if Syria and Iraq were strong supporters, since it would remove the threat of the religious radicals in Israel to expand its borders to include the conquest of Syria and Iraq as part of Greater Israel.

L. THE DISSENTERS

There is, of course, one group in Israel which would be opposed to the plan, or any other peace plan. These are the Gush Emunim and other religious nationalist extremists, including the West Bank settlers.

Their opposition would be highly vocal and, as we have discussed in detail, is based on the argument, real or pretended, that the West Bank and Gaza are sacred lands of Eretz Israel which, according to the Torah, cannot be returned.

The Israeli settlers in the occupied territories number about 70,000 people. The plan, as proposed, would give them the choice of continuing to live in their present homes in the occupied territories under Palestinian sovereignty, or selling their property and moving elsewhere.

While the welfare and survival of Israel and the peace of the world far outweigh the beliefs and comforts of this small minority, the degree of deprivation or sacrifice required of the West Bank settlers under the proposed plan should be analyzed objectively rather than emotionally. In this analysis the following factors should be considered:

1. As to the settlers, they occupy subsidized homes, most of them less than ten years old; there are no family or generational traditions connected with these habitations. There is, in a word, no *uprooting* involved.

2. Most of these settlements are not what Americans would think of as pioneer homesteads where a man is wresting a livelihood for himself and his family out of the soil in a battle with nature. Many of them are bedroom communities for office workers in Tel Aviv and Jerusalem. They are not to be confused with the Kibbutzim movement who were the original founders of Israel. These were communal organizations who worked together tilling the land and providing for their needs from the work of their hands. They were not religious zealots but were, for the most part, secular socialists.

David Shipler, in his book, *Arab & Jew: Wounded Spirits In a Promised Land,* that we have referred to earlier, has provided some illuminating comments regarding the nature of the West Bank settlers:

There were several waves of settlers. The bulk of the religious, ideologically driven Israelis took up their stations on the West Bank in the five years or so beginning with Begin's election in 1977, although small vanguards of them squatted illegally here and there from 1968 onward. That fundamentalist movement was bracketed, before and after, by mostly secular Jews who settled the West Bank for nonreligious reasons, both in the early years after 1967 and beginning in the early 1980s. The third wave, 1980s wave of settlers, went most in search of economical housing, made possible by government subsidies unavailable in major cities.

They did not need a comprehensive system of faith to move them to the satellite towns that were serving as bedroom communities for Jerusalem and Tel Aviv.

The middle group was the important one in shaping the ideological framework of the movement. Led by the Gush Emunim activists, those settlers, most of them with higher education, forged an amalgam of religious and nationalist impulses that took them to barren, stony hilltops where they practically camped in small house trailers for several years until the government built them permanent apartments. They were driven by a search for biblical heritage, military security, and personal fulfillment, with the mixture of these components varying in each individual. Some stressed the secular, pioneering objectives, and many found a modest religious revival in the new communities.

Strangely, despite these settlers' avowed reverence for the land, I never encountered any who seemed to have any feeling for it. None had the farmer's devotion to working the land they claimed to love; they used it as a place of residence, a symbol of their faith and their history, an abstraction, but they almost never turned a spade or plowed a furrow. I never saw a pious settler in the hills of Judea and Samaria hold a clump of raw earth in his hand and watch it and smell it as he crushed it and sifted it between his fingers. As the Jewish townships spread from the rocky hilltops into the more arable valleys, advancing bulldozers cut swaths and scars through the Arabs' vineyards and small fields of winter wheat, which were then left fallow by the newly arrived Jews. One settlement I know kept a herd of sheep, another grew flowers in a hothouse. Some settlements built small factories on their land, but by and large their residents commuted to work in Jerusalem or Tel Aviv.[11]

After the guerrilla war in Algeria, when the French finally decided to grant Algeria independence, they brought back more than a million of their colonists and settlers from Algeria whose ancestors had been there for up to 130 years.

Seventy thousand West Bank settlers, therefore, should not cause any great resettlement problem. Also it should not be forgotten that, for forty years, 700,00 innocent Palestinians have been uprooted from homes occupied for generations and still do not live in homes, but in camps.

As to the obligation of the religious extremists not to give back a "single foot" of the sacred lands of the West Bank and Gaza, their consciences may be alleviated somewhat by the pronouncements of a convocation of learned rabbis dealing with this question.

According to a report in the *Jerusalem Post* of August 12, 1989, there is a dispute among the rabbis as to whether, according to the Torah, it would be permissible to give up any of the occupied land. A majority said no! However, according to the *Post*:

> Citizens' Rights movement MK Dedi Zucker met with the chief rabbis and extracted from them assurances that if the government nonetheless decided on a territorial withdrawal, they would see themselves "bound" by the decision and take no action against it.[12]

Many leading scholars, according to the *Jerusalem Post,* October 28, 1989, including Ovadia Yosef (Shas) and Eliezer Schach (Degel Hatorah), "have ruled Halachically *that peace, not land, is the loftiest value.*"[13]

Reprise and Epilogue

IN CONCLUDING, we turn briefly to the beginning chapter of our thesis and quote again from Barbara Tuchman's *The March of Folly,* which she explains "is the pursuit by governments of policies contrary to their own best interests."

She cites, as a classic example, the fate of the Jewish Kingdoms of Israel and Judah and the price paid by the Jewish people for the folly of King Rehoboam:

> The Kingdom of Judah, containing Jerusalem, lived on as the land of the Jewish people. It suffered conquest, too, and exile by the waters of Babylon, then revival, civil strife, foreign sovereignty, rebellion, another conquest, another farther exile and dispersion, oppression, ghetto and massacre—but not disappearance. *The alternative course that Rehoboam might have taken, advised by the elders and so lightly rejected, exacted a long revenge that has left its mark for 2,800 years.*[1] [Emphasis supplied]

The continuing folly and failures of many of the leaders of the ancient Hebrew kingdoms and the historical consequences to the Jewish people are recounted in detail in Chapter I of this book.

We saw that the Romans first became the masters of the Jews, *not by conquest,* but because they were invited to rule the Kingdom of Judah and to settle the internecine quarrels and dissension among the Jews.

Abram Sachar comments on the phenomenon:

> Freedom was again crushed out because the Jews had not learned how to use it. The selfishness of the ruling houses and the strife of political and religious factions exhausted the strength of the State. A curse seemed to

lie on the Jews which prevented them from reaching the highest levels of moral power except when they were hammered and beaten by oppression.[2]

Today, Israel again faces a crisis of leadership and is called upon to make choices which may determine the fate of Israel forever.

In his recent book entitled *The Chosen and the Choice, Israel at the Crossroads,* author Jean-Jacques Servan-Schreiber* relates his conversations with a number of Israelis, including Shimon Peres, and expresses his views concerning the golden opportunity which the future holds for an *Israel at peace*:

> I come across urgent calls from Jews in anguish for a revision of old doctrines. The head of a religious high school in Jerusalem writes: "On this our 40th anniversary I cannot help seeing our nation as beset with pain and anguish. We feel lost. I wonder what Isaiah would say today if he were among us, leaning against the walls of Jerusalem.
>
> *"There is nothing new under the sun, have we not always destroyed our achievements with our own hands? Can we not recall before our eyes a whole two-thousand-year history of recurrent self-destruction?* I dream that some day I shall be able to tell my pupils about the rediscovery of the good life in our God-given land. We must do something more than just perpetuate our defense by military means. We have to heal the wounds in ourselves and our enemies, we have to re-invent peace. Yes, a more far-seeing form of Zionism."[3] [Emphasis supplied]

Among his other observations Servan-Schreiber states that "Something new must be created in the spiritual field by the Jewish people, if they want an Israel that is faithful to its destiny and able to fulfill its potential."[4] I share this view.

Now may be the last chance for Israel to fulfill its promise—not the promise of the Land—but the promise of its People.

I have long believed that what Israel desperately needs is a "Prophet," however, my opinion has now changed. Israel has its prophets—Abba Eban, Yehoshafat Harkabi, Simha Flapan, Amos Perlmutter, to name a few. Sadly, however, as with the Prophets of old, no one is listening.

---

*Jean-Jacques Servan-Schreiber is one of France's leading authors. He is presently Chairman of the International Committee of Carnegie-Mellon University and for a time was posted to the Hebrew University of Jerusalem.

Appendix

MUTUAL DEFENSE TREATY
BETWEEN
THE UNITED STATES OF AMERICA
AND
THE REPUBLIC OF KOREA

The Parties to this Treaty,

Reaffirming their desire to live
in peace with all peoples and all governments, and desiring to strengthen the
fabric of peace in the Pacific area,

Desiring to declare publicly
and formally their common determination to defend themselves against external armed attack so that no potential
aggressor could be under the illusion
that either of them stands alone in the
Pacific area,

Desiring further to strengthen
their efforts for collective defense for
the preservation of peace and security
pending the development of a more
comprehensive and effective system
of regional security in the Pacific area,

Have agreed as follows:

ARTICLE I

The Parties undertake to settle
any international disputes in which they
may be involved by peaceful means in
such a manner that international peace

本條約의當事國은모든國民
과모든政府와平和的으로
生活하고저하는希望을再確認
하며또한太平洋地域에있어서
의平和機構을鞏固히한것을
希望하고當事國中어느一國이
太平洋地域에있어서孤立하여
있다는幻覺을어떠한潛在的
侵略者도가지지않도록外部로
부터의武力攻擊에對하여自身
을防衛하고저하는共通의決意
를公公然히또한正式으로宣言
한것을希望하고또한太平洋
地域에있어서더욱包括的이고
効果的인地域的安全保障
組織이發達될때까지平和와
安全을維持하고저集團的防衛
을為한努力을鞏固히한것을希望
하며다음과같이同意한다.

第一條

當事國은關聯된지도모르는어
떠한國際的紛爭이라도國際
的平和와安全과正義를危殆롭
게하지않는方法으로平和的手

and security and justice are not endangered and to refrain in their international relations from the threat or use of force in any manner inconsistent with the Purposes of the United Nations, or obligations assumed by any Party toward the United Nations.

ARTICLE II

The Parties will consult together whenever, in the opinion of either of them, the political independence or security of either of the Parties is threatened by external armed attack. Separately and jointly, by self help and mutual aid, the Parties will maintain and develop appropriate means to deter armed attack and will take suitable measures in consultation and agreement to implement this Treaty and to further its purposes.

ARTICLE III

Each Party recognizes that an armed attack in the Pacific area on either of the Parties in territories now under their respective administrative

段에依하여解決하고또한國際關係에있어서國際聯合의目的이나當事國이國際聯合에對하여負擔한義務에背馳되지않는方法으로武力의威脅이나武力의行使를삼갈것을約束한다.

第 二 條

當事國中에느一國의政治的獨立또는安全이外部로부터의武力攻擊에依하여威脅을받고있다고어느當事國이든지認定한때에는언제든지當事國은서로協議한다. 當事國은單獨的으로나共同으로나自助와相互援助에依하여武力攻擊을阻止하기為한適切한手段을持續하여强化시킬것이며本條約을實行하고그目的을推進할適切한措置를協議와合意下에取할것이다.

第 三 條

各當事國은他當事國의行政支配下에있는領土와各當事國이他當事國의行政支配下에合法的으로들어갔다고認定하는今後의

control, or hereafter recognized by one
of the Parties as lawfully brought under
the administrative control of the other,
would be dangerous to its own peace
and safety and declares that it would
act to meet the common danger in accordance with its constitutional processes.

ARTICLE IV

The Republic of Korea grants,
and the United States of America accepts,
the right to dispose United States land,
air and sea forces in and about the territory of the Republic of Korea as determined by mutual agreement.

ARTICLE V

This Treaty shall be ratified
by the United States of America and
the Republic of Korea in accordance
with their respective constitutional
processes and will come into force
when instruments of ratification thereof have been exchanged by them at
Washington.

領土에있어서他當事國에對한
太平洋地域에있어서의武力攻
擊을自國의平和와安全을危
殆롭게하는것이라고認定하고
共通한危險에對處하기爲하
여各者의憲法上의手續에따라
行動할것을宣言한다.

第　四　條
相互的合意에依하여美合衆國
의陸軍海軍과空軍을大韓民國
의領土內外그附近에配備하는權
利를大韓民國은이를許與하고
美合衆國은이를受諾한다.

第　五　條
本條約은美合衆國과大韓民國
에依하여各者의憲法上의手續에
따라批准되어야하며그批准
書가兩國에依하여「와싱톤」에
서交換되었을때에效力을發生
한다.

ARTICLE VI

This Treaty shall remain in force indefinitely. Either Party may terminate it one year after notice has been given to the other Party.

IN WITNESS WHEREOF the undersigned Plenipotentiaries have signed this Treaty.

DONE in duplicate at Washington, in the English and Korean languages, this first day of October 1953.

第 六 條

本條約은 無期限으로 有效하며 어느 當事國이든지 他當事國에 通告한後 一年後에 本條約은 終止시킬수 있다.

以上의 證據로서 下記全權委員 은 本條約에 署名한다.

本條約은 一九五三年十月一日에 '와싱톤'에서 英文및 韓國文으로 두벌로 作成됨.

FOR THE UNITED STATES OF AMERICA:

美合衆國을 爲해서

[1]

FOR THE REPUBLIC OF KOREA:

大韓民國을 爲해서

[2]

---

[1] JOHN FOSTER DULLES
[2] Y. T. PYUN

WHEREAS THE SENATE of the United States of America by their resolution of January 26, 1954, two-thirds of the Senators present concurring therein, did advise and consent to the ratification of the said Treaty with the following understanding:

> "It is the understanding of the United States that neither party is obligated, under Article III of the above Treaty, to come to the aid of the other except in case of an external armed attack against such party; nor shall anything in the present Treaty be construed as requiring the United States to give assistance to Korea except in the event of an armed attack against territory which has been recognized by the United States as lawfully brought under the administrative control of the Republic of Korea."

WHEREAS the text of the aforesaid understanding was communicated by the Government of the United States of America to the Government of the Republic of Korea by a note dated January 28, 1954,* and was acknowledged by the Government of the Republic of Korea by a note dated February 1, 1954;*

WHEREAS the said Treaty was duly ratified by the President of the United States of America on February 5, 1954, in pursuance of the aforesaid advice and consent of the Senate and subject to the aforesaid understanding, and was duly ratified also on the part of the Republic of Korea on January 29, 1954;

WHEREAS the respective instruments of ratification of the said Treaty were exchanged at Washington on November 17, 1954, and a protocol of exchange, in the English and Korean languages, was signed at that place and on that date by the respective Plenipotentiaries of the United States of America and the Republic of Korea, the said protocol of exchange recording the aforesaid understanding;

AND WHEREAS it is provided in Article V of the said Treaty that the Treaty will come into force when instruments of ratification thereof have been exchanged at Washington;

NOW THEREFORE, be it known that I, Dwight D. Eisenhower, President of the United States of America, do hereby proclaim and make public the said Mutual Defense Treaty between the United States of America and the Republic of Korea to the end that the same and every article and clause thereof, subject to the understanding hereinbefore recited, shall be observed and fulfilled with good faith, on and after November 17, 1954, by the United States of America and by the citizens of the United States of America and all other persons subject to the jurisdiction thereof.

---

*not printed

Source Notes

I. The March of Folly

1. Tuchman, Barbara W. *The March of Folly*. New York: Alfred A. Knopf, 1984; 4.
2. Ibid. 5.
3. Sachar, Abram L. *A History of the Jews*. New York: Alfred A. Knopf, 1984; 43.
4. Tuchman, 10-11.
5. Sachar, 44-45.
6. Ausubel, Nathan. *Book of Jewish Knowledge*. New York: Crown, 1964.
7. Johnson, Paul. *A History of the Jews*. New York: Harper & Row, 1987; 70.
8. Sachar, 57.
9. Ibid. 74.
10. Ibid. 84.
11. Ibid. 105.
12. Ibid. 106.
13. Ibid. 107.
14. Ibid. 107.
15. Johnson, 118; *Encyclopedia Judaica*, X., 260-62.
16. Sachar, 118-19.
17. Josephus, *The Jewish War*.
18. Sachar, 120.
19. Ibid. 121.
20. *Encyclopedia Judaica*, IV.
21. Sachar, 122-23.
22. Ibid. 123.
23. Harkabi, Yehosafat. *Facing Reality*.
24. *Los Angeles Times,* 18 October 1988, Associated Press.

II. The Diaspora and Eretz Israel

1. *Encyclopedia Judaica*, VI, 8.
2. Johnson, Paul. *A History of the Jews*. New York: Harper & Row, 1987, 112.
3. Ibid. 132.

4. Ausubel, Nathan. *Book of Jewish Knowledge*. New York: Crown, 1964; 127.
5. Johnson, 118.
6. Ibid. 244.
7. Ibid. 561.
8. Ibid. 444.
9. *Jerusalem Post*, 7 October 1978: Meir Merhav, "The general with a phantom army."
10. *Jerusalem Post*, 20 June 1988.
11. *Time*, 22 November 1986: "Soviet Jews: Israel wants them all."
12. *Jerusalem Post*, 18 June 1988: "Erase disgrace of drop-outs."
13. *Los Angeles Times*, 6 July 1979: Alexander Dranov.
14. *Los Angeles Times*, 23 June 1989.

III. The Zionist Movement: 1887-1948

1. Perlmutter, Amos. *Israel: The Partitioned State: A Political History Since 1900*. New York: Scribners, 1985; 6.
2. Ibid. 9.
3. Ibid. 17-22.
4. Ibid. 23.
5. Ibid. 33.
6. Ibid. 43-44.
7. Ibid. 25.
8. Ibid. 46.
9. Ibid. 42.
10. Ibid. 55.
11. Ibid. 62-63.
12. Ibid. 76.
13. Ibid. 92.
14. Ibid. 101.
15. Ibid. 104.
16. Johnson, Paul. *A History of the Jews*. New York: Harper & Row, 1987; 521.
17. Perlmutter, 104-05.
18. Johnson, 522-23.
19. Flapan, Simha. *The Birth of Israel: Myths and Realities*. New York: Pantheon Books, 1987; 22-24.
20. Perlmutter, 113.
21. Johnson, 525.
22. Flapan, 32.
23. Ibid. 33.
24. Perlmutter, 527.

IV. The Arab-Israeli Wars

1. Flapan, Simha. *The Birth of Israel: Myths and Realities.* New York: Pantheon Books, 1987; 10.
2. Ibid. 8.
3. Ibid. 9.
4. Shipler, David. *Arab and Jew: Wounded Spirits in a Promised Land.* New York: Penguin Books, 1987; 32.
5. Flapan, 57-58.
6. Ibid. 73.
7. Ibid. 73-74.
8. Ibid. 76.
9. Ibid. 74.
10. Ibid. 47.
11. Ibid. 49.
12. Shipler, 40.
13. Ibid. 32.
14. Flapan, 83.
15. Ibid. 89.
16. Shipler, 34-35.
17. Flapan, 88.
18. Ibid. 93-94.
19. Ibid. 94.
20. Johnson, Paul. *A History of the Jews.* New York: Harper & Row, 1987; 529.
21. Flapan, 94-95.
22. Shipler, 34.
23. Flapan, 99-101.
24. Ibid. 91.
25. Ibid. 92-93.
26. Ibid. 85.
27. Ibid. 96.
28. Ibid. 106.
29. Ibid. 107.
30. Ibid. 108.
31. Ibid. 87.
32. Ibid. 117.
33. Ibid. 108.
34. Johnson, 538.
35. Ibid. 535.

V. The Search for Peace

1. *The Wall Street Journal,* 7 February 1977: "Vance's mideast trip."
2. *Los Angeles Times,* 14 February 1977: "Vance Trip."

3. *Los Angeles Times,* 9 March 1977: Ira Handelman and Yoav Peled, "Time for an eye checkup, Israel watchers'."

4. *Los Angeles Times,* 8 March, 1977: "Rabin reaffirms desire for peace on Israel's terms."

5. *Time,* 1 August 1977: "Carter's position."

6. *U.S. News & World Report,* 1977: "After Vance's trip: Peace no closer in mideast."

7. *The Wall Street Journal,* 11 August 1977: "Vance concedes that talks with Begin didn't narrow gap between Israel, Arabs."

8. *U.S. News & World Report,* 5 September 1977: re Vance's return.

9. *Los Angeles Times,* 4 September 1977: Dateline: Cairo.

10. *Time,* 19 September 1977: re Carter administration.

11. *Time,* 10 October 1977: "Geneva: The Palestinian problem."

12. *Newsweek,* 24 October 1977: re Geneva.

13. *Los Angeles Times,* : Arie Lova Eliav, "The fairy tale status of U.S. Israeli ties."

14. *Jerusalem Post,* 11 October 1977: "No cause for concern for Israel."

15. *U.S. News & World Report,* 17 October 1977: Dateline: Nablus, "Israel is in no mood to give up anything."

16. *Los Angeles Times,* Edward R.F. Sheehan, "Is Carter counting on a Geneva miracle?"

17. *Time,* 13 February 1978: "The problems Sadat left behind."

18. *Newsweek,* 13 February 1978: re Sadat's visit.

19. *U.S. News & World Report,* 20 March 1978: re Begin rejects 242.

20. *Newsweek,* 20 March 1978: "Carter and the Jews."

21. Perlmutter, Amos. *Israel: The Partitioned State: A Political History Since 1900.* New York: Scribners, 1985; 292-93.

VI. The Israeli Lobby

1. Harkabi, Yehoshafat. *Israel's Fateful Hour.* New York: Harper & Row, 1988; 69.

2. Ibid. 129.

3. *The Wall Street Journal,* 5 July 1977: "Potent persuaders."

4. Isaacs, Stephen. *Jews and American Politics.* 7-10.

5. Ibid. 46.

6. Ibid. 48.

7. Ibid. 259.

8. Ibid. 258.

9. Ibid. 257.

10. *Wall Street Journal,* "The hired hands" (editorial).

11. Isaacs, 266.

12. *Commentary,* August 1971: Podhoretz, "A certain anxiety."

13. *Commentary,* February 1972: Podhoretz, "Is it good for the Jews?"

14. Press interview, October 1976: General George Brown.

15. *Los Angeles Times,* 18 October 1976: (editorial).

16. *Los Angeles Times,* (quote) Barry Goldwater.

17. *The Wall Street Journal,* (editorial).

18. CBS: "Face the Nation," 15 April 1973: Senator Fulbright.

19. CBS: "Face the Nation," 7 October 1973: Senator Fulbright.

20. Harkabi, 68.
21. Ibid. 69.

VII. The Israeli Lobby in Action

1. CBS: "60 Minutes," 23 October 1988: (official transcript).
2. *Jerusalem Post,* 5 November 1988: Morris Abram.
3. Findley, Paul. *They Dare To Speak Out.* Westport, CT: Lawrence Hill & Co., 1985; 26-27.
4. Ibid. 32.
5. Ibid. 32-33.
6. Ibid. 35.
7. Ibid. 36-37.
8. *Village Voice,* 14 June 1983: Nat Hentoff.
9. Findley, 49.
10. Dine, Thomas: Address before Jewish community leaders, Austin, Texas, November 1982.
11. Findley, 50-52.
12. *Los Angeles Times,* 2 August 1981.
13. Findley, 56.
14. The memorandum, 1 March 1983: "To ADL regional directors from Justin J. Finger."
15. Findley, 57.
16. Ibid. 68-70.
17. Public meeting, Rm. 2200, Rayburn Building, Washington, D.C., 26 Sept. 1984.
18. Findley, 70.
19. Ibid. 71.
20. Ibid. 73.
21. Ibid. 77.
22. Ibid. 74.
23. Ibid. 74-75.
24. *The Wall Street Journal,* 24 June 1987.
25. Ibid.
26. *Jewish Chicago,* October 1982.
27. *Time,* 20 September 1982.
28. Findley, 85-87.
29. Stevenson, Adlai, III. *The Middle East: 1976.* Report to the Committee on Banking, Housing, and Urban Affairs, U.S. Senate.
30. Findley, 88.
31. *Jacksonville Journal Courier,* 31 August 1982: (a flyer distributed).
32. Findley, 90.
33. *Time,* 15 November 1983.
34. Findley, 91.
35. *Present Tense,* Spring 1983: Thomas A. Dine.
36. Findley, 92.
37. *Congressional Record,* 1 August 1963.

38. Findley, 94.
39. Ibid. 95.
40. Ibid. 95.
41. Findley, 96-97.
42. Ibid. 100-01.
43. Ibid. 102-03.
44. Ibid. 109-11.
45. Ibid. 112-13.
46. Ibid. 124.
47. *Foreign Affairs,* Winter 1975-76.
48. Findley, 125.
49. Ibid. 127.
50. Mahgoub, Mohammed.
51. *The Wall Street Journal,* Elliot Richardson.
52. *U.S. News & World Report,* 9 September 1976.
53. *Business Week,* 12 September 1977.
54. Solaim, Soliman.
55. Ashdar, Farouk.
56. Kissinger, Simon.
57. *Forbes,* 1 October 1976: "How to legislate a disaster."
58. *Business Week,* 24 May 1976: "Taking aim at the Arab boycott."
59. *Los Angeles Times,*
60. Associated Press: 9 July 1988: Dateline: London.
61. *Time,* 25 July 1988.

VIII. Israel and the United States—The Special Relationship

1. Findley, Paul. *They Dare to Speak Out.* Westport, CT: Lawrence Hill & Co., 1985; 166.
2. Ennes, James, Jr. *Assault On The Liberty.* 1980.
3. Meir, Golda. *My Life.* New York: Putnam, 1975; 431.
4. *Los Angeles Times,* 8 April 1979.
5. *Los Angeles Times,* 9 April 1979.
6. Findley, 139-40.
7. Ibid. 140-41.
8. Ibid. 141-42.
9. Ibid. 142-43.
10. Ibid. 143-44.
11. Ibid. 144.
12. Ibid. 147.
13. Ibid. 148.
14. *Newsweek,* 3 September 1979.
15. Findley, 149.
16. Ibid. 149-50.
17. Ibid. 150.

18. Ibid. 151.
19. *Washington Post,* 2 March 1977.
20. Findley, 161.
21. Ibid. 162-63.
22. Ibid. 164.
23. *Los Angeles Times,*
24. *Los Angeles Times,* Joseph Jaffee, reprint from *Suddeutsche Zeitung.*
25. *Time,* 30 March 1988: Hyman Bookbinder.
26. *Los Angeles Times,* Richard Straus.
27. *The Wall Street Journal,* 18 March 1987, Alexander Cockburn.
28. *Jerusalem Post,* 8 September 1987.
29. *Time,* 30 March 1988, Hyman Bookbinder.
30. *New Republic.*
31. Harkabi,Yehoshafat. *Israel's Fateful Hour.* New York: Harper & Row, 1988.
32. George Ball *(see Chapter VII).*
33. *Jerusalem Post,* 31 December 1988: Siegman, "The diaspora's right to intervene."
34. Ibid.

IX. American Jewry and Free Speech

1. Harkabi,Yehoshafat. *Israel's Fateful Hour.* New York: Harper & Row, 1988.
2. Findley, Paul. *They Dare to Speak Out.* Westport, CT: Lawrence Hill & Co., 1985; 282.
3. Ibid.
4. Findley, 265-66.
5. Ibid. 266-67.
6. Ibid. 267.
7. *Progressive,* August 1979: re Carolyn Toll.
8. Findley, 269.
9. *Washington Post,* 6 July 1982.
10. Findley, 270.
11. *Village Voice,* 29 June 1982.
12. Findley, 272.
13. Ibid. 272-74.
14. *The Wall Street Journal,* 7 January 1987.
15. *Jerusalem Post,* Charles Hoffman.
16. *Jerusalem Post,* 4 June 1988: "Aloni blasts Jewish leaders in U.S. for 'keep quiet' policy."
17. *Jerusalem Post,* 31 December 1988.

X. Israel in Crisis

1. Perlmutter, Amos. *Israel: The Partitioned State: A Political History Since 1900.* New York: Scribners, 1985; 316-17.

2. Ibid. 314.
3. Harkabi, Yehoshafat. *Israel's Fateful Hour.* New York: Harper & Row, 1988: 99.
4. Ibid. 100-01.
5. *Los Angeles Times,* 28 September 1988: Amos Perlmutter.
6. Harkabi, 106-07.
7. *Jerusalem Post,* 3 December 1988: Abba Eban.
8. Harkabi, 144.
9. Ibid. 143.
10. Ibid. 145.
11. Ibid. 145-46.
12. Ibid. 146.
13. Ibid. 147.
14. Ibid. 147-48.
15. Ibid. 148.
16. Ibid. 149.
17. Ibid. 149.
18. *Los Angeles Times,* 12 November 1988: John Roth.
19. Harkabi, 149-50.
20. Ibid. 150.
21. Ibid. 153.
22. *Jerusalem Post,* 19 November 1988: Abba Eban.
23. Harkabi, 153.
24. Ibid. 151-52.
25. Ibid. 154.
26. Ibid. 154.
27. Ibid. 182.
28. Ibid. 182.
29. Ibid. 159.
30. Ibid. 157.

XI. Saving Israel from Suicide

1. Yafee, James. *The American Jews.*
2. Forster & Epstein. *The New Anti-Semitism.*
3. Ibid.
4. *Jerusalem Post,* 9 November 1988: Abba Eban.
5. Harkabi, Yehoshafat. *Israel's Fateful Hour.* New York: Harper & Row, 1988; 84-85.
6. Ibid. 127.
7. Preuss, Teddy. *Begin, His Regime.*
8. Harkabi, 213-14.
9. Ibid. 219.
10. Ibid. 181.
11. Ibid. 163-64.
12. *Los Angeles Times,* 20 August 1985: Mark A. Bruzonsky.

13. *Los Angeles Times,* 5 June 1989: Dateline: Jerusalem.
14. Harkabi, 160.
15. Ibid. 177-78.
16. Ibid. 183-84.
17. Ibid. 165.
18. Ibid. 185.
19. Shipler, David. *Arab and Jew: Wounded Spirits in a Promised Land.* New York: Penguin Books, 1987; 154.
20. Ibid. 86.
21. *Los Angeles Times,* 2 February 1989: "Jewish doves see need to criticize Israel."
22. Harkabi, 183.
23. Shipler, 266-72.
24. Ibid. 189-90.
25. Ibid. 129.
26. Ibid. 195-96.
27. Ibid. 415-17.
28. Ibid. 182.
29. *Jerusalem Post,* 19 November 1988: Abba Eban, "The issues that won't go away."
30. Harkabi, 57.
31. Ibid. 58.
32. Ibid. 149.
33. Shipler, 351.
34. Ibid. 167.
35. Ibid. 169.
36. Ibid. 166.
37. Ibid. 169.
38. Harkabi, 165.
39. Ibid. 162.
40. Ibid. 168-69.
41. Johnson, Paul. *A History of the Jews.* New York: Harper & Row, 1987; 559.
42. Shipler, 158.
43. Ibid. 351-52.
44. Ibid. 137, 153.
45. *Los Angeles Times,* 9 October 1977: Dial Torgenson, "Israel thinks the unthinkable."
46. *Los Angeles Times,* 1977: Torgenson.
47. *Time,* 4 July 1988: "A deadly new missile game."
48. *Los Angeles Times,* 6 May 1989: Enrico Jacchia, "Arming the Middle East: An ominous list expands."
49. *U.S. News & World Report,* 25 September 1989: Rabin (comment).
50. *Jerusalem Post,* 23 September 1989: "Israeli missile capability causes concern in Moscow."

XII. The Issues

1. Johnson, Paul. *A History of the Jews.* New York: Harper & Row, 1987; 547.
2. Harkabi, Yehoshafat. *Israel's Fateful Hour.* New York: Harper & Row, 1988; 183.
3. *American Heritage,* "History of the Cherokees."
4. Flapan, Simha. *The Birth of Israel: Myths and Realities.* New York: Pantheon Books, 1987; 15.
5. Ibid. 15-16.
6. Ibid. 243.

XIII. Israel's Dilemma

1. *The Wall Street Journal,* 5 July 1977: "The potent persuaders."
2. Ibid.
3. Ibid.
4. *Time,* 1 August 1977.
5. *Jerusalem Post,* Abba Eban, "The threats are from within."
6. *Jerusalem Post,* Abba Eban.
7. Harkabi, Yehoshafat. *Israel's Fateful Hour.* New York: Harper & Row, 1988; 100-01.
8. Perlmutter, Amos. *Israel: The Partitioned State: A Political History Since 1900.* New York: Scribners, 1985; 314.
9. *Jerusalem Post,* 6 March 1989: Uri Avery, "The illusion of Shamir's peace plan."
10. *Time,* 17 July 1989: "Power, not peace."
11. *Jerusalem Post,* 28 October 1989: David Landau, "Moment of truth."
12. *(See chapter IV.)*
13. Shipler, David. *Arab and Jew: Wounded Spirits in a Promised Land.* New York: Penguin Books, 1987; 235.
14. Ibid. 507.
15. Harkabi, 161.
16. *Newsweek,* 6 November 1989: "Israel's deal with the devil?"

XIV. A Plan for Peace

1. *Jerusalem Post,* 23 September 1989.
2. *Foreign Affairs,* April 1977: George Ball, "How to save Israel in spite of herself."
3. *Foreign Affairs,* George Ball, response to Philip Klutznick.
4. *Jerusalem Post,* 18 February 1989: Robert Maxwell.
5. *Jerusalem Post,* 3 June 1989: Yitzhak Rabin, "Rabin praises military alliance."
6. Harkabi, Yehoshafat. *Israel's Fateful Hour.* New York: Harper & Row, 1988; 168-69.
7. *Jerusalem Post,* 18 October 1989: "Group lays cornerstone of third temple."
8. Ibid. "Engineers of Armageddon."

9. Shipler, David. *Arab and Jew: Wounded Spirits in a Promised Land.* New York: Penguin Books, 1987; 146.
10. *Jerusalem Post,* 25 November 1989: "U.S. community leaders are now ready to oppose Israeli policies openly."
11. Shipler, 144-45.
12. *Jerusalem Post,* 12 August 1989.
13. *Jerusalem Post,* 28 October 1989.

Reprise and Epilogue

1. Tuchman, Barbara W. *The March of Folly.* New York: Alfred A. Knopf, 1984; 10-11.
2. Sachar, Abram L. *A History of the Jews.* New York: Alfred A. Knopf, 1984; 107.
3. Servan-Schreiber, Jean-Jacques. *The Chosen and the Choice.* Boston: Houghton Mifflin Co., 1988; 76.
4. Ibid.